Strong Bridges

SOCIAL NETWORK MECHANISMS SERIES

The study of social networks is rapidly expanding, and the *Social Network Mechanisms* series connects this burgeoning field with network science to produce interdisciplinary insights for scholars in both areas. The series features both quantitative and qualitative books on the mechanisms by which social networks form, shape behavior, give life to institutions, and so play their role in the flow of events. Diverse in style and data, books in the series introduce or establish evidence of mechanisms consequential for the emergence, stability, or consequences of location in network structure. The series was founded by Ronald S. Burt (University of Chicago) and Mario L. Small (Columbia University). For more details on the series and its diverse editorial board, please see: www.oxfordSNMseries.com.

Current Series Editors
Ronald S. Burt, Distinguished Professor in Management and Technology, Bocconi University and Charles M. Harper Leadership Professor Emeritus of Sociology and Strategy, University of Chicago Booth School of Business

Paul Leonardi, Department Chair and Duca Family Professor of Technology Management, University of California, Santa Barbara

Series Titles
Organizational Invention in Renaissance Florence, John F. Padgett
Strong Bridges: Trust beyond Structure, Ronald S. Burt and Sonja Opper
Ctrl+Alt+Doubt: Decoding the Language of Online Conspiracy, Hayagreeva Rao and Henrich Greve
Organization: Formal and Informal Networks, Giuseppe Soda

Strong Bridges

Trust Beyond Structure

RONALD S. BURT
SONJA OPPER

OXFORD
UNIVERSITY PRESS

Oxford University Press is a department of the University of Oxford.
It furthers the University's objective of excellence in research, scholarship,
and education by publishing worldwide. Oxford is a registered trade mark of
Oxford University Press in the UK and in certain other countries.

Published in the United States of America by Oxford University Press
198 Madison Avenue, New York, NY 10016, United States of America.

© Oxford University Press 2026

CIP data is on file at the Library of Congress

ISBN 9780197834268

ISBN 9780197834251 (hbk.)

DOI: 10.1093/9780197834275.001.0001

Paperback printed by Integrated Books International, United States of America

The manufacturer's authorized representative in the EU for product safety is
Oxford University Press España S.A. of Parque Empresarial San Fernando de Henares,
Avenida de Castilla, 2 – 28830 Madrid (www.oup.es/en or product.safety@oup.com).
OUP España S.A. also acts as importer into Spain of products made by the manufacturer.

Contents

Acknowledgments

We state our argument in terms of networks anywhere, but our empirical evidence comes almost entirely from surveys of Chinese entrepreneurs in 2012, 2018, and 2021. The first author of this book had little familiarity with China before the work reported here began. What he had was considerable admiration for the second author, who was about to publish her 2012 award-winning book with Victor Nee on private enterprise in China: *Capitalism from Below*. The book made frequent reference to social networks around the people leading private enterprises, but contained none of the network data so frequently gathered on managers in the West. Much of the network module Ron wrote for inclusion in the 2012 survey is included here in the fieldwork Appendix. One thing led to another and here we are; married and living in Milan.

In the decade of work since the initial survey, we have presented results at numerous seminars and workshops, which we acknowledged in papers published over the decade. With the permission of publishers, we here draw on a few of those papers: Burt and Opper (2017) from *Management and Organization Review*; Burt, Bian, and Opper (2018) and Burt (2019b) from *Social Networks*; Burt, Opper, and Holm (2022) from *Organization Science*, Burt and Opper (2024) from the *American Journal of Sociology*. Our foundational Chapter 2 overlaps with our chapter on evaluation in network context for the *Oxford Handbook of Organisational Social Evaluation* (Burt and Opper 2026) and with a chapter on the fragility of brokerage in the Nobel Symposium volume, *Social Networks* (Burt 2026). Deserving special note are the three colleagues who served as lotsen in our Oxford workshop on the book proposal: Douglas Guilbeault, Martin Kilduff, and James Moody. Their comments triggered thought and revision in the final text. We are also grateful for able research assistance provided by colleagues during their student years: Jiongni Mao, Yujun Wang, Ke Zeng, Chenlin Zhao, and Na Zou. We are grateful also to Bocconi University and the University of Chicago Booth School of Business for financial support during the work reported here. Sonja Opper is grateful to Riksbankens Jubileumsfond for a sabbatical grant, and to the Center for East Asian Studies at the University of Chicago for hosting her as an Associate. We are both grateful to the Jan Wallanders and Tom Hedelius Foundation for their grants to Sonja supporting the three China surveys.

1

Introduction

A meritocracy is widely understood to be a governance system that distributes resources in proportion to merit. Such systems are worthy of aspiration, but are typically noted for their absence. Familiar barriers to a practical meritocracy include accidents of birth, friends, ignorance, love of one's own kind, obligations, quotas, and sloth—it is a long list. The yawning gap between aspiration and reality can generate frustration and anger. It is not surprising that people in diverse cultures have a word for relationships that provide a way around meritocracy; a manifestation of insider wisdom when you are advantaged, an indicator of corruption when someone else is advantaged: There is blat in Russia, enchufe in Spain, piston in France, guan hệ in Vietnam, raccomandazione in Italy, sifarish in India, Vitamin B in Germany, yongo in South Korea—and guanxi in China.

This category of colloquial words is a playground for social network theory. Theory defines social mechanisms responsible for the referenced advantage. In a narrow sense, this book can be read as a story of building theory around one such word, the Chinese term guanxi. We treat guanxi as an example of what Merton and Barber (2004:256) term a niche-word, a word that expresses "a familiar kind of human experience that transcends national and other cultural and linguistic boundaries." Our premise in this book is that the relationships known in China as guanxi refer to a broad category of human relationships. Elements in the category are known by other words in other cultures. The category is significant in theory and substance for its provision of strong bridges, that is to say, relationships of high trust that span structural holes. Guanxi relationships offer a strategic site for productive research on the broader category.

This is a book of two discovery stories. One is the forementioned story about guanxi. Using qualitative and quantitative data on guanxi and non-guanxi relations adjacent in the personal networks of entrepreneurs, we offer a resolution to the debilitating ambiguity of guanxi, a concept often

Strong Bridges. Ronald S. Burt and Sonja Opper, Oxford University Press. © Oxford University Press (2026).
DOI: 10.1093/9780197834275.003.0001

mentioned in studies of Chinese business, and often cited as an example of how business in China is distinct from business in the West. Beyond China, the hypotheses applied to guanxi are a template for research more generally on the meaning of colloquial words that refer to advantage.

Our second story is about network theory and research. We offer a renovation to a widely used concept in network theory. Returning to the above theme of individual advantage, fair or unfair, half a century of work on social networks has settled on bridge relations as a source of individual advantage. A bridge in graph theory is a relationship that connects two people who cannot otherwise be connected indirectly. In practice, it is customary to discuss as bridges any connection between people unlikely to coordinate with each other in the absence of the bridge—typically a person in this group connected to a person in that other group. More precisely, the lack of connection between two groups is a hole in social structure, a structural hole, and relations are a bridge when they connect across a structural hole. With information relatively homogeneous on either side of the hole, and heterogeneous across the hole, information advantages of breadth, timing, and arbitrage accrue to the person—a network broker—who bridges structural holes. Granovetter (1973), Freeman (1977), Burt (1992), and Lin (2001a) are core sources, with a burgeoning research corpus detailing the competitive advantage of network brokers arbitrating information across groups.

Coincident with the accumulating evidence of bridge relations as a source of advantage is accumulating evidence of bridge fragility. Their value is contingent on a broker's social standing. They are prone to decay. Network bridges are weak. The summary image is that brokerage is fragile. Trust is a particular concern. Can I trust this information received from someone in that group—where interests could be less virtuous, irrelevant, or contradictory to my own? Is it even worth the costly due diligence to establish the validity of the information?

We show that guanxi, a kind of relationship often referred to but not yet analytically defined, provides a case for separating tie strength from network structure. That separation relieves us of the widely held assumption that bridge relations are weak. In substantial frequency, we find strong bridges of trusted contact across groups. This is not at all to say that the strength-of-weak-ties hypothesis is incorrect so much as overstated. The hypothesis has been fruitful for so long it is easy to forget that the "forbidden triad" on which it rests was a didactic device, not a fact.

Overview of the Book

The book follows a generic research flow. We start with an empirical puzzle, move to a hunch about the puzzle, state hypotheses based on the hunch, design research to test the hypotheses, delight in empirical support for the hypotheses, then cycle back to explore more detailed and distant implications from empirical support for the hunch. We believe that the empirical journey we share in this book is best traveled along the logical path we lay out here. However, to facilitate quick access to individual chapters we allow for some repetition so that key features of the survey instrumentation and analysis are always easy to locate. Before we begin, we offer this note on language: Guanxi is both singular and plural. We use "guanxi tie" to make explicit reference to guanxi as a kind of relationship, "guanxi contact" to refer to a person who is the object of a guanxi tie, and "guanxi" to refer to the category of relationships that constitute guanxi.

In Chapter 2, we introduce an unexpected data pattern and lay a foundation that makes the pattern intriguing. The chapter is organized around four textbook ideas in network analysis, cast as stylized facts. The four facts together describe network brokerage facilitating change in the status quo, with brokerage opposed by network closure preserving the status quo. We offer a summary of thinking through the twentieth century, then drop into that context an intriguing, contradictory result: We find evidence of strong bridges—strong relations of trust across the structural holes in a network. What these contacts have in common is that respondents recall them as being particularly helpful during significant events in their personal business history. The implication is that the competitive advantage of network brokerage is less fragile than has been believed heretofore. If the contradiction survives close inspection, the outlier relationships have implications for competitive advantage with respect to broadening network theory, sharpening network research, and making network practice more effective.

In Chapter 3, we explain the survey data responsible for the contradictory result and comb through the data to better understand trust in the event contacts. We conclude that the high trust evident in event contacts comes from within—from the interpersonal history between two people. We base this conclusion on three facts: First, trust in event contacts is relatively independent of the surrounding network. Trust in other contacts, nonevent contacts, increases with mutual contacts in the usual way. Second, the high trust relatively independent of the surrounding network is robust across kinds of events. Third, years of knowing a person matter. When family is turned to for support it is most likely at founding, but family is not the primary source of support, even at founding. Rather, entrepreneurs cite people they have known for many years, typically all kinds of people beyond the entrepreneur's family. The duration association with trust is not about significant events in the life of the business or the respondent. Duration is about getting to know a person, which happens during the first four or five years of a relationship, after which trust increases at only a modest rate over additional years. In sum, events seem not to be significant in their own right. They are significant as an occasion, a context, in which an entrepreneur learns that a contact can be trusted.

Our hunch was that the unexpectedly strong bridge connections came from a category of relationships colloquially referenced in China as "guanxi." For verification, we returned to the field to talk with a new sample of entrepreneurs. In Chapter 4, we discuss our strategy, offer two hypotheses to test our hunch, and present strong empirical support for the hypotheses. Our measurement strategy is to include a guanxi name interpreter in a generic network survey instrument. This gives us network data on where guanxi occurs and where it does not. The data lead us to believe that time and significant events are the foundational predictors of guanxi. Guanxi are long-standing relations of positive sentiment deepened to a bond through exchange during one or more significant events.

We use guanxi as a strategic research site in which the unexpected tie strength is explicitly separate from network location. Network theory and research have long been hampered by the belief that relations are weak when they bridge the structural hole between groups. In fact, there is ample evidence showing that bridges between groups are often weak. But some are not, and those exceptionally strong bridges (which can be a numerous minority) are the foundation for competitive advantage.

We use two hypotheses to organize our argument and evidence. Our "strong-bridges" hypothesis states criteria for guanxi operating as a strong bridge: Relative to other ties, trust in guanxi ties is higher and less contingent on structural embedding. Our "advantage" hypothesis states that entrepreneurs are advantaged by the extent to which their guanxi are bridges. In contrast to the discussion of strong ties deriving value from corroborating relations with mutual friends and colleagues (structural embedding), guanxi ties derive value from the interpersonal history between two people (relational embedding). More structural embedding around guanxi makes it less of a network bridge, resulting in lower advantage. In short, advantage is not about weak ties, bridge connections, or trust so much as it is specifically about trusted bridge connections—what we discuss as strong bridges. Absent such bridges, we find that network brokers have no competitive advantage.

By the end of Chapter 4, we have established a beachhead. We have presented systematic evidence of an intriguing contradiction to widely-held network theories of brokerage and related social science (Chapter 2), dug into the evidence to better understand the substance of the contradiction (Chapter 3), then formalized in two hypotheses our hunch that the contradiction is an example of the proverbial Chinese guanxi, and presented new evidence providing a network description of guanxi and strongly supporting the hypotheses (Chapter 4). Guanxi bridges do not compensate for an overall closed network, but they are key to the competitive advantages of relatively open networks.

We use subsequent chapters to consolidate the beachhead. We first look for evidence of confounding explanations. Multiplexity is an obvious candidate. A relationship is "multiplex" when it is composed of more than one kind of connection. Guanxi is typically multiplex in that it is—like "love" or "respect"—an invisible quality attributed to a relationship. What are the observable qualities of relationships in which guanxi is found? For example, how often does it develop within families rather than outside of kinship circles? Is the advantage we attribute to guanxi, in fact an advantage from other kinds of connections in which guanxi tends to occur? If we feel our brother is guanxi, how much of the trust felt is because our brother is family? In Chapter 5, we show that multiplexity is not necessary to the strong bridges provided by guanxi, though it can be a helpful coincidence.

We also look into how guanxi is used. At founding, we find no difference in help between guanxi versus non-guanxi contacts, or between structurally embedded versus bridge guanxi. In short, founding is largely a story about finding contacts who can provide resources regardless of tie strength or network location. Network differences emerge subsequent to founding. Embedded guanxi are associated with help on multiple events, but no specific kind of help. Bridge guanxi performs familiar broker activities—not providing resources so much as providing referrals to helpful contacts outside the entrepreneur's immediate social circle. With respect to contact frequency, guanxi contacts are met neither less often, nor more often, than other contacts. In the extreme, however, it is unlikely that guanxi contacts are ignored for long periods of time. And in keeping with their personal nature, communication tends to be through more personal, less formal channels, especially with bridge guanxi, who are the contacts associated with business success.

In Chapter 6, we look into the language our entrepreneurs use to describe guanxi. A colloquial word such as guanxi can be used in different ways by different groups. Is our interpretation of the word peculiar, or limited to certain kinds of people? Do more educated people define the term differently from less educated people? Are there city differences, either linked to history or the institutional and cultural embedding? We asked each of our sample entrepreneurs to describe guanxi in his or her own words. We draw two conclusions: First, where complexity refers to the number and variety of words in a text, descriptions by our sample entrepreneurs do not distinguish qualitatively different kinds of speakers so much as they distinguish speakers on a continuum of complexity. Second, the complexity with which a speaker describes guanxi is predicted by the complexity of the speaker's network. Specifically, language complexity increases with the extent to which an entrepreneur's network contains guanxi bridge relations. To the extent that our understanding of a kind of relationship varies with the diversity of the situations in which we have that relationship, it is not surprising to see more complicated, nuanced descriptions of guanxi come from people with guanxi bridge relationships. In comparison, complexity is largely independent of an entrepreneur's personal characteristics (age, education, gender, etc.) or characteristics of the entrepreneur's business (industry, assets, size, profitability, etc.).

Across the chapters, we have established that strong bridges are less fragile than bridges on average. Trust is high and duration is long. More than being less fragile, they are resilient. That is the subject of Chapter 7. Weak-tie bridges dissolve under the shock of COVID. Strong bridges persist. We take three lines of attack on resilience. For these analyses, we re-interviewed in 2021 the heads of businesses interviewed in 2018 in the two capital cities: Hangzhou and Shanghai. The re-interviews took place during the COVID epidemic in China, as permitted by intermittent lockdowns. With new respondents drawn from the same sampling design, we have interviews with a stratified probability sample of 371 heads of medium and small private enterprises in the two cities.

Turning to our lines of attack, we begin by learning where COVID most disrupted each person's network. There are some close friends of our sample entrepreneurs who were severely affected by the disease, but they are a minority. The personal contacts most critically affected by COVID are rarely met individuals, disconnected from others in the network around the respondent naming them. COVID is everywhere in the environment, but the severe hardship is typically at or beyond the periphery of an entrepreneur's network. Second, we look for continuing support of the strong-bridges hypothesis. Guanxi during COVID continues to be characterized by high trust independent of network context, but the context has eroded: The structural embedding associated in 2018 with trust in routine business contacts contributes significantly less to trust in 2021. In a phrase, trust becomes more personal, less supported by context—more dependent on guanxi. Third, we look into the resilience of individual relationships. This is difficult because we assured respondents of contact anonymity. Names and addresses of contacts are unknown. Still, with some bold, carefully considered, assumptions, we match a large number of contacts cited in 2018 and 2021. Strong bridges are resilient. They are distinguished by a significantly lower risk of tie decay compared to routine bridges. More than surviving, strong bridges persist as strong bridges.

By the end of Chapter 7, we are confident in the role specified for guanxi and guanxi-like relations in network theory, research, and practice. Strong bridges forged in interpersonal history are a routine feature of networks and they are substantively less fragile and more resilient than bridges on average. They are not equally present in all networks, but they are much more familiar than currently recognized by social network theory.

We close, in Chapter 8, by taking stock of what we have learned, and looking ahead. We offer a brief summary of conclusions from the preceding chapters (now with reference to illustrative bits of evidence in the figures), and a snapshot of the process we believe is responsible for creating strong bridges.

We then look ahead to replication in a variety of forms. We discuss replication through reinterpreting results in prior research, and replication through studying colloquial words akin to guanxi outside China. Beyond colloquial words, we discuss replication through exploratory data analysis, or with strong bridges identified through significant events. We discuss replication with strong bridges defined by socially expected durations (illustrated with data on American analysts and investment bankers), and replication using data on sentiment across levels of structural embedding (illustrated with data on strong bridges in England, France, Germany, and Italy).

We close with core implications for theory and practice. Our results support a break with the last decades of network theory to separate tie strength from network structure. The two conditions are correlated, but they are separate factors in successful brokerage. By cutting through to deeper, more stable relationships responsible for competitive advantage, our results on strong bridges show that the reigning image of brokerage as a fragile advantage needs to be replaced with an image of relatively stable competitive advantage. In showing that competitive advantage is less about concrete connections than it is about a person's emotional interpretation of access, our results call for a more prominent role played by sentiment alongside structure as core to competitive advantage. Finally, our results have implications for network practice in that they show no value to abundant weak ties that are bridges; value resides in the subset of bridges that are strong.

2

Unexpectedly Strong Bridges

Our work in this book was sparked by a contradictory data pattern. Routine statistical practice would justify ignoring the pattern. But viewed in its proper context, the pattern is a fly in the ointment, a note out of tune—something to be resolved. Our purpose in this chapter is to make that context clear by sketching the foundations from which we drew inferences about the contradictory data pattern.

In the hope of communicating more effectively across disciplines, we organize the chapter around four stylized facts, each illustrated with a data display. Data patterns in the figures are the main content of this chapter. Skimming the figures should give a good sense of what is being discussed. Also, we privilege ideas and results over literature. We provide references and sources, but this is not a literature review so much as a codification of core content. Our focus is on organizational management, but implications for broader society are clear, and often explicit. We begin with the network context in which our ideas are anchored.

Network Context: Bridges and Clusters

Figure 2.1 illustrates the generic network structure on which much of social network theory is based: clusters of densely connected elements loosely connected between clusters. The sociograms in Figure 2.1 describe the relations among 227 senior managers in a large European corporation just over a decade ago. Figure 2.1A is a sociogram of the organization's formal hierarchy. Dots indicate individuals. Lines indicate reporting relations from people at the periphery up the ranks toward the CEO in the center. Figure 2.1B is a sociogram of informal organization among the managers, the social network. Lines connect colleagues who have frequent and substantial work discussions. People are close together in each sociogram to the extent that they have a strong connection with each other and with the same colleagues (Borgatti 2002).

Strong Bridges. Ronald S. Burt and Sonja Opper, Oxford University Press. © Oxford University Press (2026).
DOI: 10.1093/9780197834275.003.0002

The two structures in Figure 2.1 show different degrees of clustering. In the formal organization, there is no clustering. The density of connections between people connected to any one manager is uniformly zero.[1] The informal organization shows substantial clustering. To the east in the sociogram, company leaders in the United States are strongly connected with one another with little connection overseas. To the northeast in the sociogram, company leaders in Asia are strongly connected to one another with little connection outside Asia. To the southwest in the sociogram, an important group in the company's research and development operations, floats cut off from the rest of the company leadership.

Business practice varies between these clusters. People in the R&D cluster are guided by state-of-the-art scientific practice. They explain and describe their activities in terms of science. People in the American cluster are adapted to American legal code, business practices, and local institutions. Similarly, people in the Asian, European, front office, and back office clusters are efficient with their local language within the social and professional institutions associated with each cluster. On average, three out of four discussion colleagues discuss work with each other (.74 average density). There are

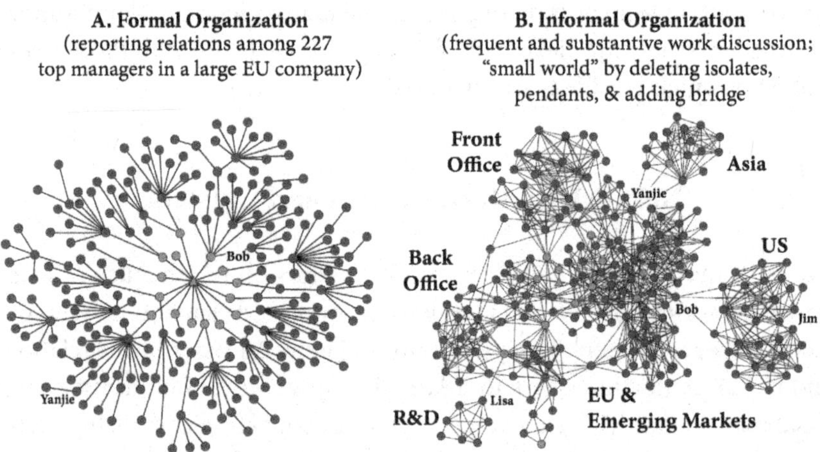

Figure 2.1 Network Context: Bridge and Cluster Structure

[1] There are 226 symmetric reporting relations in Figure 2.1A among the 227 managers (CEO reports out of the population). The ego-network around each manager is a star structure: no two of the n colleagues connected to a manager are connected to each other. Therefore, density is zero for the network around each manager (number of ties between a person's contacts divided by $n\,(n-1)$ possible ties).

occasional "bridge" relations between clusters, but relations are concentrated within clusters, often referred to in management parlance as "silos" in the organization. A bridge in graph theory is a link that connects two people who cannot otherwise be connected, but it is customary to discuss as bridges any connection between groups that are unlikely to otherwise coordinate with each other.

Clustering in Figure 2.1B illustrates the foundation for much of social network theorizing, which is based on two facts that emerged during the "golden age" of social psychology in the 1950s (e.g., Merton 1949; Festinger, Schachter, and Back 1950; Asch 1951; Katz and Lazarsfeld 1955): (1) clustering is a generic feature of social relations as a result of interaction opportunities defined by the places where people meet ("social foci" in Feld's later discussion 1981), and (2) communication is more frequent and influential within clusters than between clusters such that people in the same cluster develop similar language, behaviors and beliefs. Clustering is based on geography and function in Figure 2.1B. Those are often criteria for clustering in organizations, along with products, projects, legacy organizations, and personal characteristics such as education, ethnicity, gender, and years with the organization.

Within clusters, information drifts toward the tacit and homogeneous. People tire of repeating arguments and stories explaining why they believe and behave the way they do. They invent phrasing, opinions, symbols, and behaviors that define what it means to be a member of their group relative to people outside the group. People feel they are understood within their cluster. Beneath familiar arguments and experiences are new, emerging arguments and experiences awaiting a label, the emerging items are more understood than said. What was once explicit knowledge interpretable by anyone becomes tacit knowledge meaningful primarily to insiders. With continued time together, information in the group becomes "sticky"— nuanced, interconnected, implicit meanings difficult to understand in other groups (Von Hippel 1994; Szulanski 2003). For reasons of a division of labor in which groups specialize on separate bits of work, or variation due to the independent evolution of separate social groups (Salganik et al. 2006)— holes tear open in the flow of information between groups (see Gulati et al. 2012, on mechanisms). These holes between clusters in the social structure of communication, or more simply "structural holes," are missing relations that indicate where information is likely to differ on each side of the hole and does not flow easily across the hole (Burt 2021). In short, clustering in social networks is to be expected and serves as a proxy for the distribution of information, indicating where information is relatively homogeneous (within groups) and where information is likely heterogeneous (between groups).

Of course, people are typically involved in multiple networks, nested across levels of aggregation such that multiple clusters at one level are together a cluster at a higher level. Nevertheless, the simple bridge and cluster image in Figure 2.1B is the foundation for much that followed. It inspired Milgram's (1967) discussion of what he called a "small world" phenomenon, on which Lee (1969) and Granovetter (1974) based their corroborating dissertations, and from which Granovetter (1973) developed his weak ties paper on the importance of bridge relations across clusters. Watts and Strogatz (1998) added formal clarity, proposing elegant metrics to show that the bridge and cluster structure in Figure 2.1B can be understood as one of many such "small world" networks.[2]

In a network context of bridges and clusters, our protagonists are two people, ego and alter, as shown in Figure 2.2. Network predictions are informative across levels of analysis, so these elements could be groups or organizations, but we prefer to limit anthropomorphisms to people. Certainly, ego and alter can be agents of groups or organizations. Ego is pitching an idea to alter, or making an evaluation of alter. The two networks in Figure 2.2 differ in the extent to which their networks close around ego and alter. In Figure 2.2A, ego and alter live in separate social worlds. Ego's contacts are strongly connected to each other. Alter's contacts are strongly connected to

---

[2] The formal definition of a small world proposed by Watts and Strogatz (1998, Watts 1999) was an important step forward for network theory and analysis, but is not essential to our substantive focus here. The formal definition is irrelevant to the reporting network in Figure 2.1A because such networks are explicitly excluded by the requirement that everyone have two or more contacts (Watts and Strogatz, 1998:440; Watts, 1999:499n). The discussion network in Figure 2.1B meets the formal definition of a small world in that ego-network density (termed a "clustering coefficient" in the formal definition) is much higher than occurs if relations are distributed at random among the mangers, and the average path distance between managers is about the same as occurs if relations are distributed at random (respectively .74 average density and 4.15 average path distance in Figure 2.1B, versus .04 and 2.75 in 100 Erdös-Rényi random graphs with the same number of relations and managers). However, to make the Figure 2.1B network illustrative of the formal definition of a small world, we had to exclude several isolate managers (their discussion relations were with colleagues at lower ranks of the organization), and add a link to her boss for the director, Lisa, of the R&D unit in the lower left, a unit that is in fact isolated from the rest of management (cf. original in Burt, 2019a:23). Little is lost here by these exclusions because Figure 2.1 is here merely illustrative, but in the bigger picture of comparing these managers to senior management in other organizations, the managers in Figure 2.1A could behave as if they were one social cluster relative to the senior management of organizations, and the isolated elements absent from Figure 2.1B have substantive implications for company performance.

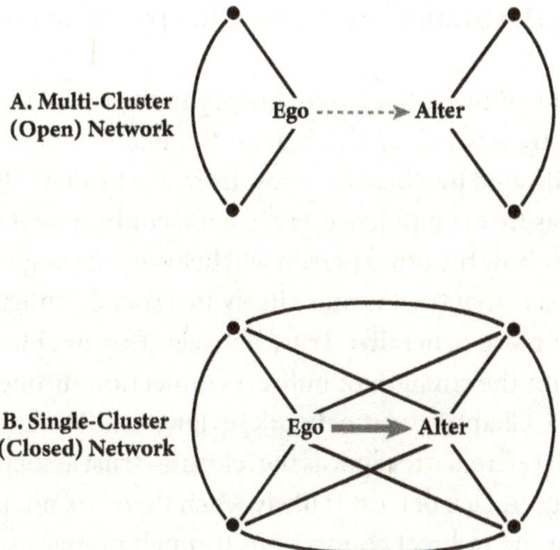

Figure 2.2 Relationship Between Clusters
Versus Within

each other (or the idea represented by alter is strongly held by people who are strongly connected to each other). Ego and alter have no mutual contacts. Ego's connection with alter is a bridge across the boundary, the structural hole, between two social worlds. In contrast, the network in Figure 2.2B closes around ego and alter, who are strongly connected indirectly through mutual contacts. Ego and alter are members of the same social world. Drawing on network theory, Putnam (2000) popularized the extremes of Figure 2.2 as bridges versus bonds, but many relations within clusters are weaker than the strength implied by the word "bond." We simply measure directly the extent to which the connection between ego and alter is embedded in relations with mutual contacts. In Figure 2.2A, they have no mutual contacts. In Figure 2.2B, they have four. The contrast between the top and bottom networks in Figure 2.2 is discussed as open versus closed, sparse versus dense, or in a variety of more technical network terms.[3]

---

[3] There is variation across disciplines; for example, density (average connection strength) is often discussed as a "clustering coefficient" in computational social science (Easley and Kleinberg 2010:44–46). In general, the network around two people closes in on them to the extent it becomes small, dense, or dominated by a central contact (Burt 2010: 293–300). We will often supplement a count of mutual contacts with the aggregate strength of indirect connections (sum across mutual contacts the product of ego's relation with the contact times alter's relation with the contact).

Preserving the Status Quo: The Closure–Trust Association

The contrast in Figure 2.2 has a long history in the social sciences. Positive and negative extremes of evaluation are more likely in Figure 2.2B than in Figure 2.2A (indicated by a heavier arrow from ego to alter). Trust, a popular benchmark measure of confidence, is a general commitment to an exchange before you know how the other person will behave. The association between closure and trust is that trust is more likely in a social configuration such as Figure 2.2B, or more generally: Trust between two people is more likely, or increases, with the strength of indirect connection through mutual contacts (Burt 2005, Chapter 3, for network review; Schilke et al. 2021 for trust review). We will reference the link as the "closure–trust association." Distrust is a mirror image. A lack of trust is likely when there are no mutual contacts (Figure 2.2A) or the indirect connections through mutual contacts are negative (e.g., I distain the people my friends distain). Given the mirror image of the association, we focus on the correlates of internal cohesion increasing within a more closed network.

The closure–trust association is to be expected with or without instrumental effort. Some arguments make association a passive result of similarity (homophily) or logistics: People who like each other are likely to like the same other people, or relationships are likely to develop between people who spend time in the same place with the same people (Heider 1958; Cartwright and Harary 1956, on balance theory; Festinger, Schachter, and Back 1950, on physical proximity facilitating social connection; Feld 1981, on social foci).

The closure–trust association is more often argued with agency in terms of reputation: The more closed the network around a relationship, the more likely misbehavior will be detected, which creates reputational costs for misbehavior, discourages misbehavior, reduces the risk of trust, and so increases the probability of trust. Thus, reputation costs in a closed network are a governance mechanism in an informal organization. In economics, the association is at the heart of business relationships, which become manageable when embedded in a formal or informal social structure (Coase 1937 to Greif 1989), and in law, the association is the basis for discussions of social order with or without formal contract (Ellickson 1991; Bernstein 1992; 2015). In sociology, the association is the basis for Blau's (1974; Blau and Schwartz 1984) work on the parameters of social structure, Granovetter's

(1985) work on relationships embedded in social structure, and Coleman's (1988) work on social capital as the control people have over each other in closed networks, later applied in Putnam's (1993; 2000) work with Coleman's social capital metaphor. More recently, in computer science, the association offers a foundation for navigating the internet as a small world (Kleinberg 2000; 2026). Following Granovetter, we refer to closure around ego and alter as "structural embedding," which we measure with a count of mutual contacts or the aggregate strength of indirect ego–alter connection through third parties.[4]

As a final note, causality runs in both directions. Mutual friends cluster around the strong connection between two people, and a strong connection is likely to develop between two people who have many mutual friends. Strong ties generate adjacent strong ties, increasing the density of ties within a social cluster and closing the network around each member.

Stylized Fact 1: Closure Facilitates Trust within, Distrust Beyond

Arguments aside, the empirical regularity is that the strength of connection between two people has a positive correlation with the strength of their indirect connection through third parties. Stronger ties manifest themselves in more extreme evaluations; close friends receive more enthusiastic evaluations than casual acquaintances. Figure 2.3 provides illustrative evidence. Figure 2.3A shows the positive association between group closure and within-group trust. The unit of analysis is a relationship, a dyad, measured by ego's evaluation of alter. The horizontal axis sorts relationships by the extent to which ego and alter are structurally embedded, i.e., members of the same group. Structural embedding is measured as a count of mutual contacts. The top line in Figure 2.3 is computed from a stratified probability sample of Chinese entrepreneurs. Survey details are not needed here. We will get into the details when we turn to our fieldwork. Each respondent

---

[4] These agency stories from economics and sociology are largely about protection. Reputation costs for bad behavior within a closed network lower the risk of trust between people in the network. This corresponds to the "exploitation" side of the strategy coin described by March (1991); people can more safely obtain the value of collaborations within the network. The other side of March's coin is "exploration," in which people obtain the value of collaborations on new ideas and practices. The stories cited in this paragraph vary in their attention to the "exploration" side of the coin. Some ignore it. Some mention it. It will emerge as a central feature of our story about guanxi and strong bridges (discussed in the conclusion to Chapter 4).

entrepreneur rated his or her connection strength with individual business contacts (on a five-point scale from low to high). Across several thousand relations with business contacts cited by a stratified probability sample of entrepreneurs running small or medium private enterprises, we regressed trust across levels of structural embedding. There are only a few relations embedded in more than six mutual contacts (in the survey), so we truncate the embedding scale at six or more. The result is the nonlinear, upward-sloping line at the top of Figure 2.3A, which is typical of the closure–trust association. The middle line shows the same entrepreneurs rating their emotional closeness to individual contacts (on a four-point scale from "distant" to "especially close"). The association with structural embedding is again positive and nonlinear. Bridge relationships, to the left of the graph, show relatively low levels of trust and emotional closeness. Embedded relationships, to the right of the graph, show the highest. Strength increases most with the addition of one or two mutual contacts. The increase is smaller for relationships already embedded in several mutual contacts. As a research design issue, note that the associations in Figure 2.3 can be obscured by sampling only close relations. Associations would be weaker if observations were concentrated to the right in the graph. The similarly positive, nonlinear association at the bottom of Figure 2.3A is for managers in two American organizations evaluating whether to include their boss among the colleagues with whom they most discuss work (Burt and Wang 2022; Jannace and Burt 2024).[5]

More generally, Figure 2.3A illustrates a tendency for ego evaluations to resemble ego's friends' views of same alter. "I think well of Bob" looks like ego's evaluation because ego expresses it. The more accurate understanding is "<u>We</u> think well of Bob." The stylized fact is similar for negative evaluations. Just as people find community in the celebration of people and ideas we jointly admire, we find community in the denigration of people and ideas we jointly distain—which grows deeper and richer as we discover more people who think like us. This is as much the social foundation for witch hunts as well as office mobbing and, more recently, social media storms, and has a long history in sociology (Burt 2005:188–196; 2010: Chapter 7).

---

[5] More specifically, the curves displayed in Figure 2.3 are regression lines through the plotted means predicting the vertical axis from the horizontal using $\log(1 + X)$ as predictor. The plotted means are computed with respondent fixed effects to remove respondent differences in mean evaluation.

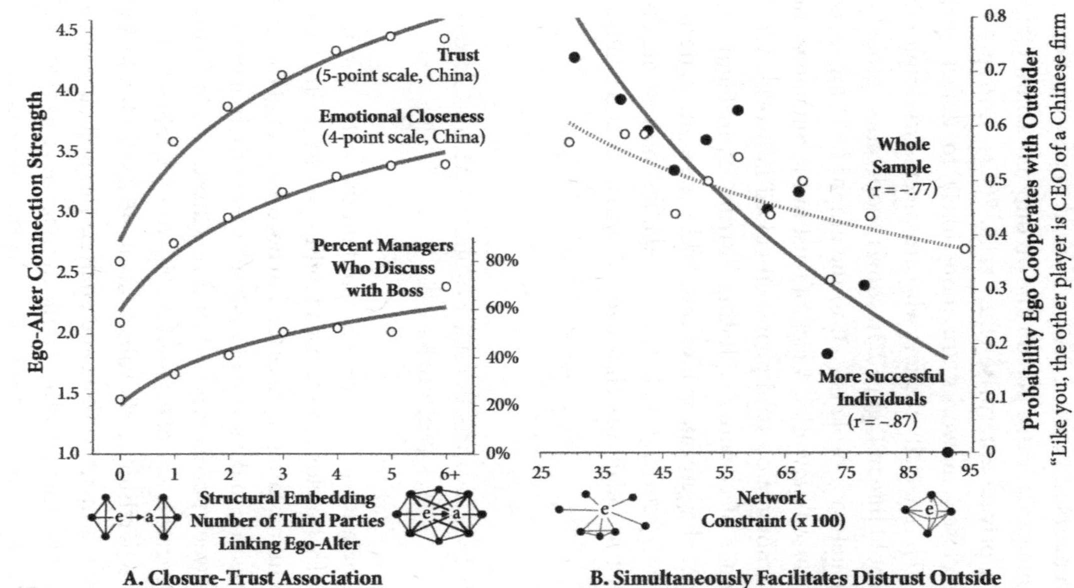

A. Closure-Trust Association

Two top lines are based on 7,166 evaluations by Chinese entrepreneurs of business contacts. Bottom line is based on 674 evaluations by American managers of discussion with corporate boss. Adapted from Burt and Opper (2026:Fig. 2).

B. Simultaneously Facilitates Distrust Outside

For a probability sample of Chinese entrepreneurs, graph plots averages for 5-point intervals on X with thin tails of X truncated for infrequency. "More Successful" are entrepreneurs whose businesses had above-median profit last year. Adapted from Burt et al. (2022:503). Regression lines in both graphs are through the plotted data.

Figure 2.3 Local Cohesion Facilitates Trust Within, Distrust Outside

As people become accustomed to the local cohesion of a closed network, relations with people and ideas outside the closed network can seem dangerous; more than just different—dangerous. As trust becomes stronger within the closed network, suspicions grow about people and ideas outside the network. Figure 2.3B illustrates closure increasing distrust of the outside world. The Chinese entrepreneurs in Figure 2.3A were asked to play one round of the Prisoner's Dilemma game with a person known only as a fellow Chinese citizen and CEO of a private enterprise (Burt et al. 2022). Entrepreneurs embedded in more closed networks are more likely to defect against the outsider ($r = -.77$), especially the few who are successful despite their closed network: The bold line in Figure 2.3B shows cooperation probability dropping from .8 for network brokers (left in the graph) to .2 for successful entrepreneurs in closed networks. A lack of trust in the outside world is particularly evident among successful people in closed networks. We prefer micro-level evidence of closure facilitating distrust, as in Figure 2.3B, but diverse bits of related aggregate evidence support the same pattern, for example, Putnam's (2007) correlation between neighborhood ethnic diversity and a lack of trust in neighbors (however, see Abascal and Baldassari 2015).

Stylized Fact 2: Evaluations Persist Longer in More Closed Networks

The closure–trust associations in Figure 2.3 maintain the status quo in that evaluations associated with closed networks tend to persist. Within closed networks, beliefs, opinions, and practices tend to become part of the shared narratives by which people make sense of themselves and their activities.

The association between persistence and closure is illustrated in Figure 2.4 at individual and aggregate levels of evaluation. Figure 2.4A, taken from Burt (2010:181), shows the persistence of evaluations in 46,231 individual relationships. These are investment bankers and analysts rating their work with individual colleagues. The horizontal axis is the number of years that ego has worked with alter. The vertical axis is the probability that this year's ego–alter relationship will end before next year. The lines in the graph are highest for young relationships. In other words, young relationships are most at risk of ending. You have professional contact with alter. You find him unpleasant, inadequate or unscrupulous, or just not interesting enough, and decide to

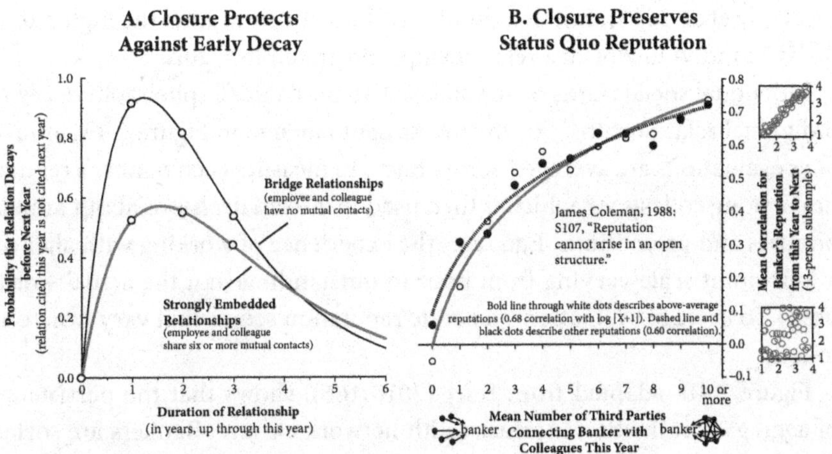

Figure 2.4 Closed Networks and Persistent Evaluations

Note: Graph A plots decay functions for colleague relations among investment bankers and analysts (based on 46,231 relations). Regression lines are through the plotted data. Graph B plots stability in banker reputations from one year to the next (based on senior bankers over four years, see footnote 6).

avoid him in the future. This is easy to do if alter is a bridge relationship in that you have no mutual contacts (as in Figure 2.2A). However, if you and alter have mutual friends (as in Figure 2.2B), you may end up interacting with alter while interacting with a mutual friend. Figure 2.4A shows very different decay curves for the two categories of relationships. Bridge relationships show strong decay within the first year. The thin line in Figure 2.4A reaches 92 percent decay in the first year. In contrast, the bold line, describing ego and alter with many mutual contacts, reaches only 53 percent decay in the first year. After two years of working together, the two lines show similar decay rates (about 50 percent in the third year). After about four years, the survival of relationships becomes independent of the surrounding social structure. In short, closure primarily protects new relationships from decay.

Rapid decay in bridge relations need not affect the advantage provided by brokerage in that some have found the value of bridge relations concentrated in new or current bridge relationships (Soda et al. 2004; Baum et al. 2012), but decay raises a question about advantage stability. One can argue that the information advantages of bridge relations create a durable advantage for an organization when the learning associated with individual bridge relations is absorbed into an organization's routines that can be deployed to new tasks

(McEvily et al. 2012). But that durability does not contradict the high rate of decay in individual bridge relationships illustrated in Figure 2.4A.

Individual social status or reputation can be stable despite rapid decay in individual relationships. For the investment bankers in Figure 2.4A, annual peer evaluations are averaged across raters to measure each banker's reputation among colleagues, which is then used to inform decisions about annual bonuses and promotions. Ego rates the experience of working with alter on a four-point scale varying from poor to outstanding (not the actual words used), so average evaluations generate reputation scores that vary from one to four.

Figure 2.4B, adapted from Burt (2010:166), shows that the persistence of aggregate evaluation increases with network closure. Bankers are sorted along the horizontal axis by the extent to which they operate in a closed network of colleagues evaluating one another. Those with open networks are to the left. Closed networks are to the right (note the sociograms under the right and left of the axis). Bankers are distinguished on the vertical axis by the stability of their reputation from one year to the next (measured as the correlation between reputation in adjacent years within a subsample of bankers similar in network closure, Burt 2005:163n). The small graph at the top of the vertical axis shows a strong correlation between four-point reputation scores this year and next. The corresponding graph at the bottom of the axis shows no persistence in reputation. The two regression lines in Figure 2.4B show a strikingly close association between reputation stability and network closure, both for below-average reputations (black dots) and above-average reputations (hollow dots).[6] As Coleman (1988:S107) so aptly asserted in his discussion of network closure as social capital, "Reputation cannot arise in an open structure."

The association between network closure and reputation persistence is critical because evaluations quickly forgotten do not have the salutary effect assumed in theories based on the closure–trust association. What good is a positive reputation if no one remembers it when resources are distributed? Why worry about a negative reputation if it is soon forgotten? Each year,

---

[6] The average rating of a banker in year t and the closeness of the network around the banker in year t are used to predict his or her average rating in year $t + 1$. The graph is based on four years of annual evaluations of bankers who reached the rank of director or above in one of the four years. There are 998 banker-years. The null hypothesis of reputation persistence independent of network closure is strongly rejected (11.39 jackknife t-test with controls for years and banker fixed effects, $P < .001$). Results for a large population of analysts are also reported in the source discussion (Burt, 2010:167).

teaching MBA students brings fresh examples. There was the earnest Army reservist who advised recruits new to his group to quickly establish their reputation for good work because first impressions seem to persist regardless of subsequent performance. First impressions persist in closed networks. Similarly, there was a new consultant advised by her McKinsey partner to follow the 3Bs: "Be bright. Be brief. Begone." Almost no one is pretty on close inspection, so dazzle quickly with brilliant work, then get out of sight. Positive stories about you will circulate within closed client networks, creating an amplified, persistent reputation for you that will be useful in future engagements. The central point: Reputation resides in the audience, not in the individual.

Contradictory Data Pattern

In the normal course of analysis, we computed residuals from the closure–trust association for our sample of Chinese entrepreneurs (shown at the top of Figure 2.3). Our intention was to rule out deviations from the familiar association so often found in the West. Most of the time deviation was random, as expected. However, given the long history of work on the closure–trust association, we were surprised to find one pattern, shown in Figure 2.5, that stood out as clearly non-random. Across levels of structural embedding, Figure 2.5A plots standardized residuals from the Figure 2.3 trust association for two kinds of relationships. Figure 2.5B is a corresponding plot of raw trust means.

The familiar upward sloping closure–trust association as in Figure 2.3, is a good description of relations defining the dashed line in Figure 2.5B. These are relations with people the respondent cites as currently important in his or her business. In other words, these are contacts typically elicited in research on manager networks. The dashed line in Figure 2.5B shows the nonlinear, upward-sloping regression line of the closure–trust association— akin to the top line in Figure 2.3, but a little steeper in Figure 2.5B because outliers have been removed. The dashed line through residual scores in Figure 2.5A is a little low for extreme bridge relations (zero structural embedding), but as expected for residuals across levels of a predictor, the line is primarily flat across levels of structural embedding, and confidence intervals overlap more often than not for adjacent levels of structural embedding.

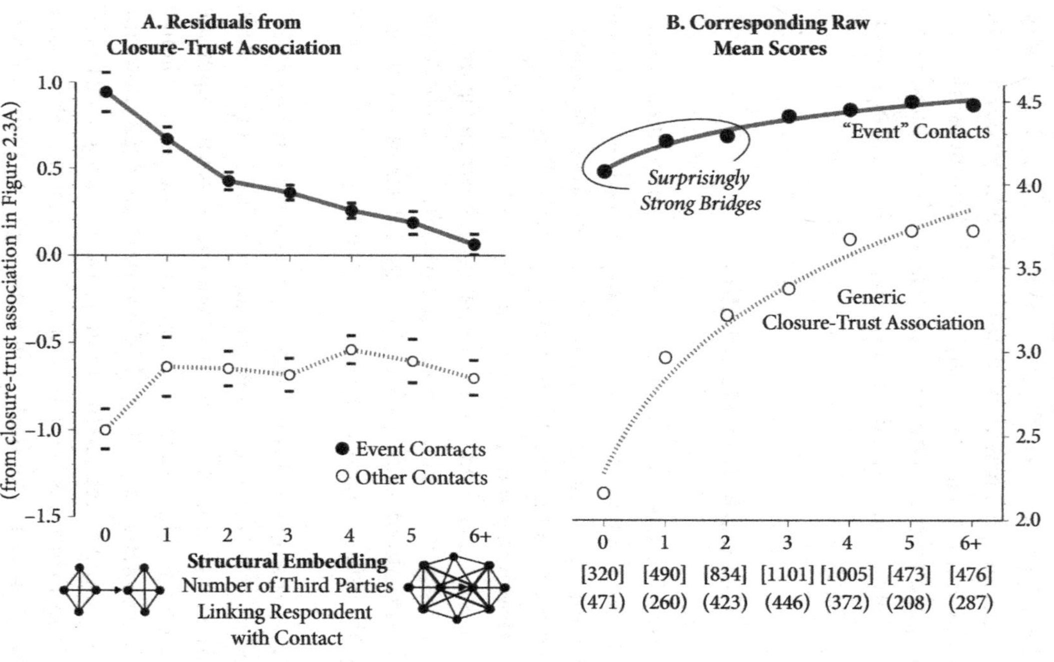

Figure 2.5 Contradictory Data Pattern

Note: Units of analysis are 7166 relationships cited by respondents in a stratified probability sample of 885 entrepreneurs leading Chinese SMEs. Horizontal axis is the number of other people in a respondent's network connected with the contact being evaluated for trust. Studentized residual z-scores on left vertical axis are defined by model M1 in Table 2.1 (± 95% confidence interval). Trust on the right vertical axis is measured in five categories ("Low" to "High"). Frequencies to the right below each level of third-party connection show number of [relations with event contacts] and (relations with other contacts).

What stands out in Figure 2.5 is the unexpectedly high trust in people labeled "event" contacts. Event contacts were identified by asking respondents to describe significant events in the history of their business. Given a history of events, we asked for the name of the person, if there was one, who was particularly helpful to the respondent in resolving each event. We discuss question details when we turn to fieldwork in the next chapter, but for the moment, anyone named as an event contact is tabulated separately along the solid lines in Figure 2.5.

The solid line in Figure 2.5B shows mean trust consistently higher than trust in other contacts. The line is almost flat across levels of structural embedding, showing little improvement from two people having numerous mutual contacts—a clear contradiction to the closure–trust association. All mean residual scores for event contacts are positive in Figure 2.5A, indexing in their own way a level of trust higher than expected from the closure–trust association. The pattern of lines in Figure 2.5A results from the different slopes of association with structural embedding: Large differences over bridge relations (where trust is predicted to be low by the lack of structural embedding, but trust in event contacts is high), and small differences over deeply embedded relations (where trust is predicted to be high by structural embedding, and it is high in event contacts). Those high-trust relations in the absence of mutual contacts are strong bridge relations. They are numerous. We find 1644 bridge relations with 4699 event contacts (indicated in Figure 2.5B). That is almost 35 percent of event contacts, or 23 percent of all contacts in our sample. Hence, strong bridges are not just a theoretical possibility. They exist, and they are far from rare.

Statistical Tests

Results in Table 2.1 show that trust in event contacts is a statistically significant outlier from the closure–trust association, but not by so much that it overshadows the fact that trust increases with network closure. The first model in Table 2.1—which defines the residual scores in Figure 2.5A—shows trust clearly increasing with structural embedding (22.17 t-test, $P < .001$). The usual closure–trust association illustrated in Figure 2.3A is supported by these data in the aggregate. The model in the second column is the same except that it includes respondent fixed effects to control for respondent differences in expressing trust (some respondents give higher ratings on average than other respondents). Explained variance is slightly larger in M2,

Table 2.1 Closure–Trust Association, Ignoring and Acknowledging Outlier Relationships

	M1	M2	M3	M4
Intercept	3.15	2.76	2.24	2.07
Structural Embedding (ln third parties)	.65 (22.17)	.96 (26.37)	.84 (22.86)	.98 (25.67)
Level Adjustment For Event Contacts	—	—	1.84 (28.91)	1.81 (26.76)
Slope Adjustment For Event Contacts	—	—	− .61 (− 14.14)	− .61 (− 14.07)
Respondent Fixed Effects	no	yes	no	yes
R^2	.12	.26	.38	.49

Note: Unit of analysis is the relationship between Chinese CEO and business contact. Across 7166 relations from 885 respondents, trust on a five-point scale is predicted by OLS from structural embedding measured by $\ln(1 + N)$, where N is the number of third parties linking respondent and contact. M1 and M3 are estimated using Stata's "cluster" option to correct for autocorrelation between contacts evaluated by same respondent. M2 and M4 are estimated with respondent fixed effects to control for respondent differences in average evaluation of contacts. Jackknife t-tests are given in parentheses. Descriptive statistics for these regressions are in Table B.1 in Appendix B.

but it hardly seems worth the hundreds of dummy variables added to the prediction by respondent fixed effects.

Explained variance increases considerably when we model trust in event contacts separately from trust in other contacts. M3 is an analysis of covariance model in which trust predicted by structural embedding (22.86 t-test, $P < .001$), is raised to a significantly higher level in relations with event contacts (28.91 t-test, $P < .001$), with a significantly lower slope across levels of structural embedding (.84 coefficient minus .61, generating a −14.14 t-test, $P < .001$). Adding respondent fixed effects in the fourth Table 2.1 model makes the three effects stand out more clearly. The first two models offer clear evidence of the closure–trust association regardless of event contacts, as the last two models clearly demonstrate the outlier status of trust in event contacts.

So What?

If the data are—on the whole—consistent with the established closure–trust association (models M1 and M2 in Table 2.1), why bother with the outliers? Many a worthy project has tumbled into anonymity because analysis was lured off message by technical details interesting only to project authors. In fact, we might not even have detected these outliers at all if our survey's name generator had not explicitly asked for milestone events in addition to the commonly reported current advisory network.

We have three reasons for digging into the outliers. First, the results in Table 2.1 show that event contacts contradict the familiar closure–trust association. They represent an opportunity to learn more about the limits of the familiar association. Second, the outliers are numerous. Of the 7166 contacts cited by the Chinese entrepreneurs, most are still being consulted (4904, or 68 percent) and are being met frequently. The others are not current contacts but were named because of their importance during one or more significant prior events. Of the current contacts, however, half are also named for their importance during prior events. Since everyone named as an event contact is tabulated above as an event contact, the solid lines in Figure 2.5 describe the majority of relations (4699, or 66 percent). Relations with event contacts are outliers in theory, but in fact, they are the majority of relations, at least for our sample entrepreneurs.

The above two reasons are concerned with getting the story right. Worthy concerns both, but they are dominated, for us, by a third reason. The outliers speak to a critical puzzle in network theory: The fragility of brokerage. We want to understand these event contacts in part for their own sake as obvious and numerous exceptions to the familiar closure–trust association. Moreover, we believe that understanding them could be a key to solving a puzzle already well known in network theory.

Changing the Status Quo: Achievement and Network Brokerage

To clarify our third reason, we need to put two more stylized facts on the table. The people labeled "Bob" and "Yanjie" in Figure 2.1 are generic senior managers in the Figure 2.1A formal structure, but they are distinct as unique connectors between clusters in the Figure 2.1B informal structure. Yanjie is the sole connection between the European and Asian clusters. Bob is the sole connection between the European and US clusters. Characterized by their location in social structure, people like Bob and Yanjie are termed "network brokers" and their network behavior "brokerage." Network brokers correspond to Merton's (1949; Gouldner 1957) "cosmopolitans," Katz and Lazarsfeld's (1955) "opinion leaders" (see Burt 1999, 2005: 84–86, on network brokers versus opinion leaders), and, more distantly, Schumpeter's (1911) and Hayek's (1937; 1945) touchstone images of what it means for a person to be an entrepreneur (Burt 2005: Chapter 5, for details; and compare Stigler's 1961:216, image of "specialized traders" in the economics of information).[7]

Network brokers like Bob and Yanjie have three information advantages over people who do not have bridge connections: breadth, timing, and arbitrage. With respect to breadth, Bob and Yanjie's bridge relations across groups give them access to more diverse information. Bob looking at European operations can see where certain practices in America could be an improvement. Yanjie looking at European operations can see where certain practices in Asia could be an improvement. With respect to timing, Bob and Yanjie are positioned at crossroads in the flow of information between groups, so they are early to learn about activities in other groups and are often the person who brings information from one group to another. There is no one other than Bob and Yanjie positioned to look at European operations through an American or Asian lens. Bob and Yanjie are more likely to know when it would be rewarding to bring together separate groups, which gives them disproportionate say in whose interests are served when the contacts come together, which brings in arbitrage: Network brokers have an advantage in translating opinion and behavior familiar from one group into the dialect of a target group. Bob and Yanjie can express their proposals from overseas in terms familiar to their European colleagues.

The information advantages are less about getting novel information than they are about applying novel interpretations to existing information and combining previously disparate bits of information into novel interpretations. For one thing, technology continues to expand our exposure to information such that getting information is not as difficult as making sense of information. Second, the benefit of access to structural holes does not come from indirect access. It comes from direct access to disconnected

---

[7] We cannot do justice here to the many productive bits of published research available. For literature, see Stovel and Shaw's (2012) review arguing that brokerage should be a more central concept in sociology, and Halevy et al.'s (2019) broad discussion of texts. For comprehensive current review, see Kwon et al. (2020), and for thinner coverage over a broader domain, Carter et al. (2015). Focusing on trust in brokers, the distrust of brokers illustrated in Figure 2.3B is perhaps less pronounced when brokers reach across larger distances (deeper structural holes), especially if brokerage involves a new contact rather than a new idea (Halevy et al. 2025). Portions of this capstone are adapted from broader introductions to the theory for other audiences: Burt (2010) for management, Burt, Kilduff, and Tasselli (2013) for psychology, Burt and Soda (2017) for strategy, and Burt (2019a) for entrepreneurship.

people (Burt 2010). It is one thing to hear about diverse knowledge and practice that defines an opportunity.[8] It is quite another to recognize and develop the opportunity. Diverse information is readily available from professionals, social media, or word of mouth. It is easy to look up a business concept in Wikipedia and cite a reputable article on the concept and, more recently, to ask an AI to solve a particular problem. It is quite another to know the concept well enough to transform it into terms familiar to a target audience. Experience coordinating people with different understandings develops one's talent for converting and synthesizing information between groups. People behaving as network brokers develop skills of analogy, metaphor, and simile. They develop tolerance for ambiguity, for conflict between contrasting colleagues' understandings, and for seeing when the time is ripe to propose a new combination of knowledge or practice. In short, the social capital of brokering structural holes is a kind of forcing function for human capital (Burt 2010). Relative to a person who has spent all their time in a single business function, a person connected to multiple business functions is more likely to see a novel solution that integrates or synthesizes knowledge and practice across functions—or industries, countries, products, or channels.

Skills developed in association with broker behavior enhance creativity. To their European colleagues, for example, Bob and Yanjie are likely to appear creative. The European colleagues are not familiar with American or Asian operations, so good ideas articulately proposed by Bob or Yanjie (from their contacts overseas) look like creative innovations to their European colleagues. For example, suppose that Bob and Jim in Figure 2.1 have the same idea for an entrepreneurial spin-off from the organization. Jim knows how to express the idea in terms of American operations. The

---

[8] Given information linked with social structure (relatively homogeneous within groups and heterogeneous between), it is often assumed that people with networks rich in structural holes have access to more diverse information. The assumption simplifies research by alleviating the need to measure information directly. In studies that do measure information, networks more closed tend to contain information more homogeneous (Rodan and Galunic 2004; Zaheer and Soda 2009; Aral and Van Alstyne 2011; Soda et al. 2021). Network diversity is only an indicator of information diversity, and it is difficult to imagine a measure of information diversity that captures its full range, so studies typically report success associations with both measures of structural diversity as well as information diversity. Nevertheless, it seems safe to say that network brokers have access to more diverse information, but allow for the risk of false negatives—Aral and Van Alstyne (2011) report that even when network and information diversity are correlated (.71 in their data), people with a closed network in which diverse information is exchanged can also show some of the success associated with network brokers (Brashears and Quintane 2018 unpack components in Aral and Van Alstyne's argument).

more nuanced the idea, the more embedded in American operations, and the more different the American versus European operations (as indicated by the structural hole between the two in Figure 2.1)—the less successful Jim will be in explaining the value of the idea to potential investors at the European headquarters. Jim can explain in terms of American operations. Bob, by being embedded in European operations and familiar with American operations, is better positioned to explain the value of the idea in terms familiar to potential investors at headquarters.

In short, network brokers are expected to generate good ideas in a target group, adapted from the brokers' familiarity with other groups (Burt 2000: 362–367; 2004). The expectation has empirical support. Network brokers score high on creativity when creativity is measured by supervisor summary opinion of a subordinate's work (Perry-Smith 2006; Jang 2017; Carnabuci and Quintane 2023), by executive opinion of a middle manager's best idea for improving the organization (Burt 2004; 2005, Chapter 2), by external critical opinion of final product (Fleming and Marx 2006; Fleming et al. 2007; deVaan et al. 2015; Tortoriello 2015; Soda et al. 2021), or captured in reverse when closed networks are associated with delayed adaptation (Gargiulo and Benassi 2000; Lee and Gargiulo 2022). More generally, brokers provide absorptive portals for creative solutions to spillover between substantively distinct networks (Padgett 2026a, 2026b, with respect to spillover between economic, kinship, and political networks in Renaissance Florence).

Of course, creating a valuable product is a process, not an event. Good ideas morph as they wind their way through colleagues and technical constraints from inception to delivery. What begins as a good idea finishes as one of many possible implementations, the original idea subject to re-framing or re-imagining each step along the way (see Lingo and O'Mahony 2010; Rahman and Barley 2017; Barley et al. 2020, for illustrative detail, Latour 2008:5 for the succinct phrasing that design "is never a process that begins from scratch: to design is always to redesign"). Network advantage at the beginning and end of the creative process is likely an advantage at critical decision points during the process (Stuart and Sorenson 2007; Sorenson and Stuart 2008; Perry-Smith and Mannucci 2017; though good ideas seem to be used to impress friends more often than improve operations, Burt 2004:389–394).

In sum, structural holes in a network are potentially valuable contexts for action, brokerage is the act of coordinating across a hole via bridges between people on opposite sides of the hole, and network brokers are the people who build the bridges and become more able brokers as they gain experience with diversity in their immediate social environment. Brokers operate somewhere between the force of corporate authority and the dexterity of markets, building bridges between disconnected parts of markets and organizations where it is valuable to do so, translating what is known here into what can be understood to be valuable over there. Network brokers are the social mechanism that clears a sticky information market.

Stylized Fact 3: Achievement is Higher in More Open Networks

Figure 2.6 contains illustrative evidence of a negative association between achievement and closed networks, sometimes discussed as "returns to brokerage." Across a variety of study populations in which achievement is indicated by compensation, annual performance evaluations, or promotions, success relative to peers is measured on the vertical axis in Figure 2.6 as a residual z-score after controlling for non-network success factors in each population, such as job rank.[9] A score of zero on the vertical axis indicates a person whose success is what would be expected in his or her study population for someone with his or her job and characteristics. Positive numbers indicate managers ahead of the average peer. Negative numbers indicate managers lagging behind peers.

The network metric across the horizontal axis is network constraint, an index measuring the extent to which a person's social contacts are limited to one group. Network constraint increases as a network becomes small, dense, or dominated by a central contact.[10] The data plotted in Figure 2.6

---

[9] Success (measured by compensation, annual evaluations, and promotions) and control variables (held constant within population to measure relative success) are described in published articles inventoried with the source figure in Burt (2019b). We here add to the source figure data from a 2006 census of avatars in the virtual world *EverQuest II* (Burt 2012: 560), and a 2018 probability sample of 384 Chinese entrepreneurs to which we turn in Chapter 4.

[10] Network constraint measures the extent to which a person's network is concentrated in one contact—in other words, it measures the lack of structural holes in the network. Given the network around a person measured as a matrix of elements z_{ij}, where z_{ij} is the strength of connection between i and j, the constraint j poses for i, c_{ij}, is the squared proportion of i's interaction spent on j ($p_{ij} = z_{ij}/(\sum_k z_{ik})$), adjusted up for i's interaction spent on others who in turn spend their time on j: $c_{ij} = (p_{ij} + \sum_k p_{ik}p_{kj})^2$, $i \neq k \neq j$. Sum the c_{ij} across contacts j to get a Herfindahl index of concentration (Burt 1992:54–56): $C = \sum_j c_{ij}$. Constraint equals one for a person who has one contact. It decreases toward zero as the person has many contacts, who have no contact with each other, and no one contact has a disproportionate share of the person's interaction. We multiply constraint scores by 100 to discuss points of constraint.

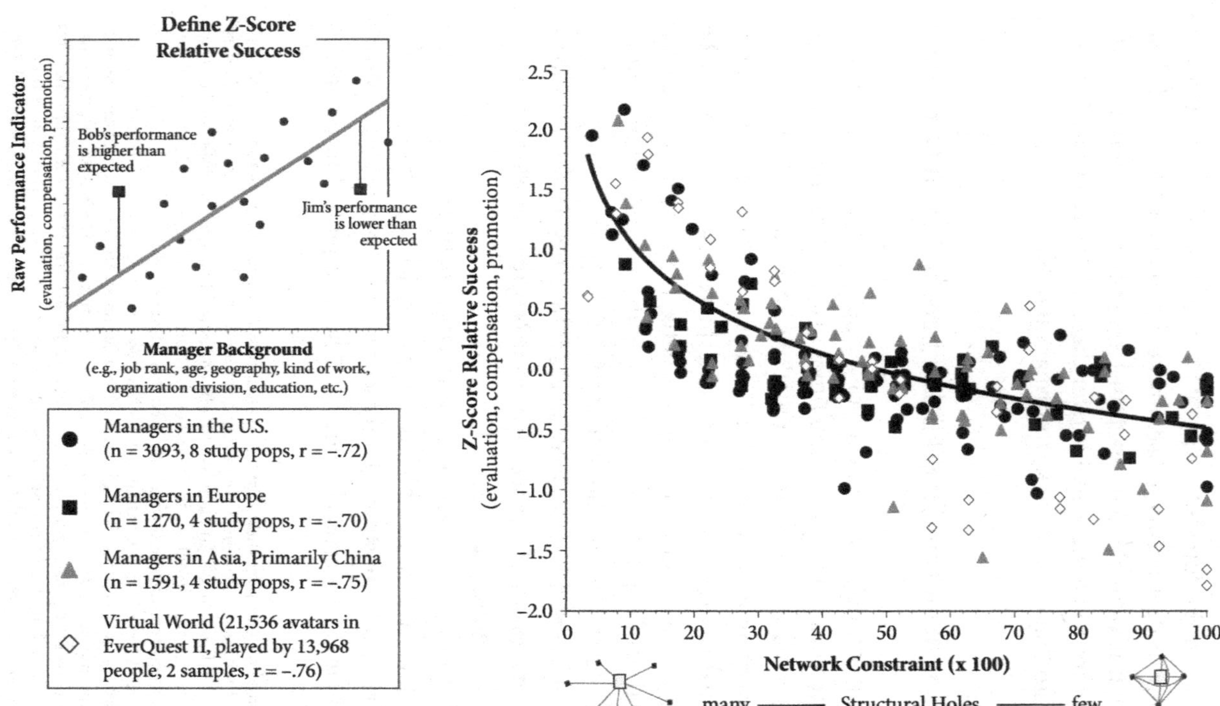

Figure 2.6 Open Networks and Achievement

Note: Plotted data are average scores within five-point intervals of network constraint within each study population. Correlations are computed from the plotted data using log network constraint. Inset graph to the upper left contains hypothetical data illustrating computation of z-score relative performance.

are averages of the horizontal and vertical axes within five-point intervals on the horizontal axis within each study population. The circles describe managers in eight American organizations. The squares describe managers in four European organizations. The triangles describe managers in Asia, mainly China, in two large organizations and three stratified probability samples of entrepreneurs leading small to medium-sized companies. The hollow diamonds describe a census of 21,536 avatars in the virtual world of *EverQuest II*. As predicted by network theory and reported in published studies of the populations, relative individual achievement decreases as a person's network becomes more closed. The pattern is similar across the four regions: −.72 partial correlation in the US, −.70 in the EU, −.75 in Asia, and −.76 in the virtual world.[11]

To the left on the horizontal axis are the network brokers, people whose networks reach across structural holes separating groups (illustrated by the sociogram of a person's network below the left side of the horizontal axis). Examples are readily found among successful people in all walks of life. For example, discussing commerce and manners, Adam Smith (1776: 539) noted that: "When the mind is employed about a variety of objects it is some how expanded and enlarged." Swedberg (1990:3) begins his book on academics working the boundary between economics and sociology with John Stuart Mill's (1848:581) opinion: "It is hardly possible to overrate the value … of placing human beings in contact with persons dissimilar to themselves, and with modes of thought and action unlike those with which they are familiar … Such communication has always been, and is peculiarly in the present age, one of the primary sources of progress." Serial entrepreneur Alex Zaffaroni is a contemporary exemplar. A former subordinate is quoted in an INSEAD video case explaining Zaffaroni's value to his organization: "… he is reading and thinking very widely. He is totally unafraid of any new technology in any area of human creativity. He has wonderful contacts with people in many different areas, so he sees the bridges between otherwise disparate fields."

---

[11] We predict achievement from the log of network constraint in order to capture the nonlinear association evident in Figure 2.6. Raw score measures of closure are sometimes used in place of log scores. Nonlinearity is evident in Figure 2.6 because we have observations widely variable in achievement and network structure. For more limited samples in which observations are concentrated to the middle or right of the horizontal axis in Figure 2.6, the association will be more linear so prediction by log constraint would be similar in explained variance to prediction by raw constraint scores. Authors likely use whichever measure provides more stable results, but the broader context deserves a note for comparisons across studies.

At the other extreme, to the right in Figure 2.6, are people embedded in a closed network of strongly interconnected colleagues (illustrated by the sociogram at the bottom right of the horizontal axis). These are the people you know who prefer to discuss ideas within a clique of friends who think similarly, and exist similarly ignorant of thoughts beyond their clique.

Stylized Fact 4: Advantage of Open Networks Is Contingent

The network advantage in Figure 2.6 can be out of reach for some individuals. When alter accepts an idea from ego, it is an act of deference. Ego has knowledge that is valuable to alter beyond what alter knows. Alter's act of deference in accepting the idea is convenient if ego is a prestigious source. But if ego is of low status within alter's group, it is status-eroding for alter to acknowledge accepting ego's idea. Instead, alter can attribute the information to an alternative, more respectable source (Menon and Pfeffer 2003) or claim to have the information without citing a source. In short, you may have a great idea, but it has no value to you if the audience for it does not want to hear it from a person who looks like you.

Let ego be termed a "legitimate" broker for alter if alter is comfortable accepting the idea or advice ego is proposing. A broker can be legitimate across audiences, but the condition is audience-specific in that a broker legitimate in this audience need not be legitimate in that other audience.

Graphs in Figure 2.7 illustrate the importance of legitimacy for successful brokerage. The axes and plotted data in Figure 2.7 are the same as in Figure 2.6, but two subpopulations are distinguished: "Legitimate" individuals have above-average social standing (solid line through dark dots). They are contrasted with other individuals (dashed line through hollow dots).

The network advantages evident across study populations in Figure 2.6 are concentrated in the brokers who have above-average social standing within each study population. This is indicated in Figure 2.7A by the authority of high job rank among supply chain managers in an electronics firm, in Figure 2.7B by high network status among HR officers in a commercial bank and managers in a software company, and in Figure 2.7C by positive reputation among investment bankers. In each graph, a solid line shows steep returns to brokerage for people with above-average

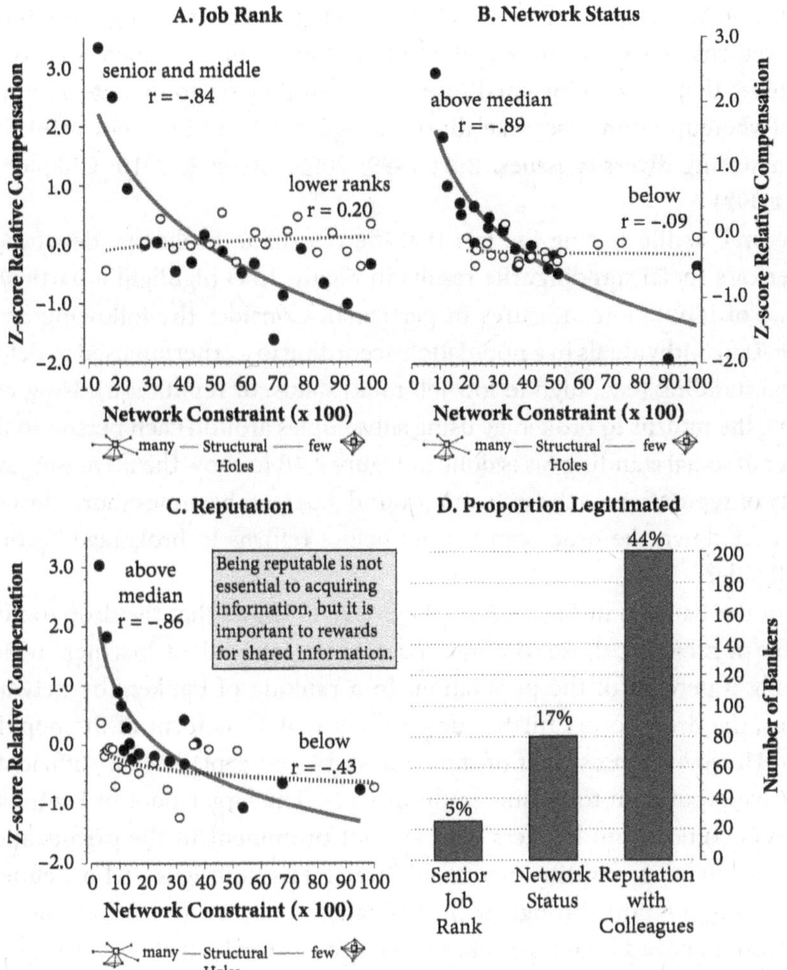

Figure 2.7 The Network-Achievement Link Is Contingent on Social Standing, Especially Reputation

Note: Plotted data here are average scores within five-point intervals of network constraint within four populations (electronics company for job rank, software company and HR in commercial bank for network status, investment bankers for reputation). Solid dots refer to people with high social standing (senior or middle job rank, above-median network status, above-median reputation). Correlations are computed from the plotted data using log network constraint.

social standing. These are people accepted to operate as legitimate brokers within their respective populations.[12] All three graphs show negligible

[12] Graphs A and B in Figure 2.7 are adapted from Burt (2021:392). See notes 6 and 7 in that text for summary details about the predictive models used to document the returns to brokerage from social status (which respectively were taken from analyses in Burt 2004 and Burt

returns to brokerage for people of below-average social standing—and those low returns can turn into negative returns for people of such low social standing that they are deemed "uppity" when they try to operate as a broker (whereupon analyses like those in Figure 2.7 can be a powerful tool for assessing diversity issues, Burt 1999; 2000:400–407; 2010: Chapter 7; 2021:392).

As well as illustrating the fact that the returns to brokerage depend on a person's social standing, the results in Figure 2.7D highlight a particular virtue of reputation measures in particular. Consider the following exercise: Rank individuals in a population according to a criterion used to define social standing (e.g., high to low job rank, status, or reputation). Now, calculate the returns to brokerage using subsamples around each person in the order of social standing (as is done in Figure 2.4B to show the increasing stability of reputation as the network around a person becomes more closed). How far down the order can you go before returns to brokerage become negligible?

For the bankers in Figure 2.7C, Figure 2.7D shows that the drop to negligible occurs after those who have risen to the job rank of "partner," which is only 5 percent of the population. In a ranking of bankers by network status, the drop occurs further down the list, at 17 percent of the population. However, almost half of the bankers (44 percent) have a sufficiently positive reputation to be successful brokers. The larger pool of legitimate brokers comes from bankers who are not prominent in the organization but who have a constituency of admirers. The colleagues who define a positive reputation through their evaluations may be few in number. In contrast, to have a high job rank, a banker must stand out above all employees. To have a high network status, a banker must be widely recognized for his or her achievements. But to have an above-average reputation, a banker only needs a constituency of people who give him or her positive ratings. Thus, reputation measured and displayed as an average colleague evaluation is a powerful tool for facilitating brokerage within a population, thereby facilitating broader participation in the achievement associated

and Merluzzi 2014). The same model is used here in Figure 2.7C to predict banker bonus compensation from log network constraint, with level and slope adjustments for the difference between bankers with above- and below-average reputations (plus controls for job rank and location, Burt 2010:92). Test statistics for the more negative associations between network and performance for people with above-average social standing are −4.24 in Graph A, −6.25 in Graph B, and −4.35 in Graph C, all statistically significant well beyond the .001 level.

with brokerage. Ironically, this condition is most likely for people embedded in closed networks.[13]

Conclusion: Strong Bridges Despite Fragile Brokerage

We have organized this chapter around four stylized facts and one contradictory data pattern. The latter two of the stylized facts concern changing the status quo. Figure 2.6 shows that across cultures and organizations, individual achievement relative to peers increases for people whose social network provides opportunities for them to move information across groups. The behavior is network brokerage, and the people who provide it are network brokers. The measures of achievement are creativity, positive evaluations from colleagues and superiors, compensation higher than peers, and promotion to more prominent positions. Network brokers with their rewarded advantages of information breadth, timing, and arbitrage are certainly positioned to change the status quo. But the rewards are not available to everyone. Rewards depend on audiences having respect for the person who brokers information. Where those audiences operate in closed networks, brokers can expect to be viewed with suspicion (Figure 2.3B). Figure 2.7 shows that returns to brokerage are contingent on a broker's social standing as indicated by authority, status, or especially reputation. Figures 2.3 and 2.4 show the intensity and stability of audience evaluation increasing with network closure, which serves to preserve the status quo against brokerage.

The four stylized facts highlight a tension in network theory: Ability to change the status quo is facilitated by open networks (Figure 2.6), but that ability is contingent on social standing (Figure 2.7), and that social standing is easier to secure, on average, in closed networks that serve to preserve the status quo (Figures 2.3 and 2.4). This is why the bridge relations on which brokers prosper are generally understood to be weak (Granovetter 1973; 1982), and brokerage often appears fragile (Stovel et al. 2011). Theoretical models are available describing the distribution of broker advantage in stable "equilibrium" networks (Ryall and Sorenson 2007; Buskens and van de Rijt 2008; Kleinberg et al. 2008), but the models are usually pessimistic about sustained advantage (though not always, Goyal and Vega-Redondo 2007).

---

[13] What we have said about status and reputation is sufficient for our purposes here, but their respective implications for returns to brokerage is a promising interface with the computer science concepts of PageRank and hubs (Kleinberg 2026).

One solution is to embed bridges in partially closed networks. A bridge can be reinforced with one or two third parties strongly connected to the individuals at either end of the bridge, thereby creating a closed-triad "Simmelian tie" (Krackhardt 1992; 1999; Tortoriello and Krackhardt 2010; Tortoriello et al. In Press), or a "wide bridge" (Centola and Macy 2007; Centola 2018; Guilbeault and Centola 2021). Aggregating up, Stovel et al. (2011) discuss examples of brokerage stabilized by embedding it in an institution: Brokerage can be made less fragile by confining it to a group that cannot abuse broker information advantage (e.g., marriage matchmakers in China), absorbing brokers into one side or the other (e.g., Protestant missionaries supporting practical community interests rather than colonial elite interests), or absorbing brokerage into the activity of an established organization (e.g., social welfare organizations that foster brokerage among members).

These proposals reinforcing bridge relations are familiar in theory, and can be supported empirically, but they are strategies for converting brokerage into closure. Adding third parties to a bridge moves it across the horizontal axis in Figure 2.3, eventually converting a bridge between groups into a relationship within a group. Third-party reinforcement has several attractive features discussed in the above references, especially for loosely connected networks across the internet. But for the general case, which includes unambiguously balkanized networks within and across organizations, we find third-party reinforcement a theoretically unsatisfactory solution to the fragility of bridge relations. Alternative solutions must exist: Despite ostensible fragility, people muddle through in that the people who have advantaged access to holes today are often the people who had advantage yesterday (Burt 2005: Chapter 5; Goyal et al. 2006; Burger and Buskens 2009; Quintane and Carnabuci 2016).

It was in this context that we were excited to see the contradictory data pattern in Figure 2.5. Connections with event contacts are strong in that they are trusted, emotionally close relationships—but many are bridge relations (indicated in Figure 2.5B). Concepts of strong bridges lie at the center of the tension between network forces facilitating versus inhibiting change to the status quo. Hence, our third and primary reason for digging into the outlier relations is to find a satisfying answer to how bridge relations can be so strong.

3

Trust in Event Contacts

To better understand the unexpectedly high trust in bridge relations with event contacts, we dig into the rich data we have on these contacts. Almost any story about them can find support somewhere in published research or practitioner anecdotes. There are professional stories: In an emergency, turn to the most recognized or most experienced experts. There are social stories: In an emergency, turn to the best people available at a good price, such as family professionals or trusted friends who owe you a favor. There are contingency stories: In an emergency, turn to a person appropriate to the specific opportunity or issue at hand.

These are difficult decisions for an entrepreneur just starting out. Move the issue to China around the turn of the century, and the situation becomes even more complex. Not only did Chinese entrepreneurs have to juggle the usual uncertainties and resource constraints rooted in the relative newness of their business venture (liability of newness, Stinchcombe 1965). The rapidly changing organizational needs during the life-cycle of a firm also coincided with dynamic changes in the firms' institutional environment. Over the decades of recent history, private firms evolved from stigmatized pariahs to legally recognized entities that have constitutional parity with publicly owned firms. Nevertheless, stories of regulatory discrimination and limited access to scarce resources such as credit, land use rights, and skilled human capital persist well into the twenty-first century (Nee and Opper 2012) and the current political regime (Lardy 2019).

Similarly, the pool of accessible experts to whom entrepreneurs can turn for help and support has changed considerably over time. Who were the people initially willing to help entrepreneurs starting new organizations to compete with state-owned enterprises and foreign ventures? Who accepted the risk, given the absence of fully developed institutional support for private firms? Even today, with a continuing shortage of skilled and highly educated labor, sought-after professionals often prefer established corporations to private start-ups. So, who are the key contacts for critical events?

Strong Bridges. Ronald S. Burt and Sonja Opper, Oxford University Press. © Oxford University Press (2026).
DOI: 10.1093/9780197834275.003.0003

Is family the most reliable source of support for entrepreneurial success in China (Huang 1990)? Should one involve prominent people such as local party or government officials to gain political protection and access to state-controlled resources (Li et al. 2008; Peng and Luo 2000)? Or, should one abstain from their involvement?

Relatedly, does the kind of event in which a respondent received help influence the level of trust placed in event contacts? In a hybrid economy such as China's, it would be understandable if respondents valued others' help more when alternatives and market solutions are not readily available. For example, the financial sector remains highly regulated, making it notoriously difficult for entrepreneurs to respond quickly and unbureaucratically to financial challenges. Many entrepreneurs therefore see access to informal finance as a critical safety net (Nee and Opper 2012). Similarly, dealing with government agencies, whether for access to government tenders, permits, or contracts, is often perceived as particularly challenging (Nee and Opper 2010). Assistance in such instances could therefore be seen as more valuable than assistance in market settings. In short, given the wide range of entrepreneurial needs and the varying degrees of institutional constraints that limit access to resources in China, we ask on what occasions did respondents rely on event contacts that now stand out as highly trustworthy, regardless of their structural embedding?

To answer such questions, one would like to have fine-grained accounts documenting the identity or social role of event contacts, the ways in which these contacts played a role in business development over time—and whether or not they continue to be an active source of support.

We have such data. Our summary conclusion from the analysis in this chapter is that the high level of trust evident in event contacts comes from within—from the interpersonal history of a relationship. Trust is relatively independent of the surrounding network, not contingent on specific kinds of events, and builds systematically over the years a contact is known. In other words, events are not significant in their own right. They are significant as an occasion for an entrepreneur to learn that a contact can be trusted. Of course, given the critical nature of these events (the respondent sees them as milestones), it is clear that the respondent did not call on a random contact. The contacts seemed trustworthy at the time, at least trustworthy enough to get involved. However, the event provided an opportunity to experience a person's trustworthiness when it truly mattered. We introduce the data, then compare event contacts with other contacts, and then compare kinds of event contacts. We wrap up with conclusions, in preparation for shifting perspective to events as the context in which guanxi develops.

Data: Social Networks of Chinese Entrepreneurs

Collecting network data from a large probability sample of entrepreneurs drawn from a heterogeneous area population is challenging. This is all the more so in the context of the Chinese economy, where entrepreneurs do not have the supportive social norms and formal institutions common in the West, so they are often careful to protect the identity of personal and professional contacts. Information on personal networks and valued business contacts is understood in China to be a key determinant of success. Information shared on even the identity of key suppliers or customers requires a certain level of trust. Experience from previous projects facilitated our data collection.

First, much was learned from the research strategy used to initially gather network data on a national probability sample of Americans for the 1984 General Social Survey (Burt 1984; Marsden 1987). The strategy is to ask the survey respondent for the names of people with whom he or she has particular relations, while specifically encouraging the respondent to use only a nickname or alias when going through the instrument. Then ask about the nature of relationships with and among the cited contacts. The former kinds of questions are "name generators," the latter "name interpreters." Name generators and interpreters have become routine in network survey research (Marsden 2011; Perry et al. 2018), in network surveys of management populations in particular (Burt 2010:281ff.), and have precedent in China (Ruan 1998, the 2003 Chinese General Social Survey, http://cgss.ruc. edu.cn/English/Home.htm, Bian and Li 2012; Xiao and Tsui 2007; Batjargal 2007a; Batjargal et al. 2013).

Another advantage was that we were able to build on established relations with a local survey organization in charge of prior firm surveys in the same region. Data for this book are taken from three surveys with stratified probability samples of small to medium-size private enterprises in the Yangtze Delta region of China. Surveys were conducted in 2012, 2018, and 2021. Establishing a baseline, the 2012 survey was the largest and most diverse sample. Based on our findings from the 2012 survey, we conducted a survey with a guanxi item in 2018 with a smaller sample including no respondents from the 2012 sample. The 2021 survey during the COVID pandemic was with a still more targeted sample, including as many respondents from the 2018 survey as could be located and agreed to participate. This chapter focuses on the 2012 survey.

Study Population

All three surveys target private firms in the Yangtze River Delta, one of the country's centers of post-reform entrepreneurial activity. Historically, the region is rich in trade networks and a commercial culture dating back to the Tang (618–907) and Song (960–1279) dynasties. The region was among the first to benefit from China's gradual market liberalization policies. Designated as the Shanghai Economic Area, the national government under Deng Xiaoping's leadership granted these cities greater autonomy and control over economic decision-making and planning, fostering more flexible policies tailored to local needs. The original zone included ten cities: Shanghai, plus four cities in Jiangsu Province (two of which are included in the network survey, Changzhou and Nantong), and five cities in Zhejiang Province (two of which are included in the network survey, Hangzhou and Ningbo), which also became founding members of the newly established Yangtze River Delta Economic Coordination Association in 1992, which now has forty-one member cities. The region is dominated by China's financial center, Shanghai, with Nanjing the capital of Jiangsu Province to the north, and Hangzhou the capital of Zhejiang Province to the south. The three provinces accounted for 20.2 percent of China's gross domestic product, and 31.9 percent of China's imports and exports in 2013, around the time of our first survey.[1]

The 2012 sample is a continuation of samples surveyed in 2006 and 2009 by Nee and Opper (2012). As they explain, participants were recruited for an initial survey in 2006 using a roster of private firms registered with China's Bureau of Industry. The registry excluded from the population small-scale household enterprises (a specific legal status reserved for firms with less than seven employees) and fly-by-night businesses—illegitimate firms in the informal economy with short life spans. Nee and Opper further

---

[1] GDP and import-export data are taken from www.chinadataonline.org. City memberships in Shanghai Economic Area and Yangtze River Delta Economic Coordination Association are taken from Wikipedia discussion of the two organizations as of November 6, 2016.

narrowed the population by excluding companies in business for less than three years and small companies (less than 10 salaried workers). The sample is stratified within the seven cities in Figure 3.1 by industry (electronics, machinery, pharmaceuticals, textiles, and transportation equipment), and size of company (following China's national classification system of small [10–100 salaried employees], medium [101–300], and large [> 300]). To maintain the original sample size, lost respondents were replaced for the subsequent two survey waves (2009 and 2012), following the same random sampling procedure described above.

One hundred firms were sampled from each city. The bar charts in Figure 3.1 show that each city provided small and large companies, with small firms more likely in Nanjing and Changzhou, less likely in Nantong (large shipping port) and Shanghai (financial hub). Wenzhou was not part of the Yangtze River Delta Economic Coordination Association at the time of the initial 2006 survey, nor the 2012 survey including the network module. Wenzhou was included in the sampling frame because it is so often referred to as the "epicenter" and model of private entrepreneurship in China—the

Sample Characteristics	N	%
Small (10 – 100)	468	67%
Medium (101 – 300)	169	24%
Large (> 300)	63	9%
Textile	170	24%
Transportation Equipment	171	24%
Machinery	180	26%
Pharmaceutical	77	11%
Electronics	102	15%
Respondent is Founder	559	80%
Year Born	1967 median, 8.4 sd, 1938–1988	
Yr Founded	2001 median, 4.6 sd, 1982–2011	

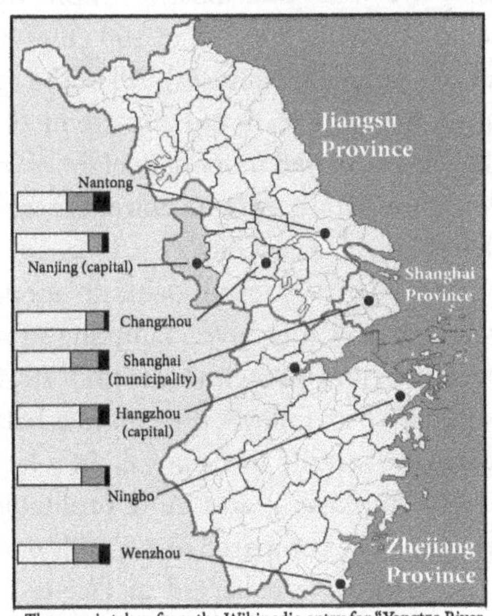

The map is taken from the Wikipedia entry for "Yangtze River Delta" with the delta proper indicated in green. Bold lines separate provinces. Bars indicate small, medium, and large firms in the sample 100 entrepreneurs from each city (respectively, light, dark grey, and black areas of city bar).

Figure 3.1 Stratified Probability Sample of 700 Chinese Entrepreneurs from Seven Cities in Three Provinces of China's Yangtze River Delta Region

so-called "Wenzhou model"—protected by its geographic isolation, from which entrepreneurial practice took hold and spread northward to the province's larger cities and beyond (Nee and Opper 2012:41ff.).

Our respondent is the general manager of a sample business.[2] Businesses were contacted by mail and phone to schedule interviews with the general manager or, for larger companies, the CEO. Replacements by the manager's deputy or other senior managers were not accepted to ensure comparable information from those actually responsible for running the business. Most of the respondents were also the founder (or co-founder) of the business for which they were sampled (80 percent); another 8 percent were owners, and the remaining 12 percent were senior managers of the business. Founders and owners were more likely to be the respondent for small businesses (91 percent), but even in large businesses, a substantial 73 percent of respondents were founders and owners. The high proportion of owners and founders—individuals present from the start of the company—provides excellent conditions for collecting network data that incorporates historical entries from the company's earlier life-course.

The means in Figure 3.1 show that the average respondent in 2012 was forty-five years old, most of whom were running a small business in the sense of having fewer than 100 employees (median is 67 employees across all 700 sample businesses). All of the sample firms are entrepreneurial ventures, but 79 percent of them are in 2012 mature ventures in the sense that they had survived more than eight years. We will refer to the respondents as entrepreneurs; surviving entrepreneurs to be sure, but entrepreneurs more than senior bureaucrats.

The 700 survey respondents do not provide a representative sample of private firms in China given sampling strata defined by affluent cities in a prosperous region, but neither are their stories peculiar. Opper et al. (2017:1512) summarize as follows the contrast between sample and national: "Specifically, the sample firms are slightly larger (with an average 130 compared to 117 employees) and more profitable (with a mean annual profit of 3.9 million CNY compared to 3.4 million nationally)."

All data were collected in face-to-face interviews conducted by teams of two professional local interviewers, who typically conducted the interview at the company's premises. The great majority of interviews were

---

[2] This means, the survey organization scheduled appointments with whoever held the role of 总经理 or CEO for the small number of large joint stock companies in our sample.

conducted in the manager's office, without additional persons present. All interviewers had previously undergone intense multi-day training workshops, received detailed manuals, and instructions that were taken to the field providing quick answers for troubleshooting and specifying the code of conduct during the interview process. Focus groups discussed the survey instrument for accuracy and the feasibility. Before taking the survey to the field, the instrument was subjected to an extended pre-test with a group of seventy entrepreneurs randomly sampled for this purpose from the same cities and industrial sectors as the main survey. The pretests were used to check on the effectiveness of the questionnaire design, as well as ensure the consistent quality of interviews and interviewers. These precautions resulted in two significant changes to the initial network module, one to protect network confidentiality, and a second to define trust in a way meaningful to the respondents (see Appendix, for further detail on survey preparations).

Survey Instrument

The survey involved two modules. One collected personal and firm information. The second asked about the respondent's network in growing the business. The network is measured in the usual way: name generators elicit the names of people helpful in building and operating the business, then name interpreters ask about relations with and among contacts. The modules differ slightly across the three surveys. In all three, respondents kept contact names confidential. In Appendix A, we display and walk you through an English version of the instrument used in the 2018 survey.

Name Generators

Six name generator questions are listed in Table 3.1, in the order of their asking. To stretch the network data back into the history of a respondent's business, we used event name generators (see Question 2). The idea is to create a timeline of concrete events, then ask for the names of contacts who were most valued during each event. The item to construct a timeline is displayed in Figure A2 (see Appendix A). The interviewer guides the respondent through the example at the top of Figure A2 as the respondent completes the timeline below for his or her business. To the left, the respondent enters the year his or her business was founded, marks the midpoint between now

Table 3.1 Name Generators

Question (number is sequence in interview, see Figure A3)	2012	2018	2021
2. (FOUNDING) Who was the one person who was most valuable to you in founding the firm?	700	384	371
3. (OTHER EVENTS) Now please do the same thing for each of the significant events you listed. The first significant event you listed was (say first event) in (say year). Who was the person most valuable to you during that event?	2701	1571	1369
5. (CURRENT) Shifting now to business this year, and thinking about people inside or outside your firm, who are the three or four people who have been most valuable to your business activities this year?	2357	1296	1824
6. (DIFFICULT) In contrast to people who help and are valued in your business activities, there are usually some people who make life difficult. Without mentioning the person's name, who was the most difficult person to deal with in your business activities this year? Just jot a name or initials in the box below. Only you are going to know who this person is.	700	384	—
7. (EMPLOYEE) Shifting to happier thoughts, who do you think was your most valuable senior employee this year?	700	383	371
8. (NEC) Now that you have a list of contacts on the roster worksheet, please look it over quickly. Is there anyone particularly significant for your business who has not been mentioned? If yes, please enter their name at the bottom of the list. There are many people you could mention. These would just be people particularly significant for your business. The roster can hold a maximum of 14 names.	16	9	563
Total Cited Contacts	4464	2702	3244
Total Respondents	700	384	371
Mean Contacts per Respondent	6.38	7.04	8.74

and then, and marks the midpoints at the quarter periods. The respondent is then asked to indicate the year and nature of significant events in the business.

We do not provide an objective definition of what makes an event "significant." We want to capture the respondent's sense of significance, not our own. However, we limit significance to events important in the overall "history of the company development." The example timeline in the questionnaire further clarifies that we are looking for milestone events in the company's development.

Upon finishing the timeline, the respondent is asked the first name generator in Table 3.1: "Who was the one person most valuable to you in founding the firm?" A similar question was posed for each of the significant events listed. All respondents named a contact most valuable when the firm was founded, then named an average of three or four contacts most valuable during subsequent events. For each of these "event" contacts, we know the event year and the kind of event in which the respondent valued the contact. Of course, the same person was sometimes named on multiple events and multiple name generators.

Questions 5, 6, and 7 list the more generic questions in management research describing a manager's current network. Question 5 asks for the names of people who the respondent feels are most valuable in his or her business activities. Many respondents used all four response slots, so an additional slot was added in the 2021 survey. Question 6 was included to ensure that at least one difficult person is included in the network. The "difficult person" generator was dropped in the 2021 survey to make room for a COVID-related name generator, which we revisit in Chapter 7. Question 7 was included to ensure that externally focused entrepreneurs named at least one valuable employee inside the business.

The final name generator in Table 3.1 is a "not elsewhere classified" generator (Question 8). Surprised by the low number of such contacts, we had interviewers add a probe in the 2021 survey ("Are you sure?"), which generated quite a few additional contacts. In total, respondents to the 2012 survey named an average of 6.38 contacts, varying from a minimum of three up to a maximum of twelve. The average is slightly higher in 2018, and rose further in 2021, aided by the additional response slot for "valued contacts" and the "not elsewhere classified" probe (for further detail, see Chapter 7).

Name Interpreters

Given a roster of key contacts, name interpreter questions were used to elicit data on contact gender, the substance of the respondent's connection with each contact (emotional closeness, duration of acquaintance, frequency of contact, trust), and the variety of roles in which respondent and contact have been linked (family, neighbor, party, childhood, classmate, military, co-worker, co-member business association; Figure A9, item 17 in Appendix A).

The Chinese word "信任" (trust) is a term as ambiguous in Chinese as "trust" is in English, so we worried respondents might take issue with its definition. To ensure that all respondents could equally relate to the question, interviewers were trained to offer examples of concrete situations illustrating norm violations and applicable to contacts with different roles. Respondents were asked to use a scale from 1 to 5, with 1 describing the lowest and 5 the highest trust level.[3]

To scale relations in the network around an entrepreneur, we ask respondents whether the respondent's own relation with each contact is "especially close," "close," "less close," or "distant" (Figure A9, item 10), then asked whether the connection between each named contact is "especially close," "distant," or "neither distant nor especially close" (Figure A9, last page). With each connection in a respondent's network scaled from 0 to 1 (see Figure A10), we can compute summary network metrics often used in studies of trust and achievement.

Illustrative Social Networks

Figure 3.2 displays a sociogram of one of the more open networks, and Figure 3.3 displays a sociogram for one of the more closed. The displays provide a quick sense of the data, and will be helpful in later discussion. Networks are visualized using a spring-embedding algorithm that locates people close together as a function of their connection with each other and through others (Borgatti 2002). Both sociograms describe the network around an entrepreneur who founded the sample business. A square dot in each diagram indicates the respondent. Line thickness indicates emotional closeness. The absence of a line indicates a "distant" relationship. Frequently used metrics summarizing network structure are displayed in each figure.

The respondent in Figure 3.2 founded his business thirteen years ago in Zhejiang province, and grew it to 467 employees by the time of the survey. He named nine contacts, largely interconnected by close relations (thin lines in sociogram) with a few especially close relations (bold lines). His nine contacts form a network slightly larger and less dense than the sample average (z-scores of 1.77 and −0.72, respectively), and his network constrains the respondent less than the average in the sample (37.1 points of network constraint, −1.38 z-score).

---

[3] It is valuable to know for our network analysis that trust scores vary primarily within rather than between networks. Trust variance across relationships is 60 percent network differences within respondents, 10 percent individual differences between respondents, and 30 percent random error (Burt et al. 2017). This is confirmed in the 2018 survey (see Appendix A, Figure A9, item 14), which used a more elaborate, situational description of trust—with no noticeable influence on response frequencies and descriptive statistics.

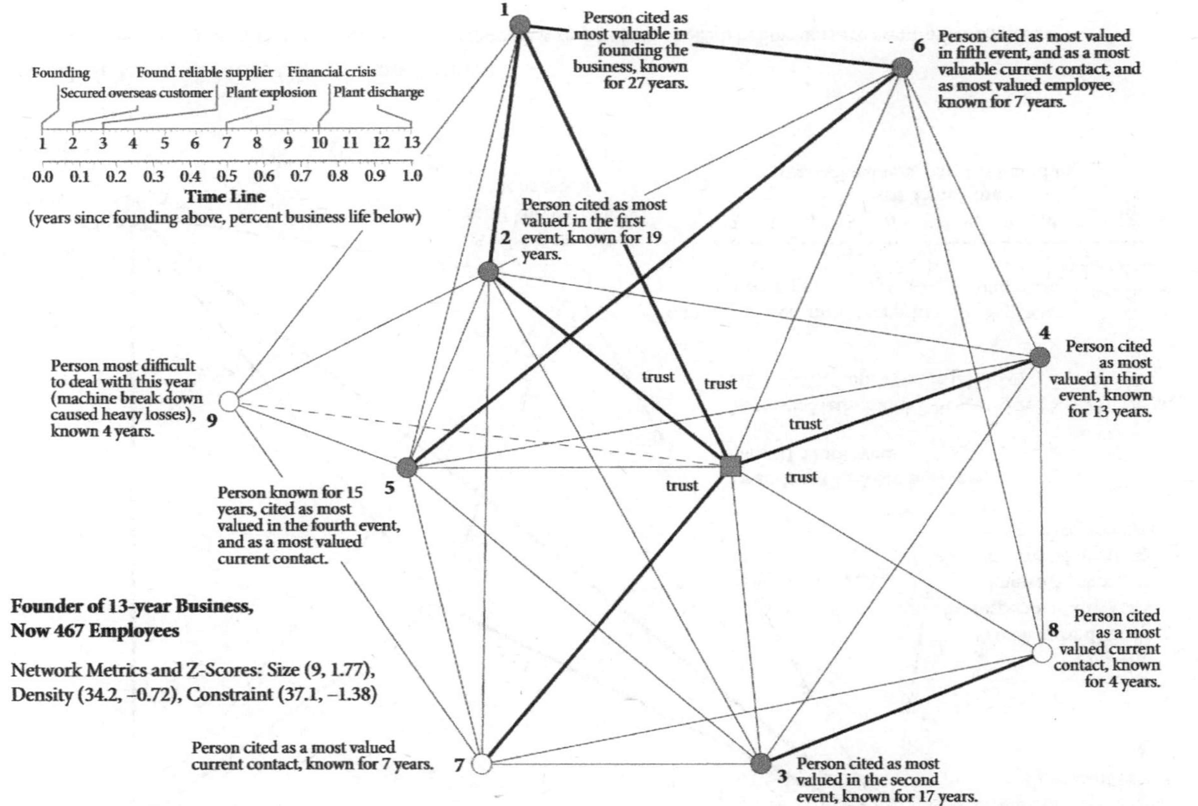

Figure 3.2 A Network Larger and More Open than Average

Note: Line thickness indicates closeness. No line is "distant" relation. Square is respondent. Shaded/hollow dots are event/other contacts.

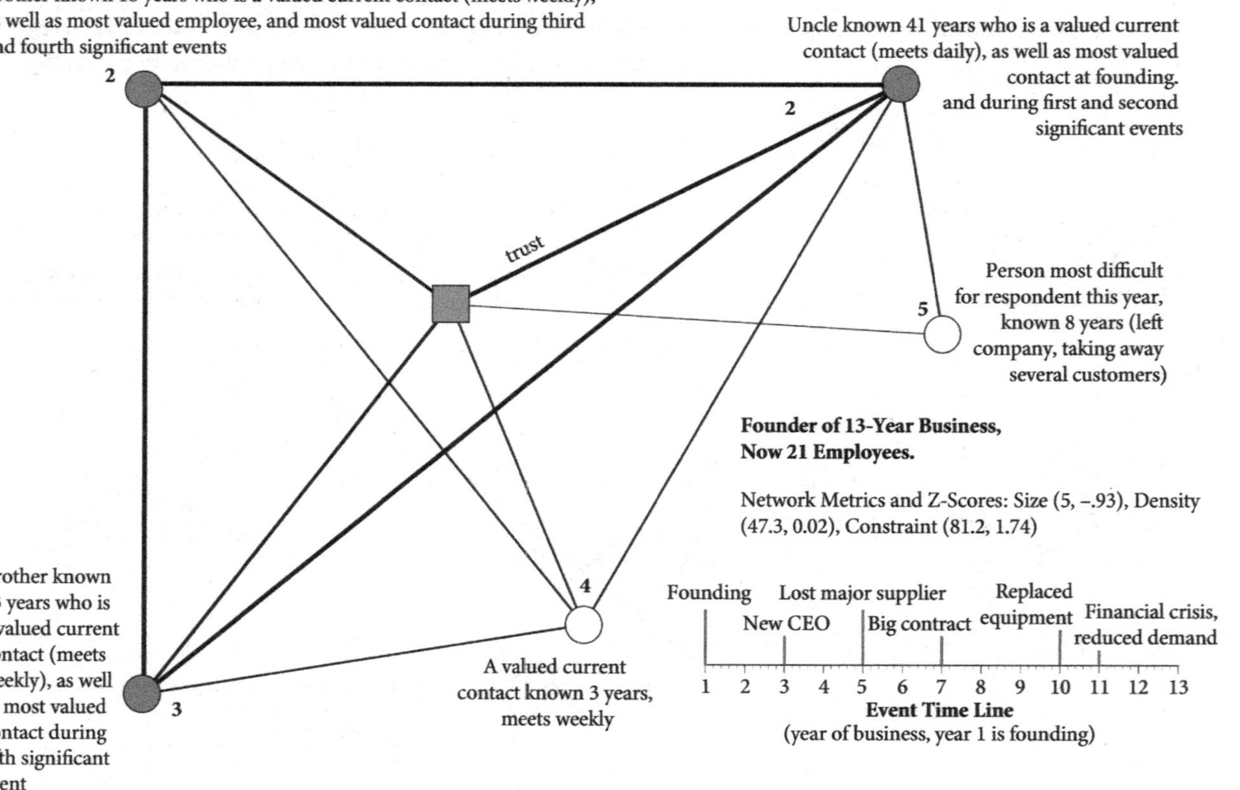

Figure 3.3 A Network More Closed than Average

Note: Line thickness closeness. No line is "distant" relation. Square is respondent. Shaded/hollow dots are event/other contacts.

People named in association with significant events, "event contacts," are indicated by solid dots in the sociogram. The hollow dots represent people named on questions other than the event name generators ("current contacts," which are the usual focus of business network research). A contact can be cited on more than one name generator, so it is often the case that a current contact is also an event contact (e.g., contacts 5 and 6).

Significant events cited during the interview with the Figure 3.2 entrepreneur are listed on a timeline to the upper-left in the figure. Contact 1 was cited as the most valued person in founding the business. Securing the first overseas customer—a key event in the second year—led to the naming of contact 2 as most valued during that event. Significant events continue across the timeline, each event eliciting the name of a person most valued during the event.

Contacts cited for the highest level of trust are indicated by the word "trust" next to their link with the respondent. Event contacts tend to be cited for the highest level of trust (contacts 1, 2, 4, and 5 in Figure 3.2). But not all are (contacts 3 and 6), while a current contact not involved in any event is cited for the highest level of trust (contact 8).

In three ways, the network in Figure 3.3 is more closed than the one in Figure 3.2. First, it is smaller with stronger connections among the contacts (5 contacts with 47.3 density versus 9 contacts in Figure 3.2 with 34.2 density). Network constraint in Figure 3.3 is high at 81.2 points, placing this network far to the right in the returns-to-brokerage graph in Figure 2.6. In contrast, network constraint in Figure 3.2 is relatively low at 37.1 points (-1.38 z-score).

Second, the network in Figure 3.3 is more family-based, which adds its own kind of closure to the structure (60 percent family in Figure 3.3 versus 0 percent in Figure 3.2). The respondent in Figure 3.3 only cites one of his contacts for the highest level of trust: His uncle, who helped him found his business.

Third, the entrepreneur in Figure 3.3 makes repeated use of the same people for support. He turned to his uncle for help in founding the business, then again when a new CEO was needed, and again when a major supplier was lost (significant events one and two in the timeline to the lower-right in the figure). He went to his brother of eighteen years for help with a particularly large contract, and when he made a large capital investment in new equipment (events three and four). The financial crisis hit China just after the equipment purchase. Company sales were hit hard. He turned to his other brother for help in dealing with the downturn. In short, the entrepreneur in Figure 3.3 relies heavily on his family—returning again and again, even to considerably younger and less experienced family members. In contrast, no contacts in Figure 3.2 are cited for more than one significant event. Most contacts cited as valued during events are met currently, but are not included among the respondent's most valued current contacts.

Event Versus Current Contacts

Research on social networks often employs multiple name generators (e.g., Wellman 1979; Fischer 1982; Bidart and Charbonneau 2011; Offer and Fischer 2018). But in projects involving diverse interests other than networks—such as early pioneering efforts with the Detroit Area Study (Laumann 1973) or the General Social Survey (Burt 1984; Marsden 1987)—time pressure often limits the interview to a single name generator, typically one that measures the current network. That makes the comparison here—between event and current name generators—valuable both for practical as well as substantive reasons. What would be lost by using one versus the other? Event and current name generators can generate the same network for an entrepreneur with a solid network that has been with her since she founded the business. In contrast, sharp differences can exist for an entrepreneur whose business involves new contacts beyond the network with which she began.

As usual, truth lies between the extremes. Table 3.2 shows that current contacts are often event contacts. The roster of contacts generated by event name generators overlaps by about half with the roster of current contacts generated by the name generators in the other rows of the table. Of the average 6.86 contacts named, 2.2 are named only as current contacts (1559/4464 equals .35, and that times 6.38 equals 2.2), 1.92 are named only as event contacts, and 2.24 are named as both event and current contacts.

Columns in Table 3.2 show that relations are stronger with event contacts, but not exclusively so. The first column of means shows that entrepreneurs have known event contacts for more years, which is not surprising since event contacts were identified from the history of the entrepreneur's business. The subsequent columns of the table describe current relationships. Event contacts are more likely to be highly trusted today, more likely to be described as especially close, and more likely to be family—though family are rare in both categories.

Table 3.2 Tie Strength with Event Versus Current Contacts

Kind of Contact	Mean Years Known	Mean Trust	Percent Especially Close	Percent Family	Contact Frequency				Total
					Daily	Weekly	Monthly	Less	
Event Only	13.10	4.29	34%	13%	572 (43%)	410 (30%)	229 (17%)	130 (10%)	1341 (100%)
Event & Current	13.33	4.46	45%	11%	1056 (68%)	397 (25%)	99 (6%)	12 (1%)	1564 (100%)
Current Only (nonevent)	5.50	3.07	5%	1%	709 (45%)	471 (30%)	135 (9%)	244 (16%)	1559 (100%)
Total	10.53	3.92	28%	8%	2337 (52%)	1278 (29%)	463 (10%)	386 (9%)	4464 (100%)
Test Statistic Rejecting No Row Difference	829.86 P < .001	1170.81 P < .001	463.28 P < .001	42.6 P < .001	208.18 P < .001	9.48 P < .01	94.90 P < .001	123.55 P < .001	

Note: Trust is measured on a five-point scale. Test statistics for difference between the rows are made with respondent fixed effects. Test statistics for trust and years known are $F_{(2,3762)}$. The other test statistics are chi-square statistics with 2 d.f. Especially close contacts are distinguished from close, less close, and distant (test statistic for ordinal regression distinguishing close, less close, and distant also rejects the null: 207.18 chi-square, 2 d.f., P < .001). Test statistic for ordinal logit predicting four categories of contact frequency also rejects the null (244.06 chi-square, 2 d.f., P < .001). Percentage of row contacts at each level of frequency is in parentheses.

In fact, the majority of people named only as event contacts still meet with the entrepreneur frequently—43 percent daily, 30 percent weekly. People named only as current contacts are equally likely to meet daily or weekly. Clearly, event contacts are of more than just historical interest. They are people entrepreneurs continue to see, and to whom they remain emotionally attached—at the same time, they are people often missed by current name generators.[4]

Kinds of Event Contacts

Given trust in event contacts significantly different from trust in current contacts, one can be curious to explore whether kinds of events establish a similar stratification among event contacts. One can think of a number of potential differences. The first milestone might be just like someone's first love. Help provided by certain kind of people may always mean more than help offered by others. And help offered in areas, in which help is particularly difficult to secure or of higher financial value than in other areas may stand out as more valuable or meaningful. Here we show that differences between kinds of events matter indeed, but less than one might expect and less than the difference between event versus current contacts.

Kinds Distinguished by Event Order

Consider Figure 3.4, predicting trust from the extent to which a relationship is embedded in mutual friends. This is the same as Figure 2.5B, except event contacts (combined in Figure 2.5B) are here distinguished by the order of the event for which they were named: founding event, first named event, second, and so on. Trust in relations with founding contacts is the bold line

---

[4] Survey network items, like other survey questions, are affected by question order. Bailey and Marsden (1999) show that preceding the General Social Survey network questions with questions about the respondent's family predispose people to think about family issues when naming network contacts, and Fischer (2009) called attention to possible problems with the 2004 General Social Survey network data because the network questions were preceded by a fatiguing battery of questions (cf. Brashears 2011). In our surveys, we build rapport with a discussion of the business history, so entrepreneurs are presented with the event name generators before being asked about current contacts. It seems likely they were primed to think about the history of the business when naming contacts significant in this year's business activities. If true, then the ratio of event-only contacts to current contacts is probably higher here than it is in fact. That ratio is not a factor in our argument, but it could be, and warrants attention in future research.

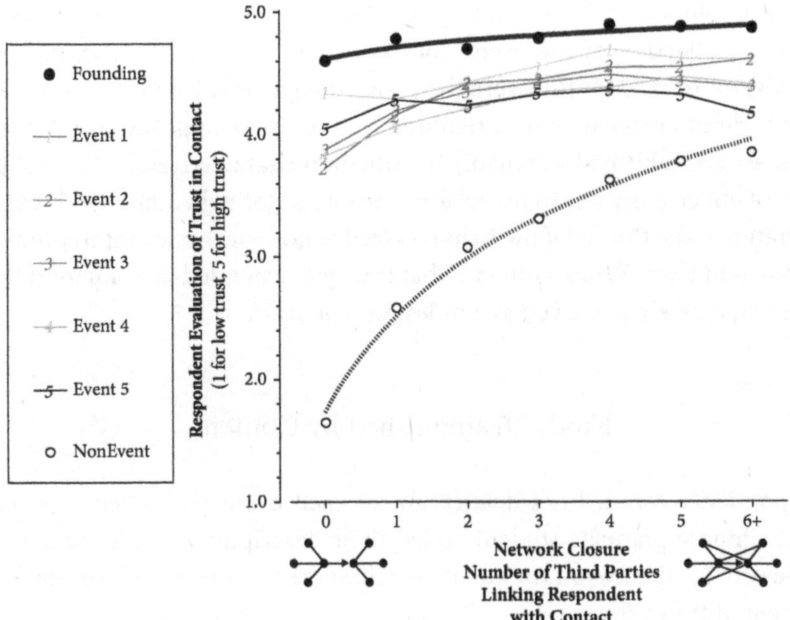

Figure 3.4 Event Contacts All Show Outlier Pattern Regardless of Event Order

Note: Dots are average Y scores at each level of X. Vertical axis is mean respondent trust in a contact, measured on a five-point scale. Horizontal axis is the number of other people in the respondent's network connected with the contact evaluated for trust.

at the top of Figure 3.4. Trust in relations with people only named as current contacts is the heavy dashed line at the bottom of the graph.

Between the top and bottom lines, the horizontal thicket of thin lines in Figure 3.4 shows that trust in all event contacts is higher than trust within relations with nonevent contacts, and—similar to the founding contact— is relatively independent of closure in the surrounding network structure. Regression analysis shows that relative to people cited only as current contacts, the level of trust with all event contacts is higher, and less associated with closure (Burt and Opper 2017). Event contacts could be named on multiple events, so we tried ordering contacts by the first event on which a contact is named. The same pattern occurs of overlapping horizontal thin lines for post-founding event contacts, and slightly higher horizontal lines indicating the highest level of trust in the contact who helped in founding the business. Beyond the founding stage, however, there is no significant difference between help for an early event and help at a later point in the firm's development. This is interesting for two reasons. First, the respondent's recollection of the event does not seem to affect the respondent's expression of trust. If this were the case, contacts involved in more recent events should receive a trust premium. Neither is the opposite true. Once a business is established—arguably the situation characterized by the highest level of uncertainty due to the relative "newness" (Stinchcombe 1965) of the operation—the timing of the help received is no longer relevant in predicting current trust. What matters is that trust was extended in a situation that is retrospectively perceived as a milestone event.

Kinds Distinguished by Content

Respondents gave a brief description of each event they cited. A mainland Chinese graduate student coded their descriptions (with the coding reviewed by the coauthor fluent in Chinese) for the broad substantive content of the event.

We began with fourteen content categories of events. Some were combined because of low frequency. Some were combined to remove unreliable distinctions. The final nine are listed in Table 3.3 with example respondent descriptions. The first kind of event is founding, about which each respondent was asked directly (name generator repeated in the first row of Table 3.3). Event categories are listed in Table 3.3 in the average order in which they occurred during the life of the sample firms. There is one founding event per respondent, which defines year one.

After founding, the next significant event tends to be one of three kinds, clustered around the fifth year of business: There are critical changes in the supplier network. The business wins or loses important customers. There are financial adjustments.

The next significant events, a few years later, include some inside the business. Examples of milestone events outside the business are receiving an award or new affiliation with a business association, or a significant exchange with the government (e.g., being granted preferential treatment regarding taxes or land, certification for a broader class of business, or sometimes imposition of a fine or restriction). The more often-cited kinds of events are inside the business. Most concern management issues, but a substantial minority concern technology adopted to improve efficiency or sell new products, so technology events are broken out as a separate kind of

Table 3.3 Kinds of Significant Events

Kinds of Events (N)	Year	Examples
1. Founding (700)	1.00	"Who was the one person who was most valuable to you in founding the firm?"
2. Supplier (255)	5.16	"replaced the main supplier" "major suppliers signed a cooperation contract" "suppliers had problems providing raw materials; resulted in serious losses"
3. Customer (833)	5.25	"company signed a big contract, which helped working capital " "company signed first export contract," "contract signed for custom product with large state-owned enterprise"
4. Financial (184)	5.44	"successfully raised money for the purchase of equipment" "obtained loans to small and medium-size private enterprises" "corporate cash flow difficulty; faced production difficulties"
5. Government (102)	6.75	"got preferential taxation policies" "enjoyed preferential land policies of the government" "obtained international agreements certification"
6. Business Management (1006)	7.13	"mismanagement; serious business losses; almost closed down" "security control group concerned with product quality was established" "established classification of job responsibilities"
7. Collaborations and Associations (215)	7.53	"established cooperative relations with the domestic textile industry" "joined the association of private entrepreneurs" "received excellent quality award of Zhejiang Province"
8. Business Technology (519)	8.18	"introduction of new technology and equipment" "adopted new technologies; developed new products" "updated production technology; improved efficiency"
9. Market Generally (349)	9.36	"price of raw materials increased, so the cost of production increased" "financial crisis in Southeast Asia; we lost some customers" "industry competition more fierce; had development difficulties"

Note: Number of events cited is in parentheses, then year on average in which the row category of events occur. A total of 4163 events are cited, which is more than the 2905 contacts in Table 3.2 cited for events because some people are cited for more than one event. Categories six and eight are events inside the business.

event. The business is up and running by year eight, when developments tied to general market conditions are cited as important.

Most of the cited events concern new opportunities—big contracts, expanded production, securing revenue or supplies. There are two exceptions: finance, is often mentioned in association with liquidity constraints or business losses; and market developments, typically cited in relation to price fluctuations and rising competition. The frequent concern with loss in market-related events likely reflects the timing of the survey—in the aftermath of the global financial crisis, amid overdue consolidation among small and medium enterprises, and increasing labor costs linked to stricter enforcement of China's Labor Contract Law, effective in 2008.

Of course, the average year in which a kind of event occurs varies between businesses, and with business age. A business founded four years ago cannot yet have an event in year eight. We focus on the order of events because respondents are free to define what constitutes a significant event, and they typically select events across the life of their business. The longer the business has been in operation, the more spread out the events.[5] The pattern is only slightly different with business age held constant.[6]

Replicating the pattern in Figure 3.4, Figure 3.5 plots trust distinguishing kinds of events by content. Here the pattern shows again that content

[5] This observation is based on a cluster analysis of time profiles. We created a time profile for each respondent defined by the years in which events occurred. For example, the time profile for the Figure 3.2 entrepreneur is 2, 3, 7, 10, 13, corresponding to the years in which the entrepreneur's five significant events occur. The squared Euclidean distance between two profiles is small to the extent that events in each profile occur in the same years after founding. Cluster analysis of profiles for the 675 entrepreneurs who reported five events, using the Ward minimum-variance method in Stata reveals three distinct clusters: a cluster of profiles that occur within the first decade of business, a cluster of profiles that occur within the first fifteen years of business, and a cluster of profiles that occur within the first twenty-two years of business. Within each cluster, events are about evenly distributed over time. The first cluster is young businesses (average 8.84 years old), the second is older businesses (average 13.95 years old), and the third is still older businesses (average 22.10 years old).

[6] Business age is held constant by measuring events as a proportion of business age. For example, an event .5 in proportional time occurred half way between founding and the 2012 survey. Cluster analysis of proportional time profiles (same method as in the previous footnote) also reveals three clusters. Events are distributed about evenly over time, differing in the first event: The first cluster spreads over the whole life of a business. The second cluster begins with the first event late (about a third of the way into the business' life). The third cluster begins at about the same time as the first cluster, but with a larger gap between the first and second events. We tested for trust and success association with time to first event. A control for time to first event adds nothing to the prediction of trust (-1.68 t-test for years to first event, 0.37 t-test for proportional time to first event), nothing to the prediction of success (respective t-tests of 1.00 and 0.41), and nothing to the prediction of success from networks limited to current, founding, and Event 1 contacts (respective t-tests of 1.28 and 0.63). Therefore, we focus in the text on event order, rather than physical or proportional time.

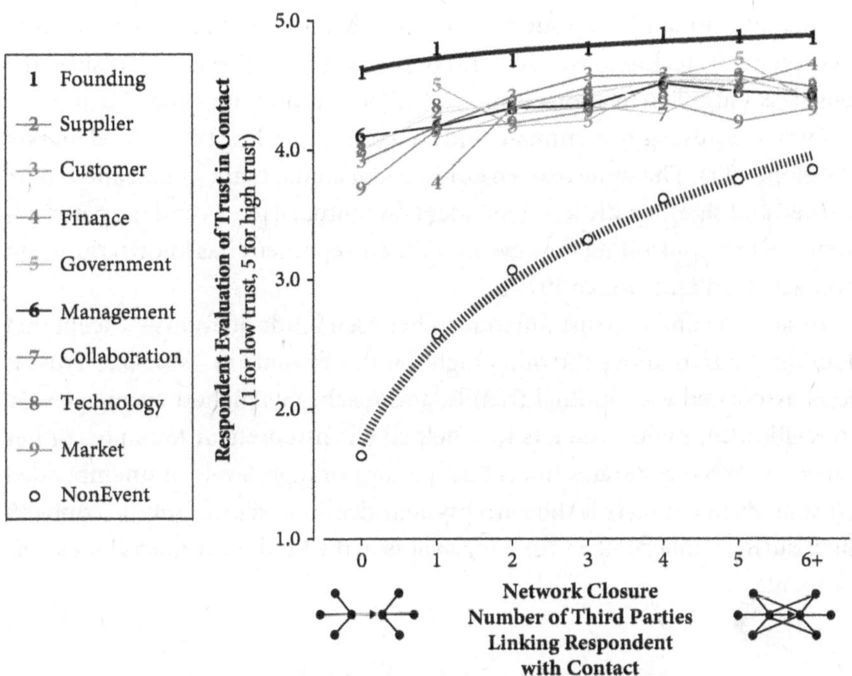

Figure 3.5 Event Contacts All Show Outlier Pattern Regardless of Event Content

Note: Dots are average Y scores at each level of X. Vertical axis is mean respondent trust in a contact, measured on a five-point scale. Horizontal axis is the number of other people in the respondent's network connected with the contact evaluated for trust.

differences between events do not matter so much as the entrepreneur deeming an event significant. Founding the business stands apart for high trust independent of mutual friends, as it does in Figure 3.4, but just beneath that is a thicket of thin lines describing high trust in event contacts regardless of the kind of event in which they were helpful. Remarkably, not even finance and assistance in dealing with government bureaucracies—both of which involve transactions in the less liberalized capital and political markets— are separate from events that take place in the highly liberalized markets for supplies and finished products. In fact, statistical tests show that trust in event contacts is generally higher, and less associated with mutual friends for each kind of event independent of the market interface in which these events occur (Burt and Opper 2017).

However, the more kinds of events we distinguish, the less reliable the distinctions. To be sure about our results, we aggregated the nine kinds of events into three kinds: founding, events "inside" the business (related to management, technology, and sales department), and events "outside" the business (supplier relations, finance, collaboration with other businesses, activities involving government, and concerns regarding the general market development). The same pattern holds: event contacts are significantly more trusted and significantly less dependent on mutual friends, and the pattern is robust when controlling for how long the entrepreneur has known the event contact (Burt and Opper 2017).[7]

In sum, we find no trust differences between kinds of events—except that founding stands above the other eight kinds of events in Table 3.3. Trust is least associated with mutual friends, and reaches its highest average levels, in relationships with contacts who helped an entrepreneur found his or her business. What generates the robust pattern of high levels of unembedded trust in event contacts is the entrepreneur deeming significant the contact's help during a milestone event—regardless of the kinds of contacts and kinds of events.

Kinds Distinguished by Multiplexity

Figure 3.6 puts the nine kinds of events into broader perspective, defined by the kinds of relationships and characteristics associated with those people who helped with each kind of event. The display is a classical multidimensional scaling of relationship characteristics. Two characteristics are close together to the extent that they often occur in the same relationships. Included in the analysis are the kind of event, the year it was cited, the kind of person, and dimensions of relationship strength in terms of contact frequency, years known, level of trust, and emotional closeness. To

[7] Distinctions between kinds of events require subjective judgments, so the irrelevance of such distinctions in Figure 3.5 gave us concern about the reliability of the distinctions in Table 3.3. The coding had been reviewed by the coauthor fluent in Chinese, and seemed sensible, but as a further check we had a second research associate in Beijing independently code all 4163 events into the Table 3.3 categories. Reliability is high on average. The two coders agreed in their assignment of 74 percent of events to the Table 3.3 categories. The coders disagreed most clearly on customer events versus collaboration events (categories 3 and 7 in Table 3.3). Entrepreneurs often collaborated with others to produce a new product or secure a customer contract. Most of the disagreements between the coders were one coding an event as a customer issue while the other coded the event as a collaboration issue. If customer and collaboration issues are combined, the two coders agreed in their assignment of 84 percent of events. Given no statistical difference between customer and collaboration issues in Figure 3.5, we are confident in our conclusion in the text: all substantive kinds of significant events have the potential to generate the outlier relations in Figure 2.5B, Figure 3.4, and Figure 3.5—containing high trust independent of mutual friends.

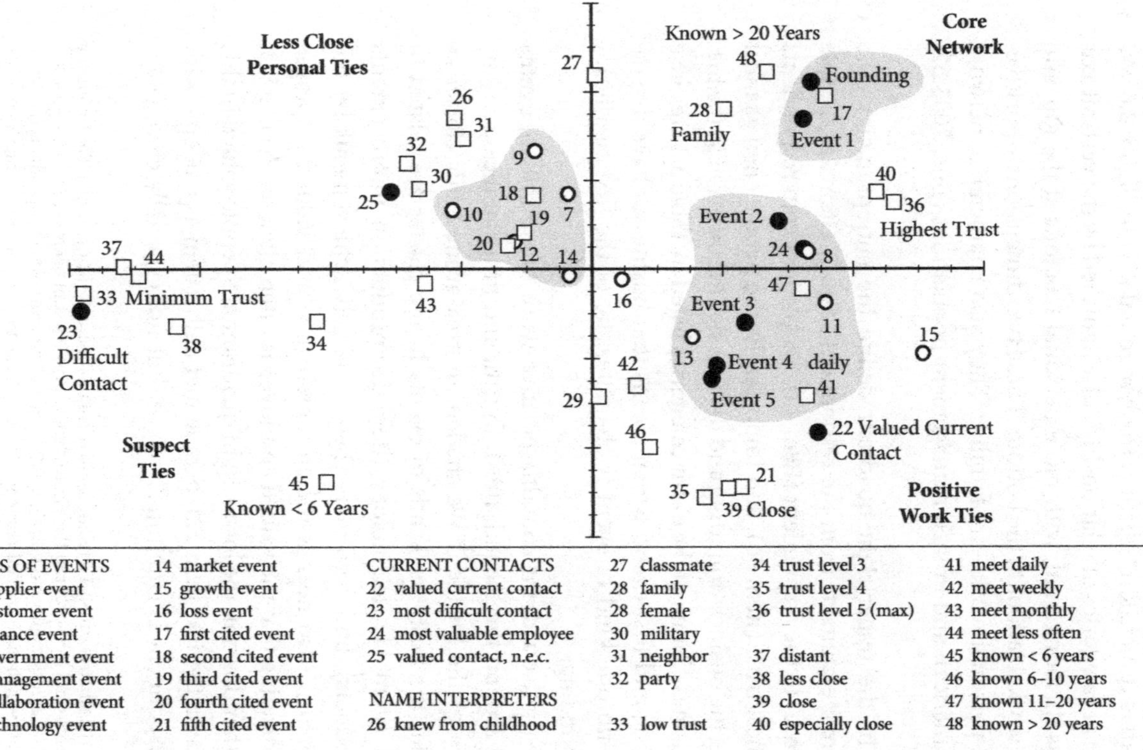

KINDS OF EVENTS		CURRENT CONTACTS	27 classmate	34 trust level 3	41 meet daily
7 supplier event	14 market event	22 valued current contact	28 family	35 trust level 4	42 meet weekly
8 customer event	15 growth event	23 most difficult contact	28 female	36 trust level 5 (max)	43 meet monthly
9 finance event	16 loss event	24 most valuable employee	30 military		44 meet less often
10 government event	17 first cited event	25 valued contact, n.e.c.	31 neighbor	37 distant	45 known < 6 years
11 management event	18 second cited event		32 party	38 less close	46 known 6–10 years
12 collaboration event	19 third cited event	NAME INTERPRETERS		39 close	47 known 11–20 years
13 technology event	20 fourth cited event	26 knew from childhood	33 low trust	40 especially close	48 known > 20 years
	21 fifth cited event				

Figure 3.6 Kinds of Events in Broader Context

Note: Classical multidimensional scaling of Jaccard coefficients measuring co-occurrence of characteristics (N = 4464). Axes are proportional in length to the eigenvalues defining them. Axes cross at their zero point. The two displayed dimensions describe 79 percent of variance in the fort-eight items. Solid circles are the six name generators in Table 3.1. Hollow circles are the Table 3.3 coded kinds of events on which event contacts were named. Squares are responses to the name interpreters.

avoid clutter, only a few of the forty-eight characteristics are labeled in the figure—enough to facilitate making sense of the space.[8]

The entrepreneurs differentiate their relationships most clearly along a positive-negative dimension, which is the horizontal axis in Figure 3.6. We label four broad categories of relationships distinguished by the vertical axis cutting across the horizontal, with more personal relations at the top, and less personal work relations at the bottom. These two dimensions—positive-negative and personal-work—are familiar. They also characterize network patterns in American and French management populations (Burt 2005:52; 2010:287).

Relations in the upper-right quadrant define the entrepreneur's core network. Here are contacts from the respondent's family (item 28), people "especially close" to the respondent (item 40), people in whom respondents have the highest trust (item 36), and importantly, the people cited as most valued during the business founding and the first significant event in the history of the business. None of the event categories listed in Table 3.3 are close to the founding and first event, which means that businesses have diverse beginnings—no one kind of event is characteristic of the first significant event after founding.

The lower-right quadrant contains positive work ties. Kinds of events are clustered around the second, third, fourth, and fifth significant events in the history of the business. We shaded an area around this cluster as events "inside" the business. Kinds of events in the cluster are related to management (item 11), technology (item 13, production improvements and new products), and customers (item 8, largely achievements by the sales department). Also near is the entrepreneur's most valued employee (item 24), indicating that the valued employee is often cited on Events 2, 3, 4, and 5. Further down in the lower-right quadrant are people valued in this year's business activities (item 22), people met daily (item 41), people with whom the respondent is emotionally close, but not especially close (item

---

[8] Cell a_{ij} in the data matrix equals 1 if relationship i contains characteristic j (else 0). The frequency with which contents j and k co-occur in the same relationships is a sum of cross products: $\sum_i a_{ij}a_{ik}$, where summation is across relations (cf. Breiger 1974:Eq. 2). The summed cross-products measures the frequency with which each pair of contents j and k occur together. To make that frequency comparable across contents, some of which occur often while others occur rarely, we normalize the frequency to be a Jaccard coefficient, which is the number of relations in which contents j and k both occur divided by the number in which either j or k occurs. Varying from zero to one, a Jaccard coefficient is zero if contents j and k never occur together, increasing up to 1.0 if contents j and k only occur together. The two-dimension solution in the figure fits the data well. The first dimension is defined by the eigenvector associated with an eigenvalue of 5.63. The second dimension corresponds to an eigenvalue of 3.23, and the third to a 1.64 eigenvalue. The first two dimensions together describe 79 percent of the association variance, and are drawn in proportion to their eigenvalues.

39), and people in whom the respondent has a high level of trust, but not the highest level (item 35).

The lower-left quadrant contains suspect ties, relations with people of whom the respondent is wary. On the left of the continuum are the person cited as causing the most difficulty for the respondent this year (item 23), people in whom the respondent has the lowest level of trust (item 33), people from whom the respondent feels emotionally "distant" (item 37), and people met less than monthly (item 37). Farther south and farther right are the people the respondent has known for the shortest period of time (item 45).

The upper-left quadrant of Figure 3.6 contains less-close personal ties. These are positive relations, but they are less intimate than core network relations to the further right. Here are people known since childhood (item 26), neighbors (item 31), people known for their role in the Communist Party (item 32), and so on. Here too are events "outside" the business, including supplier issues (item 7), financial issues (item 9), collaboration with other businesses (item 12), dealing with the government (item 10), and concerns regarding the general market development (item 14). We shaded this area to highlight the cluster, which combines events related to the world outside the firm and clearly separates the type of contacts (less close personal ties) from those involved in internal affairs (work ties) and those crucial at the founding stage (core network).

Family Versus Other Long-Standing Relationships

Given the widespread notion of family as central to Chinese life, it is tempting to expect entrepreneurs to rely on family to get the business started, and then turn to less-close friends and acquaintances for help with subsequent events (e.g., Guo and Miller 2010). The data are consistent with that image: 31 percent of entrepreneurs cite a family member as the most valued contact at founding, and family is more likely to be cited as a valued contact in the early years of a business than later (Table 3.4). In fact, family, founding contact, and the contact most valued in the first significant event cluster together in the upper-right, core-network quadrant of Figure 3.6.

Although entrepreneurs tend to turn to family at founding, it is not correct to say that entrepreneurs typically turn to family. That 31 percent of entrepreneurs cite a family member as a founding contact means that a large majority of 69 percent turned to someone outside the family. As much as

Table 3.4 The Contacts Valued at Founding Are Most Distinguished by Years Known

	Predict Founding Contact			Means	
	Coefficient	S.E.	Test Statistic	Founding Contacts	Other Contacts
Rarely Met Contacts (days between meetings, 1–90)	−.015	.005	−3.21**	5.65	14.87
Contacts Known for Many Years (ln 1–60)	.393	.023	16.87***	20.27	8.72
Number of Third Parties (ln [1+ 0–6])	−.635	.239	−2.66**	3.10	3.04
Childhood Friend (0–1)	−1.562	.923	−1.62	.04	.01
Classmate in School (0–1)	.430	.694	0.62	.16	.02
Co-Member in Business Association (0–1)	−.292	.836	−.35	.01	.03
Family Member (0–1)	.643	.694	0.93	.31	.04
Contact from the Military (0–1)	−.408	1.085	−.38	.01	.00
Neighbor (0–1)	1.509	.801	1.88	.05	.01
Contact from the Party (0–1)	.946	.913	1.04	.02	.01
None of the Above (0–1)	−.479	.710	−.67	.44	.89

Note: This is a logit regression with respondent fixed effects predicting which of a respondent's contacts is cited for help in founding the business (N = 4464 relationships chi-square = 1609.32, 11 d.f., P < .001). Categories of contact frequency are entered in days (1 for "daily," 7 for "weekly," 30 for "monthly," and 90 for "less often"). Number of third parties is increased by one and logged to capture the nonlinear association displayed in Figure 3.4 (but means here are raw counts of third parties). Contacts could be cited for multiple roles (e.g., contact could be a "neighbor" and a "classmate"). "None of the Above" is 1 if contact is none of the seven kinds of contacts listed. ** P < .01, *** P < .001.

family members are a resource on whom the entrepreneur can legitimately call, they are also people to whom the entrepreneur has a social responsibility. Entrepreneurship is, by definition, risky—especially in China at the turn of the century, under a legal system only slowly adapting to a newly evolving private enterprise economy. Many respondents were cautious not to tie up all family resources in a single venture, choosing instead to hedge their risks in an uncertain environment. The cited network contacts confirm this view. The majority of entrepreneurs found help outside the family, indeed outside the usually suspected sources of social support, such as childhood friends, classmates, neighbors, or connections to other institutions such as the military or the Chinese Communist Party.

In fact, the best predictor of who an entrepreneur cites as most helpful in founding the business is not any particular social category or institutional tie, but how long the entrepreneur has known the contact. Table 3.4 shows results from a logit equation predicting which of an entrepreneur's contacts is cited for help in founding the business. The equation includes respondent fixed effects, so respondent differences such as network size and business age are held constant to focus on the identity of contacts cited for help in founding the business. Founding contacts tend to be people still met often at the time of the survey (−3.21 test statistic for days between meetings), and people beyond the interconnected current contacts (−2.66 test statistic for number of mutual friends, the horizontal axis in Figure 3.4). None of the seven kinds of relationships has any association with being cited as helpful at founding. Particularly notable is the irrelevance of commonly discussed sources of early support—childhood friends, classmates, and family—with test statistics of −1.62, 0.62, and 0.93, respectively. The dominant predictor is duration—the number of years the entrepreneur has known the contact (16.87 test statistic).

A Careful Look at Duration

With duration the dominant predictor of who is associated with founding the business, we considered alternative ways to think about duration. Figure 3.7 offers an illustration with data on the entrepreneur whose network is displayed in Figure 3.2. Time runs from 1974, when the respondent was born, to 2012, when the respondent was interviewed about his network. The respondent graduated from high school in 1992, and founded his current business in 2000. By 2012, he had grown the business to 467 employees. The dark bars below the horizontal axis in Figure 3.7 show when contacts were cited in association with significant events in the history of the firm. Soon after founding the firm in 2000, the respondent secured an overseas customer (event 1 in 2001), and then secured a reliable supplier (event 2 in 2002). There was a plant explosion in 2006 (event 3), financial crisis in 2009 (event 4), and a plant discharge issue in 2012 (event 5). The bars above the horizontal in Figure 3.7 show when the respondent met the people who later got involved in these events. Bar height indicates the respondent's trust in each of these contacts.

Figure 3.8 shows that respondent trust increases with years known—no matter how duration is defined. Panel A in the figure applies the most generic approach. Trust is low in contacts known for only one year, higher in the second, higher still in the third year, and then increases roughly linearly. The steep increase in trust in the first few years, followed by smaller gains, is well captured by the log of years known. Predicting trust from log years known and respondent fixed effects accounts for 42 percent of the variation in trust (R^2 in Figure 3.8A).

The association between trust and duration could be linked to key events, such as the founding of the business. The respondent in Figure 3.7 met five of his nine cited contacts before founding his business in 2000, and his trust in these early contacts is higher than his trust in contacts he met after he had his business running. Across respondents, Figure 3.8B shows a linear increase in trust across years known before or after founding the business. The horizontal axis is the year when the respondent met a contact minus the year when the respondent founded his business. Positive numbers are people known before founding the business. The substantively

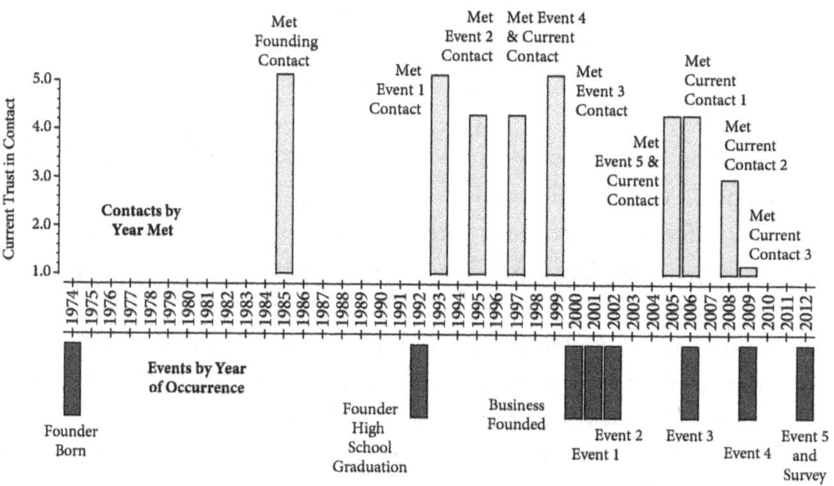

Figure 3.7 Event Sequence for Entrepreneur in Figure 3.2

Note: Dark bars below show when events occurred. Bars above indicate when each of the respondent's nine contacts were met, and the respondent's level of trust in each.

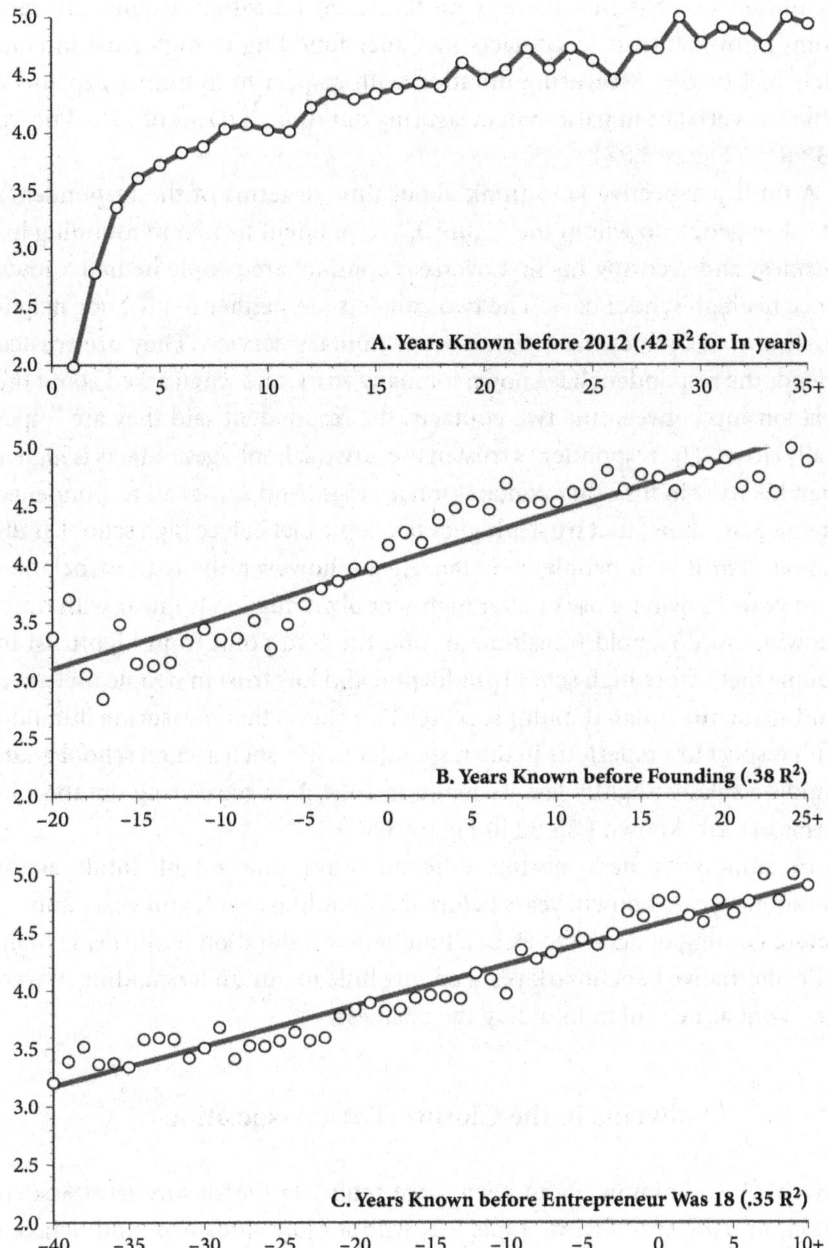

Figure 3.8 Trust Increase with Years Known

Note: Squared multiple correlations are estimated across all 4464 cited relations with respondent fixed effects, using only time on the horizontal axis as a predictor (log years in top graph).

significant point is that there is no threshold transition around the zero point from low trust in contacts met after founding to high trust in contacts met before. Measuring duration with respect to founding explains a little less variance in trust than measuring duration in terms of years known (.38 R^2 in Figure 3.8B).

A third perspective is to think about time in terms of the respondent's life. The people to whom the Figure 3.7 respondent turned in founding his business and securing his first overseas contract are people he had known since his high school days. The two contacts are neither family, nor neighbors, nor classmates, nor friends from military service. They are trusted friends the respondent has known for many years, and when asked about the relationship between the two contacts, the respondent said they are "especially close." The respondent's trust in these two school-age contacts is higher than his trust in his other contacts, on average. And across all respondents, Figure 3.8C shows that trust is higher in people met before high school graduation than it is in people met later. Again, however, the trust association with years known before or after high school graduation is linear with time, showing no threshold transition around the zero point from high trust in people met before high school graduation and low trust in people met after. And again, the squared multiple correlation shows that measuring duration with respect to a milestone in the respondent's life, such as high school graduation, explains slightly less variation in trust than measuring duration in terms of years known (.35 R2 in Figure 3.8C).

In sum, regardless of the different ways one might think about duration—years known, years before the founding event, and years known before coming of age—the association between duration and trust is high, with alternative benchmark years adding little to our understanding of who stood out as helpful in founding the business.

Events in the Closure-Trust Association

Given what we know about events, we return to the closure-trust association, initially specified in Table 2.1, with a more informed, and detailed specification. Table 3.5 contains two models we will employ in the subsequent chapters. Trust in a contact (measured on a five-point scale) is predicted by log number of mutual friends (as a measure of structural embedding)—as portrayed in Figure 2.3A, Figure 2.5B, Figure 3.4, and

Table 3.5 Predicting Trust in a Contact

	Core Model		Core With Additional Controls	
Structural Embedding (dashed line)				
Number of Third Parties (ln [1–7])	1.36	(37.76)	.80	(22.48)
Relational Embedding (solid line)				
Level Adjustment for Event Contact (0–1)	2.17	(29.72)	1.45	(21.29)
Level Adjustment for Founding Contact (0–1)	−.82	(−15.66)	.31	(9.88)
Slope Adjustment for Event Contact	—		−.52	(−11.11)
Contacts Known for Many Years (ln [1–60])	—		.23	(10.73)
Currently in Touch				
Daily Meetings Currently (0–1)	—		.36	(9.32)
Weekly Meetings Currently (0–1)	—		.17	(4.07)
Less than Monthly Meetings Currently (0–1)	—		−.90	(−17.29)
Intercept	1.50		1.71	
R^2	.61		.71	

Note: This is a regression with respondent fixed effects predicting respondent level of trust in the contact (N = 4,464 relationships). All coefficients are statistically significant at beyond a .001 level of confidence, most well beyond (jackknife t-test in parentheses). Number of third parties is increased by one and logged to capture the nonlinear association displayed in Figures 3.4 and 3.5. Duration is the log of years known. The slope adjustment is prediction by the product of event contact times log (one plus number of third parties).

Figure 3.5. All of the coefficients in Table 3.5 are statistically significant at well beyond a .001 level of confidence. The first row shows a strong closure-trust association: The 1.36 coefficient says that adding two mutual friends to a bridge relation increases trust by 1.49 levels, which is more than a standard deviation increase in trust.[9] The second row in the table shows that predicted trust increases on average by 2.17 levels for event contacts (capturing the higher average trust in event contacts). The third row in the table says that the slope of the closure-trust association has to be decreased to describe trust in event contacts, which lowers the 1.36 structural embedding effect by −.82 to .54 for event contacts (capturing the relative lack of change in trust in event contacts across levels of structural embedding).

[9] The standard deviation in five-level trust across all 4464 relationships is 1.08. Adding two mutual friends to a bridge relationship increases third parties from 0 to 2, which is an increase of 1.10 in the log predictor. The 1.36 coefficient times 1.10 says trust should increase by 1.49.

The second model in Table 3.5 adds some additional baseline controls. Trust in the contact helpful in founding the business is higher than other event contacts (bold line in Figure 3.4 and Figure 3.5). The slope adjustment for trust in the founding contact is negligible so it is not included in the table (−.74 t-test, P ~ 46). The final predictor for relational embedding is years known. The .23 coefficient says that the first decade of knowing a contact increases trust in the contact by .55 points on average. There is also an adjustment for how often a contact is met. Trust is lower in contacts with whom the entrepreneur is no longer in touch (bottom predictor in the table).

The second model in Table 3.5 predicts a .71 squared multiple correlation. As a quick summary of results, we can say that the multiple correlation is unchanged if we add a variable distinguishing family members,[10] or add five variables distinguishing the order in which events were mentioned (Figure 3.4), or add ten variables distinguishing substantively different kinds of events (Table 3.3, Figure 3.5). These additional considerations do not improve the trust prediction. The squared multiple correlation stays at .71.

Conclusion: Relational Embedding

We conclude that the high trust evident in event contacts comes from inside a relationship—from a relationship's own history. We base this conclusion on three facts. First, trust in event contacts is relatively independent of the surrounding network. In Figure 3.4 and Figure 3.5, trust in event contacts is high and relatively unchanging across increasing numbers of mutual contacts. Trust in other contacts, nonevent contacts, increases with mutual contacts as expected in the familiar closure-trust association. Second, the high trust relatively independent of the surrounding network is robust across kinds of events (allowing for the special case of founding the business). The thicket of thin lines in Figure 3.4 and Figure 3.5 display high trust—regardless of event sequence or content. Third, Figure 3.8

---

[10] We went one step further to see whether the trust prediction is different in family versus other firms. We used the common definition of family firms: owner-operated firms in which the respondent's spouse or children are employees. By this criterion, 254 of the 700 businesses are family firms. Respondents for family firms are almost twice as likely to turn to family in founding the business: 44 percent of family firms cite family as founding contacts, versus 24 percent of other firms. Regardless, the three coefficients in the first model in the table are similar for both kinds of firms (Burt and Opper 2018:534).

shows that the number of years of knowing a person matters. When family is turned to for support it is most likely at founding, but family is not the primary source of support, even at founding. Rather, entrepreneurs cite people they have known for many years, typically all kinds of people beyond the entrepreneur's family. The duration association with trust is not about milestone events in the life of the business or the respondent. Duration is about getting to know a person, which happens during the first four or five years of a relationship, after which trust increases at a slow rate over additional years. This process is reasonably captured by log years known, which we continue to use in our further analysis.

A second conclusion from the results is that events are not significant in their own right. They are significant as an occasion, a context, in which an entrepreneur learns that a contact can be trusted. Like moving in with someone—events are a situation that can develop well or poorly. Events provide an occasion that moves a relationship to a different level. Clearly, event contacts were not strangers at the time of the event as Figure 3.7 illustrates for our sample entrepreneur (initially introduced in Figure 3.2). Most event contacts were known prior to the event, often for some years. Most likely, these contacts appeared trustworthy at the time of the event, which is why they got involved in the first place. With all certainty we can make this claim for contacts who have proven helpful in founding the firm. Yet, these milestone events present an opportunity to prove oneself as a truly trustworthy and reliable contact. Asked today who was helpful during an event, you think of Susan, who you came to know you can trust from her behavior during and after the event. With more time, more behavior observed, you gain more confidence in trusting her (depending on her behavior). What matters is not the nature of the event so much as your perception of a friend's or colleague's support during the event.

These findings resonate with various pieces of research and do not stand out as culturally unique or institutionally distinct. For example, Kollock (1994) shows higher levels of trust, once trustor and trustee have experienced a "critical test" in exchanging and receiving a unilateral favor. Receiving fair, and potentially advantageous behavior can solidify trust (Hardin 1991). The effect can be stronger when help is in short supply and therefore most valuable—as in the early stages of business development characterized by weak organizational legitimacy (Suchman 1995), liability of newness (Stinchcombe 1965) and, in the case of China, weak institutional support (Nee and Opper 2012; Peng and Luo 2000; Xin and Pierce 1996).

Granovetter's (1992:41–47) phrasing is useful here. He distinguishes two forms of the context in which a relationship can be embedded: It can be embedded in a surrounding social structure such as mutual friends (structural embedding), or it can be embedded in its own history (relational embedding). The trust effect of structural embedding is what we have been discussing as the closure-trust association—long the subject of social science theory and research, and illustrated in Figure 2.3, and the dashed lines in Figure 2.5B, Figure 3.4, and Figure 3.5. Trust between two people is facilitated by surrounding mutual friends or supportive institutions. The contrast with relational embedding is useful here because relational embedding describes the trust we see in event contacts. Relational embedding does not explain the trust; it merely tells us where to look for an explanation. And our results are not a requirement of relational embedding; it is just that the results on trust in event contacts deny us the structural-embedding explanation so often invoked to explain network trust. Trust in event contacts is relatively independent of structural embedding.

4

From Events to Guanxi, to Strong Bridges

We had two initial reactions to the findings in the previous chapters. First, we were struck by the unexpectedly high frequency of strong bridges among event contacts, which challenges conventional thinking about the closure-trust association. Second, we learned from work in the previous chapter that the high level of trust in event contacts is a quality within the relationship that is rooted neither in the particular social role people play in a respondent's life, nor in the kind of the event in which they offered support. We thought: Could these highly trusted event contacts be an example of the proverbial "guanxi" so often discussed in China? Is guanxi, after all, the kind of social fabric that allows entrepreneurs to reap the benefits of brokerage while avoiding the fragility of brokerage so often discussed in the West?

In this chapter, we build on those initial reactions to propose two hypotheses. Guanxi is at once two things: a relationship and a source of individual advantage. We propose a hypothesis for each. The first locates guanxi within network structure as structure is associated with trust. The second locates guanxi within network structure as structure is associated with performance.

We begin by developing an analogy between guanxi and the results of the previous chapter on trust in event contacts. The analogy leads to a strong-bridges hypothesis defining relations that qualify as guanxi. We then report evidence strongly supporting this hypothesis. Next, we turn to guanxi as a source of individual advantage. Advantage can come in many forms: He got that job because his father works there, that contract because his uncle is the chairman of the committee, that promotion because the senior executive is a family friend. You are fortunate if you are the one who benefits from guanxi, while at the same time being an example of market corruption in the eyes of your competitors. Our second task in this chapter is to state a performance hypothesis that specifies when guanxi relations confer a comparative

Strong Bridges. Ronald S. Burt and Sonja Opper, Oxford University Press. © Oxford University Press (2026).
DOI: 10.1093/9780197834275.003.0004

advantage. This second hypothesis is central to reconciling the so widely popularized idea of guanxi advantage with social network theory. As we predict, guanxi advantage increases as guanxi embeddedness decreases, which aligns guanxi predictions with the familiar association between open networks and performance. Again, the available evidence strongly supports this hypothesis.

Before we begin, be reminded of a linguistic note from Chapter 1: Guanxi is both singular and plural. We use "guanxi tie" to make explicit reference to guanxi as a kind of relationship, "guanxi contact" to refer to a person who is the object of a guanxi tie, and "guanxi" to refer to the category of relationships that qualify as guanxi. Throughout, guanxi refers to valued relationships. There are discussions of guanxi as a network, but guanxi ties are the fundamental units of guanxi networks (Fei 1992 [1947]).

Guanxi Analogy

With China's market economy developing as it has over the past few decades, and jealous competitors being what they are, guanxi is a word often heard in China. But not only there. The word appears prominently in the global business press.

Figure 4.1 provides a quick illustration using Google's Ngram Viewer. The top graph shows mentions of guanxi in a large corpus of books written in English over the recent 100 years (American and British English show similar pattern). Guanxi is rarely mentioned until US diplomatic relations with China are established in 1979, then attention increases dramatically with Western interest in China as authors capitalize on that interest, commenting on one another's interpretations. In fact, in China, it was only under Communist leadership that the term guanxi was popularized in its current connotation as an instrumental-particularistic relationship (Barbalet 2021b). The lower graph in Figure 4.1 shows the probability of guanxi being mentioned in a large corpus of Chinese books over the same period. Guanxi is rarely mentioned in the Chinese texts until the Communists take over and make guanxi a symbol of earlier corruption, consistent with Barbalet's discussion. Attention then cycles in and out of fashion with Party interests at about one-tenth the level of attention in the West (see note to figure for details).

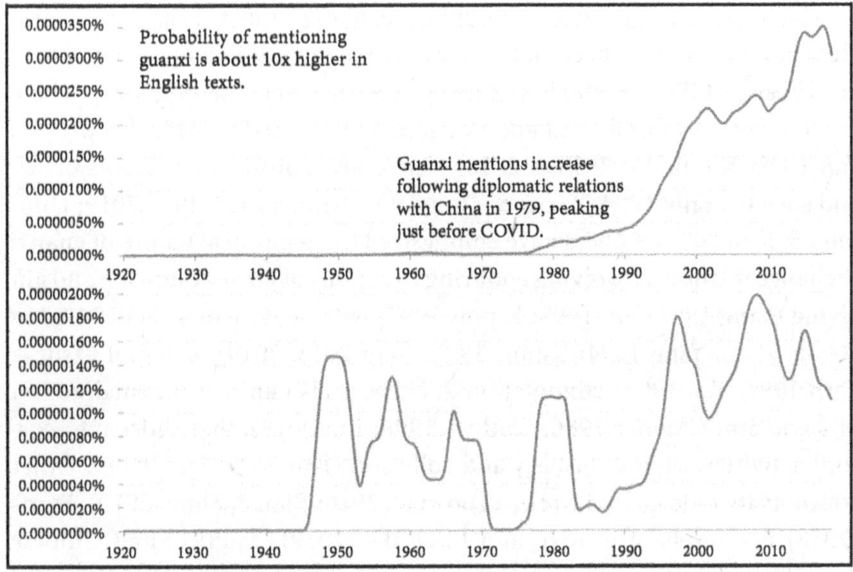

Figure 4.1 Guanxi Mentions in China and the West

Note: Google Ngram output with two-year smoothing (created on September 30, 2024). Here are some events related to peaks in Chinese attention: (early 1950s) attack on clientelist ties and feudal networks (so-called 3-Anti-campaign launched in 1951 and 5-Anti-campaign in 1952), (1957) year before Mao launches Great Leap Forward (mass mobilization and collectivization), (1966) cultural revolution begins (to purge counter revolutionaries), (1978–79) economic reforms (Deng Xiaoping begins to replace old veterans), (1997) financial crisis (in parallel 1993–1997, anti-corruption campaign by Jiang Zemin), (2008) financial crisis (in parallel 2003–2012 Hu Jintao's fairly moderate anti-corruption campaigns), (2015) height of Xi Jinping's anti-corruption campaign, started with taking office in 2012).

Too Many Meanings

A feature of the interface between social science and colloquial language is that a word often used is a word rarely used in a consistent way. Guanxi is such a word. Broadly understood to be a valuable, particularistic relationship (Tsui & Farh 1997; Chen & Chen 2004; Chen et al. 2013), guanxi is a word often found used in a variety of ways (e.g., reviews in Gold et al. 2002; Bian 2019; Nolan & Rowley 2020; Li & Bian 2024). As useful as broad cultural descriptions can be, they often overlook substantial heterogeneity between individuals within cultures (DiMaggio 1997). Depending on who you ask, and when you ask, you can get a wide variety of meanings for the word guanxi. At the time of this writing, our search for the term guanxi in the Web of Science database yielded 2604 academic works, two-thirds of which were in business, economics, or management. Search for a single definition quickly becomes mired in ambiguity and controversy. There are Hwang's (1987) metaphors for the existence and use of guanxi. There are analogies to family ties and obligations (Fei 2019 [1947]; Yang 1994; Yan 1998; Kipnis 1997; Bian 2018). There are Confucian concepts of self and society (Yang 1994; Yeung & Tung 1996; Kipnis 1997; Bian 2019; Dunning & Kim 2007). Others have emphasized the reciprocal nature of guanxi exchange relations, involving enduring traditions of favor bestowing and gift giving (Yang 1994; Yan 1998; Kipnis 1997) with sentimental (Fei 1947; Lin 2001b, 2018; Yang 1994; Kipnis 1997; Bian 2018, 2019) or moral (Tsui & Farh 1997; Yan 1998) connotations.[1] There is also an instrumental notion of favoritism (Walder 1986; Guthrie 1998; Lin 2018), that slides into corrupt activities, such as bribery and collusion (Fan 2002; Luo 2008). Other concepts include guanxi circles (Luo et al. 2016; Bian & Shuai 2019), Bian's (2018) five levels of guanxi, and Li et al.'s (2019) "multicolored Chinese knot." There are etymological stories about linguistic roots and the search for meaning in Chinese cultural traditions that distinguish guan from xi from bao (報) and shu (恕) from renqing (仁清) (for a critical review, see Barbalet 2021a). The lowest common denominator in this debate is that guanxi is generally perceived as a kind of relationship unique enough to be referred to by the Romanized term guanxi (关系), rather than translations such as "relations" or "relationships" in common parlance, or "strong ties" in network theory, characterized by emotional warmth (affection or emotional attachment), obligation (as a norm of reciprocity), and interpersonal trust (e.g., Yang 1994:111; Bian 1997:369; and for a broad review see Kipnis 1997; Luo et al. 2011; Chen et al. 2013; Bian 2019).

Within the organization's literature, two perspectives are readily distinguished, largely insulated from one another. The first consists of culturally inspired work highlighting relational strategies in which guanxi is understood as a unique, interpersonal relationship and strategy (Xin & Pearce 1996; Tsui & Farh 1997; Guthrie 1998; Peng & Luo 2000). The common

---

[1] We are mindful of widespread mention of reciprocity as a significant characteristic of guanxi, but we cannot test reciprocity because we only have guanxi data from one of the two people connected by guanxi. However, we can say from our data three things about reciprocity: Reciprocity is rarely mentioned in the guanxi descriptions offered by our sample entrepreneurs. When it is mentioned, it is mentioned in less complex texts that rarely mention other aspects of guanxi. The people who mention reciprocity as a characteristic of guanxi tend to be running an establishment with below-average economic performance. We discuss these points, and our comfort with neglecting reciprocity, when we analyze the language used to describe guanxi ("A Note on Reciprocity" section in Chapter 6).

narrative running through this literature is that companies and individuals with guanxi and associated strategies can realize financial and market benefits when accessing scarce resources, such as capital, land, or skilled labor as well as administrative services (Peng & Luo 2000; Park & Luo 2001; Luo et al. 2011; Nee & Opper 2010, 2012; Opper et al. 2017). Similarly, guanxi may offer advantages in securing legal protection and varying forms of politically motivated preferential treatment in the presence of weak and unpredictable formal institutions (Peng & Luo 2000; Park & Luo 2001; Luo 2003; Li et al. 2008; Luo et al. 2011). There is ample cumulative evidence highlighting the value of guanxi (overview in Chen et al. 2013). Arguing for the increasing importance of guanxi for the Chinese economy, Bian (2018:612) displays survey evidence of jobs obtained through social networks increasing from less than 50 percent in 1978 to 80 percent in 2009.

However, the focus on China's specific business context—often narrowly reduced to a few collectivist or Confucian elements to establish the country's cultural distinctiveness—has hindered cultural comparisons (Barbalet 2021a:Chaps. 2, 6). Among other things, this has discouraged search for similar dyads across different cultural contexts (for some exceptions, see Chua et al. 2009; Burt 2019b; Burt & Batjargal 2019), even though "affective, reciprocal, and trusting relationships" are neither culturally nor institutionally distinct (a point argued by Lin 2001b, 2018, who compares guanxi processes to familiar principles of social exchange theory). Similarly, the emphasis on relational qualities and performance outcomes has largely obscured the question of *where* managers might find productive guanxi ties within their social networks, a highly relevant question since every person has some kind of guanxi to call upon. However, not all guanxi are important or make a productive difference, a complaint often heard in China, when people regret not having the "right guanxi."

In the second perspective, typical of social network research, scholars avoid explicit operationalization of Chinese guanxi. Work in this perspective focuses on testing the validity of the network-performance hypothesis—the negative association between network closure and performance, innovation, and creativity shown in Figure 2.6—widely observed in the West. With few exceptions, the majority of studies focusing on Chinese firms and their managers confirm the negative association between closed networks and business success (Batjargal 2007a, 2007b, 2010; Batjargal et al. 2013; Burt & Burzynska 2017; Burt 2019a; Zhao & Burt 2018; Burt et al. 2021, data from some of which are the triangle observations in Figure 2.6). In this light, some observers might see little reason to care about guanxi, as a seemingly culturally specific variant of social capital. Nevertheless, skepticism remains, and cultural contingency arguments persist, raising their barrier to synthesis across the two perspectives.

We take an integrative path. Encouraged by our hunch that event contacts—and their frequent role as strong bridges—might be guanxi, we focus on the broader human experience the term captures. Rather than treating guanxi as a cultural outlier or local constraint, we examine the value of trust formed through interpersonal history, its location in a person's network, and the advantage it confers.

This reframing shifts the terms of comparison. It sidesteps the impasse between cultural specificity and structural generalization. Guanxi scholars benefit from an analytically tractable—and thus replicable—definition of guanxi. Situating guanxi within ego-centered networks offers a strategy to distinguish culturally contingent from universal social mechanisms, opening the way to cross-cultural work. More importantly, for network scholars, guanxi offers a site to explore when and how trust strengthens brokerage—insights with clear implications beyond our immediate study context. In short, we were excited by the empirical and theoretical potential of our initial hunch that event contacts were guanxi.

Cutting Through the Gordian Knot

A critical step forward is to cut through the intellectual briar patch surrounding the question of what is guanxi. We do not see a solution in meta-analysis. Authors too often articulate nuances in what they believe guanxi to be. What is already complex becomes more complex with additional publications. With a colloquial term like guanxi, making sense of the many publications is a job for poets and soothsayers. We decided to skip reports by observers inside or outside China, and take what we believe is the first-ever empirical look at who is and who is not guanxi to someone. We talked to a representative sample of entrepreneurs—seeking ground truth from the people whose businesses are directly affected by the ties they see as "their" guanxi.[2]

---

[2] From the Oxford English Dictionary, ground truth means: To confirm or validate directly, esp. by direct observation on the ground, rather than by interpretation of remotely obtained data.

2018 Survey

Our 2018 survey was conducted to ask respondents about guanxi. With limited budget, we drew a stratified probability sample of small and medium-size businesses in three of the seven cities in which 2012 interviews occurred. We employed the same survey organization we used in 2012 because the organization was, and is, uniquely experienced in interviewing heads of business and was by then already familiar with the kind of network instrument designed for the first data collection.

We chose the three large cities clustered around the mouth of the Yangtze River delta (Shanghai, Ningbo, and Hangzhou, see Figure 3.1), all three included in our previous survey. As in our prior survey, our respondent is the general manager of a sample business. None of the 384 respondents in the 2018 survey had been a respondent in the 2012 survey. To improve the odds of productive variation, sample firms were drawn from two contrasting industries prominent in the region. "Automobile and vehicle parts" (Auto) represents traditional manufacturing with a long history in the region. "Computer services and software" (IT) represents the region's proliferating computer companies dealing with rapidly evolving information technology. We maintained some key features across our survey collections. As in the 2012 survey, we stratified by size to avoid over-representing easy-to-reach, small businesses, and excluded businesses operating for less than three years, and microenterprises with fewer than ten employees.

The research was presented to respondents as "an international research collaboration to study the ways in which the people around the manager are involved in building a private company in China's Yangtze Delta region. The goal is to describe how private business contributed to the rise of modern China." As before, only the general manager or CEO (in case of larger firms) was eligible to participate. No replacements were accepted to ensure we had the best possible source of information for the firm's development and network relations over time. Securing heads of business for relatively detailed face-to-face interviews continued to be challenging. For the two survey modules—a generic company module and a network instrument—the interviews lasted on average 53 minutes (minimum of 23, maximum of 91) and 38.2 minutes (minimum of 20, maximum of 90), respectively. Nevertheless, our response rate of 33 percent is about the same as surveys of top management in the West (Baruch 1999; Mellahi & Harris 2016). As in the 2012 survey, the sample of 384 respondents is primarily composed of owners or co-owners of the business (90 percent) who originally founded or co-founded the business (84 percent). The high proportion of owners in the role of general managers is typical for the region, especially in small and medium-sized enterprises (Nee & Opper 2012), who are often reluctant to hand over their business to professional managers. Of the sampled businesses, 31 percent were launched with only the founders' personal assets. In 68 percent of them, the founders provided about half (52 percent) of the assets used to launch the business. The remaining assets came from bank loans (18 percent), family contributions (11 percent), friends (9 percent), and venture capitalists (2 percent). Only three businesses were launched without the founders' personal assets. Average gross income for the sample firms in 2017 (the most recent fiscal year preceding the survey) was 55 million CNY (slightly more than $8 million).[3] The median respondent founded the business, employs sixty-six people, and knows thirty customers personally.

We prepared for the 2018 survey based on lessons learned in the earlier survey. As before, we set up discussion groups with the local interviewer team to review the exact wording and meaning of each item to minimize interviewer-induced variation. We also conducted a two-day workshop with all field interviewers to standardize the survey implementation and to minimize potential interviewer effects. The training included trial interviews with a number of business leaders, which were attended by all interviewers and discussed during the workshop. We then conducted pilot interviews with ten managers in each of the three sample cities. Recruitment for the pilot study followed the same procedure in terms of size, location, and industry as the sampling strategy for the main survey. The results of the pilot study did not warrant any changes to the survey questionnaire, but they did provide some guidance for standardizing the interview process (see Appendix A on survey preparation).

Guanxi Data

We asked respondents to describe their business network as we did in 2012 (described in the previous chapter). The primary change in 2018 was a guanxi name interpreter. We first asked respondents about their familiarity with guanxi (Figure A9f in Appendix A). Almost everyone said they were

---

[3] China's National Industry Classification system defines manufacturing firms with annual sales of more than 20 million CNY as medium-sized (so-called companies above designated size). The corresponding threshold for IT companies is 10 million CNY.

familiar with the term (95 percent).[4] The respondent was then asked to provide his or her own definition of the word's meaning, which was written down by the interviewer. We return to the texts in Chapter 6 to analyze the rhetoric of guanxi.

Regardless of the response to familiarity with guanxi, the respondent was asked to look over the list of cited contacts to identify the person with whom the respondent has the strongest guanxi: "In general, people say that guanxi exists when two people feel morally obligated to help one another without the expectation of direct compensation. Look over the list of your business contacts. Thinking of guanxi as feeling a moral obligation to help each other, with whom do you feel you have the strongest guanxi relationship? Just read the number next to the name of the person" (row one in Table 4.1).

We then asked for comparable contacts on the roster that the respondent felt were "almost as strong" as with the first person (row two in Table 4.1). "Are there any other people on the list with whom you have almost as strong a guanxi relationship as your relationship with the person you just named?" Finally, to anchor the other end of a guanxi continuum, we asked who on the list DOES NOT have a guanxi relationship with the respondent: "In terms of the general understanding of guanxi as a feeling of moral obligation to help each other, which people on the list definitely do not have a guanxi relationship with you?" (fourth row in Table 4.1).[5] Every respondent has guanxi responses, even the 5 percent who said they were not familiar with the term.[6]

---

[4] We were surprised that any respondents claimed to be unfamiliar with guanxi. We intended the opening question to be an easy "yes," encouraging the respondent to share their description of guanxi. So we were curious about the nineteen who said they were not aware of the term. Were they unable in some way, perhaps having too few years of education? Were they self-conscious, as a person might be if asked to explain to a stranger what love means? In a logit model of various factors predicting who claimed to be unfamiliar with guanxi, the strongest predictors are city and assets. A majority of the nineteen are in the most Western of the three cities (13 in Shanghai, 2.14 test statistic, P < .05) and none are in the most traditional of the cities (Hangzhou). Number of employees and business profitability (return to assets) were negligible predictors, but entrepreneurs claiming to be unfamiliar with guanxi were more likely to run a business with few assets (2.98 test statistic, P < .01). Respondent age, gender, education are negligible predictors. Industry and network are negligible predictors. Notably, the people who said they were unfamiliar with guanxi cited the same number of guanxi contacts as the people familiar with the term (respectively 2.00 versus 2.05, 0.40 test statistic, P ~ .69).

[5] Methodological aside: Analogy with Bacon's *Novum Organum* is not accidental. To know a thing (paraphrasing here), construct three tables: A table of instances in which the thing is observed (first row in Table 4.1), a table of instances in which the thing is absent (bottom row of the table), and a table of instances in which the thing is variably present (likely present in the second row, and likely not present in the third row).

[6] Almost everyone (96 percent) had an answer to the question about the strongest guanxi, but some were troubled by the idea of singling out one contact. Fourteen people insisted they had

Table 4.1 Guanxi Responses

Guanxi Name Interpreter	Ego Networks			Strong Ties		Event Contacts		
	Mean Number	Min.	Max	% Esp. Close	% Max. Trust	Founding	Other Event	Not Event
Strongest Guanxi: Look over the list of your business contacts. Thinking about guanxi as feeling a moral obligation to help each other, with whom do you feel you have the strongest guanxi? Just read the number next to the name of the person. (n = 398)	1.04	0	4	80%	88%	69% (16.3)	22% (−6.8)	9% (−12.1)
Other Guanxi: Are there any other people on the list with whom you have guanxi almost as strong as with the person you just named, contact [interviewer says number of the top contact]. (n = 389)	1.01	0	3	58%	67%	15% (2.9)	71% (6.0)	14% (−8.8)
Not Guanxi: Contacts unnamed on the three guanxi questions (n = 1641)	4.27	0	8	16%	21%	3% (−7.5)	61% (8.2)	35% (4.2)
Definitely Not Guanxi: In terms of the general understanding of guanxi as feeling a moral obligation to help each other, with which people on the list do you definitely NOT have guanxi? (n = 274)	0.71	0	3	1%	3%	1% (−4.6)	11% (−2.8)	88% (11.5)

Note: Frequencies tabulated from 2018 interviews with 384 respondent entrepreneurs citing 2702 contacts. Guanxi name interpreter is given in Figure A9, item 16. Percentages are for each row. The last three columns are taken from the previous chapter. Parentheses contain loglinear *z*-score test statistics for each cell frequency higher or lower than expected if *guanxi* categories were independent of event categories (based on total of 2702 contacts).

The four categories of guanxi correspond to familiar indicators of strong ties, which is to be expected. At the same time, many are not strong ties. The middle two columns in Table 4.1 show the percentage of strong ties among relations in each guanxi category. For example, 80 percent of the contacts named as strongest guanxi are also named "especially close" (Figure A9, item 10), and 88 percent enjoy the "highest trust" (level 5, Figure A9, item 14). There is a substantial drop to other guanxi (58 percent especially close, 67 percent highest trust). There is an even larger drop to contacts who are not guanxi (16 percent especially close, 21 percent highest trust), and still further to contacts explicitly cited as definitely not guanxi (1 percent especially close, 3 percent highest trust). We will combine the bottom two categories and refer to them as routine business contacts to contrast routine ties with guanxi or strongest guanxi.

Guanxi, Time, and Events

The frequent representation of guanxi among event contacts is a first reassuring signal that the special quality of event contacts is indeed based on their guanxi nature. The last three columns in Table 4.1 show the percentage of contacts in each row category of guanxi cited as event contacts. To get a quick sense of high and low percentages, loglinear test statistics are given in parentheses to indicate the extent to which a cell frequency is greater than would be expected if guanxi categories were independent of event categories. For example, strongest guanxi contacts are extremely likely to be cited as a source of help in founding the business (16.3 test statistic, P < .001), and extremely unlikely to be named on another event, or unnamed on any event (−12.1 test statistic, P < .001). In contrast, other guanxi are most likely to be named as a source of help during some later event (6.0 test statistic, P < .001). They are especially unlikely to remain unnamed on any event (−8.8 test statistic, P < .001). Recall that entrepreneurs were limited to the five most significant events among all the events they had experienced, so some guanxi not named here might have been named on less significant events if respondents had been able to identify lesser events.

---

more than one strongest guanxi on their roster. All those selected as strongest guanxi were dutifully recorded as such (thus the maximum of 4 in the first row of Table 4.1 and the 398 strongest guanxi contacts named by 384 respondents). Three people did not provide a name (the minimum of 0 in the first row). Two of these three named guanxi "almost as strong" on the second question, which left one person who did not name a guanxi contact on either the first or second question. That one person, however, did name a contact who was definitely not guanxi.

Routine business contacts are also often named as a source of help with significant events (8.2 test statistic, P < .001), but rarely as a source of help in founding the business (−7.5 test statistic, P < .001). Contacts singled out as definitely not guanxi are unlikely to be named as a source of help with any significant events. They are most likely cited only as a currently valued contact not associated with any of the significant events (11.5 test statistic, P < .001).

Although most event contacts are cited as guanxi, the few cited only as one or the other highlight in their own way the importance of sentiment to guanxi. First, the 9 percent of strongest guanxi and 14 percent of other guanxi that are not cited for help during a significant event, are just as likely to be viewed as "especially close" to the respondent as guanxi contacts cited for help (69 percent each). These contacts are most often family (30 percent) or special friends (33 percent no role relation other than "friend"). In contrast, looking at other contacts not involved in any event, the corresponding share of those viewed as "especially close" drops sharply to only 14 percent (not tabulated). Second, the event contacts named as definitely not guanxi are comparatively absent sentiment. These contacts are primarily former colleagues (67 percent) who are rarely met (79 percent less than monthly), and none of them are cited as "especially close" to the respondent. A final consideration is that either kind of mismatch between event contacts and guanxi is generally rare. Of eighty respondents who cite someone as guanxi but not simultaneously as an event contact, seventy-two cite only one such case (90 percent). Of 28 respondents who cite someone as an event contact but not as guanxi, twenty-five cite only one case (89 percent). Mismatched guanxi-event contacts are not due to the kinds of respondents, but due to occasional relations that slipped through our survey instrument. Fortunately, mismatches are relatively rare.

Time tells a corroborating story. On average, guanxi contacts have been known for 17.0 years (17.0 years if cited for help with an event, 16.9 otherwise). Contacts not deemed guanxi have been known for an average of 8.5 years (9.9 years if cited for event help, 6.5 otherwise).[7]

---

[7] The mix of events and time in guanxi ties is visible in Figure 4.2, so it is no surprise to find statistical results consistent with the graph. We regressed years known over binary variables distinguishing event contacts versus guanxi contacts with an interaction between them and fixed respondent effects (n = 2702, R^2 = .56). Coefficients for event contacts, guanxi contacts, and their interaction are respectively 3.49 years, 10.64 years, and −3.32 years. All three coefficients reject the null hypothesis at beyond a .001 level of confidence. Regardless of events, in short, guanxi ties are significantly older by seven to eleven years.

Figure 4.2 offers a more detailed account. Contacts deemed guanxi are shown in Panel B on the right. Dark areas mark contacts cited as guanxi and as sources of help during one or more significant events. Lighter areas are contacts cited as guanxi, but not for help during an event. Regardless of events, guanxi contacts are concentrated at the top of the graph, among contacts known for a decade or more.

In comparison, Panel A displays contacts deemed ordinary business contacts. Grey areas mark contacts cited for help during one or more significant events; white areas mark contacts not cited for help. Compared to guanxi, both types of business contacts are more concentrated toward the bottom of the graph, among contacts met more recently.

In sum, entrepreneur responses to the guanxi name interpreter, combined with the other network data, give us a ground truth. Guanxi tend to be people known for a decade or more, often cited as sources of help during a significant event. A special bond forms during a helpful exchange in a moment of stress. For entrepreneurs, such moments reliably occur during business founding or milestone events. Different contexts define different moments—soldiers looking out for one another during combat, people surviving together a disaster that for others proved fatal, and successful graduates of the same student cohort. The phenomenon

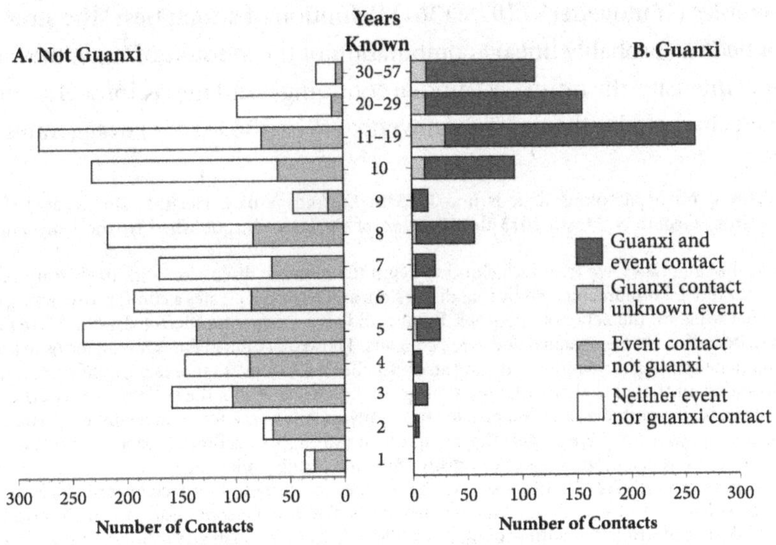

Figure 4.2 Event and Guanxi Contacts Over Time

Is neither peculiar to China nor contemporary business. The Greek playwright, Euripides, expressed it well: "Real friendship is shown in times of trouble; prosperity has friends galore."[8] Guanxi are ties marked by positive sentiment, forged to bond through felt support in a significant event.[9] They are, in short, the kind of ties from which strong bridges could emerge.

The Strong-Bridges Hypothesis

Continuing the idea of knowing a thing by knowing what it is not, a feature of event contacts is that the high trust in them is relatively independent of the surrounding network. Guanxi ties are relations of trust, warmth, and obligation, but if relations with event contacts are an example of guanxi, then positive characteristics such as trust and emotional closeness should be independent of the surrounding network. This seems eminently sensible: If you and I are guanxi, i.e., if we share a bond forged through a valued exchange, trust is not contingent on whether mutual friends are watching. You can count on my support anywhere I can provide it.

Common sense notwithstanding, analogy between event contacts and guanxi seems inherently flawed in light of widely accepted network theory. The common association of guanxi with warmth, obligation, and trust resembles Granovetter's (1973:1361) definition of strong ties: "the strength of a tie is a (probably linear) combination of the amount of time, the emotional intensity, the intimacy (mutual confiding), and the reciprocal services which characterize the tie."[10] Granovetter (1973:1363–1364) exaggerates the

[8] This is often paraphrased. It is line 1225 in Euripides's play, Hecuba. Our quoted wording is from Griffith & Most's 2013 third edition of *Euripides II*, published by the University of Chicago.

[9] In the interviews, we found it helpful to begin the network discussion with the history of significant events. Entrepreneurs enjoy that discussion, and having it creates a comfort discussing who did what when for the network questions. But it could also create a question-order effect. We find a close association between guanxi and event contacts. The association makes sense in terms of bonds strengthened through cooperation during an ordeal. But it also makes sense in terms of events affecting respondent thoughts about who are their guanxi contacts. Given the support we report below for our guanxi hypotheses, a useful task for future research is to ask for guanxi contacts before discussing business history. We suspect there will still be a strong association between guanxi and event contacts, but it is an empirical question easily answered (budget allowing).

[10] Krackhardt (1992:218–219) goes one step further to distinguish especially strong ties as *philos* ties, which are a subset of Granovetter's strong ties. Replace the commas between Granovetter's characteristics of strong ties with conjunctions: *Philos* ties are frequent and intimate and reciprocal, all over time. In distinguishing such especially strong ties and their role in response to stress, Krackhardt came close to describing guanxi ties. Operationally, however, his *philos* ties end up defined

closure-trust association to suppose there is always some strength of tie between people who have mutual friends, and that strong ties do not occur in the absence of mutual friends. So (italics in original): "it follows that, except under unlikely conditions, *no strong tie is a bridge.*" This is the basis for Granovetter's (1973:1363) "forbidden triad." From that widespread understanding, it is a short step to a common conclusion: Strong ties are likely in closed networks. Guanxi is a kind of strong tie. It follows that guanxi is more likely in closed networks. It is along these lines, that Xiao and Tsui (2007:5) reason that guanxi is associated with membership in a densely connected group, as "people who stay at the boundary of two in-groups tend to be distrusted by both groups."

Much like event contacts, we hypothesize that guanxi ties are associated with trust, independent of their structural position. To make our argument, we begin by emphasizing that Granovetter's forbidden triad was a didactic device, not a fact. By combining the strength of a relationship with its location in network structure, Granovetter could make his engaging statement that weak ties had a unique kind of strength as bridges. The more exact statement, however, is that bridges are often weak ties, but weak ties are rarely bridges (Burt 1992: 29–30). It is wise to unravel tie strength from location (cf. Kim & Fernandez 2023; Neal 2022, 2024). From his secondary analysis of network data, Neal finds numerous instances in which strong bridges are more useful than weak ties, which leads him to conclude with a recommendation we quote by way of recognition and endorsement (Neal 2024:303): "measure tie strength and bridgeness independently, then consider the roles of bridges and weak ties separately." We use strong versus weak to discuss the strength of a relationship, just as Granovetter used the terms. To discuss network location, we use measures of strong indirect connection through mutual contacts. With strength separate from location, we can study the strong ties that are bridges.

Recall the distinction in the previous chapter between two kinds of embedding; relational versus structural. Introduced in Granovetter's (1992) reflection on his (1985) discussion of embedding, relational embedding occurs when today's relationship is between people who have a history with one another. Structural embedding occurs when today's relationship is between people who have mutual friends. The two often go

in cross-section by reciprocity between ego and alter, not by their history of contact in significant events (Krackhardt 1992:222). See "A Note on Reciprocity" section in Chapter 6 on the rarely spoken role of reciprocity in guanxi.

together, of course. It is noteworthy when they do not. We find that the two kinds of embedding can operate separately, even compensating for one another.

We pull these threads together in a graph of the closure-trust association that takes into account strong bridges. Figure 4.3 is an example, patterned on similar graphs in the previous two chapters (Figure 2.5B, Figure 3.4, Figure 3.5). Trust, or some other measure of relationship strength, increases up the vertical axis from low to high. Structural embedding increases across the horizontal from none (for bridge relations) to high (for relations deeply embedded in a surrounding network of mutual contacts). The analysis-of-covariance model shown in the graph illustrates how T for trust varies with G for guanxi and SE for structural embedding.

The prediction equation for ego's trust in alter begins with the baseline level of trust in a routine bridge (alpha, α), plus the average increase in trust associated with the extent to which ego's relationship with alter is structurally embedded (beta, β, times $\ln(SE)$). Two additional terms adjust this prediction for guanxi ties: the average increase in trust when a bridge is guanxi rather than routine (gamma, γ), plus a correction that flattens the slope of the structural embedding association for guanxi (lambda, λ).

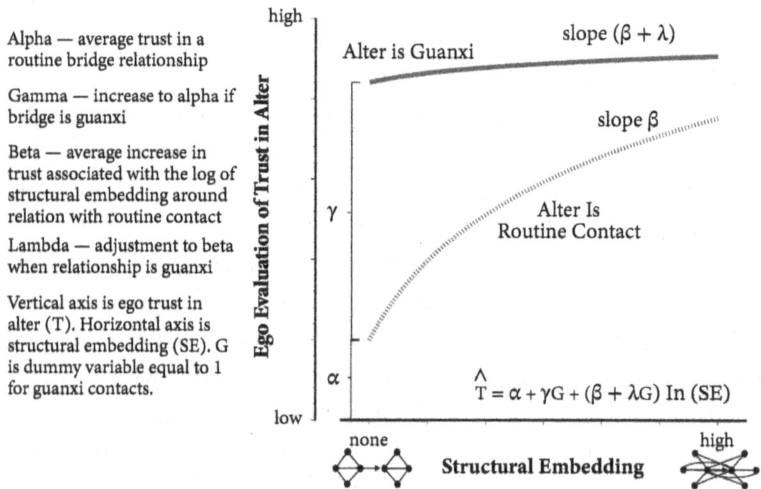

Figure 4.3 Strong-Bridges Hypothesis in Closure-Trust Association

If the analogy between event contacts and guanxi is valid, we expect trust in guanxi ties to be high on average, and relatively independent of structural embedding. This is the relatively flat solid line in Figure 4.3. In contrast, we expect trust in non-guanxi, routine business ties to increase with structural embedding as predicted by the closure-trust association, and illustrated by the dashed line. This is our strong-bridges hypothesis:

> *Strong-Bridges Hypothesis: Compared to trust in non-guanxi ties, trust in guanxi ties is higher and less contingent on structural embedding.*

With respect to Figure 4.3, the above hypothesis says that estimates of gamma should be positive and estimates of lambda should be negative for guanxi relationships. More generally, the hypothesis is a criterion for any category of relationships believed to be a source of strong bridges. A category of relations—by any name, in any population—that is consistent with the data pattern is a category of guanxi-like relations that we expect to carry the benefits and individual advantage of guanxi. We corroborate the idea in Chapter 8 by identifying guanxi-like relations among American investment bankers and an online population of college-educated adults in England, France, Germany, and Italy.

The hypothesis depends on knowing the network context of a relationship. Without context, it is difficult to know whether trust is independent of, or less dependent on, structural embedding. The answer depends on a comparative view. A guanxi tie that is a strong bridge can be distinguished from other relations by its high trust and lack of structural embedding. Over time people connected by a strong bridge may acquire mutual friends, which would move the tie to the right in Figure 4.3, making it difficult to know whether high trust observed later within the relationship is due to a history of interaction (relational embedding), or mutual friends (structural embedding).[11] But the gradual embedding of strong bridges is by no means a regularity. We return to these dynamics in Chapter 7.

---

[11] This statement does not imply that time moves from right to left in Figure 4.3, increasing with structural embedding. Mutual friends can accumulate around especially strong relationships, obscuring initial guanxi bridge relations as stated in the text. It is also possible that mutual friends in a group disappear when you leave the group, which would transform your one guanxi tie to the group into a bridge relationship. Guanxi emerge from a history of positive sentiment forged to bond in significant events. Structural embedding is a separate variable, present or absent as a function of when and where one spends time with guanxi.

Testing the Strong-Bridges Hypothesis

The simple guanxi name interpreter provides unprecedently concrete data on who is and is not guanxi. Armed with these data, we move on to determine the network location of guanxi to test our structural definition. Figure 4.4 plots mean levels of trust from the 2018 survey. The unit of analysis is a relationship. Respondent trust in a contact increases up the vertical axis. The horizontal axis distinguishes relations by structural embedding—which varies from respondent and contact with no mutual contacts in the respondent's network to contacts with six or more mutual contacts.

The data patterns are consistent with the strong-bridges hypothesis: Trust is high in guanxi and relatively independent of structural embedding. In Panel A, guanxi ties are defined by different kinds of event contacts, as in the previous chapter, but here using the 2018 survey data. The top line shows trust in contacts cited as most valued in founding the business. Trust in founding contacts is high across all levels of structural embedding. Trust is also high in contacts cited for other significant events in the history of

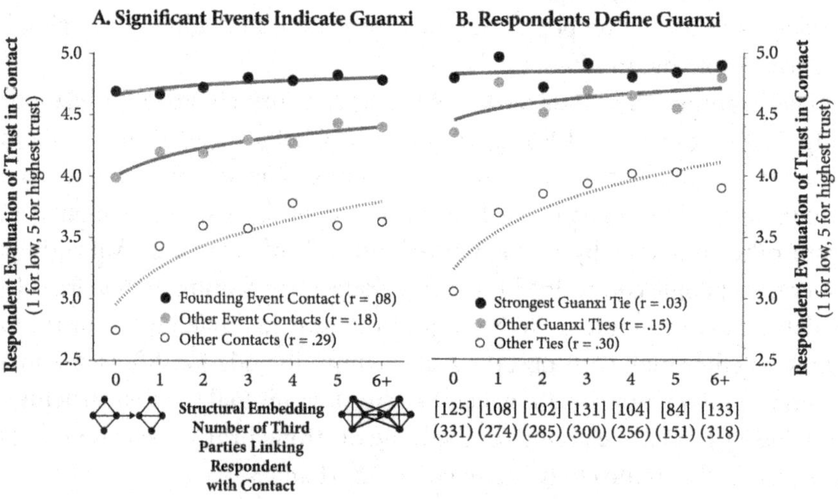

Figure 4.4 Trust Association Is More Obvious with Guanxi

Note: Dots are average Y scores at each level of X. Graphs describe relationships with 2702 contacts cited by 384 respondents. Vertical axis is respondent trust, measured on a five-point scale. Horizontal axis is the number of other people in a respondent's network connected with the contact being evaluated for trust. Correlations are computed between trust and log (number of third parties) across all relations. Frequencies to the right below each level of third-party connection show number of (guanxi ties) and (other ties).

the business, though at a lower level and more associated with structural embedding. The lowest level of trust, and strongest association with structural embedding, is in contacts not cited in connection with any event. The pattern closely replicates the results from the previous chapter and from earlier publications based on the larger 2012 sample. Thus, what we once viewed as a theoretical outlier in the earlier data now appears to be a common pattern. Panel B shows a similar, but more pronounced, pattern when we use the respondents' own definitions of who among their contacts they consider guanxi, providing initial visual support for our strong-bridges hypothesis.

High Trust Independent of Structural Embedding

Table 4.2 presents statistical tests for the above interpretation (with descriptive statistics in Appendix B, Table B.2). We use jackknife standard errors with individual fixed effects to better compare multiple relations described by each respondent. Trust differences across industries and cities are held constant by individual fixed effects, since all contacts of a respondent share the same industry-city pair. All closure-trust associations in Table 4.2 are statistically significant beyond the .001 level of confidence, so we do not distinguish coefficients by significance level in the table.

Models M1 and M2 predict trust when guanxi contacts are defined by significant events in the history of the business (as in Chapter 3, Table 3.5 using 2012 data). The other models use guanxi contacts as cited by each respondent.[12] We continue to discuss effects in terms of the number of mutual contacts, but we also include statistical tests based on a more precise measure: the strength of indirect connection between respondent and contact, measured by the sum of indirect connections within the respondent's network ($\sum_k z_{ik} z_{kg}$, $i \neq k \neq j$, for respondent i and contact j with z_{ik} the

---

[12] Given the sharp performance difference between sample firms in IT versus those in traditional manufacturing, we checked for industry effects. We re-estimated the six models in Table 4.2 without respondent fixed effects, adjusted the standard errors for autocorrelation between relations cited by the same respondent (Stata "cluster" option), and added a dummy variable to distinguish respondents in the IT industry. The explicit IT control is negligible in all six models in Table 4.2, generating t-tests of 0.81, 0.84, 1.01, 1.03, 1.01, and 1.02 in Models 1 through 6 respectively, so the probability is over .3 that trust is independent of industry.

Table 4.2 Statistical Tests for Closure-Trust Association Distinguishing Guanxi Ties (Strong-Bridges Hypothesis)

	Significant Events Define Guanxi		Respondents Define Guanxi			
	M1	M2	M3	M4	M5	M6
Intercept (alpha in Figure 4.3)	2.67	2.67	2.84	2.85	2.84	2.86
Structural embedding (beta in Figure 4.3)						
Log third parties	.67 (.07)	.67 (.07)	.78 (.06)	—	.78 (.06)	—
Log weighted third parties	—	—	—	.94 (.06)	—	.94 (.06)
Level adjustment guanxi contacts (gamma, Figure 4.3)						
All guanxi	1.25 (.10)	—	1.48 (.08)	.95 (.03)	—	—
Strongest guanxi	—	1.81 (.12)	—	—	1.63 (.09)	1.05 (.04)
Other guanxi	—	1.10 (.11)	—	—	1.33 (.10)	.84 (.04)
Slope adjustment guanxi contacts (lambda Figure 4.3)						
All guanxi	−.31 (.07)	—	−.44 (.06)	−.57 (.06)	—	—
Strongest guanxi	—	−.45 (.09)	—	—	−.48 (.06)	−.61 (.06)
Other guanxi	—	−.28 (.07)	—	—	−.40 (.07)	−.54 (.08)
R^2	.40	.43	.43	.45	.44	.46

Note: OLS results predicting trust in 2702 cited contacts measured on a five-point scale. Includes respondent fixed effects and jackknife standard errors in parentheses. Descriptive statistics are given in Table B.2 in Appendix B. All coefficients reject the null hypothesis beyond a .001 level of confidence.

fractional measure of connection strength between i and k). We find stronger associations with the more precise measure.[13]

---

[13] Contact-specific constraint, c_{ij}, is a more comprehensive measure of embedding, but it includes relational and structural embedding so using it would introduce ambiguity into our hypothesis testing. The c_{ij} score differs from the summed strength of relations in three ways: relations are weighted by their proportion within the respondent's network, strength concentrated in a subset of relations increases c_{ij}, and the respondent's own relation with contact j is included in contact-specific

Guanxi contacts are the object of high trust whether we define guanxi by events or ask respondents to identify which of their contacts they regard as guanxi. In all models, trust is higher in guanxi relations (solid lines in Figure 4.4 are higher than dashed lines). In Model M4, for example, trust in guanxi ties is on average one point higher on a five-point scale (.95 coefficient, 15.30 test statistic, which is statistically significant well beyond the .001 level).

The closure-trust association is obvious here as it has been in prior research. In all models, trust in non-guanxi relations increases with the extent to which the relation is embedded in third parties (dashed lines in Figure 4.4 have steeper slopes than the solid lines). In Model M3, for example, an embedding increase from zero to two third parties is associated with an average increase of slightly less than one point in level of five-point trust (.86 = .78 coefficient times 1.10 log score; 30.61 t-test for the coefficient, again well beyond a .001 level of confidence).

Support for the strong-bridges hypothesis comes from the interaction effects at the bottom of Table 4.2. The hypothesis is that trust within guanxi ties is less contingent on structural embedding than trust in non-guanxi contacts. The lack of contingency is visible in Figure 4.4 from the solid lines for guanxi ties being less steep than the dashed lines for non-guanxi ties. In Table 4.2, all slope adjustments for trust in guanxi ties are negative and statistically significant. In other words, trust is significantly less contingent on structural embedding around guanxi ties. In Model M4, for example, there is a .94 coefficient describing how trust increases with the strength of connection between respondent and contact through mutual colleagues. That coefficient is reduced by .57 to describe the trust association with structural embedding around guanxi ties (beta minus lambda in Figure 4.3; −9.76 t-test for the −.57 coefficient, which is statistically significant well beyond a .001 level of confidence). In fact, trust in guanxi ties can be viewed as independent of structural embedding. When we estimate the association between trust and structural embedding for relations respondents define as guanxi, test statistics do not reject the null hypothesis (1.16 t-test for number of third parties, 1.27 t-test for strength of connection through third parties, both giving more than a .20 probability to the null hypothesis).

<hr>

constraint. All three features increase multicollinearity with aggregate constraint, which is a complication for testing our second hypothesis, and the third difference means that the respondent-contact connection is on both sides of the equation in testing our first hypothesis (trust as dependent variable and emotional closeness as predictor). Not surprisingly, respondent trust in a contact is more strongly correlated with c_{ij} than it is with third parties to the relation with contact j (.39 versus .21 for a count of third parties, .28 for weighted sum of connections through third parties).

Stronger Support In Relations Respondents Define as Guanxi

While trust is independent of structural embedding for guanxi ties indicated by the respondent him or herself, that is not true for guanxi inferred from events. This is visible in Figure 4.4: the solid lines in Panel B, where respondents indicate guanxi, are flatter than the solid lines in Panel A, where we used significant events to indicate guanxi. And test statistics do reject independence when we estimate association between trust and structural embedding for guanxi inferred from events (3.06 t-test for number of third parties, 3.32 t-test for strength of connection through third parties, both giving less than .01 probability to the null hypothesis). Further, the slope adjustment for trust contingency on structural embedding is more obvious for guanxi ties in Table 4.2 when respondents indicate which of their contacts are guanxi (−7.77 test statistic for the −.44 coefficient in Model M3 and −9.76 for the −.57 coefficient in Model M4 versus −4.32 test statistic for the −.31 coefficient in Model M1). And third, Models M2, M5, and M6 in Table 4.2 show that support for the strong-bridges hypothesis is stronger for relations that respondents perceive as stronger guanxi. The models distinguish strongest guanxi from other guanxi. In Model M2, strongest guanxi is the contact most valued in founding the business. Other guanxi is any contact named as most valued for their help during significant events after founding. The trust level adjustment is higher for strongest guanxi (1.81 versus 1.10 coefficient), and the slope adjustment for strongest guanxi removes more of the closure-trust association found in routine business relations (−.45 versus −.28 coefficient). In Model M5, strongest guanxi is whoever the respondent named as his or her strongest guanxi, and other guanxi is whomever the respondent named as almost as strong. Again, the trust level adjustment is higher for strongest guanxi (1.63 vs. 1.33 coefficient), and the slope adjustment for strongest guanxi removes more of the trust-closure association found in routine business relations (−.48 versus .40 coefficient). Stronger estimates are in Model M6, when embedding is measured by the strength of connection through third parties, rather than by the count of third parties in Model M5.

In sum, the event contacts discussed in the previous chapter appear to be examples of guanxi; not perfect examples (since some are explicitly identified as not guanxi, Table 4.1), but certainly a good approximation. More importantly, Panel B of Figure 4.4 shows a modification of the closure-trust association that includes the strong bridges that guanxi contacts provide.[14]

Consistent Support in Relations Explicitly Not Guanxi

If Model M4 is extended to distinguish relations explicitly not guanxi, we get further support for the strong-bridges hypothesis. Recall that respondents were asked to identify which of their contacts were guanxi, then asked "with which people on the list do you definitely NOT have guanxi?" (bottom row in Table 4.1). A third of the sample did not distinguish any of their contacts as explicitly not guanxi (31.5 percent). The majority named one contact (66.4 percent), and eight respondents named more than one (five named two, three named three). Given the limited data we have on these least guanxi-like relationships, we do not make too much of them, but the data we have warrant mention. Add two variables to Model M4: A dummy variable distinguishing contacts identified as not guanxi, and an interaction term for the dummy variable multiplied by the log weighted third-party measure in the third row of Table 4.2. When we estimate this model with respondent fixed effects and jackknife standard errors—just as in Table 4.2— we get the following results (increasing the .45 R^2 for Model M4 to .67): First, as in Model M4, the closure-trust association is evident (.31 coefficient, 6.45 t-test). Second, as in Model M4, there is a positive level adjustment for the higher trust in guanxi bridges (.73 coefficient, 27.8 t-test), and a negative slope adjustment for guanxi trust relatively independent of structural embedding (−.23 coefficient, −4.64 t-test). Third, adding to Model M4, trust

[14] Our systematic evidence of support for guanxi providing strong bridges, brings back a reflection by Yang about her fieldwork in China during the 1980s, a period of widespread suspicion and fear. Yang (1994:24) noted how strong bridges provided by guanxi become both her subject and research strategy: "...the object of inquiry and the method of inquiry came to consist of linking up with people through networks of relationships spread around the city of Beijing and elsewhere. Doing fieldwork by replicating the very network form of the art of guanxi, hovering always between fixed sites and locations, proved a much more resilient strategy in China because it enabled me to keep my network 'connectedness' or 'density' at a low level (Bott 1957:59). In other words, the degree to which 'the members of [my] network [were] in touch with each other independently of [me]' (Boissevain 1974:37–40) was kept low to insure each person's security. Through personal introductions to a larger network of people, most of whom did not know of one another's existence, the element of trust produced by personal relationships and the feeling of security in anonymity combined to make my work much easier and more productive." Bian and Wang (2016) make a related point with their discussion of "cross-sector social capital" used by Chinese entrepreneurs.

is tenuous in contacts called out as not guanxi. The level adjustment shows trust in bridge relations with not-guanxi contacts lower than for routine business contacts (two points lower on the five-point scale; −2.08 coefficient, −20.83 t-test). The slope adjustment is positive, showing that trust in a non-guanxi contact is more dependent on mutual friends than is trust in routine business contacts (.50 coefficient, 4.16 t-test). In the Figure 4.4B graph, adding a line for trust in not-guanxi contacts would begin at 1.71 for bridge relations (below the current horizontal axis), then increase more steeply with additional mutual friends, reaching its maximum average of 2.95, which is well below the dashed line in Figure 4.4B describing trust in routine business contacts.

Structural Embedding More Broadly Considered

The business contacts cited by our sample respondents vary from one to eleven around a mean of four. In such small networks, the overall density of a network is closely correlated with the level of structural embedding around individual relations within the network. Network density—measured as the average connection strength between an entrepreneur's contacts (multiplied by 100 to vary from zero to 100)—shows the expected high correlation with our two measures of structural embedding. The relationship between a respondent and contact is structurally embedded to the extent that there is a strong indirect connection between the two through mutual friends or other third parties. We measure "strong" by either the number of third parties (correlated .68 with density) or the sum of weighted connections through third parties (correlated .72 with density).

These correlations, while high, leave roughly half of the variance in density unexplained by structural embedding around individual relationships. We expect density to enhance trust when it is consistent with structural embedding, but to reduce trust when it is inconsistent with structural embedding. The negative effect is statistically significant, yet it does not change or improve the trust prediction in Table 4.2. However, knowing that density is otherwise irrelevant keeps the trust prediction simple, so we take a brief aside to make the fact explicit.

When Network Density Differs from Structural Embedding
We are curious to know what happens when density and structural embedding come apart. The graph in Figure 4.5 plots overall network density

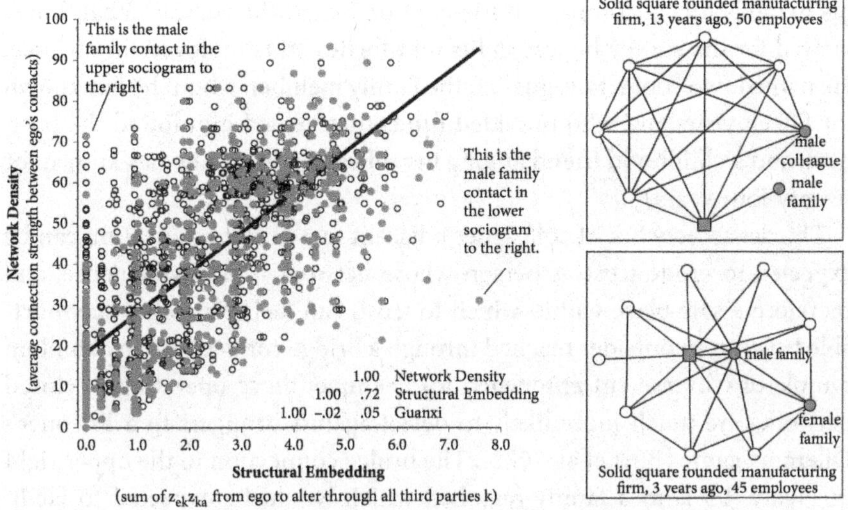

Figure 4.5 Structural Embedding within Variably Dense Networks

Note: Dots indicate 2702 contacts cited by 384 respondents. Solid dots are the 787 contacts deemed guanxi. Hollow dots are other relations. Vertical axis is average connection strength among an ego's contacts. Horizontal is strength of indirect connection to a contact through third parties ("weighted third parties" in Table 4.2). Correlations are computed across 2702 relations. The square in the sociograms is the respondent and solid dots are guanxi contacts.

on the vertical axis against structural embedding on the horizontal axis. Bridges are to the left. Deeply embedded relationships are to the right. Each dot in the graph represents one of the 2702 contacts cited by the sample entrepreneurs. Two facts stand out: First, the graph shows a close association between overall network density and structural embedding around individual relationships. Data cluster along the upward-sloping regression line (.72 correlation). Second, guanxi—the solid dots—appear independent of both network density and structural embedding, scattered across the space (correlations of −.02 and .05 respectively with density and structural embedding).

To discuss density separate from structural embedding, we pull out two extreme relationships and display the networks in which they are embedded. To the upper left in the graph, we mark a guanxi contact with zero structural embedding in a network of high density. The sociogram to the upper right shows this male family contact within the respondent's network of seven: six colleagues—almost all especially close to one another—and a bridge connection to the male family member who is disconnected from the colleagues. The sample entrepreneur, indicated by the square, founded his manufacturing company thirteen years before the survey. When interviewed for the survey he was in his mid-forties and employed fifty people. He named two contacts as guanxi; the family member, whom he has known for fifteen years and who provided funds that helped him found the business, and a childhood friend among his colleagues whom he has known for twenty-four years.

The dense network of colleagues adjacent to a bridge connection can be expected to erode trust. A person whose network is relatively dense, and therefore a safe place within which to trust, can feel relatively uncomfortable trusting an outsider reached through a bridge connection. In a random sample of Chinese entrepreneurs, for example, those operating in closed networks are much more likely to defect against strangers in a Prisoner's Dilemma game (Burt et al. 2022). The bridge connection to the upper right in Figure 4.5 is to a family member, which would be expected to facilitate trust, but it is a family member known only for the last fifteen years, which means known since the entrepreneur was in his early thirties. The adjacent dense network of colleagues could create a barrier between work and family, lowering confidence in the family member's judgment, even if the entrepreneur is grateful for the family member's early financial help in founding the business.

On the lower right side of the Figure 4.5 graph are deeply embedded relationships within otherwise open networks. We again single out one guanxi contact. The marked contact is again a male family member, now with a weighted third-party index over seven, within a network of modest density. The sociogram to the lower right shows this male family contact within the respondent's network of ten contacts: seven are colleagues the sample entrepreneur knew in the organization where he worked before founding his current manufacturing business. When interviewed for the survey, the entrepreneur was in his mid-forties and employed forty-five people. He named two people as guanxi, a man and woman, both family members, both known for about a decade. There are disconnected people in the network, but only one is disconnected from the male family member. In essence, the entrepreneur has built his network on the network of that male family member. It is his relationship with that family member which is deeply embedded in mutual contacts who are themselves relatively disconnected from one another. Networks anchored on one contact as this one is are often discussed as "partner" networks (Burt 1998). The lack of closure among contacts, combined with structural embedding around the relationship with the partner contact, make it difficult to ignore one's dependence on the partner, and the outsider status that make such a network valuable (Burt 2010: Chap. 7). At the same time, the partner's sponsorship in sharing contacts facilitates a false sense of intimacy with the contacts. In fact, the entrepreneur in the lower-right sociogram expresses trust in all his contacts—except the one person to the left who is disconnected from the partner.

In sum, we expect density to have a negative association with trust when it pulls away from structural embedding—diminishing trust in a bridge relationship within an otherwise dense network (upper sociogram in Figure 4.5), and enhancing trust in a deeply embedded relationship within an otherwise sparse network (lower sociogram). Returning to our strong-bridges hypothesis, the empirical question is whether deviation between density and structural embedding matters for trust, given their usual tendency to move together.

Trust Prediction

In Table 4.3, we add two controls for overall network density to Model M4 in Table 4.2, which we include here for ease of comparison. Metric coefficients are reported with jackknife standard errors. All coefficients reject the null hypothesis at well beyond the .001 level.

The second column, Model M4a, adds a slope adjustment for guanxi that occur in dense networks. The estimates are consistent with the strong-bridges hypothesis: Trust in guanxi is even more independent of structural embedding (slope is beta plus gamma, which is .94 − .57, or .37 in Model M4, versus 1.03 − .93 or .10 in Model M4b). Trust in guanxi has a small, but statistically significant, positive association with more dense networks (.012 coefficient, 5.53 t-test). A ten-point increase in the density of a network containing a guanxi contact is associated with a .12 increase in five-point trust in the guanxi contact. Regardless of the level of structural embedding, in other words, trust in guanxi is slightly higher in denser networks.

There is no direct effect for density in Model M4a because respondent-level variables such as the respondent's overall network density are excluded by respondent fixed effects. In Model M4b, we replace respondent fixed effects with a correction for autocorrelation between relations in the same network (Stata "cluster" option) so we can add a level effect for the overall density of an entrepreneur's network. As expected, network density has a small, but statistically significant, negative association with trust (−.013 coefficient, −7.30 t-test). The negative trust association with density

Table 4.3 Strong-Bridges Hypothesis Supported Regardless of Overall Guanxi

	M4	M4a	M4b
Intercept (alpha, Figure 4.3)	2.85	2.78	3.35
Structural embedding (beta, Figure 4.3)	.94 (.06)	1.03 (.07)	.94 (.06)
Level adjustment for guanxi contacts (gamma, Figure 4.3)	.95 (.03)	.97 (.03)	.97 (.02)
Slope adjustment for guanxi contacts (lambda Figure 4.3)	−.57 (.06)	−.93 (.09)	−.80 (.09)
Level adjustment for guanxi in dense networks	—	—	−.013 (.002)
Slope adjustment for guanxi in dense networks	—	.012 (.002)	.011 (.002)
R^2	.45	.46	.32

Note: OLS results predicting trust in 2701 cited contacts measured on a five-point scale. Structural embedding is measured by summed weighted indirect connections through third parties. Jackknife standard errors in parentheses with respondent fixed effects for Models M4 and M4a (with Stata respondent cluster option for Model M4b). All coefficients reject the null hypothesis beyond a .001 level of confidence.

balances the positive association with trust in guanxi ties (−.013 versus .011 coefficients), leaving trust in guanxi ties unaffected by network density.

In sum, when network density in these relatively small networks deviates from structural embedding, it has a small, statistically significant, negative association with trust in routine relationships. Density, however, adds nothing to structural embedding in predicting trust in guanxi ties, and thus takes nothing away from our strong-bridges hypothesis.

Strong Bridges and Competitive Advantage

We have established that guanxi, and even contacts as their surrogate, can provide strong bridge relations. To be consequential as strong bridges, however, they must provide an advantage. Business success in China is widely believed to be associated with guanxi ties (Xin & Pearce 1996; Tsui & Farh 1997; Peng & Luo 2000; Park & Luo 2001, for reviews: Luo et al. 2011; Chen et al. 2013). The literature is replete with descriptions of how managers and firms make use of guanxi. Reliance on guanxi ties helps firms secure information, financial resources, and scarce raw materials, with positive effects on performance (Peng & Luo 2000; Opper et al. 2017). These ties also help firms win public procurement contracts and succeed in tenders for state assets (Nee & Opper 2012: Chap. 9). They support access to scarce talent (Nee & Opper 2012:Chap. 7), and they can be critical in resolving legal disputes (Gong 2004). Moreover, the link between guanxi and business success is increasingly seen as neither transitory nor a mere response to weak formal institutions (Guthrie 1998; Bian 2018).

On average, bridge relations are associated with economic advantage (see Figure 2.6). This holds both in the West and in China. But how is prediction improved by distinguishing the strong bridges provided by guanxi? We expect to see the usual performance advantage among managers whose networks span structural holes—but in particular, guanxi bridges, or more generally strong bridges, should be associated with higher performance.

Individual advantage is not a question of whether an entrepreneur has guanxi. Having guanxi is like having a network; everyone has one. Recall that 96 percent of our respondents readily acknowledged having the strongest kind of guanxi relationship in their network. Against this backdrop, the common complaint that success in China is impossible without guanxi offers little analytical leverage. The real question is whether a person has the *right* guanxi (Xiao & Tsui 2007), that is, highly trusted people in the right places.

Managers turn to guanxi when internal resources are limited, and when the sole reliance on market mechanisms and formal institutions does not guarantee timely or efficient access to resources and information. Likewise, managers turn to guanxi, to secure political, legal, and market protection that are otherwise unavailable. According to network theory, the guanxi best suited to these demands are those that reach beyond the local group—bridges across structural holes, able to access, evaluate, and mobilize novel or hard-to-reach external resources (Chang 2011:318–319 on bridging guanxi).

Bridge guanxi are apparent in Figure 4.3. The solid line to the upper left describes guanxi bridges—high-trust relationships that operate with little or no structural embedding. When guanxi connects individuals across groups, they function as strong bridges. And as observed elsewhere, we expect only bridge guanxi to facilitate information transfer from one social cluster to another (Tortoriello & Krackhardt 2010), as well as broader processes of diffusion (Reagans & McEvily 2003; Centola & Macy 2007; Tortoriello et al.

2012; Centola 2018; Masuda et al. 2018; Guilbeault & Centola 2021), and, more specifically, to support job searches (Bian 1997).

Non-bridge guanxi—that is, guanxi ties to contacts who are structurally embedded in mutual friends (solid line to the right in Figure 4.3)—are less likely to offer unique insights, novel information, or access to otherwise unattainable resources (although closed networks do not preclude access to novel information, but the mechanisms differ e.g., Aral & Van Alstyne 2011; Ter Wal et al. 2016). Rather than facilitating access to resources beyond the entrepreneur's immediate social cluster, embedded guanxi are more likely to redistribute and exploit resources within a small group of like-minded actors, as is common in mutual support or microfinance groups.

When it comes to access to information, structurally embedded guanxi contacts tend to share opinions and evaluations already circulating within the manager's network. Experience in navigating competing perspectives is less likely than "echoing" the consensus view (Burt 2005, Chp. 4 on network echo). A related concern is that valued contacts shared with others can become generic go-to-contacts in moments of uncertainty. Once consultation with structurally embedded guanxi becomes routine, templates from past successes may replace novel information and search for situation-specific strategies (Levinthal & March 1993; Burt & Soda 2017; Opper & Burt 2021).

In short, we expect as an "advantage" hypothesis, consistent with the strong-bridges hypothesis, that structurally embedded guanxi provides less performance advantage than bridge guanxi:

Advantage Hypothesis: The economic performance of an entrepreneur increases more with bridge guanxi than with structurally embedded guanxi.

Testing the Advantage Hypothesis

We measure the economic performance of an entrepreneur's business using average return on assets over the three-year period from 2015 to 2017. Results are similar using return on assets from the most recent available year (2017) with a .96 correlation to the three-year average, but we prefer to report results based on the multi-year average to capture more stable differences in relative performance.

We include three types of control variables. First, we include several attributes of the sample entrepreneur: gender, age, founder status, years of education, and party membership. Second, we include company-level controls: initial assets available to grow the business (assets at firm founding), the difficulty of launching the business (measured by the number of years required to reach profitability), and an industry indicator distinguishing traditional manufacturing from the rapidly growing IT sector. Finally, we include city controls to hold constant variation in the local business environment.

Guanxi's Relevance to Performance

Before we turn to statistical tests, Figure 4.6 provides initial visual corroboration that guanxi matters for economic performance. The horizontal axis is network constraint. Entrepreneurs to the left have large, open networks rich in structural-hole opportunities for brokerage; those to the right have small, closed networks lacking such opportunities. We follow the convention of multiplying constraint scores by 100 to speak in points of constraint (see footnote 10, Chapter 2 for computation). These graphs correspond to the Figure 2.6 plot across populations. In fact, the 2018 survey data define one of the populations included in Figure 2.6 (footnote 9 in Chapter 2).

Economic performance increases up the vertical axes. Dark dots represent our performance measure return on assets. Providing corroboration, hollow dots show return on equity. Both performance measures are displayed as z-scores on the vertical axes, adjusted for business assets or equity, industry, and the time it took for the business to become profitable.[15]

Figure 4.6A shows the usual negative, nonlinear association with constrained networks (as in Figure 2.6 across study populations in the United States, Europe, and Asia): The smaller and more dense a respondent's network, the lower the relative profit returned by his or her business. The −.58 slope coefficient indicates that a one-unit increase in log network

---

[15] Regressing return on assets across value of the business' assets, industry, years after founding until the business was profitable, and log network constraint, shows a −.08 coefficient log network constraint and −3.63 t-test for lower profit margins in businesses run by people with more closed networks (P < .001). For an adjusted profit measure, we ran the regression without network constraint and use the studentized residual as the vertical axis in the figure. Regressing return on equity across value of the business' equity, industry, years after founding until the business was profitable, and log network constraint, shows a −.25 coefficient for log network constraint and −4.01 t-test for lower profit margins in businesses run by people with more closed networks (P < .001).

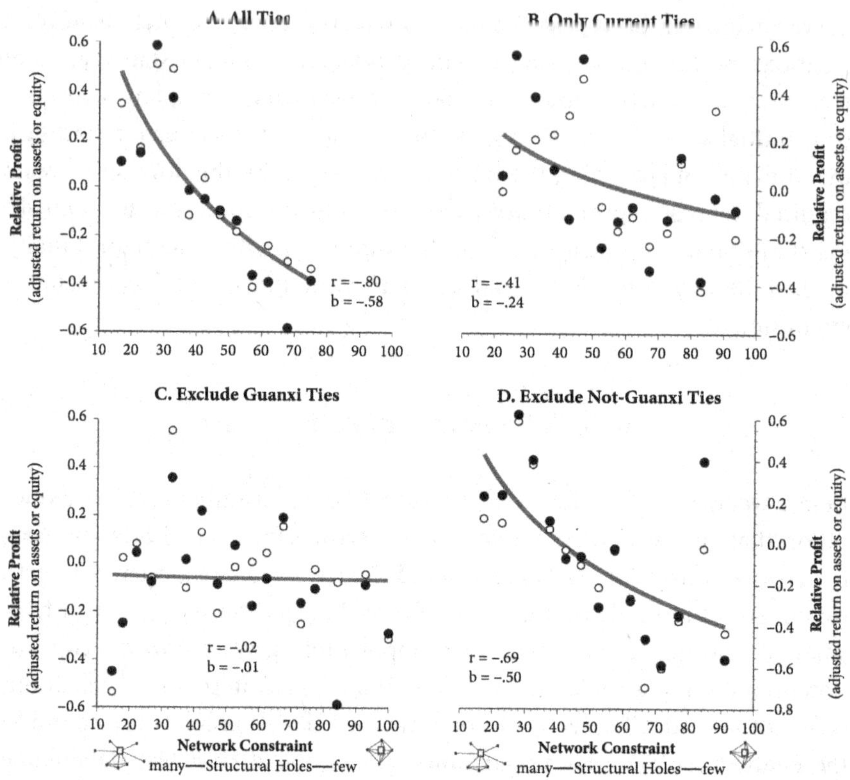

Figure 4.6 Guanxi Ties Are Critical to the Advantage Hypothesis

Note: Plotted scores are 384 individual scores on vertical and horizontal axes averaged within five-point intervals of network constraint. Dark dots show average return on assets (adjusted for value of business assets, years from founding until business was profitable, and industry). Hollow dots show average return on equity (adjusted for value of business equity, years from founding until business was profitable, and industry). Correlations are computed from plotted data with log (network constraint).

constraint—such as moving from fifteen to forty points of constraint—is associated with a drop of about half a standard deviation in returns (return on asset standard deviation is 14.20; see Table B.3, Appendix B).

Figure 4.6B shows what happens if respondent networks are limited to current contacts—which is familiar practice in social network research. Of the 787 contacts identified as guanxi ties, 456 were also named as current contacts (see name generators in Table 3.1, rows 3 to 6), so the analysis still includes many guanxi ties named as valuable contacts in the current business year. The association between network structure and performance is still evident, but there is more variation around the regression line. The −.58 slope in Figure 4.6A drops to −.24 in Figure 4.6B. The weaker association based on current contacts may help explain why some well-executed network studies in China fail to detect the expected network-performance association (e.g., Xiao & Tsui 2007).

Excluding all guanxi ties, in Figure 4.6C, wipes out the association between network structure and performance—implying the performance relevance of guanxi. This is not simply due to weaker statistical power from dropping ties. The association remains strong in Figure 4.6B but disappears in Figure 4.6C, despite more contacts being included in the latter (1915 contacts in 4.6C versus 1781 in 4.6B networks). More telling, the network-performance association is obvious again in Figure 4.6D, which excludes ties respondents identified as definitely not guanxi (fourth row of Table 4.1). The slope coefficient of −.50 in Figure 4.6D is almost the same as the slope of −.58 in Figure 4.6A, where networks include all available contacts.

In short, the four panels in Figure 4.6 point to a general conclusion: Guanxi ties are central to the network-performance association. Ties respondents consider not to be guanxi do not enhance performance, so the network-performance association is robust to their deletion. The critical question remains: Where in the respondent's network are the guanxi that offer a comparative advantage?

Performance Evidence on Strongest Guanxi

Our advantage hypothesis predicts that bridge guanxi improves performance more than embedded guanxi. Table 4.4 presents results that clearly support this hypothesis. We estimate performance from structural embedding around a respondent's strongest guanxi—measured as the number of mutual contacts connecting respondent and strongest guanxi in Model M7, and the weighted sum of indirect connections through mutual contacts in Model M8.[16] For the fourteen respondents who insisted on naming more than one strongest guanxi (12 named two contacts, one named three, and one named four), we averaged structural embedding across named contacts,

---

[16] The estimates in the table are almost identical to the ones presented in our published paper (Burt & Opper 2024:29), except we there used fixed effects to remove city differences while here we make explicit the one significant city difference. There is almost no difference between Shanghai and Ningbo in average returns to assets (−.45 t-test if Ningbo variable is added to Model M10, for example, P ~ .65). The statistically significant city difference is between inland Hangzhou versus coastal Shanghai and Ningbo with their extensive Western contact (−4.86 t-test in Model M10, P < .001).

Table 4.4 Performance Increases When Strongest Guanxi Is a Bridge (Advantage Hypothesis)

	M7	M8	M9	M10
Embedding of strongest guanxi (count third parties)	−3.66** (1.17)		−2.93* (1.17)	
Embedding of strongest guanxi (weighted sum indirect ties)		−4.20*** (1.27)		−3.23* (1.29)
Network constraint (excluding strongest guanxi)			−5.92** (1.97)	−5.65** (2.00)
Respondent is female	−.13 (1.72)	.01 (1.70)	−.05 (1.68)	.03 (1.67)
Respondent age (in years)	.07 (.13)	.09 (.13)	.08 (.13)	.09 (.13)
Respondent is founder	−.21 (2.02)	.10 (2.23)	−.43 (2.16)	−.16 (2.18)
Respondent education (years)	−.05 (.33)	−.02 (.33)	.08 (.33)	.08 (.33)
Respondent is party member	−.99 (2.15)	−1.12 (2.11)	−.84 (2.17)	−.98 (2.13)
Assets at firm founding (millions of CNY)	−.002 (.02)	.004 (.02)	.005 (.02)	.008 (.02)
Years to firm profitability	−.61** (.20)	−.60** (.20)	−.68*** (.20)	−.67*** (.20)
IT	4.79*** (1.47)	4.79*** (1.46)	4.58** (1.45)	4.59** (1.45)
Hangzhou	−7.04*** (1.45)	−7.17*** (1.44)	−6.92*** (1.43)	−6.91*** (1.42)
Constant	25.84	24.21	45.22	43.10
R^2	.14	.14	.16	.16

Note: Performance is average return on assets between 2015 and 2017. OLS estimates with jackknife standard errors in parentheses. Network constraint is entered as log constraint to capture nonlinear network-performance association (Figure 2.6 and Figure 4.6). Guanxi embedding is entered as log scores to capture nonlinear associations (Figure 4.4). Three observations are lost due to missing data (footnote 17, N = 381). Adding a control for strongest guanxi being family is negligible (1.29 to 1.44 test statistics across the four models). Descriptive statistics are given in Table B.3 in Appendix B.
*P ≤ .05, **P ≤ .01, ***P ≤ .001.

but the results hold with or without their inclusion. Performance declines as structural embedding increases around the strongest guanxi (−3.13 t-test in Model M7, −3.31 t-test in Model M8).[17]

[17] Three respondents would not distinguish strongest guanxi. Those three respondents are treated as missing data for the tests in the table. As a check on our inferences we imputed for the three missing respondents guanxi embedding using their least-weak guanxi contact, and re-estimated the models. The results are nearly identical. For example, the −3.66 coefficient for guanxi embedding

The performance erosion associated with guanxi embedding is robust to, though correlated with, the structure of the rest of a respondent's network. The correlation between log scores is .58 for network constraint and the strength of indirect connection through third parties embedding the respondent's strongest guanxi. In other words, respondents who embed their strongest guanxi in mutual contacts tend to embed their non-guanxi contacts as well. When network constraint is re-computed excluding the strongest guanxi, the correlation drops to .35. Models M9 and M10 show the usual negative performance association with network constraint—but controlling for constraint, the models support our advantage hypothesis: respondents whose strongest guanxi is more embedded in third parties experience statistically significant performance erosion (−2.51 t-test in Model M9, −2.50 in Model M10). Across the models in Table 4.4, the performance erosion of embedded guanxi is robust to controls for respondent gender, age, education, party membership, and founder status. The effect is also robust to industry and location: profit margins are significantly higher in the IT industry (by about 4.5 points), and tend to be lower in Hangzhou (by about 7 points), and tend to be lower for businesses that took longer to become profitable.[18]

Performance Evidence More Generally

Most of our sample entrepreneurs had contacts perceived as guanxi nearly as strong as the strongest guanxi in their network. To the extent that these additional guanxi are bridges, they could either reinforce or dilute the strong effects reported in Table 4.4.

in Model M7 (−3.13 t-test, P ~ .002) is −3.65 with the imputed scores for guanxi embedding (−3.20 t-test, P ~ .001).

[18] Gender deserves special mention here. The Chinese General Social Survey shows gender bias privileging men to an extent that would shock many in the West (Burt 2019b:39). Such bias can be detected in business from lower returns to brokerage (Burt 1998). There is no evidence of gender bias among the sample entrepreneurs in our 2012 survey (Burt 2019b), which suggests that entrepreneurship for women in China is a form of employment less subject to gender discrimination (cf. Hwang & Phillips 2024 on previously incarcerated African Americans using entrepreneurship in the United States to find work and income otherwise limited by employment discrimination). The test for gender bias is a slope adjustment to the negative effect on earnings from structural embedding. We replicate the 2012 results for the 2018 predictions in Table 4.4. Women entrepreneurs are no different from men in showing weaker returns to assets when their strongest guanxi is structurally embedded (−4.20 coefficient in Model M8 with its −3.31 t-test is no less negative for women, −1.05 t-test for gender difference, P ~ .29). Looking ahead to Table 4.5 with its more complete tests across all of an entrepreneur's guanxi contacts, women are no different from men in showing higher returns to assets when their guanxi is free of structural embedding (9.04 coefficient in Model M12 with its 3.69 t-test is no less positive for women, 0.61 t-test for gender difference, P ~ .54).

Measurement

There is no established method for aggregating guanxi ties in a network, so we take two contrasting approaches to frame compromises between the two. First, we measure the extent to which an entrepreneur's guanxi are all structurally embedded. For an entrepreneur with G nonzero guanxi contacts, the following is the average strength of structural embedding around the entrepreneur's guanxi:

$$\text{Embedded Guanxi} = \left(\sum_g z_{ikg} \right) / G, \tag{1}$$

where z_{ikg} is the summed strength of indirect connection from entrepreneur i to contact g through third parties k ($z_{ikg} = \sum_k z_{ik} z_{kg}$, $i \neq k \neq j$, for respondent i and contact g with z_{ik} the fractional measure of connection strength between i and k). Embedded guanxi varies from zero (if no guanxi ties are embedded) to some positive number indicating the volume of indirect connections in which guanxi ties are embedded. According to the advantage hypothesis, higher levels of embedded guanxi should be associated with lower levels of economic performance.

We take the average, rather than the sum, of embedding in the previous measure to control for number of guanxi ties (since number of guanxi should improve performance). To capture the presumed positive association with performance, our second aggregation strategy measures the absence of structural embedding—that is, the extent to which guanxi are bridges. The following fraction varies from zero to one with the extent to which the relationship between entrepreneur i and guanxi contact g is less embedded than the most embedded of the entrepreneur's relationships: $1 - z_{ikg}/\left(\max z_{ikg} \right)$, where "$\max z_{ikg}$" is the highest level of structural embedding in i's network. This expression equals one when there are no third parties to i's relation with contact g. It equals zero when the i-g relationship is the most embedded in i's network. We then sum this expression across all G guanxi contacts g to create a real number, G^*, that measures the number of guanxi bridges in i's network:

$$G^* = \text{Guanxi Bridges} = \sum_g \left(1 - z_{ikg}/\left(\max z_{ikg} \right) \right). \tag{2}$$

The guanxi bridges measure varies from zero (if there are no guanxi bridges in the network) to a positive number indicating the number of guanxi bridges in the network. In line with the advantage hypothesis, higher numbers of guanxi bridges should be associated with higher levels of economic performance.

Empirical Results

Models in Table 4.5 predict return on assets using the same variables as in Table 4.4—except that the strongest-guanxi measures are replaced with the aggregate measures of embedded guanxi and guanxi bridges. The results further support the advantage hypothesis: Performance decreases with embedded guanxi (-3.33 t-test in Model M11, $P \sim .001$) and increases with the volume of *guanxi* bridges (3.69 t-test in Model M12, $P < .001$).

Because these guanxi measures include multiple contacts, they overlap more with the aggregate measure of network constraint—even though the aggregate here excludes strongest guanxi. The correlations between network constraint and embedded strongest guanxi was .35 in Table B.3 (Appendix B); it increases to .48 for the embedded guanxi measure and becomes $-.42$ for the guanxi bridges measure. Still, both guanxi measures add significantly to predicting economic performance above and beyond constraint: Model M13 shows a negative effect for embedded guanxi (-2.12 t-test in Model M13, $P \sim .04$), and Model M14 shows a positive effect for guanxi bridges (2.82 t-test in Model M14, $P \sim .005$).

Guanxi Bridges Versus the Broader Network

There is a trade-off between guanxi bridges versus guanxi embedded in the surrounding network. A characteristic of guanxi ties is that trust is high whether the tie is a bridge or deeply embedded in mutual friends (i.e., the top lines in Figures 4.3 and 4.4B are relatively flat). Individuals are free to engage guanxi at low or high levels of embedding with no implications for trust. But there are performance costs to structurally embedded guanxi.

If we combine Models M13 and M14 to include both aggregate measures (not tabulated), we get a performance association with guanxi bridges that is statistically significant (7.92 coefficient, 2.41 t-test, $P \sim .02$), and a negligible association with embedded guanxi (-1.06 coefficient, -0.55 t-test, $P \sim .58$). In other words, guanxi bridges provide advantage regardless of embedded guanxi. These results imply that embedded guanxi have no performance implications when guanxi bridges are held constant. At the same time—because increasing one aggregate measure necessarily decreases the

Table 4.5 Performance Increases with Volume of Guanxi Bridges (Advantage Hypothesis)

	M11	M12	M13	M14
Embedded guanxi (avg. weighted sum TP, Eq. 1)	−4.88*** (1.47)		−3.37* (1.59)	
Guanxi bridges (G*, Eq. 2)		9.04*** (2.45)		7.32** (2.59)
Network constraint (excluding strongest guanxi)			−4.97* (2.12)	−4.37* (2.07)
Respondent is female	−.16 (1.71)	−.34 (1.70)	−.13 (1.69)	−.24 (1.67)
Respondent age (in years)	.09 (.13)	.08 (.13)	.08 (.13)	.08 (.13)
Respondent is founder	.58 (2.21)	.21 (2.16)	.33 (2.18)	.07 (2.15)
Respondent education (years)	−.08 (.33)	−.03 (.32)	−.01 (.33)	.04 (.33)
Respondent is party member	−1.28 (2.09)	−1.85 (2.04)	−1.18 (2.13)	−1.60 (2.08)
Assets at firm founding (millions of CNY)	.006 (.02)	−.002 (.02)	.01 (.02)	.002 (.02)
Years to firm profitability	−.63*** (.20)	−.56** (.20)	−.68*** (.19)	−.62** (.20)
IT	4.97*** (1.45)	4.85*** (1.44)	4.77*** (1.45)	4.70*** (1.45)
Hangzhou	−6.78*** (1.43)	−7.30*** (1.42)	−6.75*** (1.43)	−7.09*** (1.41)
Constant	25.52	16.21	41.99	32.37
R^2	.14	.16	.15	.17

Note: Performance is average return on assets between 2015 and 2017. OLS estimates with jackknife standard errors in parentheses. Predictors are the same as in Table 4.4 except strongest guanxi measures are here replaced by embedded guanxi and guanxi bridges (respectively defined in equations 1 and 2). Descriptive statistics are given in Table B.3 in Appendix B.
*P ≤ .05, **P ≤ .01, *** P ≤ .001.

other (−.74 correlation in Table B.3, Appendix B)—it is difficult to draw firm conclusions about their independent effects. The two predictors are too highly correlated to cleanly separate their effects.

To support a more confident conclusion, Figure 4.7 offers more detail on the guanxi-performance link. The vertical axis shows a z-score of return on assets, adjusted for business differences in years to profit, industry, and city. These three variables are the strongest non-network predictors of economic

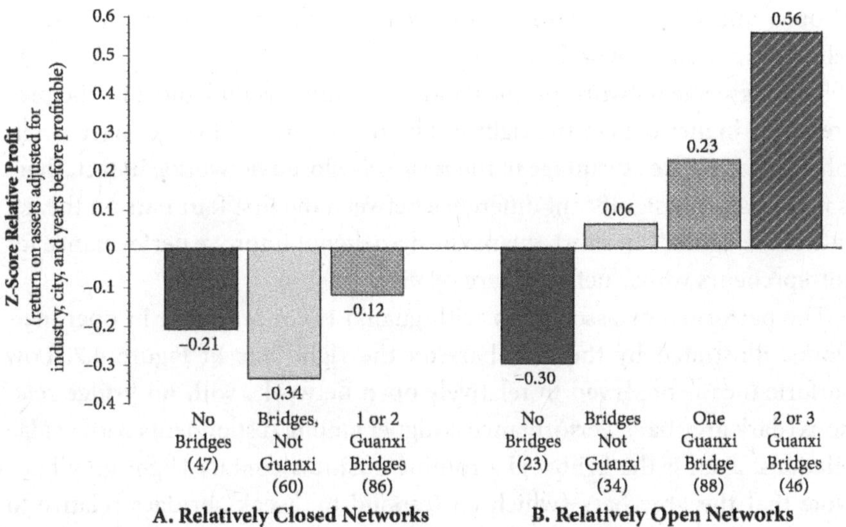

Figure 4.7 Strong Bridges in the Advantage Hypothesis

Note: Bars show z-score relative profit. Networks are sorted on the horizontal (parentheses contain number of entrepreneurs in each condition). Closed versus open networks are distinguished by median network constraint computed from all ties except the strongest guanxi (aggregate network constraint predictor in Tables 4.4 and 4.5). The count of guanxi bridges in an entrepreneur's network is the measure in equation 2 rounded to nearest integer, and "no bridges" refers to networks in which no relationship is embedded in less than a strong indirect connection. Seven entrepreneurs with two guanxi bridges are combined in the high category of relatively closed networks, and six entrepreneurs with three guanxi bridges are combined in the high category of relatively open networks.

performance in Table 4.5. An entrepreneur with a score of 1.0 runs a business that earns profits one standard deviation above what is usual for that kind of business in that city. Negative scores indicate businesses below-average profitability relative to peer firms in the same environment.

Entrepreneurs are sorted across the horizontal by network. The first cut is between relatively closed (A) and relatively open (B) networks, with relatively closed defined by a network constraint score above the median (using the constraint score in the third rows of Tables 4.4 and 4.5). Within each category, entrepreneurs are further sorted by the number of guanxi bridges—that is the guanxi-bridge measure (Eq. 2) rounded to the nearest integer. There are only six relatively open networks containing three guanxi bridges, so we combine them with the adjacent category to define a high-bridge category of "2 or 3 guanxi bridges." Among entrepreneurs with relatively closed networks, there are only seven with two guanxi bridges, so we again combine categories to define a high-bridge category of "1 or 2 guanxi bridges." At the other extreme, we distinguish within the categories of open and closed networks, entrepreneurs who have no guanxi bridge relations in their network.

The aggregate network-performance association is illustrated by the progressively higher bars to the right in Figure 4.7. Guanxi bridges have negligible performance advantage in the relatively closed networks. In fact, there is no statistically significant difference between the first four bars on the left side of the figure.[19] In short, guanxi bridges do not improve performance for entrepreneurs whose networks are relatively closed.

The performance association with guanxi is concentrated in open networks, illustrated by the four bars on the right side of Figure 4.7. Low performance is observed in relatively open networks with no bridge relations (dark grey bar). Performance is higher among respondents with bridge relations, even if the bridge is a routine business contact (light grey bar). Note that the grey bars (which correspond to "weak" bridges relative to guanxi) offer no advantage. But the highest performance is observed in relatively open networks wherein guanxi is a bridge beyond the network (light patterned bar), especially if the network includes more than one guanxi bridge (dark patterned bar).[20]

In sum, the network-performance association is concentrated in bridges, as so often observed in previous work. But not just any bridges. Advantage is concentrated in guanxi bridges—that is to say, in strong bridges—which have not been distinguished in previous research. Strong bridges are not only critical to the familiar structure-performance association shown in Figure 2.6; they are also more common than non-guanxi bridges in both open and closed networks—at least in the networks of our sample of Chinese entrepreneurs.[21]

---

[19] Specify a regression model predicting the percentage return on assets dependent variable in the figure. Include all nine control variables from the table. Replace the network predictors (first three rows in the table) with a seven-category variable distinguishing the seven bars in the figure. Take as a reference category the first bar to the far left: a relatively closed network containing no bridges. Estimating as in Table 4.5, average performance differences from the reference category are −1.34 and 1.32 for the next two categories of relatively closed networks; −1.42, 4.17, 6.33, and 10.79 for the four categories of relatively open networks. Returns on assets are up or down a few points across categories two, three, and four, but they are negligibly different from average returns in a relatively closed network containing no bridges (0.83 $F_{(3,383)}$, P ~ .48). Particularly noteworthy, guanxi bridges provide no advantage in a relatively closed network (1.32 coefficient has a 0.64 t-test, P ~ .52). High returns are associated with relatively open networks containing a guanxi bridge (6.33 coefficient has a 2.84 t-test, P ~ .005), and are highest for relatively open networks containing two or three guanxi bridges (10.79 coefficient has a 3.15 t-test, P < .002).

[20] These two network effects are the two statistically significant network-performance associations in Figure 4.7 (see previous note).

[21] As a final note to the figure, the way we aggregate relations to measure competitive advantage has alternatives, which could be of clinical interest. Our count of guanxi bridges for the figure is

Guanxi Bridges and Time

A reader informed about China's reform progress might worry that guanxi bridges have become more common as the environment has matured institutionally. If true, guanxi bridges might be concentrated in modern firms, while embedded guanxi could be a feature of traditional firms established in the earlier reform days. This is not the case. If we take the year 2003 as a cutoff—the year in which China's constitution finally granted equal rights to private firms, the share of guanxi bridges is roughly the same across firm age: 32.4 percent of highest-level guanxi are bridges in older firms, compared to 30.9 percent in more recently established firms. The pattern is similar when modernity is defined by industry. The proportion of guanxi bridges is roughly the same in IT (31.4 percent) as in the more traditional auto industry (32.8 percent). In short, guanxi bridges are peculiar to neither industry nor historical moment.

Conclusion: Strong Bridges

There are two core points to this chapter. First, we find guanxi to be a mix of time and events. Respondents tend to perceive as guanxi people they have known for a decade or more, and who are seen as a source of help during a significant event. A bond forms between people during helpful exchange in a stressful event—soldiers looking out for one another in combat, or people

---

based on values of Eq. (2) rounded to the nearest integer (for example, scores of 1.50 to 2.49 round to 2.0). We used that aggregation for consistency with the statistical estimation in Table 4.5. A more conservative recognition of guanxi bridges would be to round the index to the nearest lower integer. This would only recognize full-strength guanxi bridges (for example, 1.8 on the guanxi-bridge index would round down to 1.0).

The result of this alternative aggregation is that more entrepreneurs appear to be disadvantaged. For example, the 134 entrepreneurs in the figure who have relatively open networks that contain guanxi bridges (left-most two columns), drops to 94. Our statistical conclusions are the same with either aggregation. When we redraw the figure using the more conservative aggregation, and re-estimate the regression model in footnote 19, (a) there are no statistically significant differences in the economic performance for entrepreneurs in the first four categories of the figure (1.34 $F_{(3,383)}$, P ~ .26), (b) guanxi bridges provide no advantage for entrepreneurs with relatively closed networks (1.37 t-test, P ~ .17), and (c) the highest returns on assets are for entrepreneurs with guanxi bridges in relatively open networks (right-most two columns).

However, there is no longer a difference between the last two columns. In the figure, return on assets increases for the 134 advantaged entrepreneurs with guanxi bridges (average residual z-score return on asset in the figure of .23 for one guanxi bridge versus .56 for two or more). The corresponding z-scores for the more conservative aggregation are .42 and .46. The corresponding regression associations with return on asset are 8.96 and 8.96 (versus the difference in footnote 19). Further inference is beyond our data, but an intriguing clinical implication is that the number of guanxi bridges does not matter for an entrepreneur in a relative open network. What matters is having at least one full-strength guanxi bridge (a value of Eq. 2 greater than 1.0).

surviving together a disaster that proved fatal for others. Of course, events do not have to be threatening to be memorable or formative. They can just as easily be associated with long-awaited opportunities: Fraternity brothers pledged in the same cohort, a technological breakthrough achieved as a team, or the launch of a new business. Guanxi ties reflect positive sentiment forged to bond through felt support during significant, emotionally charged events.

The second point is more general. We use guanxi as a strategic research site where tie strength is clearly separate from network location. Network theory and research have long been hampered by the belief that relations between groups are weak. We present ample evidence showing that bridges between groups are often weak, but some are not, and those exceptional strong bridges—which can be a numerous minority—are foundation for competitive advantage. Strong bridges can exist in substantial numbers, which they do in the networks of our sample entrepreneurs. As summarized in Figure 4.8, roughly half of cited business relations are routine embedded connections, 21 percent are embedded guanxi, 31 percent are bridges, and 8 percent are guanxi bridges. Guanxi bridges are about one in ten cited relations, and one in four cited bridge relations.

We organize argument and evidence for the second point around two hypotheses. The strong-bridges hypothesis predicts that trust in guanxi ties is higher and less contingent on structural embedding than trust in non-guanxi ties (illustrated in Figure 4.3, with supporting evidence in Figure 4.4 and Table 4.2). The advantage hypothesis states that entrepreneurs are advantaged to the extent that their guanxi are bridges. In contrast to accounts

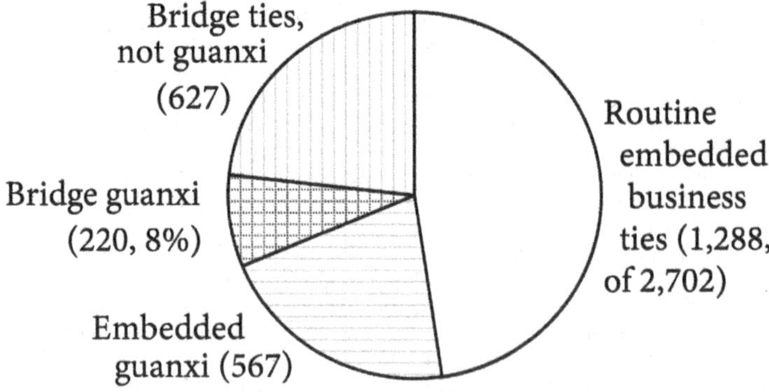

Figure 4.8 Summary Partition of Cited Business Relationships

in which strong ties derive value from corroborating relations with mutual friends and colleagues (structural embedding), guanxi ties derive value from shared personal history between two people (relational embedding). Structural embedding around guanxi makes it less of a network bridge, resulting in lower performance (Tables 4.4 and 4.5). In sum, advantage is not about weak ties, bridge connections, or trust in isolation. It is about trusted bridge connections; what we discuss as strong bridges. Without such bridges, network brokers have no discernible competitive advantage (starkly evident in Figures 4.6 and 4.7).

The chapter's two points establish a ground truth on the structural meaning of guanxi and secure for it—as a source of strong bridges—an important place in network theory.

5

Coincidental Multiplexity

We were pleased with the results in Chapter 4, but a fundamental question remains: To what extent are the documented strong bridges due not to guanxi, but to the kinds of relations in which guanxi develops? Guanxi is not an empirical connection. It is an interpretation of connection. The person we marry is defined by law to be our spouse. How we feel about that person—level of affection, level of trust, level of anger—is an interpretation. The person to whom we report at work is defined by corporate authority to be our supervisor. Our affection for, trust in, or anger toward that person is an interpretation. If we feel our brother is guanxi, how much of the trust felt is because he is family? There are facts for when we first met (childhood friend, classmate), where we usually meet (at work, at the pub, in the neighborhood), and how often we usually meet (daily, monthly, rarely). There are facts for rights and obligations enforced by contract and due legal process. Layered onto those facts are our interpretations. The facts and feelings associated with a relationship define its multiplexity. Some relations are uniplex, but the most important relationships are multiplex, a combination of multiple facts and feelings.

In the absence of network data, researchers have often distinguished guanxi using role relations associated with warmth, obligation, and trust—such as being family, or close friends from school (e.g., Farh et al. 1998). These proxies are imperfect because guanxi does not reduce to a particular role. Rather, it is more likely to develop in the context of certain roles. But it need not.

Resolving the multiplexity issue is consequential for interpreting our conclusions in the previous chapter: Are the documented strong bridges due to guanxi, or to the kinds of relations in which guanxi develops? And relatedly, is the advantage rooted in strong bridges dependent on the kinds of relations within which guanxi develops?

We take on three tasks in this chapter to ensure that the strong bridges observed in the previous chapter are not a result of multiplexity: First, we identify and describe the kinds of relations in which guanxi develops.

Strong Bridges. Ronald S. Burt and Sonja Opper, Oxford University Press. © Oxford University Press (2026).
DOI: 10.1093/9780197834275.003.0005

Beyond interpersonal history, three role relations emerge as likely foundations for guanxi—not foundations in the sense of preceding guanxi, but foundations in the sense that they are relations where guanxi is especially likely to occur. The three are family, friendship, and classmates. In addition, guanxi is especially likely in relationships where communication is direct with a wide bandwidth, as indicated by a combination of face-to-face, voice, and especially texting. Second, we show that the strong bridges associated with guanxi are not explained by multiplexity. Guanxi provides strong bridges independent of the kinds of relations in which it occurs. Third, we show that the enhanced economic performance associated with guanxi bridges is not dependent on multiplexity. Economic performance increases with the extent to which an entrepreneur has guanxi bridges in his or her network—regardless of multiplexity in those guanxi bridges. In conclusion, multiplexity is not a requirement for the strong bridges provided by guanxi. By extension, this opens all forms of connection to be viewed as strong bridges. We return to this point in the conclusion.

Foundation Relationships

There is a form/content duality to relationships. Where form refers to the strength of a relationship, content refers to emotion and activity within the relationship—advice, authority, buying/selling, casual chat, emotional closeness, cooperation, kinship, trust, and so on. A relationship is "multiplex" when it consists of more than one content. The form/content duality is crisply articulated in Breiger's (1974) discussion of the person/group duality. People are connected by their participation in the same groups, and groups are shaped by the people who participate in them. Analogously, the form/content duality identifies kinds of relational content by their co-occurrence in the same relationships, and relationships are made more or less strong by the content they contain. Co-occurrence describes how people experience—and therefore conceptualize—relationships. People who have few of their friends at work, for example, can make a clear distinction between the obligations they owe to friends and those they owe to colleagues. This distinction can be difficult to make when all of one's friends are at work. Models of network form applied to content combinations help to clarify meaning. For example, if friendship is used to describe a large number of relationships, the meaning of friendship can become ambiguous because of the different social situations in which it is applied. Form/content analysis is similar to inferring the meaning of words from the sentence context in which the word occurs.

Analysis of the form/content duality began in anthropology with discussions of relations in tribal society, where ties were reinforced by "multiplexity"—referring to people who interact in multiple activities: civic, economic, social, and spiritual (Gluckman 2012 [1965]; Mitchell 1969). Quantitative analysis took off when area probability surveys like the Northern California Community Study (Fischer 1982) and the 1985 General Social Survey provided data on multiple kinds of relations in regional and national populations (Burt 1983, 1990; Burt and Schott 1985; Marsden and Campbell 1984; Verbrugge 1979). Similar applications appeared in management (Burt 2005:50–53, 2010:285–288; Cross et al. 2001; Powell et al. 2005), with most studies limited to two or three types of content (e.g., Lee and Lee 2015), along with some novel applications on the meaning of labels for social categories (e.g., Pontikes 2012). Applications continue under the broad theme of multiplexity (Gondal 2022; Ertug et al. 2023; Lizardo 2024).

Here, we analyze the content of guanxi relations by examining the concrete kinds of interactions in which guanxi occurs. We are thus able to capture the multifaceted, complex nature of guanxi—an aspect that is often noted but seldom systematically explored. We build on our exploration of relationships strengthened by a history of positive experiences, but now shift to more specific inquiries. We want to know what kinds of interaction beyond the association with events—did guanxi typically involve? How much of what we attributed to events in the previous chapter can be attributed to other types of interactions—or to the type or quality of relationship that developed? Yang (1994:111) summarizes from her fieldwork:[1]

> …familiarity as a prerequisite for guanxixue can be found in the importance attached to relationships in which there is a shared identity or in which there are shared personal experiences. The word tong, meaning "same" or "shared," is used to designate a whole set of close personal relationships which serve as guanxi bases: "person from the same native place" (tongxiang), "classmate" (tongxue), and "coworker or colleague" (tongshi) (Jacobs 1980:41).

[1] Yang (1994:6) used the term "guanxixue" (literally "the study of connections") to refer to topics in the study of guanxi, its substance, creation, maintenance, dissolution.

Of course, these relationships cannot be reduced to guanxi relationships, for in some respects their spirit is also opposed to guanxixue. Friendship, kinship, classmates, and so forth are not coextensive with guanxi, but serve as bases or potential sites for guanxi practice. Kinship and friendship, of which all the tong or "shared" relationships above are offshoots, are understood in popular discourse as being more disinterested, less instrumental, and ethically purer than guanxi relationships.

So, what are the observable qualities of relationships in which guanxi is found? For example, how often does it develop within rather than between families? Is the advantage we attribute to guanxi, in fact, an advantage from other kinds of connections in which guanxi tends to occur? Family is particularly salient because guanxi is often introduced as analogous to kinship. Though some argue that the analogy is misleading to the detriment of theory and research (Babarlet 2021a:Chaps. 2, 6). Regardless, one can imagine a Chinese audience eager for such an analogy over the past thirty years, given the instrumental motivation to adopt the family analogy: Family analogies highlight kinship obligations that one would like to inspire in one's own guanxi contacts. With these complications in mind, it is useful to separate kinship as a system of roles and duties from kinship as actual family ties. Yang (1994:114) observed as early as the mid-1980s that family ties were rarely the foundation for guanxi in large cities. Rather, kinship labels were used to invoke images of kinship with guanxi contacts beyond the family:

> Where no actual kinship tie exists, fictive kinship ties are expressed by employing such kinship addresses as shushu (father's younger brother), bobo (father's elder brother), a-yi (mother's sister), bomu or dama (wife of father's elder brother), dajie (elder sister), xiaomei (younger sister), dage or laoxiong (elder brother), di (younger brother), and so on for friends of the family, neighbors, and personal friends. These fictive kinship extensions bring people outside the family group into the circle of familiar and trusted relationships. It can be said that in large cities like Beijing, guanxi ties based on the familiarity principle have come to supplant the centrality of agnatic and affinal kinship ties described by so many ethnographies of rural Chinese life.

Yang's inference is certainly true for our sample entrepreneurs, who operate in large, cosmopolitan cities—Shanghai, Ningbo, and Hangzhou. Family is rare in their networks (8 percent), and most guanxi ties are beyond the family (78 percent). Still, or even more so, because guanxi is inherently multiplex, it is important to know whether empirical support for our strong-bridges and advantage hypotheses is robust to tests for multiplexity, and to identify critical connections—if there are any—that facilitate the strong bridges guanxi can provide.

Fifty Kinds of Connections

With rich network data and clear respondent distinctions between contacts that are guanxi and those that are not, we can make unprecedentedly precise statements about the substantive kinds of relations and the associated qualities and reported content of social exchange that are associated with guanxi, as well as those qualities that are distant from it.

We continue to use answers to the "name generator" and "name interpreter" questions in our 2018 survey, as described in the previous two chapters and Appendix A. Our core data form a binary matrix of 57 columns and 2702 rows. The 2702 rows correspond to relationships with people cited as business contacts. The fifty-seven columns correspond to fifty-seven content categories, which are listed down the rows of Table 5.1—fifty kinds of connections, followed by seven kinds of guanxi connections. For each relationship, a content variable equals 1 if the content is present in the relationship, 0 otherwise. Percentages to the right show the frequency with which each content occurs. For example, 1296 contacts are cited as most valued contacts this year (48 percent in row four of the table), and 209 are members of the respondent's family (close to 8 percent in row eight). In the following discussion, we link specific connections back to Table 5.1 using short words and row numbers. For example, "childhood friend" is #11 for row 11.

The first seven rows in Table 5.1 are name generators. Other rows are based on name interpreters. Rows 1, 2, 3 contain the event contacts we explored in Chapter 3. Rows 4, 5, 6 contain contacts cited for their role in the current business and row 7 contains contacts the respondent wished to add to the roster. Some survey response categories are combined because the responses are redundant in multidimensional scaling that keep them separate. For example, contacts named on the most important event after founding have a different pattern of co-occurrence with other content than

Table 5.1 Roster of Network Contents

Kind of content	ID	Relation content	Percentage Relations with row content
Question on which manager cited the contact (can be more than one)	1	Valued in founding the business	14.2
	2	Valued in most important event	14.2
	3	Valued in other significant event(s)	46.6
	4	Valued current contact	48.0
	5	Most difficult contact this year	14.2
	6	Most valuable employee	14.2
	7	Valued, N.E.C.	0.3
	8	Family	7.7
	9	Neighbor	8.1
	10	Party member	0.6
	11	Childhood friend	4.2
	12	Classmate	11.6
	13	Colleague in military service	6.2
	14	Colleague in current business	47.4
Manager's role relation with the contact (can be more than one)	15	Colleague in prior business	10.0
	16	Other—investor in current business	2.7
	17	Other—partner in current business	5.3
	18	Other—customer for current business	5.8
	19	Other—supplier for current business	1.9
	20	Other—competitor to current business	1.3
	21	Other—just friend	8.4
	22	Resources	29.6
Why manager values the contact	23	Emotional support	4.7
	24	Referrals	20.8
	25	Other support	16.6
Duration of manager's relationship with the contact	26	Less than 6 years	26.2
	27	6 to 10 years	39.4
	28	11 to 20 years	25.1
	29	More than 20 years	9.3
Frequency with which manager meets the contact	30	Daily	25.5
	31	Weekly	35.5
	32	Monthly	26.4
	33	Less than monthly	12.7
How manager communicates with the contact (can be more than one)	34	Face to face	84.0
	35	Video	13.7
	36	Voice	79.7
	37	Email	46.3
	38	Text	45.9

Kind of content	ID	Relation content	Percentage Relations with row content
Manager's emotional connection with the contact	39	Especially close	29.8
	40	Close	53.7
	41	Less than close	11.4
	42	Distant	5.1
Manager's trust in the contact	43	Low Trust (1 or 2 rating)	9.0
	44	Some Trust (3 rating)	10.5
	45	Trust (4 rating)	44.7
	46	Highest Trust (5 rating)	35.8
Manager's inclination to collaborate in joint venture with the contact	47	Unlikely to collaborate (1 or 2 rating)	11.1
	48	Might collaborate (3 rating)	13.8
	49	Likely to collaborate (4 rating)	38.3
	50	Definitely collaborate (5 rating)	36.9
Manager's view of contact as guanxi	51	Not guanxi	10.1
	52	Routine business irrelevant to guanxi	60.7
	53	Other guanxi	14.4
	54	Strongest guanxi	14.7
	55	Bridge, guanxi or not guanxi	31.3
	56	Guanxi bridge	8.1
	57	Embedded guanxi	21.0

contacts named on the second to fifth events (also evident in previous work, Burt and Opper 2017:509). Therefore, in Table 5.1, we make only three distinctions between events: Cited as most valued in founding the business (row 1). Cited as most valued in dealing with the most important event after founding the business (row 2). And cited for any of the second to fifth most important events (row 3).

Moving on to name interpreters, rows 8 to 21 in the table distinguish kinds of role relations. The eight roles, from family to former colleague, are response options that reflect the variety of roles discussed in the qualitative literature as the basis for guanxi development. Each cited contact could play any of the eight roles with the respondent (rows 8 through 15).

The subsequent six roles listed in the table are extensions of the survey response categories. To ensure that no specific role was overlooked, the survey offered an "other" category with a follow-up question asking respondents to describe the nature of the specific role a contact played. The six other roles in the table (rows 16 through 21), from investor through just friend, are roles that were most frequently mentioned when a respondent selected the "other" category. Of the 2702 cited business contacts, respondents associated 767 contacts with an "other" role. If every contact cited as "other" played the same other role, the percentage of "other" would be 28 percent. Instead, the percentages are single-digit, indicating the diversity of roles for which contacts were cited. The specific other roles listed are the majority of other roles mentioned. Only twenty-nine contacts play an "other" role not listed in the table. While respondents could select multiple roles, more than 80 percent received only one role citation.

Finance people are rarely cited as key contacts. Investors account for just 3 percent of cited contacts in Table 5.1, with partners making up another 5 percent. Only one of the contacts cited as "other" was cited for a role that contained the word "bank." No one cited a venture capitalist, though they could be among the contacts cited as investors. Rare mention of financial roles may seem surprising, given the central role of finance in research on small and medium enterprises in the West but it is consistent with our context. During our study period, China's venture capital market was relatively small and underdeveloped by international standards. In addition, small and medium-sized enterprises continue to face critical barriers to securing bank loans, making formal financial contacts less central for Chinese entrepreneurs than for their Western counterparts (particularly through the first decade of the twenty-first century). Instead, financial challenges are addressed outside the formal financial system.[2] For example, more than 50

---

[2] Finance contacts might not be viewed as critical current contacts, but still could have been critical in launching the business. However, the table includes key contacts during significant events in the history of the business, including the business founding. More, a third of the sample businesses were entirely self-funded by the founders (31 percent), and the ones founded with a mix of founder and outside money were launched with founders providing an average 53 percent of the start-up money. Only three of the sample businesses were launched with no financial investment from the founders. Our median founding date is 2007. Self-reliance is even higher just six years earlier, in the larger sample of entrepreneurs in the same region described by Burt and Burzynska (2017) and Burt and Opper (2017): 65 percent of their sample businesses were entirely self-funded by founders.

Firm size is a consideration. Of our 162 sample businesses coded as "small" by Chinese authorities relying on annual sales (less than 10 million CNY for IT, 20 million for manufacturing), almost half, 48 percent, were founded entirely with founder money (versus 19 percent of the larger sample businesses), and 79 percent of their start-up funds on average came from the founders. But size is not the whole story. Founder assets are also a substantial share of start-up money for the larger sample businesses (average 59 percent of start-up money came from founders of the larger businesses), and 48 percent of small businesses self-funded means that the other 52 percent of the small businesses found start-up funds elsewhere—6 percent from venture capitalists or angel investors, 7 percent from a bank loan, and 17 percent from friends and family.

Industry is a further consideration. We included IT businesses in this sample explicitly to contrast traditional manufacturing with new technology that might be more connected to Western business

percent of respondents in our sample report financial problems during the start-up event; nearly 30 percent report that the most important post-startup event revolves around financial problems. In neither case is the person described as most helpful a financial professional, highlighting the importance of informal support from close contacts, when it comes to financial matters.

"Other – Just Friend" (#21) differs from the eight predefined roles (#8–15) as well as from the other roles respondents chose to describe their contact (#16–20). Friendship is not a concrete kind of contact so much as a sentiment. Since respondents have known contacts they describe as "just friends" for an average of 13.3 years (with a sample average of 10.5 years for all other contacts), and tend not to see them on a daily or weekly basis, it is possible that these contacts were once met in roles that no longer apply. They could be former lawyers, teachers, or investors who became friends. All we know is that these "just friends" are not childhood friends, former classmates, neighbors, someone who is a current or former colleague, or any of the concrete roles distinguished in Table 5.1.

Following the set of role relations, the table continues with kinds of help provided by event contacts (rows 22–25) and relationship duration (less than six years, six to ten years, eleven to twenty years, and more than twenty years in rows 26–29). The different periods are based on prior research on trust within a similar study population (Burt et al. 2018:15–17). This is followed by contact frequency (rows 30–33) and communication channels (rows 34–38). Using the data on emotional connection (rows 39–42), combined with a name interpreter asking for the strength of connections between cited contacts (not tabulated in Table 5.1), we scale connection strength, z_{ij}, between each pair of people i and j in a network on a continuum from zero to one (see "Scaling the Network Data" in Appendix A).

Rows 43 to 50 correspond to levels of trust. Rows 43 to 46 summarize responses to the familiar trust question, and rows 47 to 50 capture

---

models. If we regress percent start-up money from the founders across the industry and firm size sampling strata, we get a strong association for self-funding of small businesses (7.28 t-test, P < .001), but no difference between IT and manufacturing (0.10 t-test, P ~ .92). If we predict percent start-up money from venture capitalists or angel investors, we get a strong association for small businesses less likely to be launched with such funding (−3.16 t-test, P < .01), but no difference between IT and manufacturing (0.52 t-test, P ~ 60).

responses to a question about willingness to enter a formal collaboration with cited contacts. For both measures, we combine infrequent use of the lowest response items, coding them as "low trust" and "low collaboration."

Of particular note are the guanxi connections at the bottom of Table 5.1. We here preserve all four response categories from the guanxi name interpreter. As displayed in the previous chapter (Table 4.1), rows 51 to 54 respectively are strongest guanxi (398 contacts), guanxi (389 contacts), not guanxi (274 contacts), and routine business contacts (1641 contacts). The last three kinds of connections in the table concern network structure around the cited contact. Row 55 distinguishes bridges (equal to 1 if the summed indirect connection between respondent and contact is less than 1, as used in Figures 4.7 and 4.8). The final two rows distinguish bridges that are guanxi or the strongest guanxi (#56) from embedded guanxi (#57).

Spatial Display

Figure 5.1 visualizes tendencies for different kinds of connections to occur in the same relationships. As in our analysis of milestone events in Figure 3.6, characteristics that are close to each other tend to co-occur in the same relationships. Characteristics distant from one another are rarely observed in the same contact.[3] To understand the nature of guanxi, this analysis displays the kinds of relationships in which guanxi tends to develop. From the previous two chapters, we expect the various categories of guanxi (rows 51–54) to co-occur with events (rows 1–3). Which other of the fifty kinds of connections co-occur with guanxi?

The two axes of the spatial display are scaled in proportion to the variance they describe. The horizontal axis describes 71 percent of the co-occurrence variance by distinguishing negative relations to the left versus positive to the right. The vertical axis is a contrast between personal relations at the top and other business relations at the bottom (another 20 percent of variance). The two dimensions are a familiar pattern in China (Burt and Opper,

---

[3] We measure the tendency for two characteristics to appear in the same relations with a Jaccard coefficient, which is the number of relations in which the two characteristics occur together, divided by the total number of relations in which either occurs (see footnote 8 in Chapter 3 for more detail).

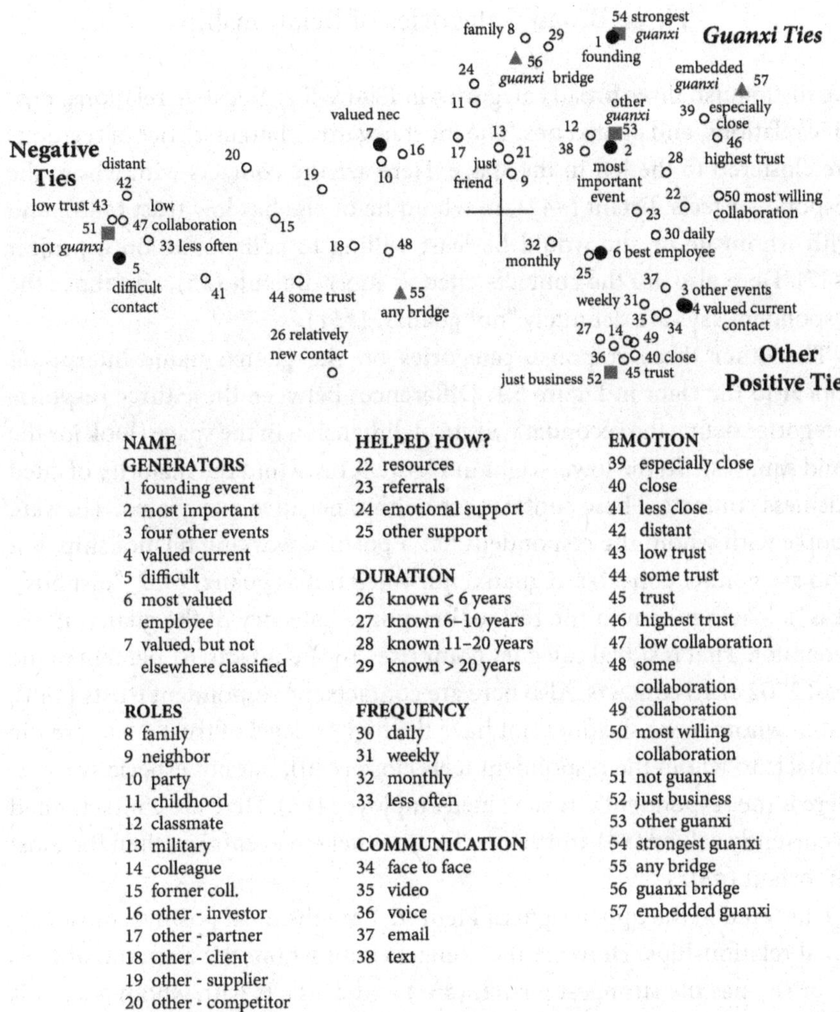

NAME GENERATORS
1 founding event
2 most important
3 four other events
4 valued current
5 difficult
6 most valued employee
7 valued, but not elsewhere classified

ROLES
8 family
9 neighbor
10 party
11 childhood
12 classmate
13 military
14 colleague
15 former coll.
16 other - investor
17 other - partner
18 other - client
19 other - supplier
20 other - competitor
21 other - just friend

HELPED HOW?
22 resources
23 referrals
24 emotional support
25 other support

DURATION
26 known < 6 years
27 known 6–10 years
28 known 11–20 years
29 known > 20 years

FREQUENCY
30 daily
31 weekly
32 monthly
33 less often

COMMUNICATION
34 face to face
35 video
36 voice
37 email
38 text

EMOTION
39 especially close
40 close
41 less close
42 distant
43 low trust
44 some trust
45 trust
46 highest trust
47 low collaboration
48 some collaboration
49 collaboration
50 most willing collaboration
51 not guanxi
52 just business
53 other guanxi
54 strongest guanxi
55 any bridge
56 guanxi bridge
57 embedded guanxi

Figure 5.1 Guanxi Is Variably Likely in Kinds of Relations

Note: Classical multidimensional scaling of Jaccard coefficients measuring co-occurrence of characteristics in same relations. Axes are proportional in length to eigenvalues defining them. Cross-hairs mark (0,0) point on the axes. The two dimensions describe 91 percent of variance in the fifty-six characteristics. Solid circles are name generators. Solid squares and triangles are guanxi categories (except #55).

2017:508–510) and the West (Burt 2005:50–53, 2010:283–288), but now with the added feature of having respondents' distinctions between guanxi categories included in the space.[4]

---

[4] Wishing to stay close to the metric of the data, we use a classical multidimensional scaling. The scaling is based on an eigenvalue decomposition as in a principal component analysis. The third

Three Broad Categories of Relationships

We distinguish three broad categories in Figure 5.1: Negative relations, positive relations, and guanxi ties. The most negative characteristics of relations are clustered to the left in the space. Here are the contacts with whom the respondent feels distant (#42), in whom he or she has low trust (#43), and with whom he or she would be least willing to collaborate on a project (#47). Here also are the contacts cited as most difficult (#5), and those the respondent says are definitely "not guanxi" (#51).

The other three response categories on the guanxi name interpreter appear to the right in Figure 5.1. Differences between these three response categories define the secondary, vertical dimension in the space (look for the solid squares). To the lower-right in Figure 5.1, we find the majority of cited business contacts. These contacts are neither negative nor guanxi. They are people with whom the respondent has a positive working relationship, but who are neither considered guanxi nor ruled out as guanxi (#52, "just business"), leaving them in the residual response category of the guanxi name generator. That residual category comprises 1641 contacts, 61 percent of the total 2702 cited contacts. Also here are contacts the respondent trusts (#45), but in whom he or she does not have the highest level of trust. Here are the contacts to whom the respondent feels close (#40), but not especially close. Here is the respondent's most valued employee (#6). Here are contacts cited as currently valued (#4) and valued for their help in events less than the most important (#3).

Clustered in the upper-right of Figure 5.1 are the most positive, most personal relationships. Here are the contacts with whom the respondent feels he or she has the strongest guanxi (#54) and contacts with whom guanxi is almost as strong as the strongest (#53). Consistent with explorations in the previous chapter, the contacts cited as most valued in founding the business (#1) are close to the strongest guanxi, and contacts most valued in helping the respondent deal with the most important event in the business's history after founding (#2) are close to other guanxi. Here are also contacts known for a long time (#29, known for more than twenty years, and #28, known for eleven to twenty years). Other characteristics in the upper-right quadrant illustrate the warmth, obligation, and trust qualities often used in qualitative

eigenvalue is much smaller than the second (1 percent of the variance), so it and all subsequent dimensions are discarded. We obtained the scaling in Figure 5.1 using Stata's "MDS" routine with the "classical" option.

work to characterize guanxi. Here are the contacts with whom the respondent feels especially close (#39), in whom he or she has the highest level of trust (#46), and with whom he or she would be most willing to collaborate on a project (#50).

Given that qualitative scholars have often distinguished guanxi ties by role relations—such as family, or close friends from school (e.g., Farh et al. 1998)—we were naturally curious about the location of different roles in the guanxi space. However, none of the fourteen role relations is as closely associated with guanxi as the attributes discussed above. A few exceptions are noteworthy. One is family (#8) which is close to the strongest guanxi (#54) at the top of Figure 5.1. Although family contacts are not cited often (less than 8 percent of all contacts), they tend to be guanxi ties when they are cited. However, family is further way from feeling especially close (#39) and highest trust (#46). In short, guanxi formed through kinship lacks some of the emotional intensity of non-kinship guanxi (we return to family in a moment). We find a similar pattern for classmates (#12), 11.6 percent of all cited contacts, who locate close to other guanxi (#53) and the most important event after founding (#2). Finally, there are contacts that respondents consider to be friends (#21), but who do not fit into any of the other role relationships. Around 8 percent of contacts fall into this category, about the same as family. Unlike family, these relations do not co-occur with the strongest guanxi, but are often described as other guanxi (#53). Like family, they are further away from being emotionally close (#39) and from being the most trusted (#46).

All three kinds of role relations have in common that they are rarely cited, even though many entrepreneurs have either a family member (42 percent of respondents have one), a classmate (45 percent), or a friend (39 percent) in their network. Only thirteen respondents cite more than one of these three categories (in each case, family and classmates). At the other extreme, fifty-three respondents (13.8 percent) cite none of these three roles.

Our tentative account from Figure 5.1 is as follows: If family, classmates, or friends are cited as noteworthy contacts, they are likely to be cited also as guanxi. This is why in the absence of network data, scholars have often distinguished guanxi ties by role relations—such as family, or close friends from school (e.g., Farh et al. 1998). Given the small number of cited family members and friends, however, it is also clear that most of a respondent's family and friends are not significant contacts, let alone guanxi.

Finally, shifting from role relations to structure, bridge relations are well away from the most positive relations (consistent with the closure-trust association). The two categories of bridge connections (#55, #56) are located in the middle of the space, midway between positive relations to the right and negative relations to the left. In other words, bridge relations are a mix of positive and negative emotions. Bridges differ in the extent to which they are dedicated to the entrepreneur's interests. Bridges in general (#55) are located at the bottom of Figure 5.1, among other positive ties. On the other hand, strong bridges that are guanxi (#56) are located to the north, among more personal ties known for more than twenty years (#29) and family (#8). Further to the right are embedded guanxi (#57), which respondents describe as especially close ties (#39) and enjoying the highest trust (#46).

Predicting Guanxi

Having identified the kinds of relations perceived as guanxi, we now turn to the combinations that warrant attention—either because of their close association with guanxi in the spatial display or because of research precedent. We begin with an overview of the most important predictors, then dig into details in the sections that follow. For the 2702 cited contacts, Table 5.2 shows results from a logit regression predicting binary guanxi (yes for strongest guanxi or other guanxi, no for just business or explicitly not guanxi). Estimates are computed with respondent fixed effects to control for individual differences.

At the top of Table 5.2, history is the strongest predictor of guanxi: History in the form of years the respondent has known a contact, and history in the form of contact help during significant events in the business' history, especially founding the business, and the most important event in the history of the business (t-tests of 9.00 and 5.54 respectively, P < .001). Help on other important events (second, fourth, and fifth) also increases the odds of a contact being named guanxi (respective test statistics of 3.64, 3.51, 2.67), but the largest increases are for help in founding the business and help during the most important event. This resonates well with trust research showing higher levels of trust when trustee and trustor have experienced a "critical test" in exchanging and receiving a unilateral favor.[5]

---

[5] Results in the table are estimated with respondent fixed effects, which means sampling strata differences are held constant. We were worried about industry differences, thinking that, relative to

Table 5.2 Which Contacts Are Guanxi?

	Predictors	Coefficient	Standard Error	Test Statistic
History	Log Years Known	2.50	.30	8.42
	Cited for Help in Founding the Business	2.24	.25	9.00
	Cited for Most Important Event (not founding)	1.03	.19	5.54
	Cited for Second Most Important Event	.66	.19	3.64
	Cited for Third Most Important Event	.31	.20	1.56
	Cited for Fourth Most Important Event	.72	.20	3.51
	Cited for Fifth Most Important Event	.73	.28	2.67
Roles	Contact is Member of Respondent's Family	2.44	.46	5.29
	Just Friend	2.19	.36	6.09
	Neighbor	.43	.39	1.10
	Party Member	.36	1.18	.30
	Childhood Friend	.50	.39	1.40
	Classmate	.84	.30	2.84
	Military	.79	.42	1.90
	Colleague in Current Organization	.24	.30	.80
	Colleague in Former Organization	−.65	.36	−1.78
	Investor	.15	.55	.78
	Partner/Collaborator	.75	.47	1.58
	Supplier/Competitor/Client	−.99	.69	−1.44
Use	Some Other Role (29 of 2702 contacts)	−.36	11.90	−.03
	Number of Communication Channels Used	.59	.15	3.95
	Days Between Communication Contact	−.01	.005	−1.92
	Structural Embedding Around Relationship	.44	.26	1.65

Note: These are estimates for a logit model predicting that a contact is named strongest guanxi or other guanxi. Pseudo R^2 is .60 with respondent fixed effects and robust standard errors (t-test statistics, Stata "jackknife" option). Structural embedding is a summed indirect connection between respondent and contact (log, as when predicting performance in Table 4.7).

Contrary to the common perception that guanxi is associated with specific favors, the nature of assistance during events (not reported here) is a marginal consideration. It adds nothing to the prediction of guanxi. Adding three dummy variables to Table 5.2 to distinguish the four kinds of

manufacturing, entrepreneurs in information technology operate smaller, more networked operations. However, number of contacts named is independent of industry and log number of employees (respectively 0.65 and 0.51 z-score test statistics in a Poisson regression across the 384 sample entrepreneurs predicting number of contacts cited). Adding controls for industry and firm size, then re-estimating without fixed effects and with standard errors adjusted for autocorrelation between contacts cited by the same respondent (Stata "cluster" option), yields negligible prediction by the two controls (0.30 and 1.35 respectively, P > .18), and the same pattern of effects displayed in the table.

help (resources, referrals, emotional support, other) does not significantly improve the prediction (0.41 $F_{(3276)}$, P ~ .74, with estimation limited to the 1794 contacts cited for help on any event). In the spatial map displayed in Figure 5.1, kinds of help are clustered close to one another to the right, among positive ties, but midway on the vertical axis between guanxi and other positive ties (#22, #23, #25). The one form of help that stands apart is emotional support (#24), which appears at the top center of Figure 5.1, clustered with family and strongest guanxi being a bridge. In short, the close association between guanxi and help during important events is less about the kind of help provided than it is about the respondent acknowledging that help was provided at a significant moment.

After history, certain role relations emerge as prone to guanxi, or unlikely to develop into guanxi. Consistent with our spatial display, family and friends are the roles with the strongest positive association (respective test statistics of 5.29 and 6.09 in Table 5.2). There is also a weaker, yet significant association between being a cited classmate and guanxi (test statistic 2.84). Other roles—such as neighbor, colleague in current or past organizations, or current business contact—are independent of guanxi or significantly unlikely to be guanxi. We dig into the family and friendship associations below, but a summary conclusion from Table 5.2 is that guanxi does not correspond directly to any specific roles. It may or may not develop in association with any particular role. In particular, the association with family does not imply that guanxi is concentrated in family. In fact, family is rarely cited as a contact. 57 percent of the sampled entrepreneurs do not cite a family member. Only 7.7 percent of all cited contacts are family, but when family is cited, the person is often cited as guanxi. Similarly, 61 percent of the sample entrepreneurs do not cite a friend. However, when friends in an entrepreneur's network are cited (8.4 percent), they are highly likely to be perceived as guanxi. Considering both categories, 37 percent of our sample entrepreneurs cite neither family nor friends. These findings speak to Yang's (1994:111) early caution against interpreting roles as anything more than a foundation from which special relationships can develop: "Friendship, kinship, classmates, and so forth are not coextensive with guanxi, but serve as bases or potential sites for guanxi practice." Similarly, Jacobs (1979:262) argued that shared identities (as family members, classmates, co-workers, neighbors, etc.) provide no more than a basis, at best a precondition, from which guanxi can develop. In extension, our data do not suggest that any of the commonly noted roles are more or less successful in providing a basis for guanxi development. The key lies in examining the nature of the interaction between the parties, since "no close guanxi (kuan-hsi, in the original) can develop without the expenditure of time in social interaction." Jacob's hunch finds empirical support in the close clustering of long duration (#29) and shared event experience (#1 and #2), a confirmation of our two previous chapters.

The three bottom rows in Table 5.2 refer to use of a relationship. The strongest predictor is the number of channels through which an entrepreneur communicates with a contact. As later analysis will show, this is largely a function of texting. Almost everyone has face-to-face contact with their core contacts, but texting, as a highly informal and convenient mode of communication, is an additional channel through which guanxi contacts are reached. The final two predictors in Table 5.2 are negligible. The number of days between communications distinguishes between daily, weekly, monthly, and less frequent. It turns out that entrepreneurs do not communicate with guanxi contacts more or less often than they communicate with other contacts (although it is unlikely that guanxi contacts are ignored for long periods of time). Level of structural embedding is also a negligible predictor. Guanxi are not limited to, or even correlated with, structural embedding.

We take from this exploration two points that we refine in the next sections: First, history is the strongest predictor of guanxi. Second, certain role relations such as family and close relations with classmates or friends, when cited as a key contact, are especially likely to be viewed as guanxi.

Guanxi Emerges from History

We take a closer look at history in Table 5.3. We extend our comparison of guanxi with other relations to include a distinction within each category between bridges and structurally embedded relations. The distinction is based on the weighted sum of the indirect connections between the respondent and the contact (the "weighted TP" measure in Chapter 4 that worked so well in predicting trust and business profits). If the weighted sum is less than one, then any indirect connection between the respondent and the contact is less than the connection strength of an especially

Table 5.3 Guanxi Emerge from More Significant Events

Contact's Most Significant Event	Routine Contacts		Guanxi		Total
	Embedded n = 1288	Bridge n = 627	Embedded n = 567	Bridge n = 220	n = 2702
Contacts helpful in founding the business	39 (3%) [−10.58]	14 (2%) [−8.05]	240 (42%) [14.36]	91 (41%) [11.54]	384 (14%)
Contacts helpful in resolving most significant event subsequent to founding	127 (10%) [−2.80]	41 (7%) [−4.01]	115 (20%) [5.73]	29 (13%) [1.28]	312 (12%)
Contacts helpful with the second most significant event	163 (13%) [0.79]	64 (10%) [0.24]	78 (14%) [2.16]	16 (7%) [−1.83]	321 (12%)
Contacts helpful with the third most significant event	195 (15%) [3.74]	76 (12%) [2.62]	38 (7%) [−3.03]	16 (7%) [−1.32]	325 (12%)
Contacts helpful with the fourth most significant event	166 (13%) [2.67]	78 (12%) [3.47]	37 (7%) [−2.61]	14 (6%) [−1.56]	295 (11%)
Contacts helpful with the fifth most significant event	97 (8%) [3.58]	36 (6%) [2.47]	20 (4%) [−0.89]	4 (2%) [−2.28]	157 (6%)
People only cited as current contacts	501 (39%) [5.82]	318 (31%) [10.59]	39 (7%) [−10.54]	50 (23%) [0.11]	908 (34%)

Note: For all 2702 cited contacts, cell entries are number of cited contacts, percentage of column contacts (in parentheses), and loglinear z-score test statistic [in brackets] for extent to which cell frequency is higher or lower than would be expected if rows and columns were independent. Contacts are treated as independent observations (see footnote 6).

close mutual friend. We define a bridge as any relationship embedded in less than one especially close mutual friend (continuous measure in Eq. 2 less than 1).

The rows in Table 5.3 distinguish contacts by the most important event on which they were cited. The first row contains contacts cited as helpful in founding the business. The second row contains contacts cited as helpful in resolving the most significant event in the history of the business (excluding anyone already cited as helpful in founding the business). The third row contains contacts cited as helpful in resolving the second most significant event (excluding anyone already cited in the two rows above). And so on for the third, fourth, and fifth most significant events. The bottom row of the table contains contacts who were not cited for their help with a significant event.

Each cell in the table contains three entries: The number of contacts in the cell, the column percentage of contacts (in parentheses), and a log-linear z-score test statistic [in brackets] for the extent to which the cell frequency is higher than what would be expected if the column categories were independent of the row categories.[6]

The first two columns of the table are similar to one another in showing that routine business contacts and people cited as explicitly "not guanxi" are associated with help on less-significant events (e.g., 3.58 and 2.47 z-scores for association with help on the fifth-mentioned event). These contacts are most associated with being cited only as current contacts (5.82 and 10.59 z-scores in the bottom row of the table).

In contrast, columns three and four show that guanxi emerges from helping in the most significant events, with slight differences between embedded and bridge guanxi. The third column of the table shows that structurally embedded guanxi are associated with help in the two most significant events—the founding of the business (14.36 z-score) and the most significant event after founding (5.73 z-score). After that, the likelihood of an embedded guanxi contact being cited for help in less significant events drops sharply. In the bottom row, embedded guanxi are strikingly absent among people only cited as current contacts (−10.54 z-score).

Bridge guanxi, or strong bridges are even more clustered. The fourth column shows that bridge guanxi are only associated with help in the most significant of all events—the founding of the business (11.54 z-score). In fact, most of these ninety-one contacts are cited as the entrepreneur's strongest guanxi (76, or 84 percent). In the other rows of column four, the frequency of bridge guanxi cited on subsequent events is about equal to the frequency to be expected if event significance were independent of the column guanxi

---

[6] The test statistics are computed with contacts treated as independent observations, which means the degrees of freedom are inflated. We checked our inferences against the pattern of effects obtained with a multinomial logit model predicting the columns from the rows and standard errors corrected for autocorrelation between contacts cited by the same respondent (Stata "cluster" option). That still overcounts degrees of freedom but less so. We find the same pattern of relative-strength effects evident in the table. We prefer to present the loglinear statistics for their simplicity and the effect normalization to the average effect rather than a reference category, which means that we have test statistics for frequencies in every category relative to independence. However, we are cautious to focus only on the strongest of interaction effects

categories. For example, in the bottom row of the table, many bridge guanxi are cited as only current contacts (50, or 23 percent), but that is in the context of many people being cited as current contacts (908, or 34 percent of cited contacts).[7]

The close association of guanxi with personal history highlights the importance of research design in uncovering specific kinds of contacts, such as guanxi. The event name generators are central to the detection of guanxi, and even more so to the detection of bridge guanxi. Thirty-nine percent of structurally embedded guanxi are only cited on the event name generators. Fifty percent of bridge guanxi are only cited on event name generators and would have otherwise been missed. In contrast, name generators on current contacts primarily elicit the names of routine business contacts and people explicitly deemed "not guanxi."

A skeptic would be correct to point out that current-contact name generators still elicit the names of most contacts deemed guanxi; 61 percent of embedded guanxi and 50 percent of bridge guanxi. So, are the event name generators adding critical information? Yes; they add key current contacts not elicited by current-contact name generators. Of the 110 strong bridges cited only on an event name generator, 40 percent are currently met daily or weekly, and another 51 percent are met monthly. Only 10, or 9 percent, are met less than monthly. Of the 221 embedded guanxi cited only on an event name generator, 69 percent are met daily or weekly, and another 29 percent are met monthly. Only 4, or 2 percent, are met less than monthly. In short, the guanxi cited only on event name generators are present in the respondent's social environment, but go unnoticed by the usual current-contact name generators. The inadequacy of current contacts to elicit the respondent's most valued guanxi, may explain why the familiar network prediction of business success is sometimes weak in China when networks are defined only by current contacts (illustrated in Figure 4.6, see Burt and Opper 2017:519–529, for more detail).

[7] We have no data independent of the respondent to indicate the relative significance of events, so we cannot test for endogeneity in the association between guanxi and event significance. For example, we cannot say whether guanxi emerge from more significant events or events are deemed more significant in the respondent's mind when a close, trusted friend helps resolve them. This is a generic issue for network studies more generally: What is the role of behavior in significant events for the conceptualization of social networks? Here, we tell the story as it exists for the entrepreneur.

Guanxi, Family, Friends and Colleagues

We have shown that role relations generally are poor predictors of guanxi. Family and friends deserve closer inspection. As relations of warmth, obligation, and trust, guanxi are often discussed as family-like, with guanxi beyond the family often described as pseudo kinship (e.g., referring to an older male guanxi contact as "uncle," Yang 1994:112–114; Lin 2001b; Bian 2018:604; 2019:7–9, 13–14, 21). In Table 5.4, columns again distinguish bridge from embedded ties among routine contacts and guanxi. The first row contains all cited family members. The second row contains past and present office colleagues beyond family. The third row contains other contacts beyond family and work, but with whom the entrepreneur has some kind of role relationship. The fourth row is contacts with no role relation for the entrepreneur; they are "just friends." As in the previous two tables, cells contain a count of contacts, the column percent in parentheses, and a loglinear test statistic in brackets.

The association with family is clear: Some unknown number of relatives are not cited as business contacts, but the relatives who are cited are likely to

Table 5.4 Family Tends To be Named as Guanxi, but Guanxi Occurs Much More Often Outside the Family

Source of Contact Citation	Routine Contacts		Guanxi		
	Embedded n = 1288	Bridge n = 627	Embedded n = 567	Bridge n = 220	Total n = 2702
Contacts inside respondent's family	24 (2%) [−6.59]	9 (1%) [−6.05]	110 (19%) [7.96]	66 (30%) [10.77]	209 (8%)
Contacts beyond family, friends who are or were colleagues at work	940 (73%) [15.38]	252 (40%) [6.05]	245 (43%) [0.88]	13 (6%) [−11.36]	1450 (54%)
Contacts beyond family, friends, and the workplace	273 (21%) [−0.675]	324 (51%) [9.42]	161 (28%) [−5.21]	58 (26%) [−3.90]	816 (30%)
Just friend	51 (4%) [−2.73]	42 (7%) [−1.79]	51 (9%) [−5.19]	83 (38%) [9.56]	227 (8%)

Note: For all 2702 cited contacts, cell entries are number of cited contacts, percentage of column contacts (in parentheses), and loglinear z-score test statistic [in brackets] for extent to which cell frequency is higher or lower than would be expected if rows and columns were independent. Contacts are treated as independent observations (see footnote 6).

be cited as guanxi, embedded or bridge (respective test statistics of 7.96 and 10.77). Cited relatives are rarely cited as routine business contacts (−6.59 and −6.05 z-scores for embedded and bridge ties).

The guanxi association with non-kin roles is less clear. From our perspective as analysts, it is true that current and former office colleagues tend to be cited as routine contacts (first two columns in Table 5.4). But from the entrepreneur's perspective, office colleagues provide the largest percentage of embedded guanxi (43 percent), and contacts beyond family and work provide another 28 percent. It is reasonable to expect that family-based guanxi is structurally embedded in mutual family contacts. But 81 percent of embedded guanxi are outside the family. Bridge guanxi, the source of strong bridges associated with business performance, rarely comes from current or former office colleagues.

Beyond family and work roles, lie the business contacts who have no role relation with the entrepreneur, the "just friends." These contacts occur with a frequency similar to family and are almost as likely as family to be guanxi bridges (9.56 test statistic).

The predominance of non-kin guanxi might reflect ongoing change in China. Twenty-five years ago, Yang (1994:114) opined: "In contemporary Chinese urban life, what is now important is the extension of such kinship principles ('familiarity,' obligation, mutual aid, sharing, and the gauging of relational or affective distance) to guanxixue." Family provides its own kind of foundation for the development of guanxi. But kinship itself is no more than a foundation from which guanxi may, but by no means must develop (Jacobs 1979; Yang 1994).[8] The 38 percent of bridge guanxi deemed "just friends," and the 26 percent who are neither family nor workplace relations corroborate these reflections.

---

[8] To be sure that support for our two hypotheses in the previous chapter is robust to family contacts, we re-estimated effects with family held constant. For the strong-bridges hypothesis predicting trust in a relationship, trust is higher with family members as expected (.22 coefficient, 3.92 t-test, P < .001), but the hypothesized effect coefficients are almost unchanged in magnitude and remain statistically significant beyond a .001 level of confidence (.94 for positive effect of structural embedding around routine business relations, .90 level adjustment for higher trust in guanxi, −.55 slope adjustment for trust in guanxi being relatively independent of structural embedding; cf. effect estimates in Model M4 in Tables 4.2 or 4.3). Effect estimates predicting trust with a control for overall network density (Model M4a in Table 4.3) similarly show a positive effect of family on trust (3.73 t-test) and similarly show effect coefficients little affected. Empirical support for the advantage hypothesis is also robust to family. Returns on assets are independent of the proportion of an entrepreneur's network drawn from family. Proportion family added to Model M12 and Model M14 (Table 4.5) yields respective t-tests of 0.39 and 0.53, P > .60.

How are Guanxi Used?

Trust in guanxi is less dependent on structural embedding than trust in ordinary business ties, and bridge guanxi—rather than embedded guanxi—are associated with the economic success of a business, as shown in Chapter 4. But what explains the advantage? Here, we show that network location has implications for how respondents use their guanxi.

We are careful with the word "used," which can imply exploitation. We refer to "used" here in the spirit of social exchange theory, mindful of the relational foundation of guanxi among practiced entrepreneurs. Well familiar with Blau's (1964:Chap. 3) social exchange foundation for status and power, Lin (2001b:161) emphasizes: "Even though guanxi are effectively used for instrumental purposes, it is the relationship that is valued and must be maintained, not the value of the favor transacted per se.... Guanxi builds reputation for the participating actors, and reputation, in turn, consolidates the guanxi. The ultimate motive of guanxi is to reinforce, sustain, and deepen relationships, rather than the instrumental goals that they serve so well."[9] We ask entrepreneurs about help during individual events, but we are mindful that each event is only one step in a social exchange process. Even so, as far as guanxi is associated with favors provided in the past, we were curious to know the network locations linked with different kinds of favors.

Kinds of Help

After citing significant events in the history of his or her business, and naming someone particularly helpful to resolution of each event, the entrepreneur was asked for each event: "What did the person do that was so helpful in that event?" A card was handed over to stimulate responses (Figure A6 in Appendix A). A named contact could have provided some kind of resource (such as money, land, skills, permits, etc.), or emotional support,

---

[9] With specific reference to bridge relations, Lin (2001b:161) notes: "the term 'bridge' (*qiao*) is not often used to describe a *guanxi*, because of its strong instrumental connotation (as in *guohe caiqiao*)." We found *guohe chaiqiao* (过河拆桥) to mean "cross the river and burn down the bridge." We assume that Lin had in mind the familiar weak-tie image of bridges. A person who behaves by *guohe chaiqiao* would violate the social exchange foundation for guanxi, and would soon find himself missing what were once his valuable bridge guanxi.

or a referral to someone who then provided needed resource, or something else. The interviewer circled in the questionnaire one or more of four kinds of help (as many as were cited) and recorded any text response. Of 1792 contacts named for help with an event, most were coded as providing one of the four kinds, but a few were coded as providing multiple kinds of help (141, or 8 percent). Most were coded as helpful on one event, but several were coded as helpful on multiple events (1.18 mean, maximum 4). We count a contact as providing a kind of help whether it is the only help provided on an event, or it is help provided in addition to other kinds.

Returning to our initial illustration of multiplex relationships in Figure 5.1 and the guanxi prediction and interpretation of Table 5.2 we already know that kind of help does not differ significantly between guanxi versus other relations. Only emotional support (#24) is closely related to guanxi bridges (#56). All other types of support are centrally located in Figure 5.1, roughly halfway between the strongest guanxi (#54) and just business (#52), while almost equidistant from guanxi bridges (#56) and embedded guanxi (#57). However, as we show in a moment, this pattern partly reflects the fact that Figure 5.1 does not account for variation across the kinds of occasions in which help was provided.

Further analysis in Figure 5.2 reveals two critical differences between contacts that were helpful at founding and contacts that were helpful at later events. First, contacts cited for help at founding are more likely to be cited again for help at a subsequent event than non-founding contacts. More than 40 percent of the contacts that helped at founding were cited for multiple events, compared to less than 10 percent of the contacts that helped after founding (first two columns on the left). Second, almost all contacts cited for help at founding provided help in the form of resources, which blurs distinctions between kinds of contacts. Given these systematic differences between helpful contacts at founding, and subsequent supporters, we distinguish both groups in our search for patterns by kinds of help, guanxi, and structural location.

Table 5.5 lists tests for kinds of relations being associated with kinds of help for the 384 contacts cited in founding the business. We return to the table shortly, but the central takeaway is simple: Most of the tests in Table 5.5 are negligible. The one exception is family being cited for emotional support at founding (4.80 t-test), though only sixty-one entrepreneurs (16 percent) reported receiving emotional support. We find no difference in help between guanxi versus non-guanxi contacts, or between structurally

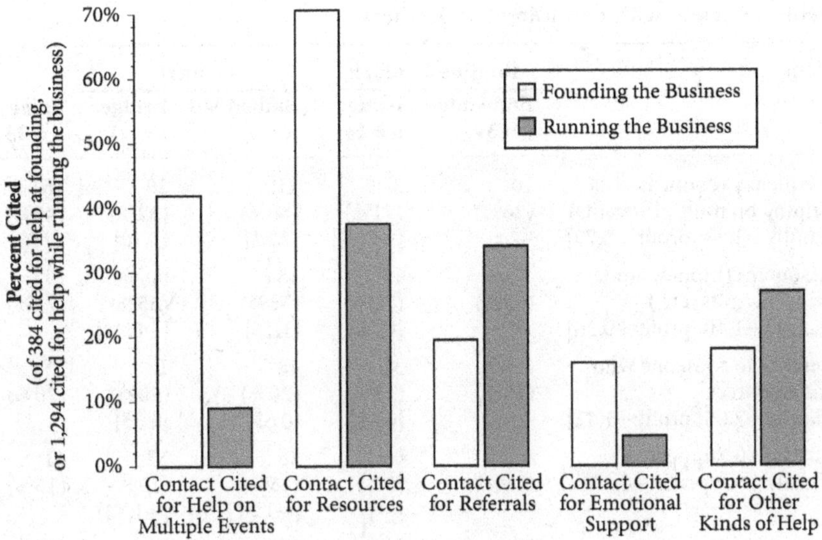

Figure 5.2 Help Founding versus Running the Business

Note: Bars show percentage of contacts cited for each kind of help. These are the 384 contacts cited for their help in founding the business (white bars) versus the 1294 contacts cited for their help with a significant event that arose while running the business (dark bars). One contact can be cited for help on more than one event.

embedded versus bridge guanxi at founding. In short, founding is largely about finding a contact willing and able to help—regardless of network tie or location.[10]

Network differences emerge subsequent to founding. The differences are documented in Table 5.6, which follows the same format as Table 5.5, but now describes the 1410 contacts cited for help with events after founding. Rows distinguish frequency of help and kinds of help. Columns distinguish contacts by network location. The first cut is binary guanxi: "yes" for strongest guanxi or other guanxi, "no" for just business or explicitly not guanxi. Within each category, a contact can be embedded within the network or a bridge beyond the network. The binary cut is based on the

[10] We initially ran the predictions across all event contacts without separating founding from subsequent events. That showed a strong association between embedded guanxi and help in the form of resources. On closer inspection, however, it became clear that help with founding the business is distinct from help with subsequent events. Family is a likely source of help at founding (4.80 t-test in left-most column of Table 5.5), and those family members tend to be structurally embedded (62 percent of cited family members provide resources at founding, 27 percent with subsequent events). But when we separate founding from subsequent events, help in the form of resources is independent of family and embedded contacts (Table 5.6).

Table 5.5 Help with Founding the Business

Help	Routine Contacts		Guanxi		
	Embedded n = 39	Bridge n = 14	Embedded n = 240	Bridge n = 91	Total n = 384
Frequency (contacts helping on multiple events) [family −1.53; profit −0.79]	10 (26%) —	3 (21%) [−0.17]	119 (50%) [2.72]	29 (32%) [1.10]	161 (42%)
Resources (money, land, skills, permits, etc.) [family −1.40; profit −0.28]	17 (69%) —	10 (71%) [0.20]	184 (76%) [1.15]	50 (55%) [−0.98]	271 (71%)
Referral to someone who has resources [family −2.05; profit −1.41]	6 (15%) —	3 (21%) [0.45]	48 (20%) [0.63]	18 (20%) [0.55]	75 (20%)
Emotional Support [family 4.80; profit −0.59]	8 (21%) —	0 (0%) [—]	36 (15%) [−1.71]	17 (19%) [−1.72]	61 (16%)
Something else [family −1.14; profit 1.60]	5 (13%) —	3 (21%) [0.51]	39 (16%) [0.64]	22 (24%) [1.40]	69 (18%)

Note: Of the 384 contacts cited for help in founding the business, these are the ones cited for the row kinds of help. Each row gives number of contacts cited for providing the row kind of help and (in parentheses) the percentage of column contacts who provided help. A contact can be cited on multiple events for providing multiple kinds of help. Under each column label is the number of contacts by kind (guanxi versus not guanxi) and network location (bridge versus structurally embedded). Brackets contain t-tests for logit prediction of row help from the column variables using embedded-not-guanxi as a reference category, with controls for contacts in the family and business profit (residual ROA in Figure 4.6). Estimation is with jackknife standard errors and correction for autocorrelation between contacts cited by same respondent (Stata "cluster" option).

weighted sum of indirect connections between respondent and contact (weighted TP in Table 4.2). As before, a relationship embedded in less than one especially close mutual friend is coded as a bridge.

Cells in Table 5.6 contain the number of contacts providing the row help, the percentage of column contacts providing the row help (in parentheses), and a test statistic [in brackets] for the extent to which the frequency is high, controlling for family contacts and relative profitability of the business (return on asset residual to industry, city, and years to profit; vertical axis in Figure 4.7).[11] The percentages do not sum to 100 down the rows because a contact can be cited on multiple events for providing multiple kinds of help.

[11] Estimation is based on a logit model predicting the row variable from the four column variables (with the first column as a reference category) plus a control for family (1 if contact is family) and relative business profit (residual return on assets in Figure 4.7). We began with respondent fixed effects but a logit model with fixed effects discards respondents who cite none of their contacts for a row resource. For example, the prediction of emotional support reduces the 1,792 event contacts

Table 5.6 Help After the Business Is Founded

Help	Routine Contacts		Guanxi		
	Embedded n = 748	Bridge n = 295	Embedded n = 288	Bridge n = 79	Total n = 1410
Frequency (contacts helping on multiple events) [family −0.59; profit −2.18]	41 (5%) —	16 (5%) [0.15]	65 (23%) [7.58]	9 (11%) [2.19]	131 (9%)
Resources (money, land, skills, permits, etc.) [family −1.44; profit 0.64]	284 (38%) —	172 (42%) [1.05]	106 (37%) [0.00]	16 (20%) [−2.87]	529 (38%)
Referral to someone who has resources [family 0.06; profit −0.83]	258 (34%) —	65 (22%) [−3.47]	103 (36%) [0.35]	54 (68%) [5.47]	480 (34%)
Emotional Support [family 3.97; profit −4.91]	28 (4%) —	9 (3%) [−0.26]	26 (9%) [2.28]	2 (3%) [−0.41]	65 (5%)
Something else [family −1.45; profit 1.90]	194 (26%) —	104 (35%) [2.57]	71 (25%) [−0.08]	10 (13%) [−2.47]	379 (27%)

Note: Of the 1410 contacts cited for help with significant events occurring after the business was founded, these are the ones cited for the row kinds of help. Each row gives number of contacts cited for providing the row kind of help and (in parentheses) the percentage of column contacts who provided help. A contact can be cited on multiple events for providing multiple kinds of help. Under each column label is the number of contacts by kind (guanxi versus not guanxi) and network location (bridge versus structurally embedded). Brackets contain t-tests for logit prediction of row help from the column variables using embedded-not-guanxi as a reference category, with controls for contacts in the family and business profit (residual return on assets in Figure 4.7). Estimation is with jackknife standard errors and correction for autocorrelation between contacts cited by the same respondent (Stata "cluster" option).

The first row of the table describes contacts cited as a source of help on more than one event after the business is founded. Most contacts are only cited on one event, but 131 are cited on more than one event. The statistical tests in brackets show that these multi-event contacts are most associated with embedded guanxi (7.58 t-test, P < .001), and slightly associated with bridge guanxi (2.19 t-test, P ~ .03). It is guanxi, not family, that predicts repeated help (−0.59 t-test for family, P ~ .56). There is also a slight tendency for less profitable entrepreneurs to cite the same contact more than once (−2.18 t-test, P ~ .03). In short, entrepreneurs tend to return to embedded

cited by 384 respondents to 517 contacts cited by 114 respondents who cited one or more contacts for emotional support. We want to include the full set of network conditions associated with not receiving a row resource, so we rely on Stata's "cluster" option to adjust jackknife standard errors for autocorrelation between contacts cited by the same respondent.

guanxi—in and beyond the family—for repeated help after founding their business, especially those with less successful businesses. It is not difficult to come up with likely explanations: peer pressure on embedded ties, moral obligation to help someone in need, and reputational cost of withholding help all likely contribute. On the supply side, less successful entrepreneurs may have limited opportunities to seek help beyond their initial circle of close supporters.

Help in the Form of Resources

Providing resources is the primary form of help in founding a business, but even after the business is founded, the second row in Table 5.6 shows that 38 percent of event contacts provide help in the form of resources such as money, skills, permits, etc.

Some example texts coded as providing resources are: "He's a relative of mine who lent me money." "He invested in me when I had financial difficulties." "(She) became a shareholder by injecting a large amount of capital into the business." "She improved the technique by consulting her friends in related businesses." "Provided significant support for the approval of bank loans." "Organized a new management system."

As in Table 5.5, resource help is independent of network tie or location. It is independent of family, and whether the business is profitable or not. The strongest association is a slight, but statistically significant, tendency for resources not to come from guanxi bridges (-2.87 t-test, P ~ .004).

Help in the Form of Referrals

In Figure 5.2, the primary change in network help after founding the business is the increased use of referrals. The third row in Table 5.6 shows contacts often cited for providing a referral (480, or 34 percent). Example texts coded as referrals are: "Recommended a friend from a state-owned enterprise, and worked with the state-owned company to develop the product." "Recommended the person in charge of the new plant and made the company's relocation smooth." "Referred a big client and the company signed a big order." "Introduced and negotiated orders from state-owned enterprises and the company began to make a profit." "Provided contacts in the government, helping the company to get several tender projects." "Recommended a friend to help the company purchase a new factory site." "Recommended a technical person for the production of HH-CD25 tools."

Referrals are to be expected of bridge guanxi. For guanxi in general, Lin (2001b:158) notes: "...an important instrumental function of guanxi is to access more guanxi. A good guanxi is characterized by its ability to reach direct or indirect social ties that can provide help in achieving an instrumental goal." Bridge guanxi in particular are likely to be a productive source of referrals because they connect entrepreneurs to people beyond embedded guanxi. The sample texts above reinforce this point. Referrals often include introductions to companies with different ownership types (state-owned firms), referrals to government officials, and connections to technical specialists. A common feature is referral across domains—to someone outside the contact's expertise or usual social circles. The signature move of bridge guanxi to a friend in need: "I cannot help you with that, but I know a guy who could." Test statistics in the third row of Table 5.6 support the expectation: Bridge guanxi stand out for providing referrals (5.47 t-test, P < .001), embedded guanxi are irrelevant to referrals (0.35 t-test, P ~ .73). The association between referrals and bridge guanxi holds for family and contacts outside the family (0.06 t-test, P ~ .95), and for businesses doing relatively well or poorly (−0.83 t-test, P ~ .41). Noteworthy is that bridge relations that are not guanxi are significantly unlikely to be cited for providing referrals (−3.47 t-test, P ~ .001). Thus, only the strong bridges provide referrals—not the standard or weak ones. This is, of course, to be expected given the positive performance effect of strong guanxi bridges reported in Chapter 4. Nevertheless, it is useful to have empirical confirmation that the network location of guanxi matters for the nature and content of social exchange. In other words, the kinds of transactions pursued with the help of strong bridges are not just more or less successful; they are substantively different from the kinds of help provided through weak bridges.

Help in the Form of Emotional Support
Emotional support is help that sustains a person under pressure—relieving stress, restoring confidence, or simply helping them to hold on. Some example texts coded as emotional support are: "Listening to me when there were problems with management, relieved me of a lot of stress." "Stressful during the mold-making period, gave me moral support and helped me hang in there." "My wife, she encouraged me to start my own business and at first I was very busy and the family depended on her."

The fourth row of Table 5.6 shows emotional support rarely acknowledged post-founding (65 of 1410 contacts are cited for providing emotional support), and independent of the network predictors—guanxi versus not guanxi, bridge versus embedded (not tabulated is a summary test statistic for the network predictors: $F_{(3,383)} = 2.29$, $P \sim .08$). The people who cite contacts for emotional support are likely to cite family and tend to be running less-profitable businesses (respective t-tests of 3.97 and −4.91 to the left in the fourth row of the table).

The rare acknowledgement of emotional support, and its association with family and profitability, made us curious to know more about the people acknowledging such help. One hundred and three entrepreneurs cited someone as a source of emotional support. Eleven cited two or more such contacts. We predicted a binary outcome (no/yes acknowledged emotional support) and an ordinal outcome ("no" versus "yes once" versus "yes multiple") from the individual attributes used in Table 4.5 to predict business success. Results are the same for both outcomes. Here we report the ordinal model: Age is the strongest predictor, with a slight tendency for younger people to acknowledge emotional support (42.4 average age for those who do, versus 44.0 average for those who do not; −2.56 t-test, $P \sim .01$). Women are no more likely than men to acknowledge emotional support (0.72 t-test, $P \sim .47$). Years of education are irrelevant (−1.69 t-test, $P \sim .09$). In fact, the three strongest non-network predictors in Table 4.5 are irrelevant (1.93 $F_{(3,364)}$, $P \sim .12$, for city, industry, and years-to-profit).

The strongest predictor is not in Table 4.5. It is a language measure that becomes central in the next chapter. The fewer Chinese characters an entrepreneur uses to describe guanxi, the more likely they are to acknowledge emotional support. The average character counts are ten for those citing emotional support from multiple contacts, fifteen for citing it once, and twenty-three for those not citing it at all (−4.61 t-test, $P < .001$). It is tempting to suspect a link between emotional stress and a simplistic understanding of guanxi. We pursue that link in the next chapter.

Help in Other Forms

The bottom row in Table 5.6 refers to kinds of help other than resources, referrals, or emotional support. The brief descriptions that respondents used to describe the nature of these "other" types of help suggest no missed category and no common theme. Examples include: "Took care of copyright approvals and made successful approvals." "A friend helped settle a contract dispute, reducing arguments." "Development and manufacture of an employee internet behavior management system." These idiosyncratic kinds of help are common (379 contacts, or 27 percent), but their diversity means entrepreneurs go outside of their network to find a contact suited to the problem. Family is irrelevant (−1.45 t-test, P ~ .15). Embedded guanxi is irrelevant (−0.08 t-test), and bridge guanxi is unlikely (−2.47 t-test, P ~ .02). The most likely source is a non-guanxi bridge relation (2.57 t-test, P ~ .02). These kinds of help also tend to be cited for less significant events. Recall that entrepreneurs listed events in order of business significance. An idiosyncratic form of help is cited in 18 percent of founding events versus 34 percent of the events mentioned fifth. When we add event order to the bottom row of Table 5.6, it is the strongest predictor (2.73 t-test, P < .01). The drift to idiosyncratic forms of help on less significant events is reassuring—it suggests the survey captured the most consequential events (bearing in mind the endogeneity inherent in these results).

How Often is Contact Made?

Much of the complication in discussions of guanxi comes from combining description of guanxi ties with description of how guanxi ties are maintained. Maintenance involves a system of social exchange in which debts are created and paid in a currency of favors, gifts, and banquets. Yang (1994) offers rich description from her conversations with people about the process. People rise in status according to the guanxi debts they can call in, and lose face according to felt or perceived defaults on guanxi debts. Social exchange with respect to guanxi seems to operate as social exchange operates outside China—Blau's (1955, 1964) version of social exchange theory providing an apt description of exchange behavior as foundation for status and power. Our concern in this book is not guanxi maintenance so much as the place of guanxi in network structure and its performance implications.

However, we have limited data on maintenance in that we know how often our sample entrepreneurs communicate with their contacts (Figure A9, item 11 in Appendix A). Three patterns stand out:

(1) Daily or weekly contact is typical of embedded contacts, regardless of guanxi. Respondent meets 75 percent of embedded guanxi and 74 percent of embedded non-guanxi contacts daily or weekly. The respective percentages for bridge contacts are 35 percent and 30 percent.

(2) Monthly contact is more typical of bridge contacts. Fifty-five percent of bridge guanxi are contacted monthly and 35 percent of bridge contacts are not cited as guanxi. The respective figures for embedded contacts are lower—22 percent and 17 percent.

(3) Infrequent contact—less than monthly—is concentrated in the non-guanxi bridge contacts. Of the 342 contacts met less than monthly, 222 are non-guanxi bridges. More specifically, people contacted less than monthly seem to be individuals discarded from, or on their way out of, the network. Of the contacts met less than monthly, almost all are not viewed as guanxi (307 of 342), and more than half of those were cited as "definitely not guanxi" or cited as the person that was most difficult to deal with in the current business year (173 of 342).

Mutual friends are shaping these patterns. Relative to meetings with bridge contacts, meetings with embedded contacts are likely to be more frequent by random chance since mutual friends increase the odds of bumping into a contact while in touch with one or more mutual friends.

In Table 5.7, we hold constant mutual friends to see whether guanxi contacts indeed consume more time and attention as some have claimed. The dependent variable is days between contacts: One for daily communication, seven for weekly communication, thirty for monthly communication, and ninety for less than monthly (assuming quarterly or less often). Model M15 shows longer intervals between meetings with bridge contacts; on average, 11.23 days longer for meetings with bridge guanxi, 28.45 days longer for meetings with bridge contacts who are not guanxi.

Model M16 introduces a control for structural embedding, which has a strong negative association with days between meetings, and controls for respondent differences in how often on average each entrepreneur meets with contacts. The multiple correlation increases because the bulk of described variance in days between meetings is due to structural embedding (14 percent) and differences between the individual entrepreneurs (25 percent).[12] With controls for respondent differences and structural embedding in place, Model M16 shows that among people who are not guanxi,

---

[12] Predicting frequency differences from respondent fixed effects generates an R^2 of .249, then adding the log count of third parties to control for structural embedding increases the R^2 to .388 (increase of .139 in the text).

Table 5.7 Predicting Days Between Contact

Network Predictors	M15	M16	M17
Intercept	15.23	49.34	27.14
Not Guanxi			
Embedded (reference category)	—	—	—
Bridge	28.45***	4.83	−.81
	(1.68)	(2.69)	(1.16)
Guanxi			
Embedded	−3.28***	−1.63	−.19
	(1.00)	(0.98)	(0.56)
Bridge	11.23***	−13.09***	−2.69
	(1.81)	(2.99)	(1.41)
Structural Embedding (log weighted third parties)	—	−28.07*** (2.35)	−12.73*** (0.98)
R^2	.19	.43	.42

Note: Regression models predicting days between meetings (1 for daily, 7 for weekly, 30 for monthly, 90 for less) from the row variables. In Model M17, "less than monthly" is coded as thirty days instead of ninety. Jackknife standard errors are given in parentheses. Model M15 is estimated using Stata's "cluster" option. The other models are estimated with respondent fixed effects. Descriptive statistics are given in Table B4 in Appendix B. * P < .05 ** P < .01 *** P ≤ .001.

communication with bridge contacts is no more frequent than with embedded contacts (1.79 t-test, P ~ .07). The same can be said of communications with structurally embedded guanxi contacts (−1.66 t-test, P ~ .10). There is a statistically significant tendency for more frequent communication with guanxi bridges (−4.39 t-test, P < .001), but the effect is due to the absence of guanxi contacts among the people with whom entrepreneurs communicate less than monthly. To be sure, we code "less than monthly" in Model M17 as a 30-day interval instead of a 90-day interval, whereupon differences in contact frequency are independent of guanxi (1.45 $F_{(3,2701)}$, P ~ .23).[13]

We conclude that communication with guanxi contacts is neither more, or less, frequent than with other contacts—with the proviso that guanxi contacts tend not to be ignored for long periods of time.

[13] We get similar results if we delete the 342 "less than monthly" contacts in Table 5.7 as contacts on their way out of the network, or already gone. Re-estimating Model M16 shows no association between kind of contact and frequency: days between meetings are independent of the four kinds of contacts (0.52 $F_{(32,359)}$, P ~ .67). The decision to set aside "less than monthly" contacts is also supported by the map in Figure 5.1. Daily, weekly, and monthly contact frequencies cluster together on the right side of the map, among positive ties. "Less than monthly" contacts form a separate cluster to the left, among negative ties.

Communication Channels

Guanxi ties are personal, so one might expect people to prefer personal modes of communication; seeing the other's face, or hearing their voice. On the other hand, guanxi ties are well-established so there might be no preference for personal communication because messages from guanxi are personal regardless of medium.

Given the variety of communication channels available, we included a name interpreter in the network instrument asking about the channels through which an entrepreneur communicates with his or her different contacts (Figure A9, item 13 in Appendix A): "With modern technology, people can communicate in many ways. During the last year, how have you communicated with the listed people?" A response card was handed to the respondent for easy reference to the six response options (Figure A7 in Appendix A): Face to face, video call, voice (by phone or computer, for example, WeChat), text (email), text (other, for example instant messaging, or some other text exchange), or something else (please specify).[14] Any combination of channels could be claimed, and any or all of the channels might be used between two people over the course of an entire year.

The white bars in Figure 5.3 are all high, showing that the entrepreneurs communicate face-to-face and by voice with almost all contacts—consistent with qualitative accounts of interaction among entrepreneurs running small and medium-size firms in the region. White bars are similar across the first three panels, then increase to 89 percent in the fourth, indicating that direct contact is especially likely over guanxi bridges. Three test statistics are below each panel. These come from a logit model predicting communication channel from the four network distinctions shown on the horizontal axis. The reference category is embedded non-guanxi contacts (far left in Figure 5.3). The first t-test in each panel corresponds to the prediction of voice/face-to-face use (white bars). Tests of -0.6, 1.2, and 3.9 document the prevalence of voice and face-to-face communication.[15]

---

[14] There are 132 contacts for whom respondents said "something else." Sixty-nine of them are contacts with whom the respondent no longer communicates. The other sixty-three are people reached through specific brands of texting software. The sixty-three are re-coded into the "text not email" category.

[15] The logit equations are estimated using the "cluster' option in Stata to increase the jackknife standard errors for autocorrelation between contacts cited by the same respondent. Each equation includes a control for whether the respondent works in the IT industry, but the control for industry is negligible in each of the three equations (0.31 t-test for face-to-face and voice, 0.89 for email, 0.05 for text and video).

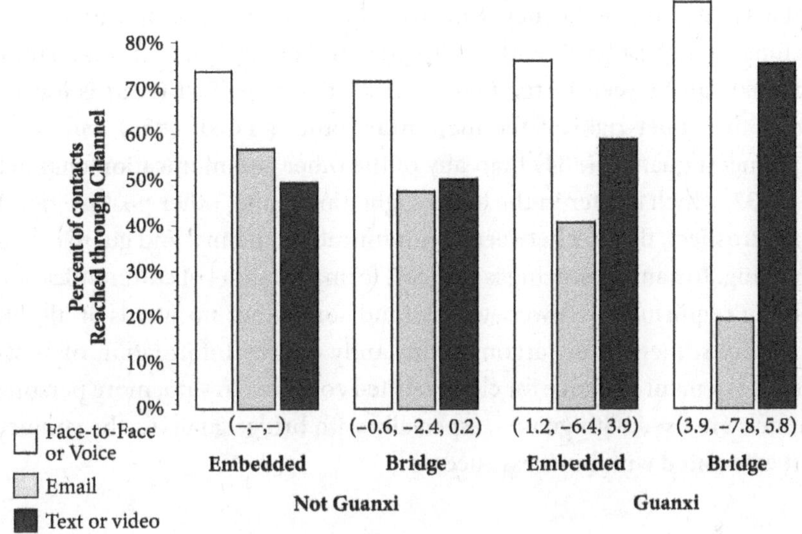

Figure 5.3 Communication Is More Personal with Guanxi

Note: Bars show percentage of column contacts accessed through each of three categories of communication channels. Parentheses contain t-tests from three logit models, each using the four network categories to predict use of one of the communication channels (embedded, not guanxi is the reference category).

Face-to-face and voice are often combined with use of other channels, and the number of channels used with a contact strongly predicts guanxi (3.95 t-test at the bottom of Table 5.2, P < .001). Figure 5.3 shows a systematic trade-off between email versus texting as a complement to direct contact. Grey bars describe use of email, the least personal of the channels, and the least likely to reach guanxi. The grey bars are highest on the left, decreasing to the right. Statistical tests of −2.4, −6.4, and −7.8 beneath the panels show decreased use of email to communicate with guanxi, especially guanxi bridges.

It is the dark bars—indicating text or video—that most increase across the figure, reaching their highest level at 75 percent of guanxi ties that are bridges to other groups.[16] The third t-test in each panel is from a logit equation predicting use of text messaging or video. Tests of 0.2, 3.9, and 5.8 from

[16] The same pattern occurs without video included. With the widely popular WeChat providing text, voice, and video, channel distinctions are not clear (especially with us explicitly mentioning WeChat with the voice option on the response card). We combine video with text here because they are both more likely with guanxi contacts, video use was the channel most often mentioned with text use (.17 Jaccard coefficient), and video is least often cited as a channel (15 percent). We think of the dark bars in the figure as instant messaging.

right to left document the increasing use of text communication with guanxi, reaching its highest levels with bridge guanxi. The relevance of this channel to guanxi can be seen in the Figure 5.1 spatial map. Text (#38) is located toward the upper-right of the map, near "other guanxi" (#53) and closer to "strongest guanxi" (#54) than any of the other communication channels (#34–#37, which cluster in the lower-right among the "other positive ties").

In retrospect, the link between communication channel and guanxi is not surprising. Instant messaging is the least formal channel of communication, typically requiring the fewest words (and sometimes no words at all, but rather icons, memes, or jargon) to instantly convey information or sentiment. It is a natural choice for close, trusted contacts. In sum, more personal channels are used with guanxi, especially with bridge guanxi—the contacts most associated with business success.[17]

How Essential is Multiplexity?

We have looked closely at multiplexity to be sure that what we learned about guanxi as a source of strong bridges is not just an artifact of the roles and attributes with which guanxi co-occurs. We now return to our two hypotheses, this time with multiplexity added to the tests. Above and beyond the history of a relationship, three role relations—family, friends, and classmates—and one communication channel—texting—stand out in Table 5.2 for their association with guanxi. For each of these four relations, discussed as "foundations" of guanxi, we now ask two questions in keeping with our hypotheses: Is trust in guanxi derivative from trust in the foundation relationship perceived as guanxi? Is economic performance higher for entrepreneurs whose bridge guanxi is embedded in a foundation relationship?

[17] A significant implication concerns what could be termed "digital guanxi" (Hong et al. 2025). We begin with personal relationships and find texting the form of communication most distinguishing guanxi from other personal ties. In contrast, suppose one starts with a sample of texting relationships, not knowing who views whom as guanxi. To say that texting distinguishes personal relations more likely to be guanxi is not to say that texting relations in general are likely to be guanxi. The set of all texting relations is a much larger pool than we analyze here. And given the importance we find for interpersonal history, the idea of "swift guanxi" seems a contradiction in terms (Ou et al. 2014). It is tempting to infer guanxi from texting because voluminous data are available on texting, and there are anecdotes in the research literature documenting instances of texting relations viewed as guanxi. What is missing is comparative analysis of network pattern in texting to distinguish guanxi texting from non-guanxi texting. Guo et al. (2026) offer an innovative validation of broker text relations in China, Goldberg et al. (2016) analyze electronic networks using manager text language to distinguish more successful network brokers), and Leonardi (2015) uses a field experiment to demonstrate enterprise social media improving employee ability to identify informal leaders in the company knowledge network.

Are the Strong Bridges Derivative?

Our strong-bridges hypothesis holds that trust in guanxi is high and relatively independent of structural embedding—that is, guanxi provides trust even when a relationship is a bridge. Figure 5.4 presents a graph linking strong bridges to guanxi with and without multiplexity. Each graph corresponds to Panel B in Figure 4.4 reporting the trust association across different kinds of relations. The difference here is that guanxi relations are separated into two categories: Guanxi that occur in foundation relationships (heavy solid line through solid triangles), versus guanxi that occur in other kinds of relationships (thin solid line through solid squares). For contrast, we also present the tendency for trust in foundation relationships that did not develop into guanxi (dashed line through hollow triangles), and the closure-trust association for all routine business contacts (dashed line through hollow circles).

Family, in Figure 5.4A, is the quintessential foundation relationship. If a contact is family, trust is high regardless of structural embedding—the three lines at the top are flat across the horizontal axis. Family is its own form of guanxi. However, the thin solid line is just as high, and just as flat, across the graph as the other two upper lines. Trust in guanxi contacts beyond the family is just as strong as trust in family contacts—and, as already noted, nine out of ten cited contacts for our sample entrepreneurs are beyond the family.

We highlight three findings across the graphs in Figure 5.4. First, for each kind of foundation relationship that is a bridge between groups (left side of each graph), trust is higher in foundation relations than it is in relations with routine business contacts (all lines higher than dashed line through hollow circles). Second, trust in guanxi relations is higher on average than trust in non-guanxi foundation relations (solid lines higher than dashed line through hollow triangles). Third, and most importantly, trust in guanxi bridge relations is similarly high regardless of whether the guanxi occurs in a foundation relationship or in some other kind of relationship (solid lines are about the same height to the left in each graph). This third finding does not extend to structurally embedded friendship relations, but it is clearly true of bridge friendships.[18] In short, the strong bridges provided

---

[18] Structurally embedded "just friends" have no role connection with the entrepreneur but they are attached to someone to whom the entrepreneur is attached. Envision the lazy brother of a close friend. Bridge "just friends," in contrast, are only in the network by choice of the entrepreneur. Most

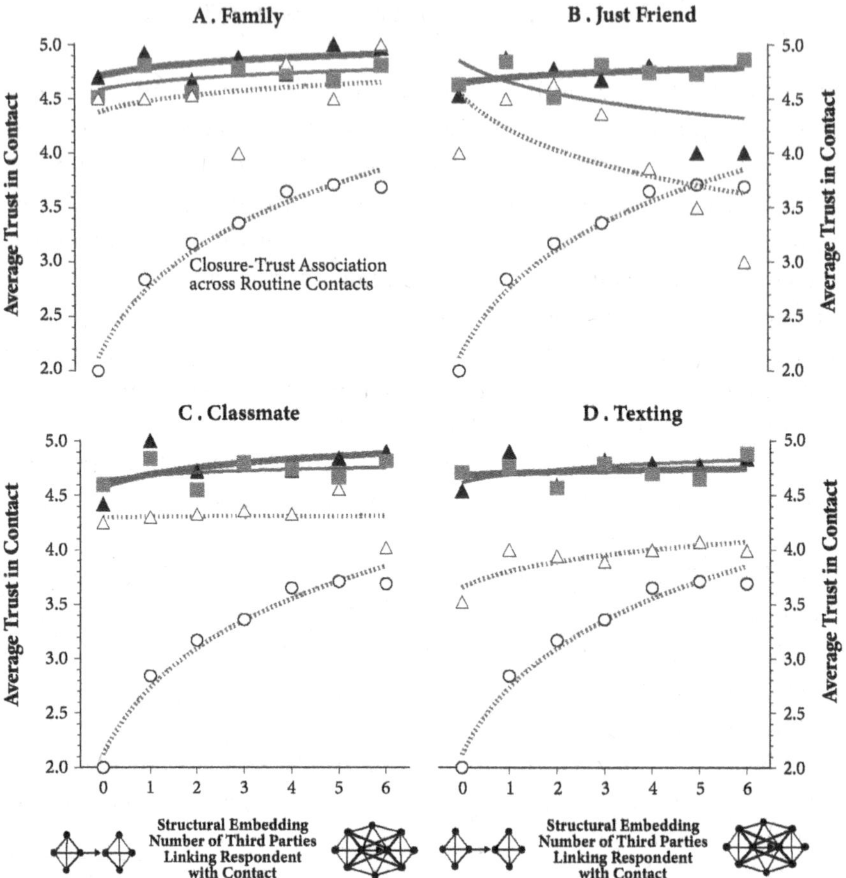

Figure 5.4 Multiplexity Irrelevant to Strong-Bridges Hypothesis

Note: These are the graph in Figure 4.4B reproduced to distinguish four kinds of relations in which guanxi tends to be found. The closure-trust association from Figure 2.5B is reproduced as a baseline in each graph (dashed line through hollow circles). Guanxi are separated into two categories: Relations mixed with the foundation relationship (heavy solid line through solid triangles) versus guanxi without the foundation (thin solid line through solid squares). Dashed line through hollow triangles describes trust in foundation relations that are not guanxi.

by guanxi do not depend on specific foundation relationships. The interpersonal history of time and events that generate guanxi seems to operate in all kinds of relationships.

"just friends" are bridge contacts (66 percent of just friends have one or no mutual contacts with the entrepreneur; 84 percent have two or fewer).

Table 5.8 reports statistical corroboration for the third point. We add multiplexity to the trust prediction reported earlier in Table 4.2. As before, jackknife standard errors are estimated with individual fixed effects. The first column is a baseline, repeating the estimates from Table 4.2 (Model M4), where multiplexity is ignored. The next five columns control for multiplexity, testing whether trust differs between guanxi with and without a foundation relationship.

Table 5.8 Multiplexity Is Largely Irrelevant to Guanxi Strong Bridges

	All Contacts (Model M4, Table 4.2)	Foundation Relationship				
		Family	Just Friend All	Just Friend Bridges	Classmate	Texting
Number of Relationships	2702	2702	2702	2016	2702	2702
R^2	.45	.45	.45	.47	.45	.45
Intercept (alpha, Figure 4.3)	2.86	2.86	2.85	2.96	2.85	2.86
Structural embedding (beta, Figure 4.3)	.94*** (.06)	.95*** (.06)	.95*** (.06)	.97*** (.07)	.95*** (.06)	.94*** (06)
Level adjustment for guanxi contacts (gamma, Figure 4.3)	.95*** (.03)	—	—	—	—	—
Guanxi with foundation	—	1.64*** (.10)	1.58*** (.10)	1.57*** (.11)	1.39*** (.17)	1.49*** (.08)
Guanxi without	—	1.44*** (.08)	1.49*** (.08)	1.52*** (.09)	1.52*** (.07)	1.53*** (.11)
P(no difference)	—	.06	.42	.65	.46	.67
Slope adjustment for guanxi contacts (lambda Figure 4.3)	−.57*** (.06)	—	—	—	—	—
Guanxi with foundation	—	−.61*** (.08)	−.87*** (.14)	−.84*** (.16)	−.39** (.13)	−.51*** (.07)
Guanxi without	—	−.54*** (.07)	−.55*** (.06)	−.66*** (.09)	−.62*** (.06)	−.65*** (.08)
P(no difference)	—	.47	.03*	.24	.08	.13

Note: OLS results predicting trust in 2,702 cited contacts measured on a five-point scale. Structural embedding is measured by summed weighted indirect connections through third parties. Jackknife standard errors in parentheses with respondent fixed effects. Probability of no difference with or without a foundation relationship is based on F-test for identical coefficients. Descriptive statistics are given in Table B.5 in Appendix B. * P < .05. ** P < .01. *** P < .001.

Across all five specifications, we replicate our baseline result. In the fourth row of the table, the closure-trust association remains a statistically significant feature of relations with routine business contacts (beta in Figure 4.3). Across the five models controlling for different kinds of multiplexity, the coefficients range from .94 to .97, all significant beyond a .001 level of confidence.

The sixth and seventh rows of the table show trust to be higher in guanxi bridges (gamma in Figure 4.3), with or without controls for multiplexity. These coefficients measure the extent to which the solid lines in Figure 5.4 are higher than the dashed line to the left in each panel. Estimates are similar across specifications and statistically significant beyond a .001 level of confidence. The eighth row, labeled "P(no difference)," reports the probability that the two coefficients above are equal. Each test fails to reject the null. In short, multiplexity does not account for the strong-bridges hypothesis.

The bottom three rows of the table report estimates for the extent to which trust in guanxi contacts is independent of structural embedding (lambda in Figure 4.3). These coefficients measure the extent to which the solid lines in Figure 5.4 remain flat across the horizontal axis in each panel. The estimates are strongly negative, adjusting the positive closure-trust association when ties involve guanxi contacts.

Probabilities of no difference in the bottom row show that estimates are similar for guanxi with or without multiplexity—with one exception. The exception is friends. Figure 5.4B shows that trust in structurally embedded guanxi contacts who are not friends is unexpectedly low (right side of graph). These contacts are in the network because of their connections to others. However, if we put aside the most deeply embedded guanxi contacts—those linked to four or more mutual friends of the entrepreneur—the probability of no difference between guanxi with or without multiplexity is high again (.24 in "Bridges" column).

Empirical support for the strong-bridges hypothesis is clear: The high trust in strong guanxi bridges is independent of multiplexity, and thus grounded in a shared history of time and events—not in the specific kinds of relations with which guanxi co-occurs.

Is the Performance Link with Strong Bridges Derivative?

Our advantage hypothesis is that economic performance increases with bridge guanxi more than with structurally embedded guanxi. This is a variation on the familiar performance association with brokerage: As bridge relations are integral to broker advantage, the strong bridges provided by guanxi should yield more economic value than embedded guanxi. The previous chapter provided empirical support for the advantage hypothesis in various ways—most clearly in Figure 4.7, where entrepreneurs with bridge guanxi show significantly higher performance than those with structurally embedded guanxi or with routine bridges.

Figure 5.5 replicates Figure 4.7, now with a multiplexity distinction between guanxi bridges. Again, the vertical axis is return on assets controlling for individual differences in industry, city, and years before the business became profitable. Again, entrepreneurs operating in relatively closed networks are to the left, and network brokers are to the right (below median network constraint). The bars to the right are higher than the bars to the left, as expected from the competitive advantage of network brokers. And again, the black bars to the left in each panel show below-average performance for entrepreneurs whose networks contain no bridges.

The bars to the right in each panel are the new element. They show the economic performance of entrepreneurs whose guanxi bridges are more or less built on foundation relations. In Panel A, economic performance is below average for entrepreneurs in relatively closed networks, whose few

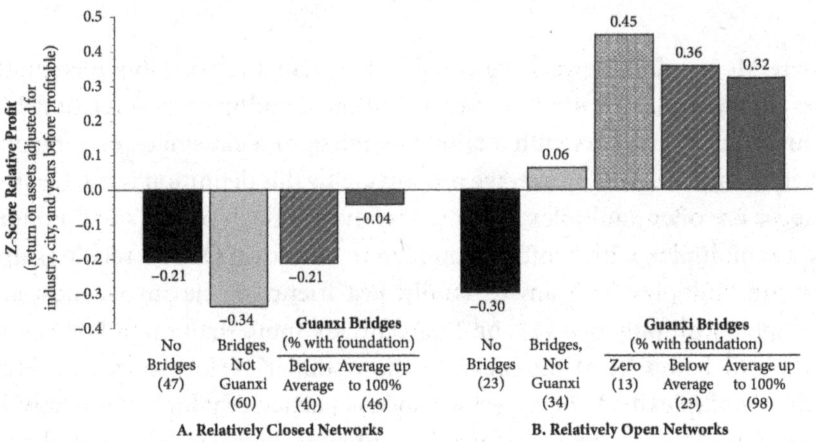

Figure 5.5 Multiplexity Is Not Essential for Advantage Hypothesis

Note: This is a replication of the network-performance association in Figure 4.7. Bars show z-score relative return on assets. Networks are sorted on the horizontal as they were sorted in Figure 4.7, with guanxi bridges here distinguished by the extent to which they co-occur with one or more foundation relations (family, classmate, or just friend in Eq. 3). Parentheses contain number of entrepreneurs in each condition.

guanxi bridges occur with or without a foundation relation. In Panel B, the right-most three bars show high economic performance for entrepreneurs with abundant guanxi bridges regardless of multiplexity. Their economic performance is high if all of their guanxi bridges are multiplex (light solid bar to the far right), if some of their guanxi bridges are multiplex (striped bar), or if none of their guanxi bridges are multiplex (light solid bar). In short, guanxi bridges with or without multiplexity are integral to the economic success of entrepreneurs.

Measurement

Testing the advantage hypothesis with a control for multiplexity requires us to aggregate guanxi bridges across an entrepreneur's network because our performance data are defined at the level of an entrepreneur's business. We aggregate by computing the proportion of an entrepreneur's guanxi bridges that are multiplex. From Chapter 4, we have a measure, G^*, of the extent to which an entrepreneur's guanxi are bridges (Eq. 2): $\sum_g (1 - z_{ikg}/(\max z_{ikg})$. To measure the proportion of guanxi bridges that are multiplex, we compute the following ratio:

$$MG^* = \sum_g \left(1 - z_{ikg}/(\max z_{ikg})\, M_g\right)/G^*, \tag{3}$$

where M_g is a dummy variable equal to 1 if guanxi relationship g is multiplex. In Figure 5.5, we used a broad definition of multiplexity. A relationship is multiplex if it occurs with a family member, or a classmate, or someone labeled just a friend. The average proportion by this definition is .62. Guanxi bridges are often multiplex in some way even though only a small minority are multiplex with multiple foundation relations. Of 736 relationships that are multiplex with any of family, just friend, or classmate, most are multiplex with only one (13, or 2 percent, are more than one). For Figure 5.5, we dichotomize at the mean to show similar performance with high or low multiplexity. Where performance is particularly high—in relatively open networks—we made a further distinction between low multiplexity (stripe) versus none at all (light solid), showing that the guanxi bridge association with performance is strong even in the complete, if rare, absence of multiplexity.

Statistical Tests

Figure 5.5 is useful to communicate that the performance association with guanxi bridges established in the last chapter does not depend on multiplexity. Table 5.9 offers more precise test.[19] The table contains the results of testing whether guanxi bridge multiplexity adds to our prediction of economic performance in Table 4.5. The top rows test whether multiplexity adds to our earlier prediction in Model M12 from the volume of guanxi bridges, G^*. To facilitate comparison, the first column in Table 5.9 repeats the result in Model M12. Table 4.5 includes nine variables controlling for background and business differences between individual entrepreneurs. Those controls are included here, but not presented because their effects are so similar for each of the different multiplexity measures. Assurance of that fact can be taken from the similarity across columns in R^2 and the effect coefficient for volume of guanxi bridges, G^*. The bottom rows in Table 5.9 add multiplexity to our earlier prediction in Model M14 from the volume of guanxi bridges and the overall network constraint in an entrepreneur's network. Again, the nine controls are included and the first column repeats the results in Model M14.

We take two conclusions from the table. First, multiplexity is not necessary for the association between guanxi bridges and economic performance. With or without the control for multiplexity, the volume of guanxi bridges, G^*, remains a statistically significant predictor of economic performance. Second, beyond being unnecessary, three forms of multiplexity are irrelevant to the prediction. The broad definition of multiplexity used in Figure 5.5

---

[19] Results in the figure are weakened by the need to partition multiplexity into categories. The strength of the figure is that our conclusion is visually obvious. It is reassuring to know that our conclusions from the corresponding Figure 4.7 are reproduced in Figure 5.5, regardless of multiplexity. Specify a regression model predicting the percentage return-on-assets dependent variable in Table 4.5 and Table 5.9. Include all nine control variables from the tables. Replace the network predictors with a nine-category variable distinguishing the nine bars in Figure 5.5. Take as a reference category the first bar to the far left: relatively closed networks containing no bridges. Estimating as in Table 5.9, average performance differences from the reference category are −1.28, 0.25, and 2.31 for the other three categories of relatively closed networks; −1.35, 4.21, 9.42, 7.86, and 7.65 for the five categories of relatively open networks. Returns on assets are up or down a few points across the first six categories in Figure 5.5, but they are negligibly different from average returns in a relatively closed network containing no bridges (1.33 $F_{(5,383)}$, P ~ .25). Particularly noteworthy, guanxi bridges with or without multiplexity provide no advantage in a relatively closed network (0.68 $F_{(2,383)}$, P ~ .51). Also noteworthy is that high returns are associated with guanxi bridges in relatively open networks regardless of multiplexity. The last three bars in the figure appear to be decreasing with higher multiplexity, but confidence intervals around the bars overlap so much that the bars are statistically indistinguishable (0.07 $F_{(2,383)}$, P ~ .93).

Table 5.9 Multiplexity Is Not Essential to Guanxi-Performance Link

	Estimates from Table 4.5	Any of Family, Just Friend, or Classmate	Foundation Relationship			
			Family	Just Friend	Classmate	Texting
Model 12: Prediction from Guanxi Bridges						
R^2	.157	.157	.158	.167	.163	.173
Guanxi bridges (G*, Eq. 2)	9.04***	8.92***	8.87***	7.27**	8.67***	7.26**
	(2.45)	(2.55)	(2.50)	(2.52)	(2.45)	(2.41)
Portion guanxi bridges multiplex (MG*, Eq. 3)	—	.28	1.00	4.70*	−3.00	4.53**
		(1.70)	(1.99)	(1.99)	(1.60)	(1.63)
P(performance independent multiplexity)	—	.83	.62	.02	.07	.01
Model 14: Prediction from Guanxi Bridges, Controlling for Aggregate Bridges						
R^2	.166	.166	.167	.173	.170	.179
Guanxi bridges (G*, Eq. 2)	7.32**	7.23**	7.13**	6.00*	7.10**	5.94*
	(2.59)	(2.69)	(2.65)	(2.62)	(2.59)	(2.56)
Network Constraint (excluding strongest guanxi)	−4.37*	−4.36*	−4.39*	−3.78	−4.09*	−3.70
	(2.07)	(2.07)	(2.08)	(2.09)	(2.06)	(2.11)
Portion guanxi bridges multiplex (MG*, Eq. 3)	—	.20	1.08	4.11*	−2.67	4.17**
		(1.69)	(1.98)	(2.01)	(1.59)	(1.64)
P(performance independent multiplexity)	—	.90	.59	.04	.09	.01

Note: Performance is average return on assets between 2015 and 2017. These are OLS estimates, jackknife standard errors in parentheses. Predictors are the same as in Table 4.5 except models here include a control for the proportion of an entrepreneur's guanxi bridges that are multiplex with the column foundation relationship (Eq. 3). Included, but not presented, are coefficients for the nine predictors in Table 4.5 controlling for background and business differences between entrepreneurs. The coefficients are little changed here (note replication of R^2 and network coefficients from Table 4.5). Descriptive statistics are given in Tables B.6 and B.7 in Appendix B. * P < .05. ** P < .01. *** P < .001

is irrelevant (.83 probability of no association in Model M12 and .90 probability in Model M14). Contrary to analogies often drawn between family and guanxi, family is irrelevant (.62 probability of no association in Model M12 and .59 probability in Model M14). Bridge guanxi with classmates borders on statistical significance, but in a negative direction—clearly not a source of advantage.

Second, the two forms of multiplexity that make a statistically significant contribution to predicting economic performance, reinforce, rather than undermine, our first conclusion. The first is "just friend." Entrepreneurs with a high proportion of their guanxi bridges "just friends" have economic performance higher than expected from the volume of their guanxi bridges (2.36 t-test in Model M12, P ~ .02, 2.05 t-test in Model M14, P ~ .04). But "just friends" are contacts without a formal role relationship. This is one sentiment (guanxi) co-occurring with another (friendship), in the absence of a concrete foundation relationship. The relationship did not emerge from a concrete role, so much as it emerged from a shared history through one or more significant events. Not surprisingly, the proportion of "just friend" guanxi bridges is more strongly correlated with the volume of an entrepreneur's guanxi bridges than any other form of multiplexity (.41 correlation between G∗ and MG∗ when MG∗ is defined by "just friend").

Texting is a similar kind of multiplexity. Entrepreneurs who text with a high proportion of their guanxi bridges have economic performance higher than what would be expected from the volume of their guanxi bridges alone (2.78 t-test in Model M12, P ~ .01; 2.54 t-test in Model M14, P ~ .01). But texting is not a foundation from which guanxi developed so much as it reflects the value of wide-bandwidth communication with especially important contacts.

Conclusion: Coincidental Multiplexity

We have done three things to determine whether the strong bridges documented in the previous chapter are derivative of multiplexity. First, we identified and described kinds of relations in which guanxi is more likely to occur (Figure 5.1 and Table 5.2). From diverse kinds of connections, history emerged as the primary predictor—both in terms of years known and in terms of help received during critical moments of the business's development. Three role relations emerged as likely foundations for guanxi;

not foundations in the sense of preceding guanxi, but in the sense that guanxi is more likely to occur within them. These are family, friendship, and classmates. In addition, guanxi is especially likely to occur in relationships characterized by direct, high-bandwidth communication—indicated by texting.

Second, we established that the strong bridges associated with guanxi are not derivative from multiplexity. Guanxi provides strong bridges independent of the kinds of relations in which it occurs. This is visually evident in Figure 5.4 and statistically corroborated in Table 5.8: trust in the strong bridges provided by guanxi is high with or without multiplexity.

Third, we established that the enhanced economic performance associated with guanxi bridges is not dependent on multiplexity. Performance increases with the extent to which an entrepreneur has guanxi bridges in his or her network—with or without multiplexity. Figure 5.5 shows that guanxi bridges offer no performance advantage in relatively closed networks, but offer substantial gains in relatively open networks—that is, to network brokers. The gains occur regardless of multiplexity. Statistical corroboration in Table 5.9 shows that this is the full story for family and classmates: their presence as foundation ties does not add to the effect. The other two foundation relations, however, do show independent positive association with performance. The guanxi bridge contacts of successful entrepreneurs are more likely to be relationships with no associated role relation ("just friends") and relationships with wide bandwidth direct communication (indicated by texting). But neither of these forms of multiplexity is essential to the association between guanxi bridges and economic performance.

We conclude that multiplexity is not necessary for the strong bridges provided by guanxi, though it can be a useful coincidence. This is a key takeaway, one that generalizes the concept of strong bridges. Guanxi has its trust and performance correlates regardless of the kind of connection interpreted to be guanxi. In principle, any form of connection can be interpreted as guanxi. When guanxi spans a structural hole, it provides a strong bridge. By implication (allowing for some research limitations, e.g., footnote 17), any form of connection can be a strong bridge.

6

Coincidental Language

In the previous two chapters, we interpreted guanxi in terms of context. Chapter 4 defined context as the structure of relations around guanxi, Chapter 5 explored the kinds of relations in which guanxi occurs. Both analyses confirmed our proposition: strong guanxi bridges are grounded in a shared personal history—time known and shared events—not in network position or specific kinds of relations.

In this chapter, we shift focus from observable characteristics to take advantage of a rare opportunity. We examine the language respondents use to describe guanxi. There has been considerable work on the mental images people construct to make sense of the social structure around them (Morgan 1986; Krackhardt 1987; Feltham et al. 2025). Our related concern in this chapter is the language people use to describe relationships, in particular guanxi relationships, especially the strong bridge relationships provided by guanxi. Language too is a familiar correlate of networks, distinguishing people by how they construct networks (Zerubavel 1991), or benefit from their networks (Goldberg et al. 2016). To our knowledge, however, no prior research has combined network and language data from a representative sample of heads of business explaining guanxi.[1] We explore the data for common themes in the language used by our entrepreneurs. More specifically, we search for language inconsistencies between subgroups, patterns that could require subgroup-specific analysis of network structure.

Our main finding is that descriptions of guanxi differ by degree, not kind; varying in their complexity, which in turn varies primarily with the network around the entrepreneur. In Japan, where rice is not a staple food but a cultural symbol present in diverse social situations, there are numerous words (distinct characters) to refer to rice in its various forms and stages, from rice as a plant (ine, 稲), to rice as uncooked grains (kome, 米), to cooked

---

[1] Yan and Yasseri (2017) analyze a collection of tweets that contain the word guanxi. The reference population is unclear (anyone tweeting during the data collection intervals) and the topics discussed when guanxi is mentioned are unknown. Nevertheless, Yan and Yasseri provide a template for intriguing analysis of guanxi texts.

Strong Bridges. Ronald S. Burt and Sonja Opper, Oxford University Press. © Oxford University Press (2026).
DOI: 10.1093/9780197834275.003.0006

rice (gohan, ご飯). Similarly, entrepreneurs in larger, more open networks describe guanxi in more nuanced terms, reflecting the broader range of social situations in which they experience guanxi. Economic performance is a correlate. The larger, more open networks associated with more complex descriptions are the same networks shown in the preceding two chapters to be associated with entrepreneurs running more profitable businesses.

Language Data

Our language data come from responses to our initial two guanxi questions (Figure A9, item 16): "Are you familiar with the word guanxi?" If yes, the interviewer continued, "When there is guanxi between two people, that tells you certain things about their relationship. In your own words, how would you describe to a foreigner the relationship between two people who have guanxi with each other?"[2] The explicit reference to foreigners served a dual purpose: We wanted to prevent respondents from neglecting the question, because they might have doubted the usefulness of explaining such a widely used term. At the same time, we wanted to elicit a level of detail in articulation that respondents might not otherwise have used in an exchange with a local interviewer.

The question asks respondents to articulate an abstract, colloquial concept, so we were concerned that people with less education would feel uncomfortable. However, guanxi is such a commonly used word that we need not have worried. Ninety-five percent of the sample respondents said they were familiar with the word. And the people who said they were not familiar with guanxi have no more or less education, along with no difference on several other respondent and business variables.[3] Therefore,

---

[2] We had interviewers write responses in the interview booklet for fear that variation in the quality of respondent handwriting would affect data transcription. The interviewer was asked to write the response verbatim, and the responses were typically short. Nevertheless, we pay extra attention to possible interviewer effects in this chapter.

[3] Being familiar with the word guanxi is independent of education years (nine to twenty-two, 10.11 chi-square, 12 d.f., P ~ .61), and independent of highest education degree (junior high, high school, junior college, college, master degree, doctoral degree, 2.62 chi-square, 5 d.f., P ~ .76). In a logit model predicting who among the sample respondents says they are not familiar with the word guanxi, respondent characteristics do not matter (age, education, gender, party membership, having founded the business, and network constraint, 2.07 chi-square, 6 d.f., P ~ .91), and characteristics of the respondent's business do not matter (IT industry, sales, assets, number of employees, return on assets, firm age, family firm, entertainment, and travel costs [for exposure to anti-corruption campaign], years between founding and the business showing a profit, 13.59 chi-square, 9 d.f., P ~ .14). The best predictor is who interviewed the respondent (15.95 chi-square, 2 d.f., P < .001). Two of the

we feel comfortable putting aside the nineteen people from whom we have no text and studying the 365 texts we have as representative of the population.

The 365 sample entrepreneurs who described guanxi used a median of 20 Chinese characters, ranging from two, up to a maximum of 101 (based on character count using Excel). A Chinese character has a distinct meaning, like a word in English, but often two characters combine to form a new word that is distinct from either of its component characters. In our case, the number translates into a median of twelve words, varying across individuals from one, up to a maximum of sixty-four. For the word count we used the simplified Chinese character dictionary for the widely-used Linguistic Inquiry and Word Count (LIWC) software (Pennebaker et al. 2015), which had most of the words used by the respondents in its Chinese dictionary version, with a median coverage of 80 percent per respondent. The software converts text into a profile of words distinguishing grammatical roles, sentiments, and topics. We use LIWC because it is easily understood, widely used in the West, and available with a Chinese dictionary (Huang et al. 2012) that we tested in prior text analysis (Opper and Zou, 2024).

There is ample network precedent with LIWC. Burt (2010:256–264) uses the LIWC's positive and negative affect categories to show that people in open networks, when proposing ideas to senior management, are more likely to mix positive and negative emotions—rather than to rely on one or the other. Measuring language style by the relative frequency with which a person's LIWC profile contains function words (e.g., pronouns, adverbs, and articles), Ireland et al. (2011) show that more successful relations (in speed dating and marital stability) occur between people who use similar language styles. Using an asymmetric measure of language style coordination defined by LIWC function words in Wikipedia and Supreme Court transcripts, Danescu-Niculescu-Mizil et al. (2012) describe language coordination correlated with hierarchy. Less powerful people talking with more powerful people quickly adopt the other's language style "in their very next reply," but coordination is markedly less from the more to the less powerful

---

nine interviewers are responsible for fourteen of the nineteen "don't know" responses to the guanxi question. The two interviewers do not have shorter texts from their respondents who said they are familiar with the word guanxi (average of 21 characters in responses for the two problem interviewers, versus the average of 20 characters in responses for the other seven interviewers, 0.52 t-test, P ~ .60), but the two interviewers did go through the network questions more quickly than their peers (34 minutes for the two versus 39 for the other seven, −2.97 t-test, P < .01). We carry a control for the two interviewers through the analysis in this chapter.

(allowing for closer coordination between justices and lawyers favoring one another's views). Goldberg et al. (2016) compare the LIWC profile of a manager's outgoing email with the profile of his or her incoming email to show that managers who broker connections across groups enjoy more success (ratings and a lower probability of involuntary exits) when their profile of outgoing language matches the profile of incoming language. Similarly, Srivastava et al. (2018) show that managers with a poor match are more likely to be fired. Burt (2017) uses LIWC language profiles to show that managers in more closed networks, argued to be suffering from more severe time compression, are less likely to use future tense when describing opportunities or problems to senior management. Burt and Reagans (2022) use LIWC profiles to measure the disappearance of function words as teammates move down a learning curve, coordinating more efficiently through shared jargon. In short, there is ample and diverse precedent supporting the productive use of LIWC profiles in network research.

To provide a first flavor of the data, Table 6.1 presents example descriptions of guanxi provided by respondents. We translate the texts into English for this discussion using the DeepL Translate service, but our analysis draws on the original Chinese texts. The phrases at the top of Table 6.1 illustrate shorter descriptions, though not the shortest in our dataset. The nineteen shortest descriptions are two characters. For example, friend (朋友), close (亲密), to be good/be on friendly terms (要好), and familiar with (熟悉). These terse descriptions have a flavor of "you know what I mean" exchanges between people reminding one another of a shared understanding of a highly familiar concept.

At the other extreme are long descriptions, as illustrated at the bottom of Table 6.1. Longer text allows for more nuanced description. For example, one of the longest descriptions (not shown in Table 6.1) came from an entrepreneur in Shanghai, who runs a medium-size business with 260 employees that manufactures auto parts. He used fifty-nine Chinese words to highlight the distinction between guanxi and routine business relations, which is similar to the one we developed in the previous section. He reasoned: "This is hard to say. When talking about two people who have guanxi with each other, there are many kinds. Guanxi depends on the depth of the relationship. Only those with deep relationships may be used. For example, family members and friends who have been known for many years so they are like brothers. Ordinary relationships are actually not very useful."

Table 6.1 Illustrative Guanxi Texts

Chars.	Words	Complex	English	Chinese
4	2	0.0	Intimacy and mutual help	亲密互助
4	2	10.4	Mutual Care	相互照顾
10	4	18.4	Mutual help, support, trust	相互帮助, 扶持, 信任
12	6	28.5	Keep in touch, communicate frequently, help each other.	有联络, 常通讯, 互相帮助
36	26	77.1	Friends who will come to my aid when I am in trouble and need help, who don't say much but offer their strength and money.	在我有困难需要帮助的时候, 会挺身而出的朋友, 话不多说, 有力出力, 有钱出钱
33	21	84.4	People who are relatively close, who have been together for a long time, who have more in common, and are easy to understand and communicate with.	关系比较近的, 相处时间比较久, 有比较多的共同之处, 好理解好沟通的人
48	30	94.3	It means that after getting to know someone, you feel that you are on the same page and can have an in-depth relationship. Then you become closer, communicate or help each other, and deepen your feelings for each other.	就是认识以后觉得大家是一路人, 可以深入交往的, 然后就是走得比较近, 沟通或者帮忙, 让彼此感情更深.
46	29	97.6	Relatives, friends, teachers, students, neighbors, people with whom you have gradually deepened your relationship since you met; apart from those related by blood, others are connections that can also be helpful.	亲戚, 朋友, 师生, 邻里, 从认识之后交往逐渐加深的人, 除了有血缘关系之外, 别的也是对你有帮助的人脉.
71	51	100.0	This term is certainly familiar, and it is inseparable from life and work. Especially when doing business in China, it is simply impossible without connections and relationships that you can use. So it refers to specific people you know you can use.	这个词当然熟悉, 生活上和工作上都离不开, 特别在中国做生意, 你没有人脉, 没有一些可以用得上的关系根本不可能, 所以就是指一些特定的你认识用得上的人

Note: Characters and word counts refer to Chinese text. Complexity score is row text's position on the horizontal axis in Figure 6.2.

LIWC Themes

Figure 6.1 shows the frequency with which respondents use words from aggregate LIWC categories. Eighty-nine percent of all words used to describe guanxi are in the LIWC simplified Chinese character dictionary (8881 words of 9980 total). The seventy-two categories distinguished in the dictionary are aggregated to the seventeen displayed in Figure 6.1. Example words in categories of the English dictionary are provided in the software manual (Pennebaker et al., 2015:3–4; see Srivastava et al., 2018:1361–1362, for example, profiles from management email). Example characters in forty-four of the more often used categories in the Chinese dictionary are provided by Qiu et al. (2017:466–468), and Chen (2019) describes overlap between the English and Chinese categories. Bars to the right in Figure 6.1 indicate the total number of words used from each category. Bars to the left indicate the number of respondents who used one or more words from each category. No bar extends all the way to the left, indicating that no category of words is used by all 365 respondents. Different individuals drew from different categories for their descriptions.

The shaded bars in Figure 6.1 show the use of words by grammatical role. A word can play multiple roles, so categories are not mutually exclusive. Most respondents used verbs, adverbs, prepositions, and multifunction words.[4] Relatively few used conjunctions (e.g., and, but, whereas) to link phrases, or negations (e.g., no, not, never) to describe what guanxi is not. This was expected. In Chinese, meaning often relies more on context, sentence structure, and simpler forms of negation, making both conjunctions and negations less salient than in English or other Western languages.

The white bars in Figure 6.1 show the use of words by content categories. Almost no respondent uses analogies to biological processes when describing guanxi, and few use analogies to perceptional processes (look, hear, feel, touch, etc.). Less than half of the respondents use informal language. At the other extreme, more than three-quarters of the respondents talk about social and cognitive processes in their descriptions (297 and 294 individuals respectively), with cognition words the more common (words about inclusion, exclusion, must, expect, insight). The affect words are usually positive

---

[4] Chinese characters can have alternative meanings depending on how they are used in a text. For example, 有 can mean "have," "there are," or "exist." The character 的 can be a preposition (of), a noun (aim), a possessive particle (someone's), an adverb (truly), an auxiliary verb (ablative cause suffix), or a suffix (-self).

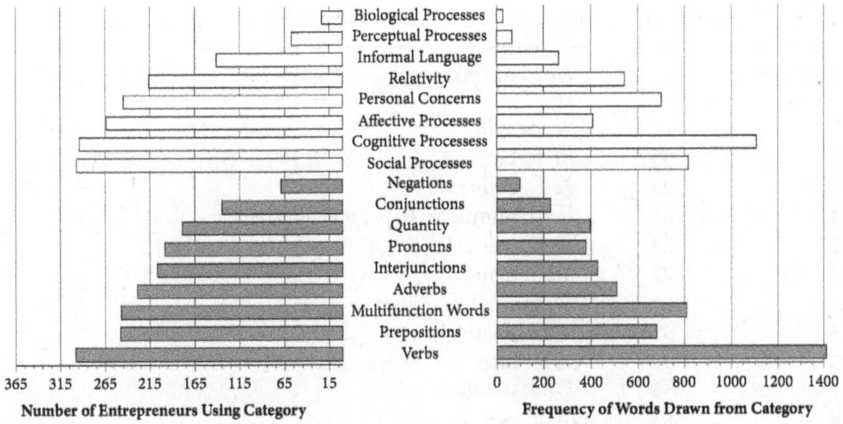

Figure 6.1 LIWC Word Categories in the Guanxi Descriptions

(255 positive emotion words versus 31 negative), but affect is used much less often than cognition (409 affect versus 1107 cognition). Almost as many respondents use affect words as use cognition words (264 versus 294 respectively). The difference lies in volume: respondents use more than twice as many cognition words as affect words. Most express personal interests primarily regarding work and achievement. Of the 701 personal-concerns words on the right in Figure 6.1, 47 percent come from the LIWC work category and 44 percent from the achievement category.

Specific Word Content

The word frequencies in Figure 6.1 describe at a high level themes and styles in respondent texts, based on LIWC categories. For more specific content, Table 6.2 lists the words and phrases used most often. The list excludes terms mentioned by fewer than 4 percent of the respondents, along with many function words that serve primarily grammatical roles. Excluded function words include multifunction terms, count suffixes, quantifiers, conjunctions, negations, progress markers, and tense markers (except for the marker for future tense). For example, the multifunction word "to have" (有) is used by 165 of the respondents, but its meaning depends on the context. It can be followed by the word for difficulties as well as the word for profits. It can be combined with trust as well as suspicion. We include a few often-used function words that carry meaning across languages (e.g., 是 "to be," see

Table 6.2 Words and Phrases Often Used in Describing Guanxi

Sequence	N	Word or Phrase
18	123	人, people
19	95	是, to be
20	95	关系, *guanxi*
21	85	互相, mutually; 相互, one another
22	73	联系, contact
23	72	帮助, help
24	62	会, future tense marker
25	57	比较, relatively
26	57	经常, often
27	53	共同, jointly
28	53	可以, can
29	45	亲密, close
30	44	朋友, friend
31	42	时候, time; 时间 time; 时 time
32	33	工作, work
33	32	认识, be acquainted
34	30	你, you (2nd person singular)
35	29	深, deep
36	28	事, thing
37	27	利益, interest, advantage
38	23	说话, speak (combinations with speak; speak honestly etc.)
39	22	信任, trust
40	20	生活, life
41	20	合作, cooperate
42	15	走, walk (combined with 近 (close), being very close)
43	13	我, me or I (1st person singular)
44	9	兄弟,家人,亲戚 (brother, family, kinship/relatives)

Note: Sequence begins after the seventeen LIWC word categories in Figure 6.1. N is the number of respondents who use the row word or phrase.

Qiu et al., 2017, for analysis of content and function words across Chinese and English). First and second person pronouns are included as indicators of individualist rather than collective perspectives. The marker for future tense is retained as a possible indicator of temporal bias associated with network structure (Burt 2017; Opper and Burt 2021).

We also identified some often-used phrases, such as "zoudejin" (走得近), which literally means "to walk close" or "to walk closely" to describe a close or strong relationship with someone, various references to time (时候, 时间, 时), and phrases including the characters for "word" (hua, 话) and "say" (shuo, 说).

All of these expressions occur in subtle variations. The theme of walking closely (走得近) commonly translated as "being close to someone" occurs once with the reinforcement "very" (走得很近), in one more extended by "together" (走到一起), and in ten explanations it is presented in a comparative perspective as "relatively closely" (as in 走得比较近/走得相对比较近/走了比较近). We add these phrases to the analysis because word counts disassemble the phrases, obscuring their colloquial meaning. For example, in LIWC the imagery of walking closely (走得近) registers with the individual characters, one in the motion category (走, "walk") and one in the space category (近, "close"), with no registration of the special affect indicated by the combination of both. This is not a failure of the software, nor a criticism of the research strategy behind the software. It is just an illustration of why we decided to augment the LIWC profiles with specific, frequently used words and phrases.

Phrases around the theme of "speaking" are more varied than the above versions of being close. Nine respondents said "talk about everything without reserve" (无话不说, or 无话不谈). Another used "just say one word (literally a sound)" (说一声), and an eleventh said "don't need to say many words" (话不多说). For six other respondents the phrase was "a shared or joint language" (共同语言) or "joint topics" (共同话题). Other variations that occurred once each are "friendly chatting" (聊天说地), "can talk" (会说话), "should not talk about" (不要说), "can tell secrets" (说一些私密的事), and "can tell everything" (都可以说), and "deep words" (深的话).

In the bottom row of Table 6.2, we include a "family" word category (the family-related words we combine in this category are the Chinese words for brother, family, and variable references to kinship or relatives), even though it is rarely used. We do this for two reasons: First, the previous chapter showed that family members tend to be rarely cited, but when cited they are often cited as guanxi. Second, further analysis in the previous chapter showed that being a family member is not a necessary foundation for strong guanxi bridges. We were curious to see, if the subjective language of the respondents matched these realities. And indeed, respondents rarely make family references when describing guanxi.

Frequencies are lower in Table 6.2 than they are for the LIWC word categories to the left in Figure 6.1. On average, the words and phrases listed in Table 6.2 occur in 46.6 texts, versus a 196.9 average for the word categories in Figure 6.1. That is to be expected since the LIWC categories contain multiple words. Still, the low frequencies in Table 6.2 might imply that we drew words from a minority of respondents. This is not the case. The average use of individual words and phrases in Table 6.2 is low, but excepting 28 respondents who used none of the expressions in Table 6.2, the other 337, or 92 percent of the sample, use multiple—varying from a median of four, up to a maximum of one respondent who used 11.

A final observation concerns what we did not find: no one referred to history, tradition, or culture as a broader framework for describing guanxi. This is notable because our prompt to explain guanxi to an imaginative foreigner could easily have triggered such references. At the very least, the complete absence of these elements suggests that business leaders—even those exposed to Shanghai's highly cosmopolitan and diverse environment—either do not perceive the concept of guanxi as rooted in a cultural or historical context, or do not consider this fact to be of primary importance in understanding it.

How Speakers Differ

The seventeen LIWC word categories in Figure 6.1, and the twenty-seven specific words and phrases in Table 6.2, together define a forty-four-variable profile of the language respondents used to describe guanxi. Since our texts are brief (median 12 words), we do not put much stock in how often a word or phrase is used. We convert frequencies to binary data to focus on the categories from which a respondent draws in his or her description. The kth variable in a respondent's profile is 1 if he or she used a word from the kth category. Two respondents offer different descriptions of guanxi to the extent that their language profiles do not match (Euclidean distance).

Figure 6.2 shows a classical multidimensional scaling of language differences. The display in Figure 6.2A contains all respondents who provided a text. The dots are individual respondents. Proximity between two dots reflects similarity in language profiles for the proximate respondents. The relative length of each axis is proportional to the variance it describes. Language varies primarily along the horizontal axis, which accounts for 78 percent of variance in language differences (based on ratio of the first eigenvalue to the total). The next two dimensions are much weaker, accounting for 5 percent and 3 percent of the variance, respectively. Subsequent

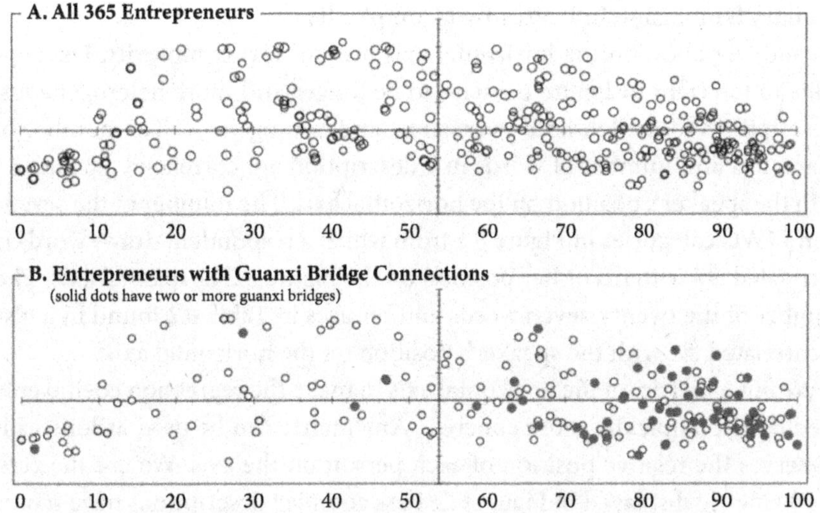

Figure 6.2 Entrepreneurs Differ In Their Language Describing Guanxi

Note: Classical multidimensional scaling of Euclidean distances measuring language differences in how respondents describe guanxi. Each dot is a respondent, 365 in all. Axes cross at their mean values and are proportional in length to the eigenvalues defining them. The two dimensions together describe 83 percent of variance in language differences.

dimensions explain little. We find nothing interesting in the third dimension, so we put it aside to focus on the first two.[5]

Predicting the Primary Dimension: Text Complexity

We note that the primary dimension to speaker differences—the horizontal axis in Figure 6.2—is continuous. The data are distributed fairly smoothly across the horizontal axis, with no obvious gaps, which would suggest discrete categories of speakers. In short, variation is more of a degree, than a kind.

[5] More than the third dimension describing little variation, we put it aside because it is largely independent of our distinctions between kinds of businesses and kinds of respondents. Looking ahead to the prediction in Table 6.3, variation on the third dimension has no association with any of the listed network, business, or personal variables (1.05 $F_{(15,348)}$, P ~ .41). The one correlate is length. Descriptions high on the third dimension tend to contain fewer characters (−3.22 t-test, P < .001). The tendency is weak relative to the strong association between description length and variation on the first dimension (25.04 t-test in Table 6.3). Therefore, we focus on the first dimension in discussing long versus short descriptions.

Primary Dimension Indicates Text Complexity

Second, variation on the horizontal axis indexes text complexity. Descriptions to the right in Figure 6.2 tend to be longer and more heterogeneous. Descriptions to the left tend to be short and homogenous. The number of characters and number of words in a description are correlated .86 and .87 with the speaker's position on the horizontal axis. The number of the seventeen LIWC categories in Figure 6.1 from which a respondent draws words is correlated .97 with his or her position on the Figure 6.2 horizontal axis. The number of the twenty-seven words and phrases in Table 6.2 found in a text is correlated .81 with the speaker's position on the horizontal axis.

We put a metric on the horizontal axis to make the regression coefficients predicting complexity more concrete. Any metric can be used as long as it preserves the relative position of each person on the axis. We use the zero to 100 metric displayed in Figure 6.2. Less complex descriptions have scores closer to zero. More complex descriptions have scores closer to 100. For illustration, Table 6.1. includes complexity scores for the sample texts. Average complexity is 53.73, with a 30.60 standard deviation.[6]

Table 6.3 shows the results of predicting language complexity from a speaker's sampling strata, network, business characteristics, and personal characteristics. Two models are presented: Model M18 predicts the horizontal axis in Figure 6.2. Model M19 predicts the length of each entrepreneur's response. Complexity is our primary interest, as it clearly differentiates speakers in Figure 6.2. Character count is a close correlate (r = .86) and the strongest predictor of complexity in Model M18 (first row in Table 6.3). Entrepreneurs with more to say have more opportunity to craft a complex text. Results are similar when controlling for word count instead of the character count, but we report character count—a control variable closer to the speaker's own language.

Text Complexity Reflects the Speaker's Social Environment

The strongest predictors are at the top of Table 6.3. First among them is city. The second row shows no difference in text volume across cities (1.18 t-test for number of characters, P ~ .24), but a sharp difference in complexity: Entrepreneurs in Hangzhou offer more complex descriptions than those in Shanghai and Ningbo (4.02 t-test, P < .001), on average eleven points higher

---

[6] The zero to 100 score is computed as 100*(D1−min)/(max−min), where D1 is a respondent's deviation score on the first dimension of the multidimensional scaling (0 mean, 1.30 standard deviation), min is the lowest D1 score (−2.287), and max is the largest D1 score (1.969).

Table 6.3 Who Has More Complex Descriptions of Guanxi?

Predictors	M18	S.E.	M19	S.E.
Number of Characters in Description	1.60***	0.17	—	—
Hangzhou (versus Shanghai & Ningbo)	10.53***	2.62	.11	.10
Network Characteristics				
Relatively Closed Network, Bridges	5.28	2.71	.18	.17
Relatively Closed Network, Guanxi Bridges	3.65	2.35	.36*	.15
Relatively Open Network, No Bridges	1.96	3.04	−.24	.20
Relatively Open Network, Bridges	5.94	4.03	.39*	.19
Relatively Open Network, Guanxi Bridges	10.15***	3.95	.80***	.14
Business Characteristics				
Information Technology (vs. Manufacturing)	−.14	2.18	−.07	.09
Current Asset Value of the Business (100,000 CNY)	.08	10.65	.004	.67
Small Firm (vs. Not Small)	−.32	2.38	.16	.10
Return on Assets (last three years)	.06	.07	.005**	.002
Years since Business Was Founded (in decades)	.11	.19	.01	.01
Research and Development Dept.	.12	1.88	.28***	.07
Founder Still Runs the Business	1.62	2.51	−.07	.11
Personal Characteristics				
Female	1.19	2.01	.03	.10
Age (in decades)	−.30	.15	−.018**	.007
College Degree	−.80	2.58	−.21	.11
Years of Education	−.65	.61	−.05	.02
Household Annual Income (10,000 CNY)	.01	.08	.002	.004
Happiness	−.67	1.74	−.02	.07

Note: M18 is an OLS regression predicting the horizontal axis in Figure 6.2. M19, is a Poisson regression predicting number of characters (N = 365). Jackknife standard errors are presented. Relatively closed networks with no bridges are the network reference category (see Figure 4.6). Intercept for M18 is 33.57 with a .78 R^2. For M19, it is 3.79 with a .28 pseudo R^2. Descriptive statistics are in Tables B.8, B.9 in Appendix B.
*P ≤ .05, **P ≤ .01, *** P ≤ .001

(10.53 coefficient in Table 6.3). Texts from Hangzhou, a city known for its more traditional business climate compared to the cosmopolitan, export-oriented coastal cities of Shanghai and Ningbo, tend to be more nuanced and richer in qualifications. Our results on guanxi, drawn largely from Shanghai and Ningbo, likely underestimate the complexity with which guanxi is discussed further inland.[7]

[7] More complex texts from Hangzhou entrepreneurs could also result from one or more interviewers in the other two cities writing abbreviated texts into the interview booklet. The two interviewers who went through the network questions quickly (see footnote 3), are no different from other interviewers in the complexity of the texts they record (add a dummy variable to Model M18

The other strong predictor at the top of Table 6.3 is the speaker's network. Figure 6.3 illustrates the pattern: Texts become shorter and less complex as the entrepreneur's network tightens. Between the number of contacts in a network and the strength of connections among them, it is connection strength that more strongly predicts complexity. Text complexity is correlated −.49 with the log of network constraint (see Figure 6.3) and −.55 with network density, measured by the average strength of connection between cited business contacts. By contrast, complexity is correlated only −.15 with the number of those contacts.[8]

The location of guanxi within a network matters. More complex descriptions come from entrepreneurs who have strong-bridge guanxi. This association is visible in Figure 6.2B, which is a duplicate of Figure 6.2A, but only displays entrepreneurs whose networks contain bridges. Relative to Figure 6.2A, the data in Figure 6.2B are concentrated to the right where descriptions are more complex. This is especially true for networks that contain guanxi bridges (dark dots). Few appear to the left.

The five network predictors in Table 6.3 support the point more authoritatively. The predictors come from our earlier analysis of how guanxi relates to an entrepreneur's economic performance. As in Figure 4.7, entrepreneurs are first sorted into closed versus open networks, then further into three subcategories: no bridge relations, some bridge relations that are not guanxi, and one or more guanxi bridge relations. Effects for the five network predictors in Model M18 measure how much more or less complex descriptions are for speakers in each category (relative to the reference category of no bridges, closed networks).

for each interviewer; null is not rejected: 0.58 $F_{(2,364)}$, P ~ .56). More, we tested for text complexity differences between all nine interviewers by adding eight interviewer dummy variables to Model M18. The six interviewers in Shanghai and Ningbo do not differ from one another in the text complexity they record (t-tests vary between −.32 and 1.47; summary $F_{(5,364)}$ of 0.94, P ~ .45), and the three interviewers in Hangzhou all record texts significantly more complex than the texts recorded in Shanghai and Ningbo (t-tests of 3.90, 3.96, and 3.48; summary $F_{(3,364)}$ of 5.59, P < .001). We conclude that the complex guanxi texts in Hangzhou likely reflect the city's more traditional business culture, rather than interviewer bias.

[8] We looked into the possibility that the association between complex text and complex network is a spurious result of chatty respondents—a talkative respondent winding on about guanxi, and indulging in a fulsome discussion of his or her social network. The possibility seems unlikely because of inconsistency across the interview. The number of characters in a respondent's guanxi text is independent of the number of characters in his or her description of the most important event in the history of the business (r = −.01). The lack of correlation could be taken to imply that respondents offering longer guanxi texts spend more time on the network questions. No, the number of characters in a respondent's guanxi text is shorter for people who use more time to respond to the network items (r = −.52).

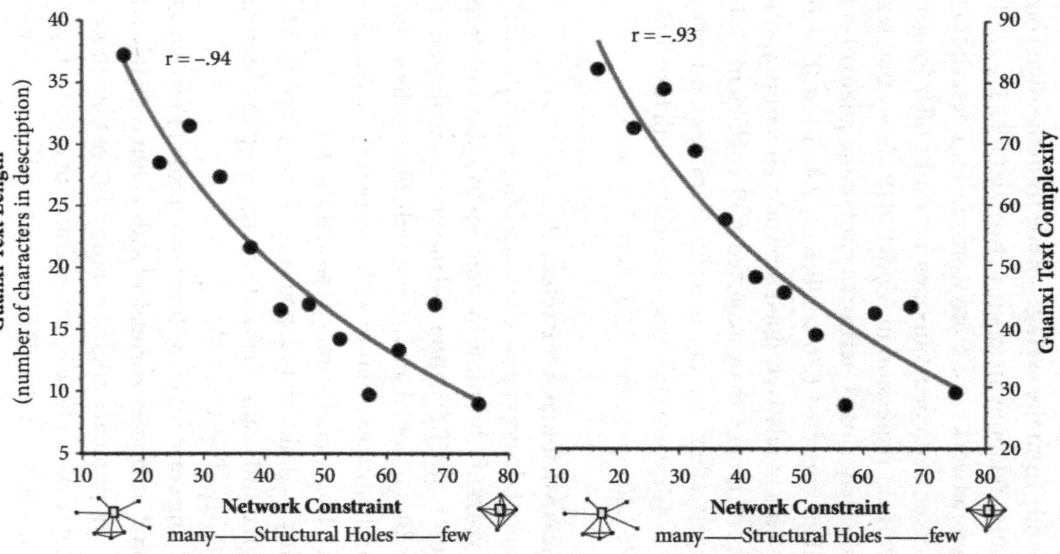

Figure 6.3 Entrepreneurs in More Complex Social Networks Offer More Complex Guanxi Texts

Note: Plotted scores are 365 individual scores on vertical and horizontal axes averaged within five-point intervals of network constraint. Correlations are computed from the plotted data with log (network constraint).

One network category stands out: Complexity is especially high among speakers in relatively open networks where one or more guanxi relations are bridges. Complexity is ten points higher in these networks (3.40 t-test, P ~ .001). Guanxi bridges in relatively closed networks are independent of complexity (3.65 coefficient, 1.55 t-test, P ~ .12), and no other network category differs significantly from the average—aside from the high complexity associated with guanxi relations in open networks (1.20 $F_{(4364)}$, P ~ .31). As managers in open networks use more words in idea descriptions (Burt 2010: 262), so too do entrepreneurs in open networks offer longer guanxi descriptions. The Poisson regression in Model M19 shows that texts from entrepreneurs in relatively closed networks containing guanxi bridges are 42 percent longer than expected (.36 coefficient, 2.45 t-test, P ~ .02), and texts from entrepreneurs in relatively open networks containing non-guanxi bridges are 46 percent longer than expected (.39 coefficient, 2.01 t-test, P ~ .05). The strongest effect, by far, is again from respondents in relatively open networks with guanxi bridges—associated with texts 123 percent longer than expected (.80 coefficient, 5.70 t-test, P < .001).[9]

Personal and Business Attributes Are Irrelevant
We used five respondent demographic characteristics as predictors: gender, age, college degree, years of education, income—plus a check on respondent mood (GSS happiness item). Education and income, in particular, are familiar explanatory variables in social science research, but results at the bottom of Table 6.3 show negligible association with complexity. None are relevant to text complexity (1.12 $F_{(6364)}$ summary test statistic for the six predictors, with a .35 probability that all are independent of complexity). The irrelevance of college degree and years of education argues against human capital explanations (1.65 $F_{(2364)}$, P ~ .19).

Of course, by holding constant the volume of a speaker's text, we also hold constant any personal attributes correlated with volume. Better-educated, wealthier, happier entrepreneurs might be more effusive than those who are ignorant, poor, or depressed. There is something to this, but not much. One personal characteristic shows a statistically significant association with text

---

[9] Role relations with guanxi contacts adds nothing to the prediction. Adding to Model M18 multiplexity measured as the portion of guanxi ties that are also family, or classmate, or just friend (Eq. 3, Table 5.9) does not improve the prediction (1.11 t-test, P ~ .27). Adding three measures for each kind of foundation relationship does not improve the prediction (2.08 $F_{(3,364)}$, P ~ .10). In sum, and reassuringly given our findings in Chapter 5, respondent descriptions of guanxi do not reflect underlying role relations with their contacts, just as roles did not predict in the preceding chapter who is and who is not guanxi.

length: Age. Older entrepreneurs give shorter descriptions (-2.59 t-test for age in Model M19, $P \sim .01$).

Similarly, business characteristics are irrelevant to text complexity. Whether entrepreneurs are in manufacturing or information technology, texts are equally complex in both small and large organizations. Text complexity is also independent of returns on assets, and of the three business characteristics previously found to predict success among Chinese business leaders in the same region (Burt and Burzynska, 2017; Burt and Opper, 2017): years since the business was founded, presence of a research and development unit, and whether the founder still runs the business. Entrepreneurs with a research and development unit do offer longer descriptions (3.62 t-test in Model M19), but a summary test for the irrelevance of all seven of the business characteristics fails decisively to reject the null hypothesis (0.23 $F_{(7364)}$ in Model M18, $P \sim .98$).

Predicting the Other Dimension of Speaker Differences

Variation on the vertical axis in Figure 6.2 is less systematic than variation on the horizontal. The .78 R^2 for Model M18 in Table 6.3 drops to .16 when the same 20 variables are used to predict variation on the vertical axis. All but one of the business and personal predictors in Table 6.3 are unrelated to vertical variation. The one is the current asset value: Entrepreneurs higher on the vertical axis tend to run more valuable businesses (2.27 t-test, $P \sim .03$). But there is no significant difference by industry (0.54 t-test), firm size ($-.66$ t-test), or profit (-1.84 t-test for ROA, $P \sim .07$). Scores are slightly higher in Hangzhou (.23 coefficient, 2.88 t-test), but that reflects the effect of a single interviewer. Scores for the other eight interviewers show no difference by interviewers on the vertical axis, regardless of city (1.54 $F_{(7,364)}$, $P \sim .15$), and controlling for interviewer differences eliminates the Hangzhou difference (0.74 t-test, $P \sim .46$). The other six of the seven predictors at the top of Table 6.3—those controlling for guanxi text length and the entrepreneur's network—are unrelated to variation on the vertical axis (1.28 $F_{(6364)}$, $P \sim .26$).

How Words Differ

We know that the length and complexity of respondents' descriptions increase with the complexity of their social network, but so far we know nothing about the words used to describe guanxi. One possibility is that the forty-four categories of words, phrases, and word categories in Figure 6.1 and Table 6.2 are randomly distributed across descriptions in proportion to their prevalence in the population. That statistical possibility would be expected if respondents share one concept of guanxi, but when asked to describe it, draw specific words/phrases at random from a shared pool. The lack of clustering in Figure 6.2 makes it unlikely that different groups hold on to different definitions of guanxi. Still, it remains possible that certain words or phrases appear more often in more complex descriptions—as might happen if specific words only came into play once a description crosses a threshold of detail or sophistication.[10]

Words in Complex Versus Simple Texts

To identify words/phrases/categories associated with text complexity, we use each of the forty-four binary content variables listed in Figure 6.1 and Table 6.2 to predict complexity, holding constant the probability of a content variable being in the text (number of characters in the text and number of the 44 content variables in the text), and controlling for the network complexity around the speaker (network constraint).

Table 6.4 lists the words, phrases and categories most associated with text complexity. These are the nineteen items for which we can reject the no-association null hypothesis beyond a .001 probability (t-test greater than 3.29). The remaining twenty-five items, which would appear in the middle of the table, show weaker or less obvious associations with complexity. Items are listed in order of their test statistic rejecting the null. We refer to the words most strongly associated with complexity as "guanxi words."

Negative coefficients for the first nine items in Table 6.4 show that these items occur in significantly less complex descriptions. For example, when a text contains one or more LIWC emotion words (affective processes), complexity drops by about eight points (−7.98 coefficient, −10.46 t-test,

---

[10] We stay close to the spoken word in comparing texts. Such conservative treatment runs a risk of missing instances in which different categories of words are used to describe the same topic. We looked into topic models, which are less constrained by specific words, and found the analysis useful in reinforcing what we learned from studying word-count profiles, and for identifying particularly good indicator texts, but little new emerged. Still, topic models are a popular strategy within the expanding domain of language analysis, so we include our exploration of the strategy, but out of the main text, in Appendix C. Of course, we would not have confidence in topic modelling corroborating our analysis of word-count profiles if we had not run the topic models.

Table 6.4 Guanxi Words, Phrases, and Word Categories

Coefficient	Test Statistic	N	Word/Phrase/Category
−7.98	−10.46	264	Affective Processes (LIWC)
−8.46	−7.59	45	亲密, Close (guanxi word in Table 6.2)
−6.62	−7.06	72	帮助, Help (guanxi word in Table 6.2)
−6.00	−6.74	85	互相, 相互, Mutual, One Another (guanxi word in Table 6.2)
−5.75	−4.72	297	Social Processes (LIWC)
−7.15	−4.61	23	说话, to speak (guanxi word in Table 6.2)
−9.82	−3.93	9	兄弟, 家人, 亲戚, Family (guanxi word in Table 6.2)
−4.55	−3.91	44	朋友, Friend (guanxi word in Table 6.2)
−5.89	−3.69	22	信任, Trust (guanxi word in Table 6.2)
...	...	...	25 Nondiscriminatory Words/Phrases/Categories (deleted)
3.65	3.66	135	Conjunctions (LIWC)
4.08	3.87	216	Relativity (LIWC)
4.04	4.17	179	Quantity (LIWC)
4.92	4.31	95	是, To be (guanxi word in Table 6.2)
5.63	5.17	141	Informal Language (LIWC)
6.14	6.53	123	人, People (guanxi word in Table 6.2)
9.00	8.04	248	Prepositions (LIWC)
9.34	9.45	198	Pronouns (LIWC)
10.69	10.45	207	Modal words (LIWC)
12.71	12.84	247	Multifunction Words (LIWC)

Note: When these words/phrases/categories are used in a description, language complexity changes by a statistically significant amount (holding constant text length, content categories in text, and network constraint). Rows are ordered by test statistic rejecting null hypothesis (P < .001). N is number of respondents who used the row word/phrase/category.

P < .001). Example descriptions with low complexity scores are listed at the top of Table 6.1. The nine items at the top of Table 6.4 mirror the three qualities most often associated with guanxi in prior research: emotional closeness ("close," "friend"), trust ("trust," "honest language"), and an expectation of support ("help," "mutual," "family"). Most of these are emotion words in the LIWC "affective processes" category.

Positive coefficients at the bottom of Table 6.4 identify items that occur in more complex descriptions. For example, texts containing multifunction words are about thirteen points more complex than texts without them (12.71 coefficient, 12.84 t-test, P < .001). Most of the ten items associated with high complexity relate to sentence structure: conjunctions, quantifying words, prepositions, pronouns, modal particles, and multifunction words. This is no surprise—these categories tend to appear in more complex statements.

The two specific words associated with high complexity are broad references: one to a state (是, "to be") and one to people in general (人, "person"). The latter contrasts directly with the specific role relations—"friend" and various words for family relations—that correlate with low complexity. In other words, more complex descriptions go hand in hand with a broader view of guanxi as embedded in human exchange generally, and not limited to specific types of relations.

The five illustrative high-complexity texts listed in Table 6.1 are not only longer than the low-complexity texts, but they also show more variable structure. Low-complexity descriptions tend to be short phrases. High-complexity descriptions often contain multiple thoughts strung together in run-on sentences—as in the most complex description at the bottom of Table 6.1: "This word is of course familiar, both life and work are inseparable from (it), especially doing business in China is impossible if you do not have connections, (if) you don't have some guanxi which can be used, therefore, guanxi refers to some specific people you know and can use." Note also that four of the five sample texts refer to "people" or "persons" rather than to any specific kind of relation.

In sum, the complex texts contain more ideas and opportunities, but their core content overlaps with that of the low-complexity texts. All sample descriptions refer to closeness, trust, and mutual assistance. Respondents with high-complexity texts just see more variation in finding and experiencing guanxi.

How Words Combine

Our second conclusion from studying the texts concerns how words are combined. Consistent with the image of random draws from a pool of alternative words and phrases, we see that words combine in texts as a function of frequency rather than content. The more often a word is used, the more likely it appears in a complex text. Figure 6.4 is a multidimensional display of word co-occurrence, similar to Figure 5.1 in the previous chapter, which showed kinds of connections occurring within the same relationships. Co-occurrence between the forty-eight words and phrases is well described by the two dimensions in Figure 6.4, which account for 71 percent of the variance in co-occurrence. Two words or categories appear close together to the extent they occur in the same texts. Axis length is proportional to the magnitude of the eigenvector defining it. The horizontal axis is more than twice the vertical, and is strongly correlated with how many entrepreneurs use a given word or phrase (.84 correlation).

Clustering in the space is concentrated on the far right, where we find words and sentence elements used together in complex texts. Note the squares densely packed on the right side—many on top of one another. These are the sentence-structure elements most strongly associated with complexity, as listed at the bottom of Table 6.4. The only individual word that stands out in the right-hand cluster of Figure 6.4 is the abstract reference to "people" (#18), rather than a specific kind of role like friend or family.

Also on the right are the complex texts (above-median complexity) and the very complex texts (top 25 percent). This is where we find texts from entrepreneurs whose networks include bridges beyond the network (item "C" in the figure), and whose strongest guanxi is a bridge relationship (item "D").

Infrequently used words appear on the left side of the space. They do not cluster with one another so much as they are set apart by their failure to mix with the elements on the right. Their lack of clustering is clear from the extensive empty spaces between them. What they represent is a variety of synonyms for the core elements of guanxi—randomly picked as a brief explanation.

This property of randomly drawing from an urn of descriptive words is nicely illustrated by the word "often," which appears in fifty-seven texts that describe frequent contact as a feature of guanxi (item 26 in Table 6.2). The word is useful as an illustration because we have data on how often people actually meet their contacts. "Often" appears near the center of the spatial map in Figure 6.4. The texts in which it appears are slightly more complex and slightly longer than average. Texts without "often" are slightly less complex and shorter than average. The word does not appear in Table 6.4 because it sits in the middle—one of the twenty-five words and phrases that do not discriminate between more and less complex texts.

In fact, in the previous chapter we did not see more frequent communication with guanxi contacts. Communication was neither more, or less, frequent than with other contacts (Table 5.7). We revisit the issue by comparing whether entrepreneurs who use the word "often" interact with their guanxi contacts differently than others. In a regression predicting the

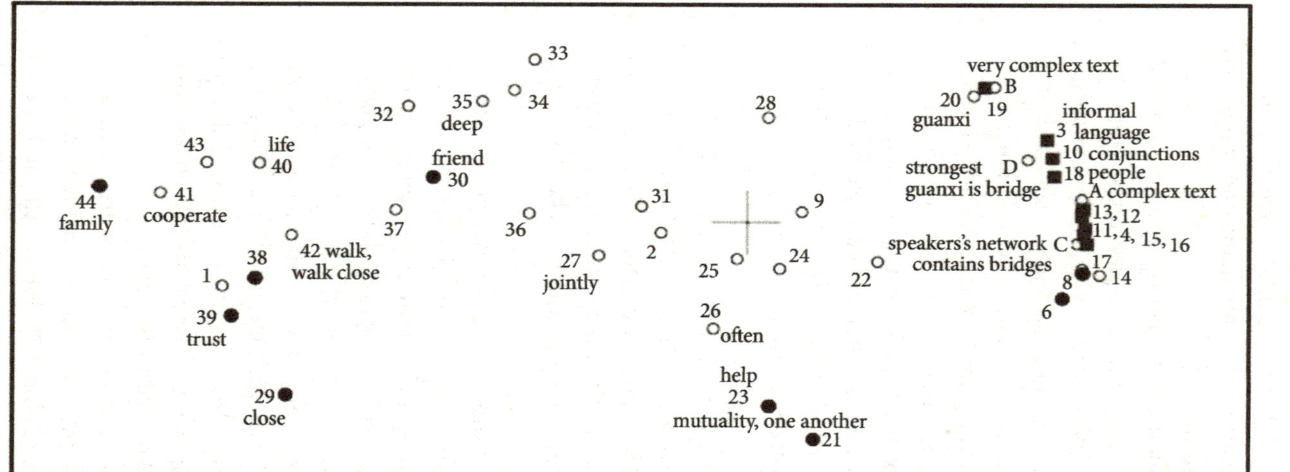

LIWC Categories (Figure 6.1)

1 Biological processes
2 Perceptual processes
3 Informal language
4 Relativity
5 Personal concerns
6 Affective processes
7 Cognitive processes
8 Social processes
9 Negations
10 Conjunctions

11 Quantity
12 Pronouns
13 Interjunctions
14 Adverbs
15 Multifunction words
16 Prepositions
17 Verbs

Words/Phrases (Table 6.2)

18 People
19 To be

20 Guanxi
21 Mutuality, One another
22 Contact
23 Help
24 Future tense
25 Relatively
26 Often
27 Jointly
28 Can
29 Close
30 Friend
31 Time

32 Work
33 Be acquainted
34 You
35 Deep
36 Thing
37 Interest, advantage
38 Speak, language
39 Trust
40 Life
41 Cooperate
42 Walk
43 Me or I

44 Family

Other

A Complex guanxi text

B Very complex text

C Speaker's network contains bridges

D Strongest guanxi in speaker's network is a bridge

Figure 6.4 Co-Occurrence Varies with Frequency, Not Content

Note: Classical multidimensional scaling of Jaccard coefficients measuring co-occurrence of word categories in same guanxi texts. Axis length is proportional to eigenvalue defining it. Cross-hairs mark (0,0) on the axes. Two dimensions describe 71 percent of variance in the forty-eight word categories. First dimension is correlated .84 with use frequency. Solid squares/circles are positive/negative characteristics in Table 6.4

number of days between exchanges, contact frequency does not differ for entrepreneurs who describe guanxi as involving frequent contact.[11] Returns on assets are independent of both mentioning "often" and the actual frequency of contacts.[12] In short, entrepreneurs who mentioned "often" were simply drawing from the urn of colloquial guanxi descriptors—an example pulled at random during the interview.

Frequency of usage again displays a continuous transition from simple to complex texts. Figure 6.5 is a box plot of complexity scores adjusted for the likelihood that one of the forty-four content items appears in a text.[13] Thirty-one respondents use none of the words in Table 6.2, and do not mention any words from the LIWC social category or the LIWC affect category. These are the texts to the far left in Figure 6.5. Complexity is lower in the descriptions from the 127 respondents who mentioned a LIWC social or affect word, but none of the commonly used words. Complexity is lower still in descriptions from the 130 respondents who mentioned one of the commonly used guanxi words. Mentioning just two words is associated with still lower complexity, and mentioning three with the lowest complexity. No explanation contained more than three of these words. The scatter of elements to the far left in the Figure 6.4 space results from infrequent combined use of typical words.

The point in Figure 6.5 is that complexity decreases gradually across the columns. Adjacent boxes overlap along the vertical axis, and there is no sharp drop in complexity when one or more guanxi words appear in a description. Nor did we find any combination of these words associated with a sharp drop in complexity. It is certainly not the case that every text contains the same words. Imagine an urn with balls of different colors, each representing a different aspect of guanxi. In any given discussion, a person draws from the urn to form their description. A random draw might yield a description largely about emotional closeness, or on trust, or some mix of the elements.

[11] For this test, we predict contact frequency (Table 5.7) from three variables: Whether a contact is guanxi, whether the respondent included "often" in his or her guanxi description, and an interaction term for whether guanxi are met more often than non-guanxi. The "often" variable and interaction are independent of contact frequency (1.54 $F_{(2,364)}$, P ~ .21).

[12] For this test, we begin with the five statistically significant predictors of returns on assets from Model M10 in Table 4.4 (two network variables, years to profit, industry, and city) then add two predictors: A binary variable distinguishing entrepreneurs who mention "often" in their guanxi text, and the continuous measure of days between contact. The two added predictors are negligible (0.01 $F_{(2,361)}$, P ~ .99).

[13] We regress raw complexity scores across network constraint, number of characters in a description, and number of the forty-four content categories in the description (17 in Figure 6.1 and 27 in Table 6.2), then compute a residual complexity score. For the zero to 100 metric in Figure 6.5, we normalize the residual scores to vary from zero to 100 (see footnote 6).

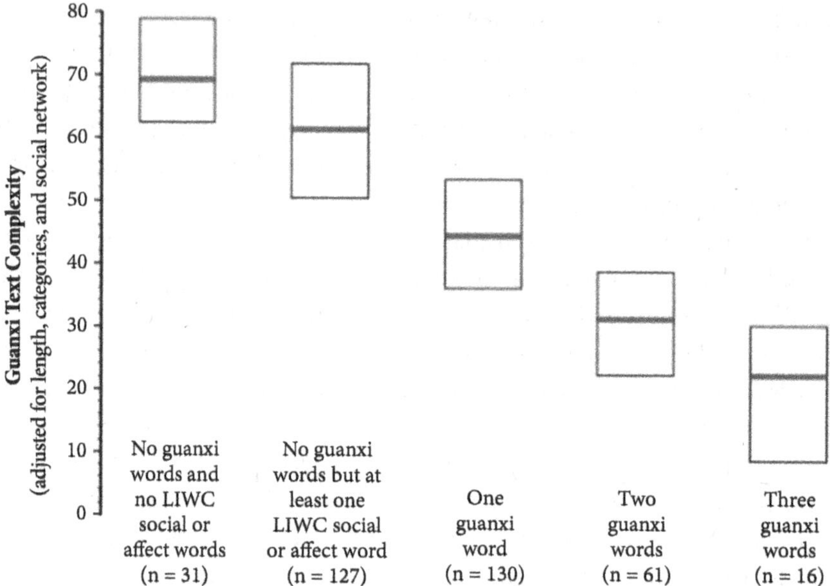

Figure 6.5 Guanxi Words Show Gradual Transition in Complexity

Note: Columns distinguish number of guanxi words in an entrepreneur's description. Vertical axis is text complexity (horizontal axis in Figure 6.2), adjusted for number of characters in description, number of forty-four categories in description, and level of network constraint (see footnote 13). Boxes show interquartile range of complexity in each column of descriptions, 25th percentile, to the mean, to 75th percentile.

But there is no evidence that one group of entrepreneurs draws primarily emotion words while another draws primarily trust words. Different texts contain different words, but whether drawn for a simple phrase or a complex sentence, guanxi is consistently about emotional closeness and trust. We conclude that respondents chose words as substitutable references within a shared understanding—a semantic field—describing what guanxi is.

A Note on Reciprocity

From previous work, much of which is summarized in Bian's (2019) authoritative review, guanxi ties are described as a mix of warmth, obligation, and trust. The sample entrepreneurs, at varying levels of complexity, focus on emotional closeness and trust between people who feel kinship—or pseudo-kinship—with one another. Obligation is not often mentioned.

Some texts stand apart for mentioning obligation. At the bottom center of the spatial map in Figure 6.4 the two words "help" (item 23) and "mutuality" or "one another" (item 21) cluster together. These words occur in less complex texts (negative t-tests in Table 6.4, dark circles in Figure 6.4, two example texts at the top of Table 6.1). When either word appears in a text, that text is less likely to include any of the other words in Table 6.2 (-2.42 test statistic for Poisson regression predicting number of other words, $P \sim .02$)—and especially less likely to include any of the complexity-associated words in Table 6.4 (-3.24 test statistic, $P \sim .001$). Of the 365 texts provided by our sample entrepreneurs, 24 include "help" alone, 37 include "mutuality" alone, and 48 include both as defining qualities to guanxi. In sum, the two words stand together and apart from others in the map—yet together, they are mentioned by a third of the sample (109 of 365), a substantial minority.

It makes sense that obligation stands apart. When asked to describe our relationships, we describe what we know. Ego's view is separate from alter's view. Each view can affect the other, but we can like and trust a person without the other reciprocating. In contrast, obligation involves more symmetry, more reciprocity, especially in the case of guanxi since the obligation is not the kind of short-run obligation familiar in economic exchange: "What is the price to compensate you for your help?" Guanxi is not about the immediate, transactional duties familiar in legal and commercial contexts. It is a social debt—an obligation in exchange where both the timing and kind of reciprocation remain unspecified: "I owe you one." Yang (1994:144) notes the foolishness of repaying such debts too quickly: "Even though one may be in the disadvantageous position of the debtor, the extension of a debt is what one should aim for in the art of guanxi, because a debt keeps a relationship open." I do a favor for you, then you owe me. You later reciprocate with a favor for me, then I owe you. I later do a favor for you … and so on. Yang's text is completely consistent with social exchange theory from Mauss (1925) to Blau (1964; see Ekeh 1974 for broad review). The general rule applies in China as it does in the West: Social standing depends on the repayment of debt. As Lin (2001b:157–158) summarizes (cf. Yang 1994:7–8; Yan 1998:80–91):

> …gestures can never match or be seen as a 'payment' for the favor rendered. They merely reflect deference and gratification on the part of the favor seeker for being granted a favor by the giver. Guanxi does not expect a balance in repeated transactions; in fact, it is built on the assumption that

transactions will always be imbalanced both in each exchange episode and even in the long run. What, then, is the payoff for the favor giver in guanxi?

Proper payback, in fact, takes a form totally detached from the interaction between the two parties. It takes on the form of the favor seeker's spreading the word to others that favors have been rendered by the giver. Public recognition of favors rendered by a giver is the payoff for the giver.

Because of the perpetual asymmetric transactions, imbalance of favors is the perpetual state of guanxi—it is always understood that one party owes another party some favors. Since transactions involve goods different in kind and magnitude, it may also be the case that both parties understand that each owes the other some favors.

Accepting a needed favor, and carrying the debt, serves the same purpose as doing the favor that creates the debt: Guanxi maintenance. In short, guanxi implies reciprocal obligation.

The implicit symmetry, or reciprocity, of guanxi ties is not something we can test directly with our data. We have data only on ego's side of the ego-alter relationship. In our data, guanxi is an invisible quality attributed by ego to a relationship. There can be aspirations for, even expectations of, reciprocity; but whether reciprocity actually exists is an empirical question we cannot answer without alter's view. Knowing that ego sees alter as guanxi need not mean that alter sees ego the same way. The question of reciprocity and its social enforcement, calls for future network research.

We can, however, say something about the people who choose to make help or mutuality explicit in their description of guanxi. The minority who do so are scattered across the population. We used the predictors in Table 6.3 to identify who mentions help or mutuality. None of the individual predictors generates a statistically significant association (strongest is −1.88 jackknife t-test for entrepreneurs with relatively closed networks containing no bridges, P ~ .06), and all twenty predictors together are independent of mentioning help or mutuality (1.38 $F_{(20,364)}$, P ~ .13).

Although entrepreneurs are explicit about help or mutuality existing throughout the population, where they appear, they tend to run less successful businesses. Table 6.5 shows the statistically significant predictors of business success in Chapter 4 (Table 4.4, Model M10)—with one new predictor added in the top row—a binary indicator for entrepreneurs who include help or mutuality in their guanxi text. The earlier predictors remain statistically significant: Structural embedding continues to have a negative association with returns on assets (negative for strongest guanxi embedded

Table 6.5 Mutual Help Explicit in Texts from Heads of Less Successful Businesses

	Coefficient	S.E.	Test Statistic
Includes "help" or "mutual" in guanxi text	−2.97	1.44	2.06
Embedding of strongest guanxi (weighted sum indirect ties)	−3.03	1.29	−2.35
Network constraint (excluding strongest guanxi)	−5.50	1.97	−2.97
Years to firm profitability	−.69	.19	−3.53
IT	4.81	1.40	3.45
Hangzhou	−6.81	1.33	−5.12
Constant	48.23		
R^2	.17		

Note: These are OLS estimates predicting return on assets from statistically significant predictors in Model M10, Table 4.4—with the addition of a binary predictor in the first-row distinguishing entrepreneurs explicit about "help" or "mutual" in their guanxi text. Jackknife standard errors are presented (N = 365).

in third parties and high network constraint). Returns are higher in the IT industry, lower in Hangzhou, and lower for businesses that took longer to become profitable. Holding these factors constant, returns are three points lower for businesses run by entrepreneurs who mention help or mutuality (−2.97 coefficient, −2.06 t-test, P ~ .04). Perhaps the claim expresses a hope that guanxi contacts will feel obligated to help.[14] As Wang et al. (2016:3) point out: "The particularistic relationship between partners is not equal; it is always the weaker side that wants to build a closer relationship through gift-giving in exchange for service."

Robust Hypotheses

Support for our hypotheses is robust to differences in respondent language complexity—though not independent of it. Given the association between text and network complexity described above, some correlation is expected, since our hypotheses use network-complexity variables to predict trust and

---

[14] Our decision here to put "help" and "mutual" aside from emotional closeness and trust as key words for guanxi is reinforced by the topic analysis in Appendix C. The word "help" loads primarily on topic T5 (Table C.1), which is strongly associated with the relatively minor and eclectic vertical axis in Figure 6.2 (Factor 2 in Table C.3). The word "mutual" loads primarily on topic T3 (Table C.1), which is associated with closed networks, a lack of complexity in describing guanxi, and a lack of guanxi bridges (negative correlation with Factor 1 in Table C.3).

economic performance. However, the correlations between text complexity and trust or performance are driven more by text length than by text complexity itself. American managers with larger, more open networks have also been found to use longer texts when pitching ideas (Burt 2010: 262, 2017:425).

With respect to economic performance, return on assets has a positive association with text complexity (Model M19 in Table 6.3), but the association disappears when we control for the number of characters in a speaker's text (Model M18 in the same table). If we replace network constraint with text complexity in our test of the advantage hypothesis (Model M14 in Table 4.5), the coefficient for guanxi bridges has a slightly smaller positive association with performance (6.63 versus the 7.32 in Table 4.5) and a slightly larger standard error (2.69 versus 2.59 in the same table), but the association is still there (2.09 t-test, P < .05). Text complexity is associated with higher economic performance in the prediction (3.38 t-test), but as in Table 6.3, the association disappears when we hold constant text length (1.08 t-test).

Turning to the strong-bridges hypothesis, we get no prediction from text complexity if we add complexity to our tests in Table 4.2 because our tests are estimated with respondent fixed effects to control for differences between respondents in reporting trust. However, if we replace the fixed-effects estimation with each respondent's mean level of trust, and use ordinary least squares estimates with jackknife standard errors, we get about the same R^2 (.41 compared to .45 for Model M4 in Table 4.2), and trust is positively associated with text complexity (4.96 t-test). This is to be expected: More complex texts come from respondents with larger, more open networks (Table 6.3), and people with larger, more open networks display higher trust in people beyond their network (Figure 2.3B). But again, the association is more about text volume than structure: When we add the number of characters to the model, the association between trust and text complexity is negligible (1.91 t-test, P ~ .06). There is some association there, but it is weak, and additional controls for network structure wipe it out (e.g., the 1.91 t-test drops to 0.30 if we add network constraint to the prediction).

Through it all, support for the strong-bridges hypothesis holds. In the prediction above—which includes text complexity, character count, and network constraint—the closure-trust association across routine business contacts is only slightly reduced from Chapter 4 (.94 in Model M4 in Table 4.2 drops to .72, 15.46 t-test). The level adjustment for unexpectedly high trust in guanxi bridges remains stable (.95 becomes .97, 31.65 t-test). The slope adjustment for trust being less dependent on structural embedding is somewhat dampened (−.57 in Model M4 decreases to −.47), but remains a strong effect (−8.14 t-test). In sum, the strong-bridges hypothesis is in effect for all the entrepreneurs, regardless of differences in language complexity and the way people think or talk about guanxi.

Conclusion: Language Complexity Mirrors Network Complexity

To our knowledge, no previous research has had network and language data from a representative sample of business leaders describing guanxi. From this initial study we draw three conclusions (mindful that the language variation we have spans statistically significant differences between Hangzhou and the coastal cities of Shanghai and Ningbo, but is likely not representative of China in general).

First, the guanxi texts vary primarily along a continuum of complexity. Where complexity refers to the number and variety of words in a text, descriptions offered by our sample entrepreneurs do not reveal qualitatively distinct kinds of speakers. Rather they position speakers along a continuum. We see this first in complexity emerging as the main axis of differentiation in language profiles, and in the lack of subgroups in the distribution of complexity (Figure 6.2). We see it again in the way frequently cited keywords appear together. Words co-occur in proportion to their popularity across the sample, consistent with a population urn of guanxi descriptors from which speakers draw at random—with draw probability increasing with word popularity (Figure 6.4 and Figure 6.5).

Second, text complexity varies primarily with the complexity of the speaker's network (Table 6.3). It is largely unrelated to personal characteristics such as age, education, or gender and independent of business characteristics like industry, asset value, firm size, or profitability.

Third, our two hypotheses about strong bridges are robust to language complexity. While it is difficult to test cleanly—given how deeply text complexity is entwined with network structure—our results show that support for both the strong-bridges and advantage hypotheses holds even when controlling for variation in language complexity.

These results secure our hypotheses at the same time that they leave wide open questions for future research. The network correlates of text complexity we have reported make sense in terms of what we know about social networks. Much of communication within dense networks of strongly connected contacts involves shared assumptions and understandings; tacit knowledge, often in the form of jargon (see "Network Context" section in Chapter 2). The fewer and more densely connected the people in a person's network, the more the network is a social straitjacket limiting the person's exposure to diverse opinion and practice. Within a dense network, guanxi's meaning can be taken for granted because it is so similarly understood. People therein experience such relations in a homogeneous way. Alternative definitions are irrelevant to their social experience.

Information diversity is the defining characteristic of the networks associated with text complexity. On average, relatively open networks bridge across social groups, in whatever way those groups are defined by location, affiliation, or practice. When bridges in those networks are guanxi, the network not only bridges group boundaries, but it is a fulcrum for trust across the groups. Each guanxi bridge in a network involves exposure to a close relationship exercised with some other kind of contact. To the extent that our understanding of a kind of relationship varies with the diversity of situations in which we experience it, more complicated, nuanced understandings of guanxi are to be expected from people with guanxi bridge relationships. It is reasonable to conclude that these respondents see, cultivate, maintain, and activate guanxi more broadly and that experience, in turn, fuels more complex, nuanced descriptions of what guanxi is.

Moreover, these are the kinds of strong-bridge relations integral to economic performance, as documented in the preceding two chapters. When an entrepreneur with guanxi bridge relations describes what guanxi means, he or she is describing something central to their success—a topic on which any of us can be eloquent. It is easy to see how a broader search for guanxi could be a success factor. People with a broader understanding of guanxi may recognize it whereas those in closed networks do not. Different levels of complexity can matter. If one person defines guanxi simply as "a very close friend" and another defines it as "a trusted person with whom one can discuss confidential matters," both share a core understanding centered on trust. But the second allows for a broader space in which guanxi can be found.[15] Causality remains elusive. Does a broader and more complex understanding of guanxi encourage the development of strong bridges—or does positive experience with strong bridges broaden one's understanding of guanxi? Either way, the correlation between network and text complexity is an important issue that deserves future attention.

[15] There is more to be done with the language of network brokers. Consider Zhang's (2015) concept of elastic language. Language is elastic to the extent that it is consistent with alternative interpretations. Examples are descriptions that involve words like "approximately," "sometimes," "kind of," "suppose." For the same reason that network brokers are more aware of contrasting views held by contacts in different groups, they can be expected to more often use elastic language acceptable in different groups, and by so doing find more acceptance for their ideas in different groups.

We looked through the guanxi texts for words associated with elastic language. Most guanxi texts contain none (258), some contain one (77), and a few contain more than one (30). Across these three categories, text complexity increases with elastic language (averaging 45, 72, and 82 points across the horizontal in Figure 6.2), and network constraint is lower for speakers who use elastic language (averaging 44, 37, and 36 points). In short, more complex texts tend to contain more elastic language, and network brokers tend to use more elastic language in their more complex texts. Our exploratory measure of elastic language is only a rough indicator based on translations of the Chinese texts into English, and the measure is not as strongly associated with complexity as the variables we discuss in the text (e.g., the three-category measure of elastic words has negligible association with complexity against the controls in Table 6.4 [$-.83$ t-test, P ~ .41]). Nevertheless, text complexity is correlated with the three categories of elastic language (.45) and the continuous measure of network constraint ($-.48$). There is signal there for future research.

7

Strong-Bridge Resilience

With the existence of strong bridges corroborated, we return to our original intuition and ask directly: Are the strong bridges resilient? The familiar closure-trust association discussed in Chapter 2 predicts that trust within a relationship is facilitated when the relationship is embedded in third parties such as mutual friends, shared colleagues, or deference to the same authority. These forms of structural embedding imply shared interests, and create reputation costs for bad behavior. But the closure-trust association simultaneously describes weakness increasing with the lack of structural embedding (Figures 2.3B, 2.4A). By implication, bridge relations are expected to be fragile, not resilient.

Resilience can be conceptualized in more or less sophisticated ways (for a history of research on the subject, see the chapters assembled in Lazega et al. 2022, especially the Introduction). Here is the simplest: A relationship is resilient if it is observed today and observed again in future. Through normal wear and tear, through minor or severe exogenous shocks, resilient relations endure.

A variety of studies show that bridge relations tend not to endure. Bridge relations are more prone to decay (Figure 2.4A), and more likely to be forgotten (Brashears and Quintane 2015). Bridge relations are more likely to disappear in the wake of a natural disaster (Islam and Walkerden 2014), or the imposition of remote work during the COVID pandemic (Yang et al. 2022; Zuzul et al. 2025). Further commenting on the COVID pandemic, Völker (2023:1) summarizes from a Dutch household panel interviewed in 2019 and 2020: "We find that networks become smaller and more focused on stronger ties, while weaker ties more often decayed." Jo et al. (2021) report similar declines in friendship and advice ties. As the closure-trust association says that structural embedding facilitates trust, dissolution of such embedding can erode future cooperation and trust (Samila et al. 2022).

Strong Bridges. Ronald S. Burt and Sonja Opper, Oxford University Press. © Oxford University Press (2026).
DOI: 10.1093/9780197834275.003.0007

For informed counsel on such research, we turn to Fischer and Offer (2020). Drawing on unusually good data (stratified probability samples of older and younger adults in the San Francisco Bay Area) they report results from seven name generators in panel network surveys conducted one year apart. On average, half the contacts cited in the first interview are not cited in the second—a high level of decay consistent with past work (Fischer and Offer 2020: 79). The authors probe reasons for the decay. When a contact from the first interview is missing in the second, respondents are asked (Fischer and Offer 2020:81): "Before finishing our discussion of your social ties, we ask about people you named in the last interview but did not name in this one." For each missing contact (NAME), respondents are asked to choose between reasons why they did not cite NAME in the second survey: "(1) You did mention NAME, but gave a different name [this time]; (2) You just forgot to mention NAME; (3) NAME passed away; (4) There has not been any occasion for you to be in touch; or (5) Your relationship changed." This exceptional information shows far less than 50 percent network change. Fischer and Offer (2020:85) conclude: "...the percentage of truly sundered ties could be as high as 27 percent (all those neither relisted nor forgotten) or as low as four percent (dropped only by death or disagreement) or nine percent (adding in those who 'drifted' away.) . . . If, as we suggested earlier, each [name generator] question prompts a partly random draw from a pool of qualifying ties, then there is greater stability in network membership than previously presumed." And yet, even with greater-than-expected network stability, certain ties are more likely to be dropped: non-kin contacts, and contacts with an unfavorable balance of support and burden. Both qualities likely correlate with structure, but are not a concern in the analysis above.

Returning to our study, informed by the above, the strong bridges in Chapter 4 are with people known for three to fifty-seven years, with a median of fifteen years. Strong ties known for a long time invoke an image of resilience. By resilient, we mean ties that endure regardless of visibility. They may or may not be cited as relevant to current activities, but they are not gone—and they bounce back from exogenous shock. When you turn to them, they are there. The event name generator was key to discovering strong bridges. Four-fifths of the strong bridges were cited in connection with significant events. Half were not cited among currently valued contacts. Here, we make explicit the resilience of strong bridges implicit in earlier chapters.

Three Lines of Attack

To look into resilience, we re-interviewed in 2021 the respondents interviewed in 2018 in the two capital cities: Hangzhou and Shanghai. We began preparations at the end of 2019. By early 2020, preparations were underway as COVID began to surface in Europe and America. As the exogenous shock unfolded and disrupted social life, the case for testing the resilience of strong bridges grew more compelling. Still unaware of the crisis's full scope and severity, we moved forward with equal parts naïveté and optimism. Of course, there were instances of respondent indifference, and businesses gone bankrupt, sold, or shuttered. Still, the field operations did well. Of respondents to the 2018 survey in the two cities, 71 percent were re-interviewed. We describe the 2021 survey in the next section.

Armed with the re-survey data, we take three lines of attack on resilience. We begin by learning where COVID most disrupted each person's network. There are some close friends of our sample entrepreneurs who were severely affected by the disease, but they are a minority. The personal contacts most affected by COVID are rarely met individuals, disconnected from others in the network around the respondent naming them. Stories about how a victim was affected are not about illness so much as damage to business, a shared interest between entrepreneurs. Network brokers are more aware of people affected by the pandemic, but what they know is about distant people. It is the rare respondent who has close, regular contact with the person they cite as a COVID victim. Our conclusion from this first analysis is that COVID is everywhere in the environment, but the severe hardship is typically at or beyond the periphery of our sample entrepreneur networks.

Second, we look for continuing support of the strong-bridges hypothesis. The 2021 survey results show that guanxi during COVID continued to be characterized by high trust independent of network context, but the context eroded: The structural embedding associated with 2018 trust in routine business contacts contributes significantly less to trust in 2021. In essence, trust becomes more personal, less supported by network context.

Third, we look to the resilience of individual relationships. This is difficult, because names and addresses of contacts are unknown. With some considered assumptions, however, we match a large number of contacts. Strong bridges turn out to be resilient. They face a significantly lower risk of tie decay than routine bridges. More than surviving, strong bridges persist as strong bridges. The caveat is that resilience does not imply stasis. Some ties once considered guanxi no longer are. These shifts are not explained by structural embedding. The risk of change is similar for both embedded and bridging ties. What matters is that respondents' trust in these ties shifted during the pandemic, underscoring the purely interpersonal foundation of trust in strong bridges.

Follow-Up Survey in 2021

We briefly introduce our follow-up survey and map how COVID left its mark on respondent networks. For the follow-up survey, we focused on two of the original three cities: Shanghai and Hangzhou. This decision was driven by practical considerations. With headquarters in Shanghai, and long-experienced staff in the Hangzhou branch, our local partner was most able to ensure high-quality execution in these two cities. The ability to rely on long-time interviewers familiar with the project and survey instruments proved critical, as international travel restrictions required that all training and coordination for interviews and data collection be conducted online. Second, as local COVID policies shifted rapidly, rescheduling interviews became the norm rather than the exception, necessitating a team of experienced and trusted on-site personnel. In response, we accepted that the timing of both pilot and main interviews would be determined entirely by national and local COVID protocols. As a result, the survey of returning firms extended from January through December 2021, with the addition of new firms continuing through the winter and into 2022. Two conditions were maintained: All interviews were conducted face-to-face, and no interviews were conducted with anyone less than the general manager or CEO.

Respondents

We began by recruiting respondents who had participated in the 2018 survey. Of the 256 respondents interviewed in Shanghai and Hangzhou in 2018, 181 (71 percent) agreed to participate again, with comparable re-survey rates in Shanghai (69.5 percent) and Hangzhou (71.8 percent).

Fifty-five declined to participate a second time, and twenty invitations went unanswered because the firms were "dormant"—that is, operations had been suspended without formal closure or liquidation (see Zhao and Burt 2018).

A comparison of respondents in 2018 who participated again versus those who did not reveals no substantial differences in network structure. Both re-survey respondents and those who did not participate a second time report on average 7.3 contacts in 2018. The average network constraint is forty among re-survey firms, versus forty-four for the others. The average share of strong bridges is 9.5 percent among re-survey respondents, compared to 6.8 percent. If anything, the data suggests that respondents with slightly more open networks were slightly more likely to participate again. The two groups did not differ in firm success, as measured by average return on assets.

To maintain the original sample size, we added 190 new respondents (90 in Shanghai and 100 in Hangzhou) using the same sampling procedure described in Chapter 4. In all, we have 371 respondents in the 2021 survey.

Survey Instrument

The 2021 questionnaire retained the core name generator questions used in the two previous surveys (see Table 3.1), with three notable changes. First, we dropped item 6 from the earlier surveys, which asked respondents to name a difficult contact. In its place, we introduced two new name generators. Respondents were asked: "Without saying the person's name, fill in the name of the person who is the CCP secretary in your company." Only a few respondents cited a Party secretary in their business (48, 13 percent). We also asked: "Were any of the people you know personally affected by the virus?" Eighty-one people answered "no." That seems unlikely given the pervasive effects of the pandemic, however, closer inspection of the data makes sensible such seemingly implausible isolation. Those 290 (78 percent) who answered "yes" were prompted: "Without giving a person's name, who is the person you know personally who has been most affected by the virus?" This second question was intentionally open-ended, allowing respondents to name either a contact whose health was affected or one who had experienced business consequences. A follow-up question asked how

COVID had affected this person's life. We return to those contacts and their network location shortly to get a better handle on what COVID meant to our respondents.

The survey continued with the name interpreter questions used in the 2018 survey (given in Appendix A) to elicit data on each contact's gender, the substance of the tie (emotional closeness, duration of acquaintance, frequency of contact, trust), and the role through which the contact was known (e.g., family, neighbor, party, childhood, classmate, military, co-worker, or co-member in a business association). As in the prior survey, respondents were asked to rate each contact as "especially close," "distant," or "neither distant nor especially close." Importantly, for the focus on strong bridges and their stability, the guanxi question was repeated exactly.

Contacts

The average respondent in Shanghai and Hangzhou cited 7.26 contacts in 2018, 10.04 in 2021. The increase is equally present for respondents re-interviewed in 2021 and respondents new to the survey (though with 10.5 and 9.6 contacts on average, with a statistically significant difference between resurveyed and new respondents). Respondents were limited by the survey instrument to fourteen contacts in both surveys. With so few people citing a Party secretary, the effective number of name generators are the same for the two surveys. Average numbers of names are similar in the two surveys where the instruments are similar. The questions for event contacts (with probes), most-valued employee, and guanxi give little response flexibility. Accordingly, number of contacts cited on these questions are similar in 2018 and 2021: Respectively, averages of 4.83 versus 5.17 names on events, 2.04 versus 2.11 on guanxi contacts, and one on most-valued employee in both surveys. The most-valued current contacts question asked for three or four names in 2018 (Figure A3, item 5, Appendix A), then four or five names in the 2021 instrument. Accordingly, the question in 2021 elicits an additional contact: an average of 3.54 valued current contacts in 2018 versus 4.92 in 2021.

Unexpected difference came from the final name generator asking for valuable contacts not already cited. After assembling a non-redundant roster of cited contacts, the respondent was asked (Figure A3, item 8, Appendix A): "Is there anyone particularly significant for your business who has not been mentioned?" Additional names could be added up to the interview maximum of fourteen. In 2018, the not-already-cited question seems to have been ignored. Only nine contacts were cited across all respondents. In 2021, the same question elicited names for 562 additional people. We attribute the additional names to field staff responding to our inquiries about why response to the question was so low in 2018.

We cannot be certain that the difference is due solely to interviewer engagement. The shift could also reflect broader contextual change. The pandemic may have changed how people thought about their contacts. With businesses slowing ties, personal ties may have mattered more. That shift could have made it more likely that respondents wanted to add contacts not mentioned earlier, when questions were more narrowly focused on business activities.

We looked into kinds of people added by the not-already-cited question. In a logit equation estimated with respondent fixed effects and jackknife standard errors, the odds of a contact being delayed until the not-already-cited question are most strongly predicted by three variables: (1) the contact is not associated with work (−5.91 t-test for current or former work colleagues), (2) the contact is family (5.10 t-test for family), and (3) the respondent has known the contact for many years (5.10 t-test for log years known). Other roles are independent of appearing on the not-already-cited question (neighbors, party members, classmates, military). As in 2018, family tends not to be cited in 2021 (9 percent of contacts), but if family is cited on the not-already-cited question, it tends to be a woman (two-thirds of family cited on the question are women). Two additional variables have statistically significant associations with contacts named on the not-already-cited question: (4) being especially close to the respondent (2.55 t-test), and (5) being someone the respondent speaks to frequently (2.12 t-test). In other words, these final names are active, meaningful ties in the respondent's current life.

We believe the additional contacts are valuable in the data. Looking over the roster of assembled contacts, respondents answered the not-already-cited question by adding one or two long-term, especially close contacts with whom communication is currently frequent. In the probabilistic draw of contact citing (Fischer and Offer 2020), these final citations didn't come up until the respondent reflected on earlier-named individuals. They might be named sooner in subsequent interviews. Important for this book, the last-named contacts often contain guanxi. Guanxi contacts are no less likely to appear among the added contacts (0.25 t-test in the above logit prediction).

More specifically, 34 percent of the 782 contacts deemed guanxi in 2021 are only named on the not-already-cited question. We return to these ties in a moment.

Where Is COVID in the Network?

We expected disruption from the COVID pandemic. The stringent zero-COVID response in China is well documented. However, regional implementation varied considerably in response to local infection rates. There is clear contrast between our two 2021 study sites, which are separated by only 100 miles. To get a better sense of these regulatory differences, we calculated the cumulative number of months that a respondent's district had been subject to stringent lockdown policies at the time of the interview.[1] Shanghai was repeatedly designated a "lockdown closed area" (封控区) for extended periods. This designation represented the most severe policy response, involving temporary home confinement, regular testing, and intensive monitoring, including patrols and surveillance. By the time interviews could be scheduled in Shanghai, respondents had experienced closed confinement for periods ranging from 1 to 8 months, with interruptions averaging 3.5 months. In contrast, Hangzhou was classified only as a "lockdown prevention area" (管控区), a designation involving relatively mild restrictions, comparable to those implemented in Western contexts. These included controlled intra-area movement and social distancing, but no general suspension of business operations.

Locating COVID Contacts

Our data are not about regions or even districts; they are about the personal networks of individual entrepreneurs. Many suffered under COVID, but there are also individuals who prospered by shifting their business to items

---

[1] Information on district level COVID policies was collected from municipal Shanghai Health Commission Website and Shanghai Release WeChat Official Account. Information on district level COVID policies for Hangzhou was collected at Hangzhou Health Commission Website and Hangzhou Release WeChat Official Account. In Shanghai and Hangzhou, our resurvey respondents are located in eleven different districts respectively. For Shanghai, these are: Baoshan, Changning, Fengxian, Huangpu, Jiading, Jinshan, Minhang, Pudong, Qingpu, Songjiang and Yangpu. For Hangzhou, they include Binjiang, Fuyang, Gongshu, Jianggan, Shangcheng, Tonglu, Xiacheng, Xiaoshan, Xihu, Yuhang and the Technology Zone.

for which COVID increased demand, like surgical masks. To get a handle on individual variations, we turn to the identity and network location of the contacts, respondents had named as the one most severely affected contact they know personally.

First, as might be expected from accurate reporting, entrepreneurs less exposed to lockdown are less likely to cite a personal contact affected by COVID. In the less-affected Hangzhou, 27 percent of respondents did not cite a personal contact affected. In the more-affected Shanghai, the percentage takes a statistically significant drop to 16 percent (6.43 chi-square, P ~ .01). The city difference becomes even stronger when months of lockdown are held constant, since local areas within each city varied in exposure (3.28 t-test for Shanghai, P < .001). More relevant to this study, entrepreneurs operating in closed networks are less likely to be aware. The networks around respondents aware of a personal contact severely affected by COVID are relatively open (29.65 mean network density, 32.18 mean network constraint). The networks around entrepreneurs who are unaware are relatively closed: Mean density and constraint for respondents who do not name a personal contact affected by COVID are 46.52 and 39.38 (respective t-tests of 8.51 and 9.01, P < .001).

Table 7.1 shows networks absorbing shocks. The logit model predicts which contacts respondents cited as most severely affected COVID victims.[2] The first two rows report area controls for exposure to disruption. Respondents in harder-hit areas were more likely to name someone severely affected. Controlling for city, the second row shows that each additional month of lockdown significantly raised the odds that a respondent cited a personal contact affected.

With city and local area held constant, the other rows in the table describe kinds of contacts cited as COVID victims. The point established in the third and fourth rows of the table is that the cited COVID victims are often isolated from the rest of the network. Figure 7.1 is a visual display of the COVID association with tie strength and structural embedding. Embedding varies on the horizontal axis measured by mutual friends with the respondent; none, one, two, and so on. This is the axis used in Chapters 4 and 5 to

---

[2] We have a stratified probability sample of respondents, so we treat the 3726 contacts they cite as a probability sample of contacts. This means we include contacts in Table 7.1 who are not cited because the respondent citing them did not cite a COVID victim. Fortunately, we get the same pattern of results if we limit Table 7.1 to the 2976 contacts cited by the 290 respondents who did cite a personal contact affected by COVID.

Table 7.1 Who Gets Cited as a COVID Victim?

	Coefficient	S.E.	t-test
Cited by a Hangzhou (vs. Shanghai) entrepreneur	.42	.22	1.91
Months respondent's district in lockdown (footnote 2)	.07	.03	2.63**
Structural Embedding (see Figure 7.1)			
Bridge (no mutual contacts of any strength)	.85	.25	3.46***
Log weighted strength of indirect connection (Eq. 2)	−.06	.23	−.27
Contact frequency			
Daily (reference category)	—	—	—
Weekly	.56	.43	1.30
Monthly	.81	.46	1.81
Less than monthly	1.36	.46	3.04***
Emotional closeness			
Less than close (reference category)	—	—	—
Close	−.03	.21	−0.13
Especially close	−.43	.28	−1.55
Cited as an event contact	−3.16	.29	−10.85***
Cited as most valued contact	−2.87	.28	−10.12***
Years known	−.03	.02	−1.06
Family	−.58	.35	−1.64
Colleague, current	−1.17	.31	−3.77***
Colleague, previous	−1.23	.27	−4.56***

Note: These are logit regression results predicting which of the 3726 contacts are among the 290 cited on the COVID name generator (jackknife standard errors −1.37 intercept, .38 R^2). Descriptive statistics are given in Table B.10, Appendix B.
* P < .05, ** P < .01, *** P < .001.

display variation in structural embedding. The vertical axis in Figure 7.1 is the proportion of contacts cited as a COVID victim. The bars show a non-linear, negative association: The more deeply a contact is embedded in a respondent's network, the less likely the contact is the cited COVID victim.[3] At every level of structural embedding, there are contacts especially close

---

[3] This holds whether or not the respondent claimed that his or her own business was affected. We asked respondents whether the pandemic had affected their business in terms of business mission, restructuring, merger, scale of production, or outsourcing. A little over half said it had affected their business, with manufacturing business more likely affected than IT. We added that dummy variable to Table 7.1 as a direct effect and interaction with the two structural embedding predictors. All three are negligible (0.93 $F_{(33,725)}$, P ~ .42).

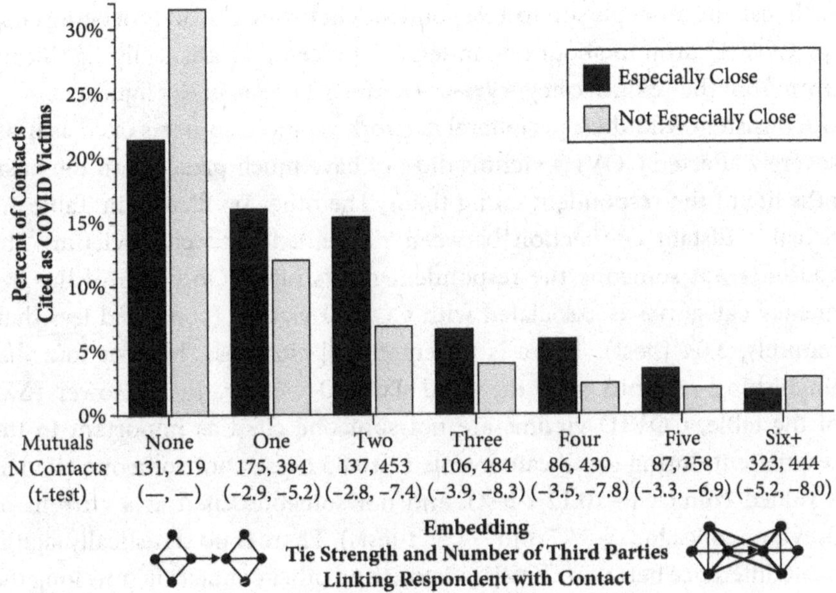

Figure 7.1 Contacts Cited for COVID Are Separate from Other Contacts

Note: These are the 3726 contacts cited in 2021 varying across levels of tie strength and structural embedding. Vertical axis is the percent of contacts at each level cited in response to the COVID name generator. Parentheses contain t-tests (jackknife standard errors) for COVID at each level relative to bridge relations ("None" categories, far left), which here are relations free of any mutual contacts within the cited network.

to the respondent and less close, but the difference is negligible relative to structural embedding.[4]

The visible association between COVID victim and structural embedding in Figure 7.1 is absent in the Table 7.1 logit model (−.27 t-test, P ~ .79). The difference between table and figure is due to the "None" categories, which is why we specify the association the way we do in the table. Contacts in the "None" categories to the far left in the figure have no connection at all with the other cited people in the respondent's network. One in four (28 percent) of these people are cited as personal contacts affected by COVID. Their tendency to be cited for COVID is the primary association between network and citation (3.46 t-test in the table, P < .001). If a cited person is connected

---

[4] Across the 3,726 cited contacts, a logit model predicting COVID citation from the categories in Figure 7.1 yields a −14.83 t-test for association with structural embedding (P < .001), and a 1.38 t-test for association with especially close contacts (P ~ .17). In Table 7.1, the categories of emotional closeness are negligible predictors (1.98 $F_{(23,725)}$, P ~ .14).

with just one other person in a respondent's network, the odds of being cited for COVID drop to about one in ten (13 percent, a statistically significant drop from the "None" category; −2.9 and −5.2 t-tests in the figure) .

Consistent with their peripheral network position, contacts cited as most severely affected COVID victims did not have much presence in the business life of the respondent citing them. The other predictors in Table 7.1 reveal a distant connection between respondent and cited victim. The victim is not someone the respondent meets often. Only one of the frequency categories is associated with COVID victims (contacted less than monthly, 3.04 t-test). There is no emotional closeness, high or low, distinguishing relations with the cited COVID victims. In the lower rows of the table, COVID victims are not someone cited as important to the respondent during significant events (−10.85 t-test), not someone cited as a valued contact (−10.12 t-test), and not someone cited as a current or previous colleague (−3.77 and −4.56 t-tests). There is no statistically significant difference between COVID victims and other contacts in how long the respondent has known them (−1.06 t-test) or whether the contact is family (−1.64 t-test).[5] In sum, the people cited as personal contacts most severely affected by COVID tend to be contacts at or beyond the edge of the network around a respondent. They are not central players in the respondent's world. They are reminders of how bad the impact could be.

How Was the Cited COVID Contact Affected?

Table 7.2 breaks down how respondents described the impact of COVID on the contact they named as most affected. The table excludes the eighty-one entrepreneurs who did not cite a COVID contact. The columns distinguish who was affected: the contact's business or family. Some stories were about personal consequences for the contact or the contact's family. Most stories (70 percent) concerned the contact's business.

Rows in Table 7.2 distinguish a range of disruptions—from illness and death to stories about how COVID quarantine affected the contact's business. A substantial minority of stories focused on COVID as a serious disease and its health consequences. In the second row, those stories escalate to fatal outcomes. One entrepreneur cited a supplier who died from the

---

[5] We suspect that family members who are cited are more distant relatives since COVID victims generally are not especially close to the respondent, met rarely by the respondent, and not cited as important or valued for the respondent's business.

Table 7.2 Who and What in COVID Stories

	Contact's Business Was Affected	Contact's Family Was Affected	Total
COVID is a serious disease	3 (15.0)	17 (85.0)	20 (100%)
COVID resulted in deaths	2 (8.3)	22 (91.7)	24 (100%)
Quarantine had positive effects	5 (100)	0 (0)	5 (100%)
Quarantine had negative effects	193 (80.1)	48 (19.9)	241 (100%)
Total	203 (70.0)	87 (30.0)	290 (100%)

Note: These are the 290 explanations given for how a personal contact was affected by COVID pandemic. The other eighty-one respondents did not have a personal contact affected.

disease, but most death-related stories involved the contact's family members (92 percent). The majority of stories, however, were not about the disease itself, but about the quarantine imposed to contain it—246 of the 290 total (85 percent). Most of the quarantine stories centered on the contact's business (198 of 246, 80 percent). A handful describe positive outcomes, like rising online sales, or a well-timed investment in a mask factory. But aside from those few, the typical quarantine story was negative. Some stories touched on family disruptions—feelings of depression, boredom, and the toll of immobility. But by far the most common theme was the economic damage to business. The lower-left cell of Table 7.2 holds the largest share: 193 stories describe business setbacks ranging from staff being locked out and factory shutdowns to stalled custom processing, collapsed demand, and a lingering recession.

Social Function of the COVID Victim

The situation of our sample entrepreneurs during the pandemic involved fear and an acutely felt loss of control. Lockdowns loomed large, imposed unpredictably by authorities. Disease roamed through colleagues, friends, and neighbors. People were dying. In response, one can find community by sharing stories about whatever fragments of experience one has to affirm the common fate of speaker and audience.

Our conclusion from the results in this section is that stories about COVID victims served such a function: The personal contacts named as COVID victims are rarely seen individuals, disconnected from people in the network around the respondent naming them (Figure 7.1, Table 7.1). The gist of the stories is: "I know a person seriously affected by events around COVID." Most stories describe damage to business—a core topic among entrepreneurs. One has the image of entrepreneurs sharing such stories to the accompaniment of bobbing heads visually expressing agreement, "Yes, that's the way of it."[6] Network brokers appear more aware of people affected by the pandemic, but what they know is about people on the periphery. Few respondents have close, regular contact with the person they cite as a COVID victim.

Erosion of Closure-Trust Association

Opportunities for informal exchange with business friends and casual acquaintances declined sharply during the COVID pandemic. Business meals, late-night entertainment, KTV sessions, drinking rituals, mutual visits, and business travel—the informal infrastructure of trust—were disabled by the state's zero-COVID policy. These settings for maintaining closure and reaffirming community disappeared for extended periods. As these exchanges disappeared, so did the trust they supported. Structural embedding that predicted trust in routine business contacts in 2018 had weaker effects in 2021. Trust became more personal, less grounded in network position—more reliant on guanxi.

The point is illustrated in Figure 7.2. The graphs match the initial display in Chapter 4 with Figure 7.2A identical to Figure 4.4B for easy comparison. The vertical axis tracks respondent trust in a contact, measured on a five-point scale. The horizontal axis captures structural embedding, measured by the number of cited contacts connected to both respondent and target contact. Averages are plotted for three categories of relationships: strongest guanxi (solid line through solid dots), almost as strong guanxi

---

[6] Consistent with this image of COVID stories patterned by mutual interests of speaker and audience, respondents whose own business has been affected by COVID are more likely to cite a COVID victim whose business was also affected. They are particularly likely to tell a negative quarantine story about their cited COVID victim (3.30 test statistic, $P \leq .001$), and the story is unlikely to mention family (-2.17 test statistic, $P \sim .03$).

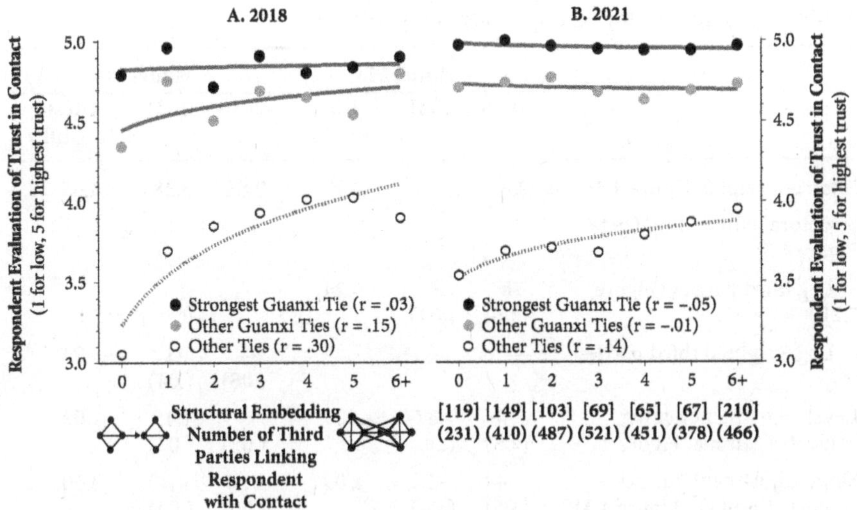

Figure 7.2 Closure-Trust Association in 2018 and 2021

Note: Dots are average Y scores at each level of X. Left graph describes relations with 2702 contacts cited in 2018 by 384 respondents, taken from Figure 4.4B. Right graph describes relations with 3726 contacts cited in 2021 by 371 respondents. Vertical axis is respondent trust, measured on a five-point scale. Horizontal axis is the number of other people in a respondent's network connected with the contact being evaluated for trust. Correlations are computed between trust and log (number of third parties) across all relations. Frequencies below each level of third-party connection show number of (guanxi ties) and (other ties) in 2021.

(solid line through light shaded dots), and other relationships (dashed line through hollow dots).

The strong-bridges hypothesis is supported by the solid lines at the top of each graph. Trust is consistently high for guanxi ties across levels of structural embedding, from bridges (to the left) to deeply embedded relations (to the right). Support for the strong-bridges hypothesis is strong in 2018 and in 2021. If anything, it is even stronger during COVID in that solid lines in Figure 7.2B are higher and flatter than the corresponding lines in Figure 7.2A.

Erosion of the closure-trust association is illustrated by the dashed lines. Both lines slope up, showing higher trust with more structural embedding. But the dashed line in 2018 is much steeper than in 2021. Trust during COVID does not vary as closely with structural embedding as it did before COVID.

The statements illustrated in Figure 7.2 are grounded in the Table 7.3 statistical results. The results for 2018 are from Table 4.2. Model M3 in Table 4.2

Table 7.3 Estimates for Strong-Bridges Hypothesis

	Model M3			Model M4		
	2018	2021	t-test (no diff.)	2018	2021	t-test (no diff.)
Intercept (alpha, Figure 4.3)	2.84	3.55	4.19	2.85	3.38	4.65
Structural embedding (beta, Figure 4.3)						
Log third parties (Figure 7.2B)	.78 (.06)	.16 (.04)	−5.24	—	—	
Log weighted third parties	—	—		.94 (.08)	.41 (.04)	−5.94
Level adjustment guanxi contacts (gamma, Figure 4.3)	1.48 (.08)	1.37 (.06)	−.52	.95 (.03)	1.45 (.05)	−1.02
Slope adjustment guanxi contacts (lambda, Figure 4.3)	−.44 (.06)	−.22 (.04)	2.09	−.57 (.06)	−.40 (.04)	3.50
R^2	.43	.44		.45	.46	

Note: These are OLS results predicting trust in cited contacts measured on a five-point scale (Figure 7.2). Estimates for 2018 are taken from Table 4.2. Estimates for 2021 are computed across the 3726 cited contacts (and include respondent fixed effects and jackknife standard errors). Descriptive statistics for 2021 are given in Table B.11, Appendix B. Excluding the t-tests for difference between the two points in time, all coefficients reject the null hypothesis beyond a .001 level of confidence.

uses a count of third parties to measure structural embedding. Model M4 uses a weighted strength of indirect connection (Eq. 2 in Chapter 4). The results for 2021 are estimated in the same way using the 2021 survey data (and we get the same pattern of estimates if we exclude the additional contacts cited in 2021 in response to the not-already-cited name generator).[7] Similar levels of trust variance are described by the model in 2018 and 2021 (bottom row in Table 7.3).

The intercept terms (first row in Table 7.3) show that respondents are reporting trust scores about half an interval higher during COVID (e.g., 3.38 in 2021 versus 2.85 in 2018). The difference is statistically significant, and

[7] Excluding the 562 contacts cited only on the not-already-cited name generator, yields for Model M3 an intercept of 3.36, a statistically significant estimate of .27 for beta (7.16 t-test) smaller than the .78 estimate in 2018, a statistically significant estimate of 1.49 for gamma (22.18 t-test) about the same magnitude as the 1.48 estimate in 2018, and a statistically significant estimate of −.28 for the guanxi slope adjustment (−6.44 t-test) that describes the near-zero slope of the solid lines in Figure 7.2B. The three effect estimates are the same when estimated with structural embedding measured by weighted indirect connection, except they reject the null hypothesis more strongly (10.97, 27.34, and −8.92 t-tests respectively).

perhaps interesting as an expression of hope that contacts are as trustworthy as rated, but the strong-bridges hypothesis makes no statement about the intercept.

Erosion of the closure-trust association is shown in the second and third rows of Table 7.3. These are slopes for the dashed lines in Figure 7.2. The slope for the dashed line in Figure 7.2A (when estimated through dyads instead of the aggregate values in the graph) is .78 with a standard error of .06, which together define a statistically significant positive association between trust and structural embedding (13.51 t-test, P < .001). The same is true for results corresponding to the dashed line in Figure 7.2B during COVID: .16 coefficient with .04 standard error (4.62 t-test, P < .001). As in Chapter 4, larger estimates of beta occur when structural embedding is measured as the weighted indirect connection through mutual friends (Model M4 in Table 7.3, t-tests of 15.30 and 9.48 for 2018 and 2021, respectively).

Although there is a statistically significant association between closure and trust in both 2018 and 2021, they occur with a substantial difference in magnitude of association. As the dashed line is flatter in Figure 7.2B during COVID than it is in Figure 7.2A for 2018, the estimates of beta are .78 and .94 in 2018, but much lower in 2021: .16 and .41. The drop in magnitude is statistically significant.[8] Thus, we conclude that structural embedding provides less security during COVID.

In contrast, trust in guanxi contacts is similarly high in 2018 and 2021. This is shown in the fourth row of Table 7.3. These gamma coefficients show the magnitude by which trust within a guanxi bridge exceeds trust within a routine bridge. All four coefficients are well above zero (e.g., 1.37 with a .06 standard error in Model M3 during COVID, 24.27 t-test, P < .001). There is no significant difference between coefficients for 2018 and 2021 (t-tests of −.52 and −1.02 respectively, P > .30). In short, guanxi provides similarly strong bridges before and during COVID.

The fifth row in Table 7.3 contains slope adjustments for trust in guanxi as structural embedding increases. The lambda coefficients are all statistically significant, showing that trust in guanxi contacts is less dependent on structural embedding than is trust in other contacts. The slope adjustments are less negative in 2021 because structural embedding provides less security in

---

[8] The drop from .78 to .16 generates a −5.24 t-test in Table 7.3. The drop from .94 to .41 generates a −5.94 t-test. These jackknife t-tests were obtained by adding to the prediction an interaction term between structural embedding and time to test the statistical significance of the drop in beta magnitude.

2021. In Model M3, a .78 estimate of beta in 2018 is corrected by a −.44 slope adjustment to describe the solid lines in Figure 7.2A as less steeply sloped than the dashed line. In 2021, the .16 smaller estimate of beta is entirely eliminated by a −.22 slope adjustment to describe the flat solid lines at the top of Figure 7.2B.

The comparison between two points in time does not support a causal claim. But we can note that the results are consistent with our argument. If trust in ordinary business contacts depends on structural embedding, then the effect may weaken when social gatherings and personal interactions are restricted. If, on the other hand, trust is largely independent of structural embedding—as appears to be the case with guanxi ties—then limitations on social life experienced during the pandemic matter less. Again, we are not using the displayed patterns to claim causality, but it is worth pointing out that the observed shift in respondent trust aligns with the distinction we draw.

Bridge Resilience

Now to the resilience of individual relationships. Matching contacts named in both the 2018 and 2021 surveys is complicated by the confidentiality we promised respondents. Entrepreneurs are generally unwilling to disclose identifying information on their most valuable business contacts, making anonymous reporting a preferred method for studying the networks around entrepreneurs. With some considered assumptions, however, we can match a large number of contacts. The results lead us to conclude that strong bridges are resilient. We begin with making matches.

Matching Contacts Across Surveys

For respondents with whom we conducted a follow-up interview, we have the same person in the same role naming contacts who have been, or are, important to the respondent. We do not know contact names or addresses, but we do have limited identifying data on the contacts.

Gender Score
We used a hierarchical decision rule to match contacts across surveys. We started with gender, which has a high likelihood of stability between 2018

and 2021. Gender only offers coarse matching since many contacts can be the same gender, but it is a start. Contacts without a gender match were immediately excluded—a contact who is male in 2018 is not the same person as a contact who is female in 2021.

Duration Score

We then looked at how long the respondent knew a contact. Depending on the exact interview date, reported length of acquaintance should differ by three to four years (2018 to 2021). However, time recall is fraught with inaccuracy, and respondents often round to salient numbers (e.g., 5, 10, 15, or 20 years). We coded a difference of three to four years as an exact match (1.0). Larger discrepancies (two or five years), were treated as near matches (.75 score). Contacts showing larger discrepancies were excluded from further matching analysis.

Role Score

We then looked at the respondent's role relationship(s) with a contact. A family member known for five years in 2018 is likely the same family member known for eight years in 2021. Roles are more subject to changes inconsistent across respondents (relative to gender or years known), so role-match served as a third level of refinement. Family is usually cited as family, and neighbor as neighbor, but neighbor is more optional, more likely to be skipped if multiple roles apply and the respondent is tired or distracted. Further, a contact cited as a neighbor in one survey might not be cited as such in the other survey, because the neighbor is now considered a friend. We took a conservative approach: we calculated the percentage of roles recorded in 2021 that were also recorded for the same contact in 2018. For the 83 percent of cited contacts that only received one role label in 2021, it had to be identical to the one used in 2018. For multiple roles, we calculated retention. If a contact had four roles in 2021 (e.g., family, neighbor, employee, and other), and three of those matched roles recorded in 2018, we coded a retention rate of 75 percent. Retention rates of 75 percent or higher were classified as high similarity (1.0); rates from 50 percent to 74 percent as medium similarity (0.75); and rates below 50 percent as low similarity (0.5).

Citation Score

As a final criterion—less certain than the above and so kept for last—we looked at the order in which a contact was cited. Within a survey, citation order is a strong predictor of strength of tie, which is our dependent variable in this exercise. Contacts cited earlier within a roster tend to be stronger connections than contacts cited later. It is natural for narratives around the importance of events (as reflected in the first six name generator questions) and the sequence of currently valued employees to shift over time; however, large deviations are less common. We coded identical citation order and differences of ±3 positions as a high match (1.0). All other cases were coded as medium similarity (0.75). For example, if a contact was cited as the second alter in 2018 and as the fourth in 2021, the case qualifies as a high match; if the same contact appeared as the sixth, it was coded as medium. Building on these matching scores, we turned to defining who is the same as whom.

Making Matches

Reflecting greater natural volatility in the role and citation scores, we constructed a summary index for each same-gender pair that assigns 50 percent weight to the length score, 30 percent to the role score, and 20 percent to the citation score. Applying this procedure, 432 of the 1313 contacts listed by the 181 re-surveyed respondents in Shanghai and Hangzhou yielded exactly one possible match in the 2021 survey, with an average accuracy score of 0.86 (on a scale from 0 to 1). An additional 560 contacts resembled two contacts listed in 2021, with an average match probability of 0.83. In these cases, we selected the contact with the highest probability, ensuring that no alter cited in 2021 was matched to more than one contact from 2018. This process produced a total of 622 matches between 2018 and 2021. With 622 out of 1313 contacts cited again, the resulting "survival rate" of 47 percent resembles results from past research (multiple studies compared in Fischer and Offer 2020: 79).

The average accuracy index across all matches is 0.9, with 244 of the 622 matches—nearly 40 percent—achieving a perfect score of 1.0. As a reminder, a score of 0.875 could result from a perfect role score and citation score, combined with a reported contact duration of five years instead of the expected three to four years. Such minor deviations were most common in the set of cited social roles, typically involving one mismatched or missing role (41 percent), followed by contact duration differences of two or five years (24 percent), and least common in citation order (under 20 percent).

Given an average accuracy of 0.9, we are reasonably confident that the procedure errs on the side of caution. Nevertheless, in the analyses that follow, we subject each result to additional scrutiny using the subsample of 244 contacts with a perfect accuracy score.

Guanxi Stability

Our discussion of guanxi as a relationship from which strong bridges emerge implies stability and resilience. If that is the case, contacts cited as guanxi in 2018 should be more likely than other contacts to be cited again as guanxi in the 2021 survey.

In fact, guanxi do tend to continue as guanxi. Of the 622 relations with matched contacts, 424 are routine relations in the sense that the contacts were not cited as guanxi in 2018. The survey was not an inventory of guanxi. Some guanxi can easily be overlooked in any one interview. Of the 424 relations cited as routine in 2018, one in ten is cited as guanxi in 2021 (11 percent). Those odds are much higher—one in two—if a contact was cited as guanxi in 2018 (55 percent). Not surprisingly, the logit regression coefficient in the first column of Table 7.4 shows that guanxi in 2018 is a good predictor of guanxi in 2021 (10.78 t-test, P < .001). The 2.28 coefficient says that the odds of a 2018 guanxi relationship being cited as guanxi in 2021 are 9.76 times higher than the odds of a routine relationship emerging as guanxi. If we limit the data to perfect matches (1.0 matching score), the tendency for guanxi to be re-cited as guanxi is more pronounced: Three out of four 2018 guanxi relations with contacts perfectly matched in 2021 are re-cited as guanxi in 2021 (75 percent, reflected in the Table 7.4 logit coefficient increasing from the 2.28 coefficient in the first column to a 2.82 coefficient in the second column).

The third column in Table 7.4 includes controls for possible confounding factors. The most important point is that the tendency for guanxi to continue as guanxi is the dominant association in the table. The association is statistically significant (8.28 t-test, P < .001), and the coefficient is only slightly lower than in the first column, where controls are ignored (2.28 coefficient lowers to 1.99).

We note three points about the controls. First, structural embedding is irrelevant to the prediction. The second row in Table 7.4 shows no association with the continuous measure of structural embedding (−1.07 t-test), and we get a similar result if we use number of mutual friends to measure embedding (−1.06 t-test). These are the measures used in Chapter 4 to test the strong-bridges hypothesis (e.g., second and third rows in Table 4.2). We also checked for an interaction effect by which structural embedding would increase the stability of guanxi continuing as guanxi. The interaction effect is

Table 7.4 Are Guanxi Resilient?

	All Matched Contacts (n = 622)	High-Match Contacts (n = 244)	All Matched, With Controls (n = 622)
Guanxi in 2018	2.28***	2.82***	1.99***
	(10.78)	(8.47)	(8.28)
Structural embedding			−.21
			(−1.07)
Contact is family			1.29**
			(2.82)
Contact is just friend			.33
			(0.86)
Contact is classmate			.79*
			(2.26)
Contact reached via multiple communication channels			.19
			(1.44)
IT industry			.23
			(1.05)
Hangzhou			−.65
			(−1.28)
Months of lockdown			−.25*
			(−2.02)
Intercept	−2.08	−1.75	−1.97
Pseudo R^2	.19	.28	.23

Note: Estimates are from a logit model predicting which of 622 contacts matched across surveys in 2018 and 2021 are cited as guanxi in 2021 (jackknife t-tests in parentheses). Structural embedding is log of indirect connection from respondent to contact. High-match contacts are contacts who match perfectly on all factors considered. Third column includes respondent random effects (pseudo R^2 is without random effects). Descriptive statistics are in Table B.12, Appendix B.
*P < .05, **P < .01, ***P < .001.

negligible (−.99 t-test, P ~ .33). In short, guanxi tends to continue as guanxi regardless of the connected people having mutual friends.

Second, we tested for the stabilizing effect of the foundation relations found in Chapter 5 to be likely places where guanxi develops. For example, family increases the odds of a contact being cited as guanxi in 2021, regardless of the contact being cited as guanxi in 2018 (2.82 t-test, P < .01). The key question here is whether guanxi continues as guanxi regardless of family, just friends, classmates, or number of communication channels. The 8.28 t-test in the first row of the third column shows that it does.

Finally, we tested against some basic environmental conditions. Industry and city do not matter in the prediction, but entrepreneurs in areas under more extensive COVID lockdown were less likely to cite guanxi in 2021 (-2.02 t-test, P $\sim$ .05). We tested for an interaction effect on former guanxi being cited again as guanxi, but the interaction effect is negligible (-1.01 t-test, P $\sim$ .31).

Resilience Is Not Stasis: The Case of Demoted Guanxi

If resilience is expected, why are nearly half (89 of 198) of former guanxi not still guanxi in 2021? It is tempting to attribute the missing guanxi citations to limited opportunities for social exchange during the pandemic, but the contact-frequency data suggest otherwise. Among the eighty-nine contacts no longer classified as guanxi, respondents communicate with 55 percent daily or weekly. Only 10 percent were contacted less than once a month, compared to 6 percent of newly added guanxi.

One explanation is measurement error. As in any network survey, some omissions reflect respondent inattention, that is, guanxi ties simply overlooked in the 2021 interview. If so, these contacts would still be highly trusted and valued contacts, but not recited as guanxi.

An alternative explanation concerns eroded trust. Guanxi are closely associated with a high level of trust. If trust in a contact has been damaged in some way, we would expect the contact to no longer be viewed as guanxi.

The trust explanation seems more likely. Figure 7.3 shows how trust drops in contacts demoted from guanxi. Former guanxi are sorted on the horizontal axis by change in trust from 2018 to 2021. Change ranges from a decrease of two points on the five-point trust scale up to an increase of one point. (The high mean level of trust in these key contacts leaves more room to lose trust than to increase it.) At each level of trust change in the graph, the vertical axis shows the percent of contacts demoted from guanxi to routine contact.

The association is clear. Of the contacts in whom trust dropped the most, all former guanxi are demoted to routine contacts. Among the fifty-one contacts whose trust scores dropped by one point, 86 percent are no longer guanxi. Only 24 percent of those who maintained the same trust score are no longer cited as guanxi. The steeper the drop in trust, the less likely a contact remains guanxi.

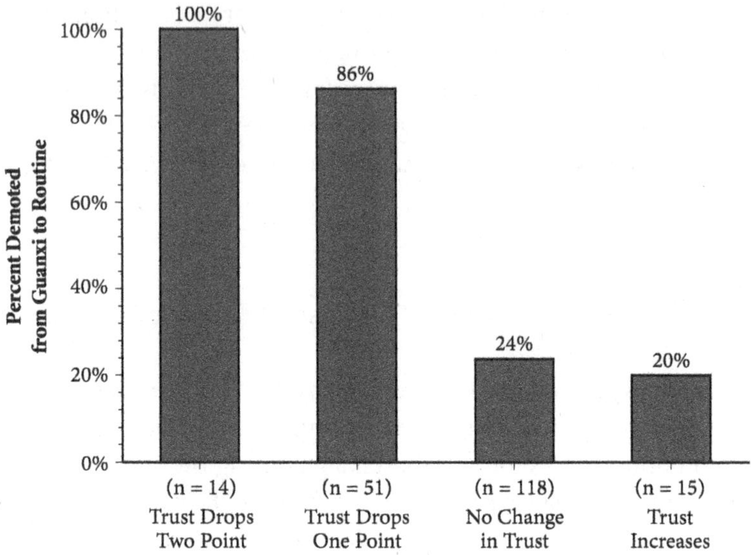

Figure 7.3 Trust Change and Guanxi Demotion

Note: These are the 198 contacts cited as guanxi in 2018. Horizontal shows trust in 2021 minus trust in 2018. "Drops Two Points" contains one relationship that dropped three points. "Trust Increases" includes one relationship that increased by two points. Vertical is percentage of contacts in each category who are demoted from guanxi to routine.

Table 7.5 offers statistical corroboration. The first column shows a strong tendency for former guanxi to be demoted when trust decreases (−5.56 t-test, P < .001). The negative association is about the same for the extreme case of contacts perfectly matched between the surveys. And in the third column of the table, adding controls does not diminish the negative association. The −2.48 coefficient says that a unit increase in trust is associated with a 2.48 decrease in the log-odds that a contact is demoted from guanxi, which is a 92 percent decrease in the odds that a guanxi contact will continue as guanxi.

Other predictors in the table are irrelevant to guanxi demotion. Consistent with the strong-bridges hypothesis, mutual friends are irrelevant (−.67 t-test in second row of table, P ~ .51, and we get a similar result if we replace the embedding measure with log number of mutual friends, −.94, P ~ .35). Guanxi demotion is between respondent and contact, regardless of mutual friends. More notable is the absence of protection from foundation relations such as family, friend, or classmate. Family comes closest to limiting

Table 7.5 Change in Trust and Guanxi Demotion

	All Matched 2018 Guanxi Contacts (n = 198)	High-Match 2018 Guanxi Contacts (n = 102)	All Matched, With Controls (n = 198)
Change in trust (2018–2021)	−2.48*** (−5.56)	−2.46** (−3.14)	−2.48*** (−5.40)
Structural embedding			−.27 (−.67)
Contact is family			−1.22 (−1.96)
Contact is just friend			−1.00 (−1.51)
Contact is classmate			−.44 (−.71)
Contact reached via multiple communication channels			−.20 (−.89)
IT industry			−.17 (−.41)
Hangzhou			−.78 (−.91)
Months of lock-down			−.04 (−.19)
Intercept	−.95	−1.63	1.00
Pseudo R^2	.29	.23	.34

Note: Estimates are from a logit model predicting which of 198 guanxi contacts in 2018 are no longer cited as guanxi in 2021 (jackknife t-tests in parentheses). Structural embedding is log of indirect connection from respondent to contact. High-match contacts are contacts who match perfectly on all factors considered. Third column includes respondent random effects (pseudo R^2 in third column is without random effects).
*P < .05 **P < .01, ***P < .001.

demotion (−1.96 t-test, P ~ .06), but clearly does not offer statistically significant protection from demotion. Other role relations are irrelevant. Controls for local environment tell a similar story. Industry, geography, and months under COVID lockdown are irrelevant to guanxi demotion.

The strong link between trust decay and guanxi demotion is reassuring. The demoted contacts were not overlooked by accident, stress, or poor recall. They were re-evaluated. Moreover, the findings reinforce a central claim: Being guanxi to someone, or no longer being guanxi, is not anchored in a social role or the surrounding network. It is a personal judgment. He is a valued business contact, but I no longer have highest trust in him. He is not one of my people. With respect to the spatial map of kinds of relations in Figure 5.1, the contact has moved from the upper-right containing one's core positive ties down to the lower-right of valued, but more routine contacts.[9]

Whether the COVID-19 pandemic contributed to these dynamics remains unclear. One can certainly assume so. Like other significant events in an entrepreneur's business history, the pandemic acted as a stress test: some ties held, others failed. In sum: Guanxi ties are clearly resilient, but they are not static. Guanxi are resilient as long as they continue to be deemed trustworthy. How this applies to strong bridges is the critical next question.

Bridge Stability

The results in Table 7.4 are encouraging in that they show the stability of guanxi relations. The critical test for this book concerns strong-bridge stability. To support the claim that strong bridges rise above the fragility typical of bridge relationships, we need to show that these ties endure, persisting beyond routine bridges that lack comparable depth.

That is precisely the evidence in Figure 7.4. The horizontal axis distinguishes four categories of relationships in 2018 by guanxi (yes, no), and bridge (yes, no), where a bridge is a contact with little or no indirect connection to the respondent through other contacts (weighted indirect connection through third parties is less than 1). The vertical axis is the percent of relationships in a category that are strong bridges when the respondent is interviewed three years later, in 2021. Two indicators are used. A relationship in 2021 can be a strong bridge because it is a bridge (weighted indirect connection less than 1 within the 2021 network) and the contact is cited as guanxi (those are the striped bars in Figure 7.4), or because the relationship is a bridge and the contact is cited as someone in whom the respondent has maximum trust (level 5 in Figure 4.4 and Figure 5.4; the solid bars in Figure 7.4). These two conditions are related in the strong-bridges hypothesis, but

---

[9] Half of the eighty-nine former guanxi were cited in 2021 as valued contacts (Question 5 in Figure A3, Appendix A). If we add that variable to the controls in Table 7.5, the fact of being cited as valued is strongly associated with guanxi demotion (3.40 t-test, P < .001). In other words, demoted guanxi in particular tend to be cited as valued. But they are not trusted. With valued contact in the table 7.5 prediction, change in trust continues to be the strongest predictor of guanxi demotion (−2.46 coefficient, −5.06 t-test, P < .001).

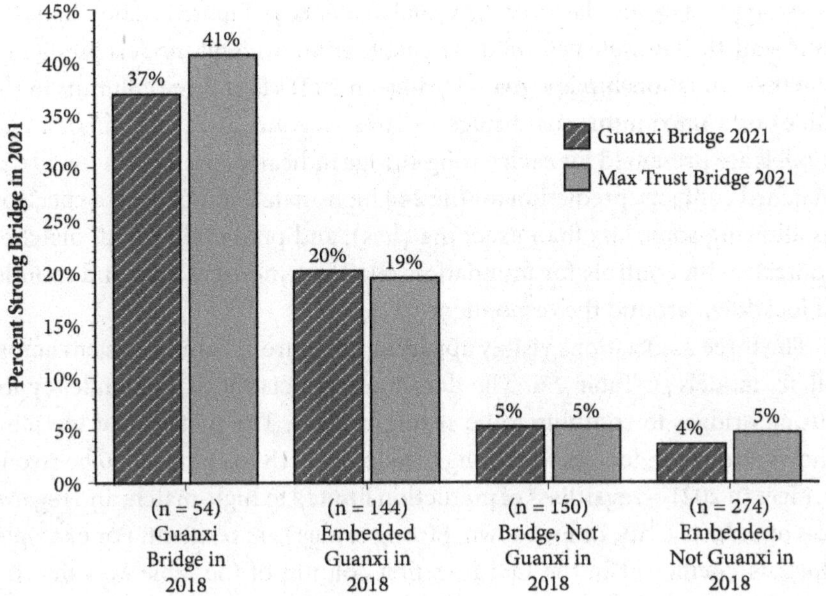

Figure 7.4 Strong Bridge Resilience

Note: Columns show percentage of matched contacts in 2018 who are strong bridges in 2021. Bridges are contacts with weighted indirect connections to respondent through third parties less than 1). Striped bars are bridges also cited as guanxi. Solid bars are bridges to contacts in whom the respondent has maximum trust. Number of relations in parentheses sum to 622 matched contacts.

they are not identical. Sixteen percent of guanxi bridges are not contacts cited for maximum trust, and 21 percent of maximum-trust bridges are not cited as guanxi.

Our conclusion from analyzing the two indicators is that strong bridges are resilient. Three associations are illustrated in Figure 7.4. First, relations that were guanxi bridges in 2018 are the most likely relationships to be strong bridges in 2021. The two bars to the left in Figure 7.4 are by far the highest. Second, guanxi contacts, even if embedded in mutual friends, can emerge three years later as a bridge in an entrepreneur's network—and still be guanxi. But the odds of embedded guanxi emerging as a bridge are much lower than the odds for a former guanxi bridge (20 percent versus 37 percent). Third, non-guanxi are unlikely to emerge later as a strong bridge. Neither weak bridges (5 percent), nor embedded routine ties (4 percent), emerge in the strong-bridge category. In short, former strong bridges are most likely to be current strong bridges.

We appreciate the clarity of the visual evidence in Figure 7.4, but Table 7.6 puts statistical muscle behind it. The table contains logit models predicting whether a relationship is a guanxi bridge in 2021 (first three columns in the table) or a maximum-trust bridge in 2021 (second three columns). Three models are presented for each strong-bridge indicator: prediction for all 622 matched contacts, prediction for the 244 high-match contacts (as a check on us allowing some less than exact matches), and prediction for all matched contacts with controls for foundation relations, industry, city, and months of lockdown around the respondent.

The three associations visibly apparent in Figure 7.4 are consistent across all six models in Table 7.6. The dominant association is the tendency for strong bridges to continue to be strong bridges. The first row of the table shows strong tendencies for strong bridges in 2018 to continue to be strong bridges in 2021—regardless of prediction limited to high-match, and regardless of industry, city, or lockdown. Strong bridges are resilient. For example, the 2.74 coefficient in the first row, first column of the table says that the odds of a guanxi bridge emerging from a former guanxi bridge are 15.5 times higher than the odds of seeing a guanxi bridge emerge from the reference category (an embedded non-guanxi relationship in 2018).[10]

The second row of the table shows the second effect visible in Figure 7.4. Strong bridges are likely to emerge from guanxi, even if the guanxi was not a bridge in the earlier survey. The coefficients in the second row of the table are not as large as the coefficients in the first row, but they are all statistically significant. As an example, the 1.90 coefficient in the second row of the first column says that the odds of a guanxi bridge emerging from a former embedded-guanxi tie are 6.7 times higher than the odds of seeing a guanxi bridge emerge from the 2018 reference category of relations.

The third row of the table shows the third effect visible in Figure 7.4. Strong bridges are unlikely to emerge from weak bridges. The final four bars in Figure 7.4 are similarly close to zero. All coefficients in the third row of Table 7.6 are negligible. To take an example, the .40 coefficient in the third row, first column of the table says that the odds of a guanxi bride emerging

---

[10] We model as we do to test the statistical significance of differences visually apparent in Figure 7.4. When we estimate models that distinguish level effects for former bridges versus former guanxi, the bridge effect is absorbed in the guanxi effect because the bridge effect is a combination of high association with former bridge guanxi and negligible association with former non-guanxi bridges. For example, level effects for the first column in Table 7.6 generate a 4.95 t-test for former guanxi and a negligible 0.75 t-test for former bridges.

Table 7.6 Former Strong Bridges Continue To Be Strong Bridges

	Predict Guanxi Bridges in 2021			Predict Max Trust Bridges in 2021		
	All Matched Contacts (n = 622)	High-Match Contacts (n = 244)	All Matched, With Controls (n = 622)	All Matched Contacts (n = 622)	High-Match Contacts (n = 244)	All Matched, With Controls (n = 622)
2018 Relationship						
Guanxi bridge	2.74*** (6.17)	2.68*** (3.83)	2.39*** (4.86)	2.62*** (6.43)	2.71*** (4.26)	2.43*** (3.65)
Embedded guanxi	1.90*** (4.75)	2.05** (3.20)	1.46** (3.33)	1.38*** (4.33)	1.82** (3.16)	1.21** (2.59)
Bridge, not guanxi	.40 (0.77)	−.03 (−.04)	.55 (1.15)	.12 (0.25)	−.69 (−.62)	.09 (0.15)
Embedded, not guanxi (reference)	—	—	—	—	—	—
2018 Controls						
Contact is family			1.71*** (4.03)			2.93*** (3.86)
Contact is just friend			.56 (1.12)			1.44 (1.60)
Contact is classmate			.23 (0.48)			.92 (1.46)
Contact reached via multiple channels			.03 (0.18)			−.19 (−.96)

continued

Table 7.6 *continued*

	Predict Guanxi Bridges in 2021			Predict Max Trust Bridges in 2021		
	All Matched Contacts (n = 622)	High-Match Contacts (n = 244)	All Matched, With Controls (n = 622)	All Matched Contacts (n = 622)	High-Match Contacts (n = 244)	All Matched, With Controls (n = 622)
IT industry			.17 (0.57)			.16 (0.40)
Hangzhou			−.08 (−.11)			−.69 (−.61)
Months of lock-down			−.23 (−1.11)			−.46 (−1.43)
Intercept	−3.27	−2.94	−3.22	−3.00	−2.71	−2.51
Pseudo R^2	.14	.17	.21	.14	.19	.24

Note: Estimates are from a logit model predicting which of the 622 contacts matched across surveys in 2018 and 2021 are cited as strong bridges in 2021 (jackknife t-tests in parentheses). Relationship categories are taken from Figure 7.4. High-match contacts are contacts who match perfectly on all factors considered. Third and sixth columns include respondent random effects (pseudo R^2 is without random effects). Descriptive statistics are in Table B.12, Appendix B.

*$P < .05$, **$P < .01$, ***$P < .001$.

from a former non-guanxi bridge are about equal to (1.5 times) the odds of seeing a guanxi bridge emerge from the 2018 reference category of relations.

The final point to note about the table is the irrelevance of the controls in the third and sixth columns. Contacts who were family in 2018 are significantly more likely to be cited as guanxi bridges in 2021. The connection with family is not surprising, given the history of work on guanxi and the results on multiplexity in Chapter 5. What is important here is strong bridge resilience. The control for family does not eliminate the tendency for strong bridges to continue. We also tested for an interaction effect that previous strong bridges tend to be cited again as strong bridges—if they are family, but the interaction is negligible. Family does not increase the likelihood of a former guanxi bridge being cited later as a guanxi bridge (0.65 t-test for family interaction effect in third column of Table 7.6, P ~ .32). In the same way, family does not increase the likelihood of a guanxi bridge in 2018 being cited as bridge relation of maximum trust in 2021 (0.16 t-test for family interaction effect in sixth column, P ~ .87). The other controls in the table for foundation relations and environment are negligible predictors.

In sum, being guanxi or a strong bridge is not a transient condition. Strong bridges are resilient, showing significantly lower risk of decay than routine bridges. More importantly, strong bridges persist as bridges, regardless of environment or foundation relations carrying them over time. The role of the specific political context and observation window is unclear, of course. Still, observing bridge stability under China's highly disruptive COVID policies suggests that their resilience may be even more pronounced in normal times, when constraints on personal interaction are relaxed.

Conclusion: Strong Bridges Are Resilient

Bridge ties are often presumed fragile—situational, thinly reinforced, prone to decay. Throughout this book, we have implied that such is not a necessity. We claim that strong bridges defy that expectation. To test that claim in this chapter, we returned to the field. Re-engaging respondents three to four years after the original survey posed obvious challenges. Added to this was the exogenous shock of COVID, which served as a natural stress test. We pursued resilience through three lines of attack. The findings converge on a simple conclusion: Strong bridges are resilient.

We begin by learning where COVID most disrupted each person's network. There are some close friends of our sample entrepreneurs who were severely affected by the disease, but they are a minority. The personal contacts most affected by COVID are rarely met individuals, disconnected from others in the network around the respondent naming them (Figure 7.1, Table 7.1). Stories about how a victim was affected are not about illness so much as damage to business, a shared interest between entrepreneurs (Table 7.2). Our conclusion from this first analysis is that COVID is everywhere in the environment, but the severe hardship is typically at or beyond the periphery of entrepreneur networks.

Second, we looked for continuing support of the strong-bridges hypothesis. The protective scaffolding of structural embedding eroded during COVID. Closure no longer served as an anchor for trust. Routine contacts, once supported by shared third parties, gained little trust from structural embedding. But guanxi ties—including those functioning as bridges—sustained high levels of trust regardless of network context. Figure 7.2A versus 7.2B, and Table 7.3, make this visible: as the slope of trust with respect to embedding for ordinary contacts becomes less steep, trust in guanxi remains consistently high and less dependent on structure. The mechanism is relational, not structural. The exogenous shock of COVID revealed a limit to trust from structural embedding. In a phrase, trust became more personal, less supported by context—more dependent on interpersonal history with a contact.

Third, we dug further into the data to study the persistence of individual ties over time. Matching contacts across surveys—absent names but anchored in gender, duration, role, and citation order—strong bridges exhibit remarkable resilience. Ties cited as guanxi in 2018 were significantly more likely to be re-cited in 2021 (Table 7.4). More importantly, they were more likely to persist as strong bridges rather than sliding into embeddedness or decay (Figure 7.4, Table 7.6). This is not to say that strong bridges are cast in concrete. Networks changed. Ties shifted. Some were lost, some gained, and others redefined. But the sorting mechanism remained intact, with trust the fulcrum: Contacts demoted from guanxi status were accompanied by a drop in trust (Figure 7.3, Table 7.5). And throughout, structural embedding is irrelevant to the resilience or change in strong bridges. This is not about mutual friends. It is about interpersonal history.

8
Taking Stock and Looking Ahead

We do four things in this closing chapter: We summarize conclusions from what we've done ("Evidence of Strong Bridges"). We speculate more abstractly about what we've done ("The Origin of Strong Bridges"). We discuss and illustrate work related to what we've done ("Strong Bridges in Other Study Populations"). We speculate beyond what we've done ("Other Implications of Recognizing Strong Bridges").

Evidence of Strong Bridges

We have the advantage, at this point, of being able to state our conclusions linked to evidence presented in preceding chapters. We began, in Chapter 2, describing the state of the art against which our results with event contacts were a contradiction. Here is the core network theory of brokerage through the twentieth century (and into much of contemporary work): The bridge and cluster structure of social networks creates information advantages of breadth, timing, and arbitrage that are the competitive advantage of network brokers, the people whose social connections bridge the structural holes between groups (Figures 2.1, 2.6). The efforts of network brokers to change the status quo are opposed by the social pressures of local cohesion within groups—that is to say, network closure. Closure facilitates trust within the structurally embedded ties inside groups, as the relative lack of structural embedding between groups fosters suspicion of ideas and people beyond the group (Figures 2.3, 2.4). This closure-trust association limits successful brokerage to individuals with sufficient social standing to overcome the suspicion (Figure 2.7). With respect to the pipes and prisms metaphor often used in network theory, advantage is created by holding a broker position in the flow of information, but harvesting the value of that advantage is contingent on perception of the broker as an appropriate source. In short, bridges are weak and brokerage is fragile.

Strong Bridges. Ronald S. Burt and Sonja Opper, Oxford University Press. © Oxford University Press (2026).
DOI: 10.1093/9780197834275.003.0008

It was in this context that we were excited to see the contradictory data pattern in Figure 2.5. As expected from past research, connections with event contacts are strong in that they are trusting, emotionally close relationships. But unexpectedly, many are bridge relations (enumerated in Figures 2.5B and 4.8). What these contacts have in common is that respondents recall them as being particularly helpful during significant events in their personal business history. The implication is that network brokerage is less fragile than has been believed heretofore. If the contradiction survives close inspection, the outlier relationships have implications for competitive advantage with respect to broadening network theory, sharpening network research, and making network practice more effective.

In Chapter 3, we analyzed data from probability samples of Chinese entrepreneurs to better understand the strong bridges with event contacts. We began by describing the data (details in Appendix A) and illustrating some example networks (Figures 3.2, 3.3). We then described variation in the evidence of strong bridges depending on the kind of event on which a contact was cited, the kind of help provided, and the number of years the contact was known to the respondent. The evidence of strong bridges is stronger for contacts who helped with events deemed more significant by the respondent, especially the founding event—but evidence of strong bridges can be seen regardless of kind of event, kind of help, or source of help (Figures 3.4, 3.5). When family is turned to for support it is most likely at founding, but family is not the primary source of support, even at founding. Entrepreneurs cite all kinds of people beyond the entrepreneur's family. Time emerges as a key variable. The duration of a relationship is about getting to know a person, which happens during the first four or five years of a relationship, after which trust increases at a slow rate over additional years (Figure 3.8). In sum, events seem not to be significant in their own right. They are significant as an occasion, a context, in which an entrepreneur comes to believe that a contact is a reliable ally.

In Chapter 4, we formalized the concept of strong bridges with an analogy to the colloquial Chinese word, guanxi, and offered empirical support for two hypotheses broadly applicable to such words. We use guanxi as a strategic research site in which the unexpected strength of relations with event contacts is explicitly separate from network location. Our measurement strategy was to include a guanxi name interpreter in a generic network survey instrument of name generators and interpreters. This gave us network data on where guanxi occurs within a network and where it does not.

We use two hypotheses to organize our argument and evidence. Our "strong-bridges" hypothesis states criteria for guanxi operating as a strong bridge: Relative to non-guanxi ties, trust in guanxi ties is higher and less contingent on structural embedding (Figures 4.3, 4.4). Our "advantage" hypothesis states that entrepreneurs are advantaged by the extent to which their guanxi are bridges (Figures 4.6, 4.7). In contrast to the discussion of ties strong as a result of corroborating relations with mutual friends and colleagues (structural embedding), guanxi ties are strong as a result of the interpersonal history between two people (relational embedding). Each form of embedding can contribute to tie strength, even one compensating for the other. Bridge relations are typically weak, but some are not. Those exceptions turn out to be a numerous minority (Figure 4.8; 8 percent of all cited ties, 26 percent of cited bridge ties), and essential to the competitive advantage associated with brokerage (Figures 4.6, 4.7). Strong bridges do not compensate for an overall closed network, but they are key to the known competitive advantages of open networks (Figure 4.7).

Thus, the competitive advantage of brokerage is much less fragile than has been assumed. The oft-cited link between tie strength and network structure can create the impression of fragility, but the link is merely a correlation. Separating tie strength from network structure reveals substantial evidence of strong bridges providing competitive advantage and high trust across the structural holes between groups. Advantage isn't about weak ties, bridge connections, or trust so much as it is specifically about trusted bridge connections—what we discuss as strong bridges. Absent such bridges, network brokers have no discernible competitive advantage (Figure 4.7).

In subsequent chapters, we consolidate the beachhead established in Chapter 4. We first looked for evidence of confounding explanations. Multiplexity is an obvious candidate. A relationship is "multiplex" when it is composed of more than one kind of connection. Guanxi is typically multiplex in that it is—like "love" or "respect"—an invisible quality attributed to a relationship. What are the observable qualities of relationships in which guanxi is found? If we feel our brother is guanxi, how much of that trust in guanxi is because our brother is family? In Chapter 5, we identified kinds of relationships associated with a contact being viewed as guanxi (Figure 5.1). Beyond help in significant events and knowing the contact for years, four kinds of "foundation" relations emerge as statistically significant correlates of guanxi: family, just-friends (the absence of a connection other than friend), classmates, and contacts with whom an entrepreneur has multiple communication channels, especially texting (Table 5.2). Given these four foundation relations, we asked whether empirical support for the strong-bridges hypothesis depends on guanxi occurring with one of the foundation relations. The answer is "no" (Figure 5.4, mirroring Figure 4.4). We then asked whether empirical support for the advantage hypothesis depends on guanxi occurring with one of the foundation relations. Again, the answer is "no" (Figure 5.5, corresponding to Figure 4.7). Strong bridges operate as stated in the two hypotheses regardless of other sentiments or roles with which they occur.

Cognition is another likely confounding variable. As a respondent's interpretation, guanxi and its correlates could vary with how a respondent thinks about guanxi. If there are groups within which respondents understand guanxi similarly, and between which respondents understand guanxi differently, then the empirical support in Chapters 4 and 5 might not generalize. In Chapter 6, we studied cognition in terms of the language people use to describe guanxi. We drew two conclusions: First, descriptions by our sample entrepreneurs do not distinguish qualitatively different kinds of speakers so much as they locate speakers on a continuum of complexity (Figures 6.2, 6.5)—where complexity refers to the number and variety of words in a text. Second, the complexity with which a speaker describes guanxi is predicted by the complexity of the speaker's social network, specifically, by the extent to which a speaker's network contains strong bridges (Figure 6.3). We took this to mean that speakers are more articulate about a condition with which they are more familiar. In comparison (Table 6.3), complexity is largely independent of an entrepreneur's personal characteristics (age, education, gender, etc.) and characteristics of his or her business (industry, assets, size, profitability, etc.). Here again, strong bridges operate as stated in the two hypotheses regardless of how an entrepreneur understands guanxi—assuming the brief text we obtained captures a speaker's understanding, acknowledging the difficulty of separating language from network (wherein our strong-bridge predictors are defined), and allowing for the loquacity of network brokers (broker texts tend to be longer).

We then turned to the resilience implicit in strong relations. The stronger a connection, the less subject it should be to decay from exogenous shocks, or normal wear and tear. Not impervious to decay, but resilient. Resilience is a familiar characteristic of strength derived from structural embedding: Such relations are less subject to decay than are bridge relations (e.g., Figure 2.4A).

In Chapter 7, we took three lines of attack on network resilience. Armed with a re-survey in 2021, we began by learning where COVID most disrupted each person's network. There are some close friends of our sample entrepreneurs who were severely affected by the disease, but they are a minority. The personal contacts most critically affected by COVID are rarely met individuals, disconnected from others in the network around the respondent naming them. COVID is everywhere in the environment, but the severe hardship is typically at or beyond the periphery of an entrepreneur's network (Figure 7.1). Second, we looked for continuing support of the strong-bridges hypothesis. Guanxi during COVID continues to be characterized by high trust independent of network context, but the context eroded: The structural embedding associated in 2018 with trust in routine business contacts contributes significantly less to trust in 2021. In a phrase, trust becomes more personal, less supported by context—more dependent on guanxi (Figure 7.2). Third, we looked into the resilience of individual relationships. This is difficult because we assured respondents of contact anonymity. Names and addresses of contacts are unknown. Still, with some carefully considered assumptions, we match a large number of contacts cited in 2018 and 2021. Strong bridges are resilient. They are distinguished by a significantly lower risk of tie decay compared to routine bridges (Figure 7.4). In short, both structural and relational embedding are associated with tie resilience, but it is the strong bridges emblematic of relational embedding that stand out as resilient to COVID's disruptions.

At this point, we are confident that strong bridges are recognizable and less fragile than typical bridge relations. Strong bridges are not equally present in all networks, of course, but when present we find they are the active ingredient in network structure that provides competitive advantage.

The Origin of Strong Bridges

What can we say about origins? An origins story is valuable in its own right, but also for crafting strategies to develop strong bridges, or for designing research. For example, we noted in Chapter 4 that guanxi has been discussed as a family, or family-like relationship. But results in Chapter 5 show that family is rarely a source of guanxi, and not essential to the strong bridges guanxi can provide.

The origins story implied by our research is anchored in cognition; specifically, in your interpretation of your past. Your perception of someone as guanxi—a trustworthy source of support—is triggered by an event in which you felt at risk, exposed. The other person offered support that relieved your felt exposure. Subsequent corroborating moments solidified your perception. This is the process we believe generates relationships described by our two hypotheses: High trust relatively independent of structural embedding (the strong-bridges hypothesis), and high performance—when the process occurs with respect to someone on the far side of a structural hole (the advantage hypothesis).

The process is robust. We find no variation in support for the hypotheses across kinds of events, kinds of help, or kinds of people. What matters is your feeling at risk, and your perception of support from the other person, reinforced by corroborating evidence in the years that follow. When a respondent is asked to enumerate significant events for the event name generator (Figure A2), we do not test for accurate recollection. We facilitate accuracy by locating each event in real time relative to other events, but event significance is left to the respondent. An event significant to one person need not be significant to another. What we are after is the people who were perceived as helpful to the respondent during events that he or she deems significant. It is similar for the General Social Survey (GSS) name generator, which asks for the names of people with whom important events are discussed. The respondent defines what is important. What the GSS overseers were after with the GSS generator is the extent to which the respondent discusses whatever he or she deems important within a closed circle of friends or colleagues. We do not ask respondents to find important what observers deem important. In the same vein, the event name generator does not ask respondents to focus on events that everyone would consider significant.

The above origins process is free of causality in linear time. Your belief in the other person could result from an accurate recollection of concrete events in which you were, in fact, at risk. But it could just as well result from a memory you construct to support your desire for a trustworthy source of support—as might happen in a current period of risk, a stretch of loneliness, or the haze after that fourth Negroni (ripping us back to Zerubavel's 1991 discussion). Historical accounts are similarly fair game. To what extent is distrust of strangers based on socially constructed accounts of historical events? For example, Nunn and Wantchekon (2011) show distrust of others is higher in areas of Africa more heavily raided years ago by slave traders. On the positive side, to what extent is trust in strangers based on socially constructed accounts of historical events? For example, Opper et al. (2025) show that the Chinese cities that developed as trade centers (which includes our survey cities) tend to be places where years ago missionaries taught outsider language and values, facilitating early trade with the outsiders.[1]

It is a short step to draw an analogy with imprinting and attachment (Hinde 1966; Bowlby 1969), in which a baby—at mortal risk if left to its own survival—bonds with a mother or surrogate. The bond improves the baby's odds of survival and diminishes feelings of risk. Imprinting is usually attributed to a period of neuroplasticity in the baby's brain, during which it seeks the nearest mother-like object it can find ("critical-period plasticity," Horn 2004).

The analogy with imprinting is intriguing, but unnecessary at the moment. This observation does not rule out the possibility of creating perceptions of strong bridges by directly manipulating the brain with drugs or therapy. However, the process we infer from our results is more general. Feeling at risk at one time or another is a familiar occurrence for most people; even a frequent occurrence for some people. It is a relief when such emotions feel managed. In short, we expect strong bridges to exist in a wide variety of situations, real and imagined.

Strong Bridges in Other Study Populations

Research on structural holes and network brokerage has benefitted from replication in diverse study populations—different kinds of activity, different kinds of organizations, and different cultures. Again and again, we see higher achievement and creativity from network brokers, illustrated in Figure 2.6. These replicated results are attractive because individual research

---

[1] There is also intriguing analogy between significant events as we describe them and epiphanies as studied by Dane (2020; Dane et al. In Press). Epiphanies are a kind of event (Dane et al. In Press:4–5, page 10 for event operationalization): "Epiphanies resolve psychological tensions people have been wrestling with in some way ... By resolving psychological tensions, epiphanies reconcile matters that previously felt troubling, vexing, or even intractable." And the people more likely to report having epiphanies are managers who daydream about alternatives. From this, we believe epiphany-prone managers are network brokers, since brokers are more exposed to alternative perspectives from bridge contacts. That implies brokers are more likely to recognize the transformational substance of significant events, which implies that not only do brokers prosper because of their strong bridges (as we have shown); they are also more likely to recognize events from which strong bridges are formed.

projects provide limited generality. Regardless of data quality and analytical rigor, the generality of results from an individual project are limited because social networks and their correlates are so strongly affected by the culture and institutions in a study population. Network patterns and correlates in this population are often different in another population. What recurs across populations are the general network predictions. The limited-generality issue is particularly severe in studies of management networks, which are often conducted within a single organization.

This book is but one study. The preceding chapters document the existence, correlates, and abundance of strong bridges in the networks of Chinese entrepreneurs during the early twenty-first century in large cities within the Yangtze River delta, particularly Shanghai and Hangzhou. Observations are well sampled, and data quality is high, but it is just one study. We are reassured by the fact that much of what we report is consistent with the conclusion in Nee and Opper (2012) that China's emergence was a "bottom up" process (at least until a business grew large enough to warrant attention from local or national government). In the absence of institutional support, Chinese entrepreneurs constructed in their social networks personal institutions to support their businesses, especially during difficult events. Our results support the claim in certain ways, but with a critical qualification. Contrary to the common stereotype that guanxi generates advantage, we find—consistent with network theory across cultures—that advantage is specifically rooted in having access to bridge guanxi, that is to say strong bridges.

Comparison with Nee and Opper is reassuring, but less than replication. Our results on strong bridges are more precise network predictions than what was possible in the absence of network data, and our results are based on interviews with sample entrepreneurs in the same Yangtze River cities in which Nee and Opper interviewed years before. The need for replication calls for studies of strong bridges in the networks around Chinese entrepreneurs in other large cities at other times, and Chinese entrepreneurs in smaller cities, and managers in the bureaucracies of state-owned organizations (Xin and Pearce 1996 offer a pioneering effort; also case studies in Wang and Hsung 2016).

And there is the broader world outside China. We have two reasons to expect our results on strong bridges to replicate in populations outside China. First, bridge connections are known to provide competitive advantage outside China, in much the same way they do in Chinese populations

(Figure 2.6). Second, we have uncovered nothing about guanxi that prohibits guanxi-like relations outside China. Discussion of guanxi is often rich in Chinese metaphors, but the substance discussed is consistent with social exchange theory, especially theory along the lines of Blau (1964) that emphasizes the macro implications of micro exchange (see related work in anthropology, Ekeh 1974). Commenting early on guanxi in Chinese economic life, Walder (1986:179) noted: "…the concept is by no means culturally unique; the terms blat in Russia and pratik in Haiti refer to the same type of instrumental-personal tie." What seems to be exceptional about guanxi in China is its ubiquity. As a leading Chinese network scholar summarizes (Lin 2001b:159): "What is so unique about guanxi in the Chinese context is that it has been so pervasive and dominant in the entire society throughout much of its historical, political, and economic contexts." In short, China can be a uniquely informative laboratory for learning about the substance and implications of the bridge relations provided by guanxi—in preparation for work on strong bridges outside China.

"Replication" in Previous Research

A great deal of replication work has already been published. These are studies in which evidence of strong bridges is presented without being discussed as evidence of strong bridges. This is not a claim that such work was interpreted incorrectly. Multiple perspectives are always possible on research evidence. We have in mind research focused on one or another topic, but containing evidence of strong bridges.

One of our favorite examples is Brian Uzzi's dissertation research, used in two widely-cited papers. Uzzi (1996) presents argument and evidence on the point that embedding lowers the probability of an apparel firm failing. Uzzi (1997) corroborates with qualitative material. These two papers were early, prominent empirical support for the embeddedness metaphor. Their conclusions continue to be correct, their frequent citation well deserved. At the same time, they offer corroborating evidence of strong bridges. Begin with the study population: Unionized "better apparel" firms in New York City in 1990. It is a difficult business. One in four firms fail in 1991 (Uzzi 1996:686). Uzzi (1996:675) traces the odds of failure to: "the concept of structural embeddedness that concerns the material quality and structure of ties among actors." Uzzi measures embedding with three variables: A group variable (1 if a firm is part of a business group, 0 otherwise), and two network variables based on purchase patterns among the firms (termed first- and second-order coupling). All three variables have a negative association with firm failure (Uzzi 1996:691). The group membership variable has a modest association (z-score test statistics of −1.69 and −1.72), but associations with the network variables clearly reject the null. In particular, first-order coupling is the network variable most clearly rejecting the null hypothesis (z-score test statistics of −2.54 and −2.37). The variable is a Herfindahl index measuring the extent to which a contractor's business is concentrated in a single trading partner (sum across manufacturers j, the squared proportion of contractor i's business that is with manufacturer j, Uzzi 1996:686). There is no reference to third parties supporting the bridge (i.e., structural embedding). First-order coupling is a measure of business concentrated within the relationship between one contractor and one manufacturer (i.e., relational embedding). Such concentration is a strong bridge between a single contractor and a single manufacturer. The odds of failure decrease for the contractor who concentrates his business on one trading partner, versus spreading business across a portfolio of manufacturers. The measure of second-order coupling is similarly a measure of business concentration in a single relationship from the manufacturer's perspective (Uzzi 1996:687). Qualitative material in both articles describes the high trust and experience to be expected in such bridges. In short, the evidence can be interpreted in terms of strong bridges protecting against the risk of economic failure, corroborating our evidence showing that strong bridges are associated with high economic performance.

We were drawn to the two Uzzi articles for their quality and prominence, but they are merely an example. Advances in research often lead to people discovering that they already knew the advance under a different label (Merton 1961; Stigler 1980). In the wake of writing this book, we often see evidence of strong bridges when re-reading classic favorites (an edited collection in the making?).

Replication with Other Colloquial Words

With respect to new research, a short step to replication would be to study the network structure of trust and advantage associated with words that function in other cultures as guanxi functions in China. The incomplete roster in Table 8.1 extends the list with which we began this book in Chapter 1. Consider a replication in Germany. By asking a sample of German respondents to name important contacts, then asking the respondents to identify the contacts they deem "Vitamin B," research could proceed as we have done with guanxi in China. With such data, research could determine the extent to which Vitamin B provides strong bridges in the form of high trust relatively independent of structural embedding (strong-bridges hypothesis, as in Figure 4.4), and whether those strong bridges are the core of the network association with achievement (advantage hypothesis, as in Figure 4.7). People in Japan are reputed to put a premium on stable interpersonal connections (e.g., Yamagishi and Yamagishi 1994; Kuwabara et al. 2007). To what extent are strong bridges the core of the social harmony associated with kankei ties in Japan?

Two Cautions

Refer to a category of relations selected for study as "special" relations (versus "routine" relations). We have used guanxi as a special relationship. The use of Vitamin B as a special relationship would be another example. Prior work offers two cautions regarding the design of research on such relationships. Weak sampling of relationships or people can obscure evidence of strong bridges.

Sampling Relationships

On the first point, sample special and routine relations for study that vary widely in trust and structural embedding. The sharp drop in trust over bridge relations (to the left in Figure 4.3) is more obvious if the name generators in a study include one or more negative relationships. Also, finding high trust within deeply embedded relations neither supports nor contradicts the strong-bridges hypothesis: High trust is expected there from the familiar closure-trust association (Figure 2.3). More, there is relatively low variation in trust within relations at high levels of structural embedding (to the right in Figure 4.3), so there is less opportunity for a trust difference between special versus routine bridge relations. The clearest evidence for or against the strong-bridges hypothesis will be in relationships that are lightly, or not at all, embedded in mutual friends. We all have such relations. The challenge is not to miss them when crafting a network name generator (see Chapter 3, Table 3.1).

Table 8.1 Possible Guanxi Analogues Elsewhere

Country	Word	Meaning
France	Réseau, Piston	First means "network," when describing advantage through personal connections. Second means "piston," when describing advantage forced through personal connections.
Germany	Vitamin B	Literally means "Vitamin B," where B stands for Beziehungen which means connections or relationships.
Greece	Meson	Translates to "middle" or "intermediary" referring to the advantage one can gain through personal connections.
India	Sifarish (सिफारिश)	Term means "recommendation," and often refers to leveraging personal connections for advantage.
Indonesia	Jaringan	Refers to "network," highlighting personal relationships in achieving goals.
Italy	Raccomandazione	Translates to "recommendation," and often implies advantage from a personal endorsement or connection.
Japan	Kankei (関係)	Term means "relationship" or "connection," highlighting advantage from personal networks.
Mexico	Palanca	Literally means "lever," and is used to describe connections providing advantage.
Philippines	Pakikisama	Term means "to get along with others," to highlight building harmonious relationships that can lead to mutual benefits.
Poland	Znajomosci	Literally means "acquaintances," and refers to the personal connections providing advantage.
Portugal	Cunha	Term means "wedge," and is used to describe a connection or recommendation that provides advantage.
Russia	Blat	Refers to the use of personal networks to gain advantage.
South Korea	Yongo (연고)	Refers to personal connections, often emphasizing regional, educational, or familial ties.
Spain	Enchufe	Literally means "plug," and is used to describe having an inside connection or contact that provides advantage (plugs you in).
Thailand	Cha-ya (ชะยา)	Term refers to the network of contacts that can be used for mutual benefit.
The United Kingdom	Networking	Not unique to the United Kingdom, but the term "networking" is widely used to describe leveraging connections for advantage.

Country	Word	Meaning
The United States & Canada	Old Boys' Club	Refers to a network of people, typically men, advantaged by their connections with one another.
Vietnam	Quan hệ	Literally means "relationship" or "connection," emphasizing the importance of personal networks.

Sampling People

Bear in mind the contingent advantage of network brokerage when sampling people for a study. Research can be conducted in any population to test *whether* network brokerage matters, but to test hypotheses about *how* it matters, one needs a study population in which brokerage does in fact matter.

For example, there is little evidence of broker advantage among people in relatively closed networks, and strong bridges do not change that fact (to the left in Figure 4.7). There is considerable evidence of advantage among people in relatively open networks; specifically among people with strong bridges in their open network (to the right in Figure 4.7).

More generally, returns to brokerage are contingent on the social standing of would-be brokers. Flow is from high to low: Brokerage into a target audience is more likely to be successful when a would-be broker is viewed in the audience as a person of appropriate social standing—appropriate authority, status, or reputed expertise. Brokerage is inhibited when it threatens social standing in the target audience. Of course, a person with good social standing in one audience can be a suspect in another audience. Broker legitimacy—whether defined by gender, age, ethnicity, kind of work, previous employer, or any other characteristic—is not universal. It is an empirical question to be answered for a specific study population.

Consider the concrete examples in Figure 8.1. The graph to the right shows returns to brokerage in our 2012 and 2018 samples of Chinese entrepreneurs analyzed in prior chapters. The graph to the left shows returns to brokerage in a 1989 probability sample of managers in the four job ranks below the C-suite in a large U.S. computer-equipment organization. Managers in Figure 8.1A are distinguished on the vertical axes by early promotion (details on the managers are provided in the source study, Burt 1992: Chap. 4). A score of zero indicates a manager promoted to his or her

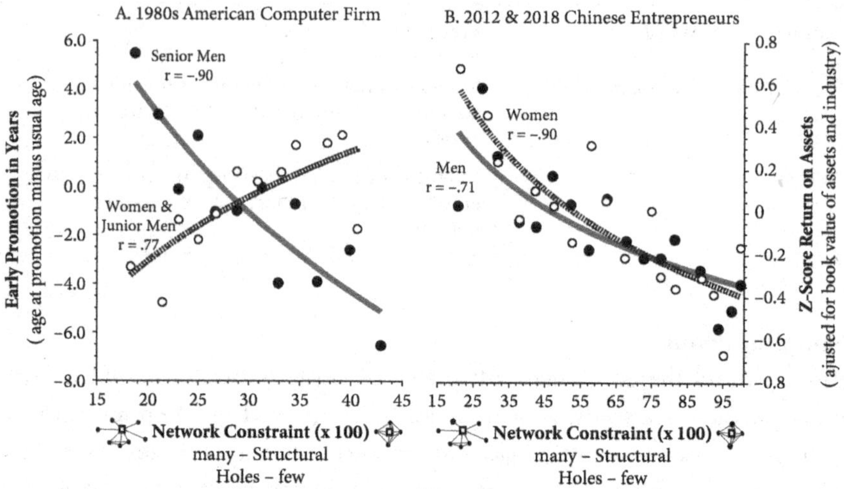

Figure 8.1 To Study How Brokerage Works, Look Where It Works

Note: Graph A displays top managers in an American computer equipment organization. Solid dots are men in the top three ranks below the C-suite. Hollow dots are men in the fourth rank (new to senior rank) and women in any rank. Graph B combines our 2012 and 2018 samples of Chinese entrepreneurs. Hollow/solid dots are male/female CEOs. The plotted data are average values of X and Y within 5-point intervals of the X axis. Correlations are computed from the plotted data.

current rank at the age typical for his or her kind of work and personal background.[2] Positive scores indicate early promotion. Negative scores indicate late promotion. Managers are distinguished on the horizontal axes by network constraint measuring the extent to which each operated in a closed network. These are all senior people, so they have relatively open networks: The data lie within fifteen to fifty points of network constraint (in contrast to the full range up to 100 points in Figure 8.1B, consistent with study populations in Figure 2.6).

The study was commissioned by the head of HR, who was curious to know how personal networks were involved in the process generating promotions. In this organization, at the time of the study, the top four ranks were deemed a political arena, the realm of senior decision makers. Their work was to execute well, but more to wisely decide on what to execute. Occupants of these ranks were, relative to lower ranks, the authors of their jobs.

[2] Regress age at promotion to current rank across the following predictors: Job rank, function, plant location, education, race, gender, and seniority. The vertical axes plot residuals from predicted age (see Burt 1992:126–131 for details).

For men in the highest three of the four ranks, the solid line in Figure 8.1A has the usual downward, nonlinear regression slope illustrating returns to brokerage (cf. Figure 2.6). Managers who operated as network brokers tended to be promoted early. There is a −.90 correlation for the solid line in Figure 8.1A, and a statistically significant −5.36 t-test in Table 8.2. Reconfiguring a senior man's network so as to decrease constraint from forty to fifteen points would correspond to a unit decrease in log constraint, which is associated with a promotion ten years earlier than expected on average (−10.32 coefficient in Table 8.2).

The dashed line in Figure 8.1A shows the opposite pattern. Early promotion for men in the lowest of the four ranks, and women in any of the four ranks, is associated with closed networks. There is a .77 correlation for the dashed line in Figure 8.1A. The analysis of covariance model in Table 8.2 shows that the reversal is more severe for women. For men in the lowest of the four ranks, the −10.32 years early-promotion effect for senior men is slope-adjusted by 13.29 to define a barely positive 2.97

Table 8.2 Returns to Brokerage in Figure 8.1

	Figure 8.1A	Figure 8.1B
Ln (Constraint)	−10.32 (−5.36, P < .001)	−.30 (−3.10, P ~ .002)
Level adjustment, junior men	−.27 (−0.39, P ~ .70)	
Level adjustment, women	.64 (0.85, P ~ 40)	0.03 (0.38, P ~ .70)
Slope adjustment, junior men	13.29 (3.94, P < .001)	
Slope adjustment, women	22.99 (5.61, P < .001)	−.26 (−.94, P ~ .35)
Intercept	33.99	1.16

Note: Performance variable is predicted by row variables using OLS estimates with jackknife standard errors, generating the t-tests in parentheses. Constraint scores are multiplied by 100 as in Figure 8.1. Performance across 284 managers in the 1989 computer firm (Figure 8.1A) is early promotion (age at promotion to current rank minus the age typical for people doing the same work with the same background, see footnote 2). Performance across 1084 sample Chinese entrepreneurs in the 2012 and 2018 Yangtze River delta cities (Figure 8.1B) is return on assets adjusted for industry and book value of assets (see footnote 3). Interaction predictors are computed as (log constraint—mean log constraint) times a binary variable distinguishing women or junior men, so level adjustments are estimated at the average level of constraint (rather than zero constraint, which is outside the observed data).

slope for returns to brokerage among junior men. For women in any rank, the -10.32 effect for senior men is completely reversed. Suppose a woman emulates successful senior men by broadening her network to reduce constraint from forty to fifteen points (reducing log constraint by one unit). She could expect to be promoted thirteen years later than peers to her next rank ($22.99 - 10.32 = 12.67$). Note that the hollow dots to the left in Figure 8.1A—representing women and junior men operating as network brokers—correspond to negative numbers on the early promotion measure. For these people, brokerage was associated with delay rather than acceleration in promotion.

Details are provided in the source study (Burt 1992: Chap. 4) and elaborated in Burt (1998), but the gist of the story is that men in ranks below the top four, and women in all four top ranks, seem not to have been treated as legitimate network brokers. The closed networks associated with early promotion are not cliquish networks in which everyone is strongly connected to everyone else. They are networks in which a senior sponsor is central and has introduced a manager to the sponsor's colleagues in multiple parts of the organization (Burt 1998:32, 2010:206). For men, promotion into the fourth rank, the junior of the senior ranks, was an act of accepting a newcomer into the fold, akin to promoting a professor to tenure in a university, or an associate to partner. Men in the fourth rank are not junior in an absolute sense. They are 39 years old on average, and have made it into one of the top 3000 jobs in an organization of more than 100,000 employees. They are junior only in the relative sense of being new to the political arena. Acceptance was about sponsorship as much as ability. Once in the top ranks, however, men had to become their own person since network brokers are promoted early into higher ranks. The picture is darker for women: Their early promotion required sponsorship at each of the four top ranks.

The need for sponsorship is a fascinating subject for study. But it would be unproductive to test our brokerage hypotheses with data on men in the fourth or lower ranks of this organization. Brokerage was not a source of advantage until a person reached the top three ranks. Care is needed when interpreting results from study populations in which people have low autonomy—settings where brokerage provides no advantage (Burt 2010: 61n, for illustration). The success of senior women in the organization could be an interesting topic for strong-bridges research, with the relationship between a woman and her sponsor analyzed as a strong bridge. But the issue lies outside our current focus. The strong bridges we found among the

Chinese entrepreneurs do not concern gender so much as they concern the vicissitudes of launching a venture in the nascent Chinese private economy.

Of course, we tested for gender differences (Burt 2019b). One in five of our sample entrepreneurs were women (a total of 175 of 1084 in the 2012 and 2018 surveys combined). A priori, there was reason to expect women to be disadvantaged as network brokers. China was "male-oriented" in the sense that leadership roles were expected to be held by men and seen as more appropriate for men than women. This will be obvious to some, anathema to others, so consider Figure 8.2. The figure displays responses from two World Values Surveys (Inglehart et al., 2014): One a national probability sample of Chinese adults in 2013, the other a comparable national probability sample of American adults in 2011. Chinese respondents were more likely to agree that "men make better business executives than women do," that "a university education is more important for a boy than for a girl," and that "men should have more right to a job than women when jobs are scarce." More specifically, Chinese respondents were more likely to strongly agree (6.70 loglinear test statistic) and agree (14.32 test statistic) with the opinion that men make better business executives. Despite gender equality being politically correct in China, traditional attitudes about gender persist, perhaps diminished, but still discernible (Ji and Wu, 2018 is a portal into literature).

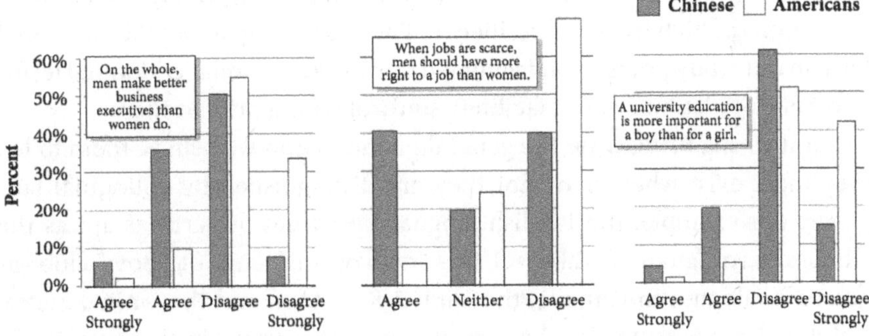

Figure 8.2 Gendered Opinion in China and the United States

Note: These are responses to World Values Surveys of national probability samples in China (2300 respondents in 2013) and the United States (2232 respondents in 2011). Bars show the percent of each sample giving the indicated response (excluding the few "no answer" and "don't know" responses). Chinese opinions on gender are significantly more conservative than American opinion: 709.03 chi-square on men make better business executives, 765.72 on men have more right to a job, 510.49 on college is more important for a boy than a girl. All reject the null hypothesis of no difference at well beyond a .001 level of confidence.

All the more surprising, therefore, that the gender effect so obvious among senior American managers in Figure 8.1A is absent in Figure 8.1B among our Chinese sample entrepreneurs. Performance is measured in the figure as a z-score return on assets for an entrepreneur's business.[3] As shown in prior chapters, entrepreneurs with more open networks ran more profitable businesses. The point here is that the solid line for men and the dashed line for women show similarly negative associations between network constraint and performance. The probability of identical associations for men and women is an acceptable .35 (Table 8.2). In short, Chinese women who leave formal organizations to create their own ventures can prosper just like men even in a context that remains relatively sexist. Of course, the gender neutrality we observe may be limited to entrepreneurs, or to the East Coast population from which our probability samples were drawn. Either way, the broader question is for subsequent research. Our point here is only to say that our observations are not obscured by the lack of, or reversal of, brokerage returns so visible in Figure 8.1A.

Beyond Colloquial Words: Exploratory Data Analysis

Our analysis shows that strong bridges exist in consequential, substantial numbers. Our evidence comes from network data on entrepreneurs in a society within which there is a colloquial term, guanxi, widely used to refer to relations of high trust and resilience. The widespread use of the colloquial term in our study population facilitated our work, as similar colloquial terms in other populations would facilitate study of strong bridges there.

But if strong bridges are the general phenomenon we believe them to be, they must exist whether or not they are distinguished by colloquial language. For example, the English language provides no term as apt as the Chinese term "guanxi." Table 8.1 lists "networking" and "old boys' club" as guanxi analogues in Canada, the United Kingdom, and the United States. But how lame is that? Yes, they are analogous to guanxi in that they imply special advantage for people included, but "networking" is used to label all kinds of relationships from casual socializing to guanxi-like bonds. And "old

---

[3] Within each sample, 2012 and 2018, we regressed return on assets across book value of assets and industry (five categories in the 2012 sample, two in the 2018 sample). The vertical axis in Figure 8.1B is the Studentized residual from those regressions.

boys' club" is an affiliation-based guanxi analogue, leaving many guanxi-like personal ties outside the club.

Absent colloquial clues, or substantive wisdom about a population, the strong-bridges hypothesis can be reverse-engineered to identify relationships likely to provide strong bridges. Gather representative network data sufficient to measure each relationship for trust or cooperation (vertical axis in the hypothesis, as in Figure 4.3) and an indicator of structural embedding (horizontal axis). Estimate the rate at which scores on the vertical axis increase with scores on the horizontal. The rate is expected by the closure-trust association to be positive (dashed line in Figure 4.3). Now analyze the extent to which categories of relations deviate from the average. Guanxi-like relations will be deviant because they are unexpectedly high on the vertical axis and poorly predicted by the horizontal (as illustrated in Figure 2.5A for relations with event contacts). The guanxi-like relations can be studied for the advantage they provide (as we have done subsequent to Figure 2.5).

Beyond Colloquial Words: Significant Events

Alternatively, if language does not provide a window for research, known correlates of guanxi might. We have established that the guanxi ties providing strong bridges have three primary correlates: Strength, time, and events. They are strong ties in the familiar sense of emotional closeness and trust, emphasizing resilience through time, forged in a positive connection during one or more past events that were stressful to one or both parties in the relationship. Most importantly, guanxi ties are relations of high trust relatively independent of structural embedding such as mutual friends.

The three correlates—strength, time, and events—are listed in ascending order of research effort required. Strength in the form of emotional closeness and trust is a current condition easily, and often, recorded in network surveys. Years known requires a survey respondent to think back in time—which is more demanding than asking how the respondent currently feels, so we facilitated the task for our Chinese entrepreneurs with an event name generator (Figure A2 and A3 in Appendix A) to build up a frame of reference for the years-known name interpreter (Figure A9, item 11 in Appendix A). Events are the most demanding. Questions about what, where, when, and who require interview time and can try a respondent's patience, so we focused on significant events in a person's history, which we felt the person is likely to recall vividly, and perhaps accurately. More, respondents seemed to enjoy telling their history.

In the absence of colloquial hints at strong bridges, adding an event name generator to an interview instrument is an engaging and reliable way to anchor network data in a person's life history, and identify likely strong bridges. The history can be a person's career (Burt 2001; Merluzzi and Burt 2021), or a project as we did with our sample entrepreneur businesses. Relations with event contacts resemble guanxi in fitting the strong-bridges hypothesis (Figure 4.4, Table 4.2). Of the contacts our entrepreneurs cited as guanxi, 87 percent had already been identified in the interview as event contacts. In part, the high percentage is because we asked for contacts helpful in multiple events. The complication is that event contacts are often not guanxi. The less significant the event, the less likely guanxi were named as helpful with the event: Of the 384 people named as helpful in founding the business, 86 percent were named as guanxi. Of the 384 people named as helpful with the most significant event other than founding, 55 percent were named as guanxi. Of the 384 people helpful with the next-most-significant event, 38 percent were named as guanxi, and a lower 27 percent were named as guanxi from the 932 people named as helpful on less significant events. Two or three milestone events are likely to generate more guanxi-like contacts than a broad inventory of events. The preceding chapters are an illustration of using events to identify guanxi-like relations, so we turn to the next-most complex correlate, time.

Beyond Colloquial Words: Socially Expected Duration

Merton's (1984) concept of a "socially expected duration," or SED, can be useful to identify guanxi-like relations. A SED is a socially prescribed or collectively patterned expectation about temporal duration embedded in social structure (cf. Merton 1984:265–266). The SED for your position in a firm is how long people like you can expect to spend in the position (not how long you actually stay, but how long you are expected to stay).

SEDs in an organization can be studied in two ways: as a description of the organization, or as a baseline from which individuals deviate. For example, Ph.D. programs typically last about six years, and academics in North America spend three to four years on average at the associate rank before promotion to full professor. People with certain demographic and human capital characteristics can expect to spend more or less time in specific positions in their firm, in their industry, in their economy. Figure 8.1A makes the alternative use of SEDs to capture performance by measuring how quickly a person is promoted relative to peers. These are people about whom peers say, "She was certainly young to get that promotion!" or, "Yes, John has been waiting a long time for his promotion."

SEDs apply equally well to relations. For example, Quintane and Carnabuci (2016:1348) identify long-term relations by email exchanges that last more than a week. The one-week criterion was selected because the study population's activities had a "weekly rhythm" and employees often spoke of work in terms of weekly intervals. On a related note, SEDs are implicit in our Figure 2.4A on relationship duration. Bridge relations are compared to embedded relations in terms of their socially expected durations in a population of American analysts and investment bankers. On average, 92 percent of bridge relations end within the first year they are formed. The average for structurally embedded relations is much lower, 53 percent. Bridges that survive the first year, however, decay more slowly thereafter: 82 percent before they reach second year, 52 percent before they reach third year. By the third year, bridge relations and structurally embedded relations decay at statistically indistinguishable rates before their fourth year. Thus, if a relationship between bankers survives beyond two years, it is relatively independent of structural embedding. Such relations could be viewed as resilient guanxi analogues.

Results in Figure 8.3 support that speculation. As a reminder, Figure 8.3A displays levels of trust in guanxi versus other contacts across levels of structural embedding for the Chinese entrepreneurs (cf. Figure 4.4B). Consistent with the closure-trust association, there is a statistically significant positive association between structural embedding and trust in routine contacts (dashed line). Consistent with the strong-bridges hypothesis, trust is high in guanxi contacts and relatively independent of structural embedding (solid line).[4]

---

[4] Test statistics in Figure 8.3 are estimated across relationships with respondent fixed effects and jackknife standard errors generating the reported t-test statistics. All relationships are included in the China test statistics (Figure 8.3A), and parameter estimates across all relations are displayed as Model M3 in Table 4.2. Corresponding to Model M3, estimates for a logit model with individual fixed effects and jackknife standard errors predicting strong analyst and banker relations generates the following three parameter estimates across all 46,342 relationships in Figure 8.3B (see Figure 4.3 for parameter names): 0.81 for the slope β of the closure-trust association in routine relations

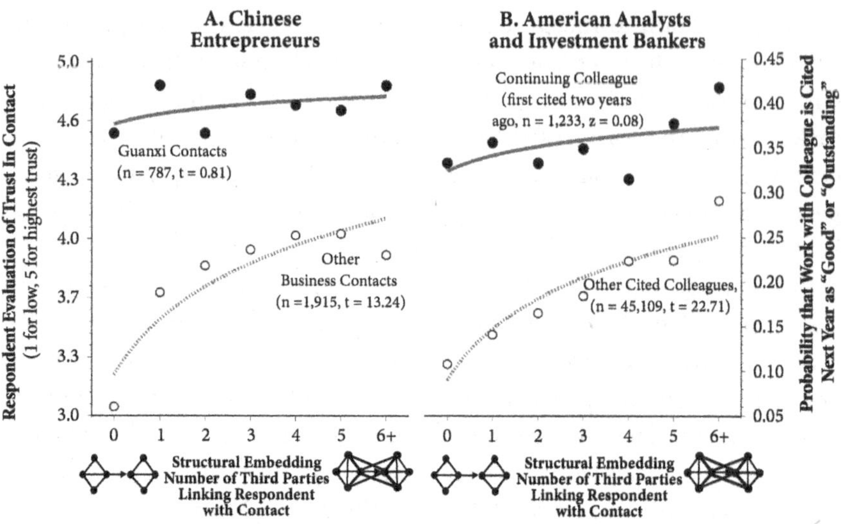

Figure 8.3 Strong Bridges in Very Different Populations

Note: Dots are average Y scores at each level of X. Regression lines go through the plotted data.

The term guanxi would be alien in name to most American analysts and investment bankers, but Figure 8.3B shows that relationships that have survived for more than two years among the study analysts and bankers are guanxi-like according to the strong-bridges hypothesis. The network data (adapted from Burt 2010:174–175) are annual evaluations of colleagues in which the evaluator chooses colleagues to evaluate. The vertical axis indicates the probability that the evaluator chooses to work with a colleague again next year and gives him or her a top evaluation. The horizontal axis varies from left to right with increasing closure around the evaluator-colleague relationship this year. To the left, the sociogram beneath the axis shows evaluator and colleague with no mutual contacts (bridge relationship). To the right, evaluator and colleague have many contacts in common (deep structural embedding).

(21.54 t-test), .34 for the γ level adjustment describing the higher trust in guanxi-like long-term relationships (3.42 t-test), and −.45 for the λ slope adjustment describing trust less dependent on structural embedding around the guanxi-like long-term relationships (−2.75 t-test). The 1233 analyst and banker relations that are guanxi-like for surviving beyond two years are reduced to 937 observations in the estimation because so few relations survive that long. Where an analyst or banker had only one such relation, it is absorbed in the fixed effects. Regardless, the test statistics in both Figure 8.3 graphs show strong difference between the positive closure-trust association for routine relations, and negligible association with structural embedding for guanxi and guanxi-like relations.

Only a small minority of working relationships survive past two years (1233 of 46,342, just under 3 percent). Routine relations that do not reach two years show the usual positive association between structural embedding and trust in routine contacts (dashed line in Figure 8.3B). Those that survive past two years show guanxi-like characteristics of high trust, relatively independent of structural embedding (0.81 t-test for the solid line in Figure 8.3B). These longer-lasting relations would be our selection to analyze as a source of strong bridges across groups in the financial organization.

Beyond Colloquial Words: Sentiment and Structural Embedding

A fourth strategy for identifying guanxi-like relations absent colloquial language is to use relationship strength combined with structural embedding. Here we report findings from four online surveys targeting college-educated adults aged thirty to sixty-five in four European countries during the Winter and Spring of 2023: England, France, Germany, and Italy.[5] The surveys were distributed to non-representative samples through an international market research firm. Absent the rigor of representative samples conducted under survey protocols like the GSS, we limit our use of these data to illustration. Still, the European results are valuable as replication because they display a pattern consistent with the Chinese results in Chapter 4. The European results are also valuable as illustrative replication for the behavioral measure of trust employed in the surveys.

Network Data in Four European Populations

We used the General Social Survey (GSS) network name generator to get a rough cut on respondent networks. We asked for six to seven contacts with whom respondents had discussed over the past six months matters important to them. We did not ask about specific events or guanxi-like characteristics. A name-interpreter question asked about emotional closeness with each cited contact. We collected complete surveys from 3382 participants citing a total of 19,275 contacts (4176 in England, 4488 in Germany, 4588 in Italy, and 6023 in France). We scaled the network data

---

[5] The instrument was developed in English, then translated into Italian, German, and French. We used professional translation services and verified the quality of the translated text through back-translation and pre-piloting with native speakers to ensure that each survey conveyed the same meaning and achieved comparable natural language flow and accessibility.

as described in Chapter 4 to measure the strength of indirect connection between respondent and each contact (Eq. 2). Respondents feel "especially close" to about half of their cited contacts (43 percent are deemed especially close, 37 percent close, 20 percent less than close). We operationalize strong bridges in these data as relations with contacts that meet two criteria: (a) the respondent deems the contact especially close, and (b) there is low structural embedding around the respondent's tie to the contact (weighted indirect connection less than one, as in Chapter 4, which means less than one especially close mutual friend).[6]

Behavioral Measure of Trust

In Chapter 4, we used an opinion measure of trust. For each contact, respondents said 1 for low trust, 2, 3, 4, or 5 for high trust. It is common practice to ask respondents to express trust on multi-point scales, but a skeptic could worry about two kinds of contamination when the trust opinion is response to a name-interpreter question in a network survey.

First, the respondent is asked to repeatedly sort contacts for whom she likes, how long she has known each person, how often she speaks with them, and so on. Given the fixed citation order of names presented to respondents to evaluate with respect to name interpreters, does simultaneously asking multiple name-interpreter questions including trust affect the trust ratings?[7]

Second, a skeptic could worry about implicit social norms, especially in closed networks. We described in Chapter 2 two reasons to expect the closure-trust association: inertia (similarity/proximity of people with mutual friends), and reputation (mutual friends ensure awareness of good and bad behavior). I know Sam well enough from past behavior not to trust

---

[6] Two reassuring points here: First, we get similar results using a more stringent criterion for strong bridges (indirect connection less than .5), but many fewer observations of strong bridges. Second, we went back to the results in Chapter 4 to see whether we would see the same support for the strong-bridges hypothesis if we distinguished the category of especially close ties in the same way we here distinguish the category of guanxi ties. The pattern of results is quite similar (with respondent fixed effects and jackknife standard errors), which gives us confidence in the European surveys as replication: There is strong evidence of trust facilitated by structural embedding (beta estimate is .95, 15.25 t-test, versus the .94 estimate in Model M4, Table 4.2, 15.30 t-test). In addition, there is strong evidence of trust in bridge contacts with whom the respondent feels especially close (gamma estimate is 1.61, 19.90 t-test, versus the .95 in Model M4, 30.61 t-test). Most importantly, trust in especially close contacts is relatively independent of structural embedding (lambda estimate is −.62, −9.42 t-test, versus the −.57 in Model M4, −9.76 t-test).

[7] Correlation between the name-interpreters suggests a "yes" answer to the question. Across the 2702 contacts cited by respondents in the 2018 survey, 73 percent of variance in trust can be predicted from respondent differences (14 percent for respondent fixed effects) and how a respondent answered closeness, years known, and contact frequency (59 percent).

him, but I keep that knowledge to myself within our circle of mutual friends to avoid the discord that would result from my opinion becoming known. Keep that knowledge to yourself often enough, and it becomes an unspoken social norm. Our respondents were assured of confidentiality, but why take a risk? Just say you trust Sam. There is no cost. The risk of blowback from friends is zero. So are trust ratings biased up for respondents accustomed to making positive public statements about trustworthy colleagues and friends?

We see potential in combining network data with behavioral games to lessen both forms of contamination. We had some success with that in the 2012 survey (reported in Figure 2.3B), so we went a step further in the 2023 survey. We had respondents play the trust game (described in a moment) with an anonymous other respondent, then play a round of the game with each cited contact. With respect to contamination from prior name-interpreter questions, the behavioral game is a break from opinion name interpreters to a new kind of question. With respect to implicit social norms, behavior in the virtual game is fully anonymous. None of a respondent's contacts will ever know how the respondent behaved in the virtual games with contacts. In this situation of a cash outcome free of social monitoring, we expect more discrimination in trust. Indeed, 4 percent of contacts in Chapter 4 were labeled "low trust" in the sense that the contact had in the past "often misled people from who he asked favors." That percentage is about the same in the 2012 survey (5 percent), lower in the 2021 survey (2 percent). In contrast, 38 percent of contacts in our European surveys were deemed untrustworthy in the behavioral games. These are different populations observed at different times under different circumstances, but trust seems clearly less likely in the behavioral games. All the more pleasant to see replication of the Chapter 4 results on strong bridges.

The Game

Respondents were primed by having them play one round of the trust game with an anonymous stranger (whose decision had been previously recorded). The widely-used game consists of one player sending money to the other, which is multiplied, then the second player decides how much to return.[8] The goal was to ground decisions in real financial

---

[8] The procedure is similar to the "strategy method" described by Fehr et al. (2002), in which the second player (trustee) makes the decision prior to the respondent's decision, so that both decisions can be matched without delay and without a counterpart playing the game simultaneously

stakes—encouraging more deliberate, consequential choices—before playing a hypothetical variant of the game with the respondents' own network contacts.[9]

The trust game is widely recognized for its effectiveness (Alós-Ferrer and Farolfi, 2019; Johnson and Mislin, 2011). The game simulates an economic interaction between two roles: An investor (trustor), and a receiver (trustee), where the participant's decisions can lead to monetary gains. In our surveys, respondents begin with an endowment of 200 points (100 points convert to 1 euro) and face a binary choice: Keep their points, or invest them with the other player. Choosing to invest is an act of trust. The initial 200 points are doubled to 400, and transferred to the other person. The other person, now holding 600 points, decides whether to keep it all or return half to the respondent. If the respondent suspects that the other person will keep it all, then the respondent can keep the initial 200 points, and the game ends—leaving the other person with nothing.[10]

Four characteristics of the game make the decision to invest a choice of trust as outlined by Rousseau et al. (1998), distinguishing the choice from mere coordination (Coleman 1990:97–99): (1) The respondent's decision to invest gives complete control of the respondent's investment to the other player to use as the other sees fit. (2) If the other player is trustworthy (shares the gains), the respondent will be better off than if he or she did not invest. (3) Respondent's decision to trust is voluntary. (4) The respondent has to make his or her decision before knowing what the other will do.

(Johnson and Mislin, 2011 find no association between method and behavioral decisions). In this study, informants were first paired with a computer simulation to ensure a diverse yet controlled set of responses for the actual survey respondents. The selection of informants in the game is then randomized, maintaining the anonymity of the game and ensuring that no personal biases influence the trust decision. This approach not only avoids ethical concerns related to deception, but also mimics real-life trust scenarios where synchronous decisions are often made without specific information about the other party. Furthermore, using a pool of informants for the second move in the trust game means that data collection in behavioral experiments with large random populations does not require coordination between respondent interviews (for difficulties, see Fehr et al., 2002). Finally, we should note that we are not concerned with whether the trust placed in the other was reciprocated. We focus entirely on the respondent's initial move.

[9] In previous research, Falk et al. (2023) confirmed a high within-sample correlation between actual game decisions and survey decisions, particularly for first-mover behavior in trust games.

[10] We adopted a binary variation of the game (Berg et al. 1995). Similar to Ermisch and Gambetta (2010), we prohibit partial investments to emphasize a clear distinction between trust and distrust, trustworthy and untrustworthy actions. In doing so, we limit the influence of other motives, such as risk aversion, which might predict how respondents divide the amount they are willing to return. That is, respondents are not allowed to "risk a little" of their resources by trusting the other person, or to be "a little" trustworthy in response to the other person. This methodological choice ensures that trust is measured as an absolute value and not as a gradient. Respondents either trust or do not, which allows clearer interpretation of the responses.

After the respondents registered their game decision, and before they learned what the other person had decided, they were asked: "Now that you know how the game is played, what choices would you make if you knew the other person in the game was one of the people you named earlier as someone with whom you often discuss important matters? For each name listed below, click whether you would KEEP or INVEST if you were playing the game with the row person. As before, the row person will not know your game choice."

Results

Trust varies as expected across contacts, as illustrated in Figure 8.4. Relationships are sorted on two dimensions. The first is especially close relations versus relations less than especially close. The second is bridge relations versus embedded relations (bridges defined as in prior chapters by weighted strength of indirect connection less than one especially close mutual friend, Eq. 2 in Chapter 4). The vertical axis is the probability of trust in a contact.[11]

Two points are illustrated. First, the closure-trust association is apparent. Trust increases from left to right across the solid bars—lowest in weak bridge relations (.28 for white bar), higher in weak embedded relations (.35 for grey bar), and highest in strong embedded relations (.49 for black bar). Second, strong bridges are a marked exception to the closure-trust association. Trust is high in strong bridges (.47 for striped bar), almost as high as trust in the traditional strong ties embedded in mutual friends (.49 for black bar). More, there are quite a few strong bridges. Of the 11,578 contacts cited by respondents who trusted some contacts but not others, 1077 are strong bridges. That is one in ten cited relations, a ratio interestingly similar to what we found among the Chinese entrepreneurs (Figure 4.8).

The differences apparent in Figure 8.4 are statistically strong. Table 8.3 contains estimates for Model M4 in Table 4.2 with respondent differences

---

[11] Contact-specific trust is computed as the probability of displaying trust by sending the 200 points to the contact, adjusted for contact citation order (less trust expected in contacts cited later) and a respondent's average probability of trusting contacts (some respondents display more trust than other respondents). We want to see where trust varies across network locations, so we control for citation order differences and respondent differences, and we exclude respondents who trust everyone or trust no one (see next footnote on the excluded respondents).

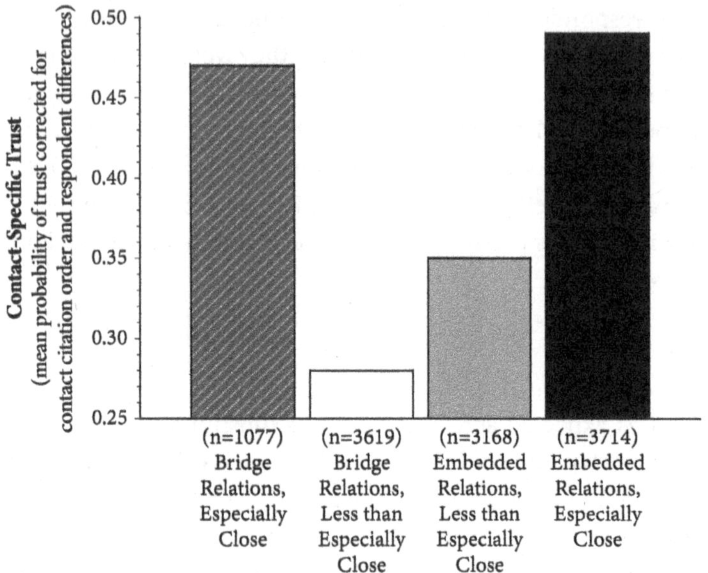

Figure 8.4 Trust Behavior in Four European Countries

Note: Vertical axis is average of observed trust minus baseline trust predicted by contact citation order and the respondent's average observed trust. Respondents who show no variation in trust across their contacts are excluded (trust all contacts or none).

held constant as random effects.[12] We control for the order in which contacts were mentioned. Both models in Table 8.3 show trust is more likely in relations with the first two or three people named.[13]

As in Table 4.2, there is a statistically significant association between trust and structural embedding (3.59 t-test, P < .001). Trust is more likely in contacts with whom the respondent feels especially close (11.96 t-test,

---

[12] We use random effects instead of respondent fixed effects because a large number of respondents do not vary in their trust behavior toward cited contacts. Of the 3382 respondents across the four surveys, 388 did not trust any of their contacts, and 1038 trusted all of their contacts. The other respondents, who expressed variable trust in their contacts, cited 11,578 contacts, down from the 19,275 cited across all contacts. We ran the model in the first column of the table using fixed effects (11,578 dyads), then random effects (19,275 dyads), and found negligible difference between coefficients (6.86 Hausman chi-square with 10 d.f., P ~ .74, and 13.92 Hausman chi-square with 10 d.f., for coefficients estimated from only respondents who trusted some contacts but not others, P ~ .18). We are comfortable with random effects across all 19,275 dyads substituting here for fixed effects.

[13] We control for citation order with dummy variables but the three key estimates in Model M4 are only slightly different if citation order is not held constant (.14 for beta, 3.20 t-test; .94 for gamma, 13.38 t-test, and −.39 for lambda, −5.89 t-test). Since stronger connections tended to be cited earlier, controlling for citation order throws away some differences that are substantive rather than methodological. In current surveys, we display contacts in random order for game play.

Table 8.3 Trusting Behavior Toward Which Contacts?

	Continuous Predictors (as in Model M4 Table 4.2)		Categorical Predictors	
	Coefficient	t-test	Coefficient	t-test
Intercept	.33		.49	
Structural Embedding (beta, weighted third parties)	.16	3.59	—	—
Level Adjustment for Especially Close (gamma)	.85	11.96	—	—
Slope Adjustment for Especially Close (lambda)	−.36	−5.48	—	—
Strong Bridge (bridge, especially close)	—	—	.51	8.09
Weak Bridge (bridge, less than esp. close)	—	—	−.08	−2.10
Embedded Strong Tie	—	—	.46	11.25
Embedded Weak Tie (reference category)	—	—	—	—
Contact One (reference category)	—	—	—	—
	−.01	−.28	−.02	−.43
Contact Two	−.12	−2.26	−.13	−2.45
Contact Three	−.18	−3.47	−.19	−3.70
Contact Four	−.27	−4.53	−.28	−4.80
Contact Five	−.23	−3.66	−.25	−3.91
Contact Six	−.40	−5.51	−.42	−5.76
Contact Seven	−.41	−5.17	−.43	−5.40
Contact Eight				

Note: These are logit models predicting trust behavior from 3382 respondents in England, France, Germany, and Italy toward their 19,275 contacts. Respondent random effects are used to control for respondent differences, and jackknife standard errors define t-tests.

$P < .001$). Trusting people to whom one feels especially close is not surprising, but it is important to hold the sentiment constant when estimating the slope adjustment to structural embedding. The positive closure-trust association is reversed and eliminated by the slope adjustment for especially close relationships (−5.48 t-test, $P < .001$). When a respondent is especially close to someone, they trust the person despite an absence of mutual friends.

The second model in Table 8.3 replaces the continuous network measures with the four-category measure shown in Figure 8.4. With embedded weak ties as the reference category, trust is high in embedded strong ties (.46 coefficient, 11.25 t-test, P < .001), and low in weak bridges (routine contacts reached by a bridge relation (embedded weak ties −2.10 t-test, P ~ .04). The key point is that strong bridges—that is, especially close contacts with whom the respondent does not have a mutual friend—offer the same high level of trust found in strong embedded relations (.51 coefficient, 8.09 t-test, P < .001).

In the spirit of replication, there is a third point to be emphasized: The pattern of results in Figure 8.4 across the four European countries is consistent within each country. Figure 8.5 shows the Figure 8.4 data displayed repeatedly within each country. The closure-trust association is evident in the increasing heights of white, to grey, to black bars. The outlier high trust in strong bridges is evident in the substantial height of the striped bars. This is least pronounced in France, but strong bridges in England and Germany are associated with higher levels of trust than even the trust in especially close relations embedded in especially close mutual friends (striped bars versus black bars). It is tempting to speculate about why trust in strong bridges is higher in some countries, but it is important to recall that the marketing firm did not use professional probability sampling. Still, the results are

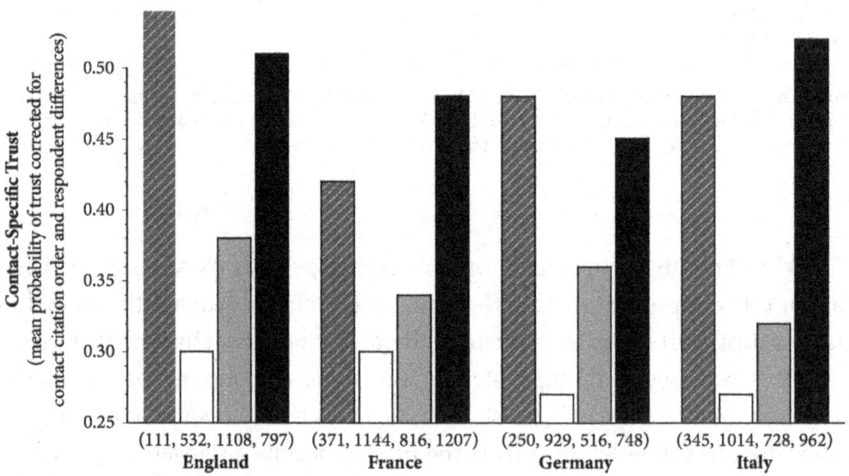

Figure 8.5 Trust Behavior within Each European Country
Note: See Figure 8.4 for category labels and note.

sufficient for our purposes: clear, consistent evidence of the familiar closure-trust association, matched by clear, consistent support for the strong-bridges hypothesis.[14]

Other Implications of Recognizing Strong Bridges

We have spoken at length about replication because we see that as the most pressing implication of our results on strong bridges. Replication will determine the extent to which, and the conditions under which, strong bridges are a routine feature of social networks (strong-bridges hypothesis) and a source of competitive advantage (advantage hypothesis). Beyond replication, we close with four other implications—three concerning network theory, one concerning network practice.

Tie Strength Is Separate from Network Structure

A theme throughout this book has been that tie strength is correlated with, but distinct from, network structure. As discussed in Chapter 2, research during the 1950s "golden age" of social psychology established that mutual friends are associated with stronger relationships. Milgram (1967) and Granovetter (1973) popularized the implication that the weak connections between groups are important for the spread of information—hence Granovetter's widely familiar metaphor: the strength of weak ties. Indeed, relations between groups are weaker on average than relations within groups, but most weak ties are within group, and some between group relations are strong (Burt 1992:29–30).

---

[14] The virtual game play in this section is all in the respondent's imagination, so it should not be surprising to learn that how a respondent believes contacts will behave is shaped by how he himself behaves. Untrustworthy respondents tend to perceive contacts as untrustworthy. For example, from the priming game played by respondents (before they play games with the cited contacts), we know whether the respondent would share with a stranger who trusted him. Among the respondents who trust some, but not all, their contacts, 43 percent are untrustworthy in the priming game (i.e., they do not share the funds transferred to them by the stranger). The percentage is lower for respondents who trust all of their cited contacts (35 percent of 1038 respondents) and considerably higher for respondents who trust none of their cited contacts (67 percent of 388 respondents). Given this reflection of self in respondent perceptions of probable contact behavior, we added to the continuous model in Table 8.3 the binary variable of whether a respondent was trustworthy in the priming game. Statistically, that variable emerges the strongest predictor of respondent trust in contacts (18.72 t-test). However, estimates of the coefficients in the strong-bridge hypothesis remain similar to the estimates reported in Table 8.3 (.16 for beta, 3.66 t-test; .84 for gamma, 11.73 t-test, and −.36 for lambda, −5.41 t-test.

This book has been about those occasional strong bridges beyond one's own group. When presenting this work at conferences, someone typically remarks that the point is obvious from structural hole theory. It is true that structural hole theory emphasizes the advantage of any relationship that provides access to non-redundant information (Borgatti and Halgin 2011 for a succinct statement). But debates persist over how to separate tie strength from network structure (Kim and Fernandez 2023; Neal 2022, 2024). A central purpose in this book has been to clarify that distinction—and to drive it home by digging through layer after layer of data from probability samples of Chinese entrepreneurs. As has so often been argued and demonstrated, advantage is associated with bridge relations—but not weak-tie bridges; only strong bridges. The evidence corroborates an early suspicion: Brokerage is most valuable where task ambiguity is highest. That is precisely where trusted brokers—not fleeting contacts—are best positioned to turn uncertainty into advantage (Burt 2005:94).

Resilient Competitive Advantage

Strong bridges are the active ingredient in competitive advantage (Chapters 4 and 5), and strong bridges are relatively resilient (Chapter 7). Together, the two statements imply that the competitive advantage provided by strong bridges can be stable. This is in contrast to the claim often made that brokerage is a fragile advantage, as we discussed in Chapter 2 (Stovel et al. 2011; Burt 2026). For temporal resilience, we only have the evidence in Chapter 7, which could be unique to COVID, or affected by our difficulty matching confidential contacts over time. As with the rest of the book, we are eager to see replication results on the resilience of strong bridges. Pending that work, we expect people advantaged by strong bridges to be advantaged again and again over time.

Extreme change could be an exception to our expectations. Suppose the collapse—of a political system, a regulatory regime, an institutional order—is such that existing strong bridges no longer produce value. An American investor's privileged access to Chinese markets is suddenly devalued by a policy shift. A lobbyist's influence evaporates when electoral turnover replaces familiar policymakers with new actors and new rules. The reflex is to argue that brokers adapt. Brokerage, after all, offers not just a structural advantage but a learned behavioral foundation of access and adaptation that endures (Burt 2010). But what if even the network itself disappears? Creating strong ties is a long-term strategy. Relational embedding takes time. To the extent that time and events are necessary ingredients in developing relational strength independent of structural embedding, such ties are going to develop more slowly than strong ties supported by the structural embedding created by joining an existing group of interconnected friends.

We cannot resolve this issue with our cross-sectional data, but we can sharpen the question. Across levels of structural embedding, Figure 8.6 shows how long our sample entrepreneurs knew their contacts. Dark bars describe relations with guanxi. White bars describe relations with non-guanxi contacts.

Two points stand out. First, relations with guanxi are older. The dark bars show double-digit years known versus single-digit for relations with non-guanxi contacts. Second, the dark bars show that structural embedding around guanxi is independent of relationship age. It is non-guanxi relations

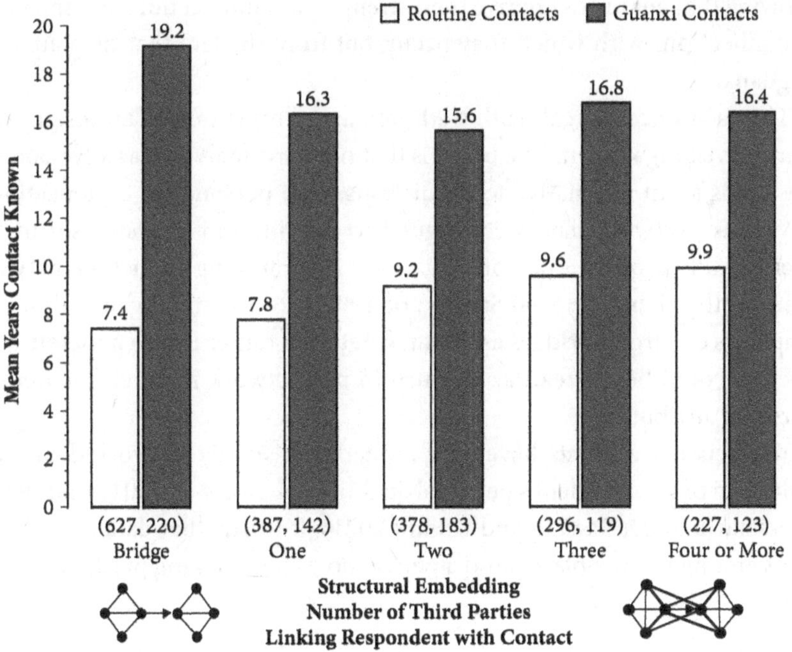

Figure 8.6 Years Known Across Levels of Structural Embedding

Note: From the 2018 survey, structural embedding is indirect connection through third parties, rounded to lower integer (footnote 22, Chapter 4). A bridge is a connection with less than one especially close mutual friend (embedding < 1).

that accumulate third parties over time, or tend to emerge within social circles of mutual friends. Among these, relations embedded in four or more mutual friends are, on average, two years older than unembedded bridge relations.[15] Two years is statistically significant, but the marginal change puts the difference in perspective. Even these bridge relations were known, on average, for seven years—compared to nine years for deeply embedded relations. That difference is irrelevant to someone who needs a network today. In sum, we expect a stable competitive advantage for people with strong bridges—but set aside as uncertain the value of strong bridges in the face of extreme exogenous shock.

Sentiment Versus Structure

Strong bridges are less a social connection than an individual's interpretation of connection. The analysis of multiplexity in Chapter 5 is valuable for showing that guanxi ties derive their strength and impact not from the kinds of connections with which they occur, but from the fact that they are seen as guanxi.

This is at once a break with tradition, and a repetition of an insight that some have long known. The break is that network analysis was advocated in the 1980s as an alternative to predictions from personal or organizational attributes. Network data were argued to provide indicators closer to the social reality around a person (e.g., Burt 1984 arguing to include network items in the General Social Survey; or 1992:186–192 more generally). Our emphasis on strong bridges as an interpretation rather than a concrete connection could be misread as a return to pre-network research focused on personal attributes.

Yet, network analysts have long argued that survey network data are a reflection of a respondent's personal qualities (Mehra et al. 2001; Kilduff and Krackhardt 2009; Tasselli and Kilduff 2021). It is true that data on connections among key people around a person do well in making predictions, but

---

[15] The horizontal axis in the figure is defined by intervals of the strength of indirect connection between respondent and contact through mutual friends (Eq. 2). Regress years known across the continuous predictor, using respondent fixed effects to hold constant respondent differences in age, industry, city, etc. When we run that regression across the 1915 non-guanxi relations, we get a jackknife t-test of 5.69 (P < .001). Structural embedding increases with years known. Across the 787 guanxi ties, structural embedding is independent of years known (0.01 t-test, P ~ .99).

the data are not about reality so much as an indicator of how the respondent is looking at the world. We need not worry about accurate recall of relations, or whether the respondent selected appropriately important topics for discussion. However accurate the respondent or esoteric the discussion, network data distinguish respondents who live in a closed, homogeneous social world from respondents who live in an open, heterogeneous world. That variation is associated with respondent sentiment, whether enduring as respondent personality, or a fleeting shadow of mood. There is wisdom in viewing the contacts named in an interview as a probabilistic sample drawn from a broader set of respondent contacts (Fischer and Offer 2020), with probabilities affected by respondent mood. Make respondents feel threatened, and their reported networks are likely to change—toward the support of closure for lower-status respondents, or toward the freedom of an open network for higher-status respondents (Smith et al. 2012).

We are not troubled by our focus on a category of relations independent of concrete connection, but we acknowledge that strong bridges as we have sketched them are more subject than concrete connections to respondent sentiment and beliefs. Walking one step further down that path, new questions arise: To what extent is the advantage associated with strong bridges due to the self-confidence and stamina needed to form and maintain such relations; or to an ability to trust people beyond one's own group?

Network Practice

One of the consequences of academic progress in linking advantage to network structure has been the broad use of the noun as a verb. What was once socializing, is now "networking," which we understand to be socializing to get ahead. Nasty imagery in common parlance (Casciaro et al. 2014). The above implications for network theory have implications for networking, the theory's stepchild: Do not expect too much from weak ties. Weak-tie bridges index contact. Strong bridges index integration.

The typical goals for networking events are to build a sense of community and improve personal well-being. Reasoning from the strength of weak ties, the advice for such events is that participants should strike up conversations with new contacts. You learn new things from new people, and at the same time discover things you have in common.

But we do not welcome information contrary to our beliefs or understandings. We are each of us fully armed with rationalizations that protect (indeed, isolate) us from information inconsistent with what we know. Networking events can end up doing little more than reinforcing existing connections (Ingram and Morris 2010). To any one individual, new acquaintances are frightening, obnoxious, or trivial. Time spent with them increases one's felt distance from them, providing anecdotal illustration of the distance. Casual contact imposed by networking events can result in deeper structural holes.

It is certainly true that new information is more likely to be encountered in discussion with someone beyond one's group, but it is more likely to be accepted if the source is trusted. To the extent that feelings about the source matter, which we know it does, network training puts too much emphasis on adding casual ties beyond one's group, and not enough on building strong bridges. Connections beyond your group are, on average, not the goal. Those are just weak ties; more sources of email to discard. Sift through the many weak ties to find people with the potential to be strong bridges.

Time is an issue. To the extent that time and events are primary ingredients in developing strong bridges, such ties are going to develop more slowly than casual ties. But to say existing strong bridges developed slowly over time and through events is not to say that they must develop that way. In this book we ask where strong bridges exist. Imagine asking where they could exist, and how quickly (Frank et al. 1993; Meyerson et al.1996).

With a recognition of strong bridges in mind, sort through the constant influx of weak ties for individuals who have the potential to be strong bridges—people beyond your group, but in some way admirable in skills, spirit, or understanding. You do not care for many in that group, but John is a sound person, and Helen is a solid source of advice. As so many social scientists have said before, local cohesion varies inversely with societal fragmentation. What makes you feel more closely connected to people like you makes you feel more distant from outsiders. In the resulting bridge-and-cluster structure, so characteristic of contemporary society, integration across clusters requires the occasional strong bridge.

Fieldwork and Network Interview Instrument

Data for this book are taken primarily from three surveys conducted in 2012, 2018, and 2021 with stratified probability samples of heads of business leading small to medium size private enterprises in the Yangtze River Delta region of China. For most firms in this category, the target role is typically held by one of the founders or current owners. In the 2012 survey, 88 percent of respondents were owners; in 2018, 90 percent; and in 2021, 89 percent. The remaining CEOs were professional managers, typically hired by the founders after a few years of operation. In 2018, there was no significant difference in company size (as indicated by company assets) or age, between owners and professional managers. In 2012 and 2021, however, professional managers tended to lead slightly older, significantly larger firms.[1] Sample stratification by city, industry, and firm age is described at the beginning of Chapter 3 for the 2012 sample, Chapter 4 for the 2018 sample, and Chapter 7 for the 2021 sample. This Appendix details collaboration with the Chinese survey organization, and the interview process.

Survey Preparations

Collecting personal and company information is a matter of trust. Respondents need to trust that the research is relevant and worthy of their time and attention—a critical factor for busy and successful business leaders. They also need to trust that data protocols will be followed precisely as communicated and agreed upon. Researchers, on the other hand, need to be confident that the survey organization and interviewers they hire will conduct sampling, interview invitations, interviews, and data handling as specified. This is a challenge in general, but even more so when face-to-face surveys are conducted in cultural and institutional settings outside the researcher's home environment. The liability of foreignness, well-documented in international business, can be a critical barrier in international research.

We were fortunate to build on a long-standing business relationship with a Chinese survey organization that one of the authors had worked with since 2005. Since then, and through continuous collaboration on various projects, both parties had developed a mutually reliable relationship based on honest feedback and joint problem-solving. This

---

[1] In 2012, the mean firm age was 11.6 years for owner CEOs and 13.2 for professional CEOs. Owner CEOs reported a market value of firm assets of 19.1 million CNY, while professional CEOs estimated their assets to be 50.2 million CNY. In 2021, there is no significant age difference between both groups, yet professional managers run larger companies with an estimated asset value of 430 million CNY compared to an estimated asset value of 134 million run by owner CEOs.

foundation allowed us to introduce increasingly sophisticated, often novel types of survey questions—even some that our local partner and professional interviewers had not previously used, or in some cases, not even heard of.

Certainly, lack of familiarity with unconventional survey methods is a challenge, but a surmountable one. To ensure the quality and validity of the data collection, we relied on three processes. First, each part of the survey (company module, network instrument, and lab-in-the-field games) was reviewed in team meetings that included not only the team leaders but also all field interviewers and data entry staff. Our discussions went beyond verifying the linguistic accuracy and natural flow of the Chinese survey instruments. Drawing on the extensive experience of professional field staff who frequently interviewed business leaders, the meetings also helped to identify potential sensitivities— questions that our respondents might not feel comfortable answering as phrased—or even questions that seemed either too obvious or too remote and would therefore undermine the credibility of the study. Our discussions highlighted the use or avoidance of certain words that had positive or negative connotations and could therefore bias the respondent's answer. More, the team actively participated in discussing the wording and value of interviewer instructions to ensure that all team members were able to handle the relatively complex material in an efficient and professional manner—an important concern when interviewing business leaders, who are notoriously short of time.

Second, we conducted multi-day training workshops with all team members. The interviewers conducted a series of mock interviews with each other, which helped them internalize the flow and proper use of the interview and supporting materials. These interviews also provided an opportunity to experience the interview—and its challenges—from the respondent's point of view, and to learn how to respond to questions and queries without compromising the quality of the interviewee's answers. The training workshops were supported by written manuals and were led and supervised by at least one of the authors alongside research assistants. The aim of the workshops was to ensure that each interviewer felt able to conduct all parts of the survey in a professional and confident manner and, importantly, within approximately the same time frame— though events during an on-site interview at the company premises could always lead to delays or brief interruptions. The workshops usually ended with a series of mock interviews with local businesspeople who had agreed to be observed and then discussed by the whole team.

Third, to test the questionnaires and interviewer skills under real conditions, we conducted pilot interviews with business leaders located in the same cities and active in the same sectors as the intended target population of the main survey. The sampling of respondents followed the same procedure as in the main survey. The number of pilot interviews was set at 10 percent of the expected size of the main survey to ensure that we would have sufficient data to identify three types of problems.

(1) Poor handling of the questionnaire by interviewers—including errors in survey entries or overlooked interviewer instructions and interviewer bias visible in survey responses. This bias could result from a rushed presentation of the survey, or from an interviewer's particular attitude or behavioral style. For example, over the years, pilots have helped identify interviewers who rushed respondents through the network questionnaire, evidenced by systematically smaller-than-average networks. We identified interviewers who took an excessive amount of time—and risked losing the respondent's interest in the process.

(2) Questions flagged as problematic because interviewers reported a higher-than-usual number of respondent inquiries during the interview. This had not occurred in our 2018 and 2021 surveys.
(3) A lack of variation in responses, which made it clear that some newly introduced questions were simply not worth pursuing.

In sum, when we deployed the survey in the field, we were reasonably confident that we had a well-trained and dedicated team of field interviewers, along with survey instruments that were well-designed, competently administered, easily understood by respondents, and structured to generate meaningful variation in the data.

Company Module

All interviews were conducted face-to-face on the company premises. For the purpose of the interview, respondents were asked to provide a private room or office to ensure privacy from onlookers, but were invited to call in specialist staff if they needed confirmation or verification of information that was not immediately available—as was occasionally the case with financial company data.

Each survey began with a brief introduction covering the purpose of the study, privacy information, and the signing of a confidentiality agreement. Once the respondent confirmed that they understood all aspects of the interview process and privacy policy, the interviewer initiated the actual interview by recording the interview date, respondent code, and interviewer ID code—with signature—on the cover page of the questionnaire. A clock was started to record the total interview time at the conclusion of the company module.

The company module begins with questions about the respondent's personal and professional background. Whenever useful, these questions distinguished between the career paths of owner CEOs and professional CEOs. For many personal questions, we relied on tested wording from the Chinese version of the General Social Survey; a few personal questions were specifically designed for our surveys. For questions related to a firm's business development and strategies, we again drew on a corpus of questions that had been used successfully in surveys such as the China version of the World Bank Enterprise Surveys and the Chinese Private Enterprise Surveys. We added customized questions in response to insights gained from qualitative interviews with local business owners and other stakeholders. As our research evolved over several years, other questions emerged naturally from previous quantitative survey results. For example, where there was a notable clustering of responses, we followed up with more fine-grained response options, including opportunities for free-text explanations or entirely new questions. Finally, we included a number of items related to recent events. The most critical of these was the COVID pandemic, which we addressed in our 2021 survey with a dedicated set of questions exploring company strategic responses.

Because all three surveys covered a range of different industries (five in 2012, and two each in 2018 and 2021), all business-related questions about strategy, operations, and performance remained intentionally generic, framed to be equally applicable and relevant across industries.

Network Instrument

The network interview began after rapport was established with the respondent during the company module. The interviewer took out a booklet of materials under a separate cover (Figure A1 stapled along the dashed line), wrote the respondent's ID (identifying city and person) and interviewer's name on the cover, started the clock for the network interview, and then opened the booklet to begin a conversation about the history of the respondent's business. Figure A2 shows the two-page spread for this conversation, which was usually engaging and energizing for the respondent. A timeline is created that begins in the year the respondent's business was founded and runs through the previous year— 2017 in Figure A2, since we display the 2018 instrument in this Appendix.[2] To make it easier for the respondent to place dates, the timeline at the bottom of Figure A2 is divided in half, then divided in half again. The conversation then turns to significant events in the history of the business. The events, and their dates, are written on the respondent's timeline as indicated in the example.

Name Generators

The interviewer turns the page to name-generator questions (Figure A3) and hands a "network roster worksheet" to the respondent (Figure A4). The purpose of the network worksheet is to preserve the confidentiality of the respondent's business contacts. The interviewer asks questions 2, 3, 5, 6, and 7 in Figure A3, and the respondent writes names on their worksheet. After the questions are answered, the respondent constructs a nonredundant list of contacts on the "network roster" worksheet (Figure A5) following the instructions on page 6 of the interview, with assistance from the interviewer if needed. With the nonredundant list in hand, the respondent is directed to question 8 (in Figure A3), which asks to add "anyone particularly significant for your business who has not been mentioned."

At this point, the respondent's network roster worksheet contains up to fourteen names. There is a sequential ID number next to each name. The interviewer now goes back to the blank name generators on the interviewer's booklet and asks for the number of each contact named on each item (see Figure A3). Table 3.1 shows the number of contacts elicited by each name generator in the 2012 survey. The 700 respondents to the 2012 survey generated a total of 4,464 different contacts, averaging 6.38 contacts per network.

The final task of the name generators is to understand the events that the respondent deems important. Question 4, contains text in the interviewer's copy (upper right in Figure A3a), but not in the respondent's worksheet (upper right in Figure A4). For each contact that was helpful during a significant event, the interviewer asks, "Very briefly, what did the person do that was so helpful?" The interviewer records the response on the "Events Worksheet" and circles a code indicating whether the help provided was a resource, emotional support, a referral, or something else (Figure A6).

---

[2] The 2012 instrument was the same, except the timeline ended earlier and three name interpreters were not included (guanxi, collaboration, communication channels). The 2021 instrument was the same as in 2018, except that the collaboration interpreter and communication channels were dropped, and a behavioral game interpreter was added at the end.

Name Interpreters

The above concludes the name generation. Notice the greyed-out area on the right-hand side of pages in the network booklet (to the right in Figure A3). The greyed-out areas of the network instrument are cut away, leaving an open space to the right of each two-page spread. The network roster of names slides under a page from the right, providing a list of names next to the response options. Respondents answer each name interpreter for the listed names. For example, question 9 of the network booklet (right side in Figure A3) asks for gender. The respondent lines up the network roster with the response options and circles the appropriate gender for each person on the roster.

This continues for each subsequent page of the booklet. The interviewer turns a page and the respondent slides the network roster under the page to the right and answers the question about each person on the roster. Figure A9, items 11 to 18, show the subsequent name interpreters: emotional closeness, years known, contact frequency, communication channels (2018), trust, collaboration (2018), guanxi (2018 and 2021), kinds of connections between respondent and contact, and strength of connection between contacts. Two of the questions allow for multiple possible responses, so the interviewer hands the respondent a card to help with those questions: the Comms Card in Figure A7, and the Roles Card in Figure A8.

The name interpreter items are generic to the survey network data, except for the trust item. Two versions of the trust item were pre-tested: one based on full disclosure in Figure A9, item 14, and an alternative based on reciprocity: "For example, suppose one of the listed people asked for your help. The help is not extreme, but it is substantial. It is a level of help you cannot offer to many people. To what extent would you trust each person to do the right thing in returning a comparable favor in the future, either by helping you is a similarly significant way, or providing suitable compensation for your help?" Respondents in the pre-test had no difficulty with the idea of reciprocity; however, the "right thing" to do varied across respondents and kinds of contacts. The full disclosure version in Figure A9, item 14, had a consistent meaning for the respondents, so it became the version used in the survey.

The usual name generator/interpreter format was slightly modified to ensure respondent comfort talking about network contacts. First, as learned with the network items in the General Social Survey, respondents often stopped at three names in response to multi-name questions, so interviewers were trained to prompt with "Anybody else?" Second, the pre-test revealed discomfort in naming contacts, even though the respondents were encouraged to use nicknames and it would have been prohibitively expensive to track down a contact with the limited information elicited. The discomfort could have been linked to how the name generators were asked. Batjargal et al. (2013:1034n) found it sufficient to limit contacts to surnames in telephone interviews with Chinese entrepreneurs in Beijing, as did Zhang and Wong (2008:418), who relied on surnames because they found: "it is difficult to find businessman willing to talk openly about their network utilization. In particular, in recent years, using personal ties for venture fundraising from government agency or banks may be considered improper behavior." Whatever the reason, respondent comfort in this study was secured through the use of worksheets. Assisted by the interviewer, the respondent wrote his or her responses in the interview booklet using their own words. For the name generators, however, the respondent wrote contact names on a separate worksheet (Figure A4). Once the name generator items were complete, a sequential, non-redundant roster of contact names was created on a second worksheet (Figure A5) for reference when answering the subsequent name interpreter items. The respondent kept both worksheets after the interview. In the interview booklet sent for data entry, contacts were referenced only by ID number. The interviewer took away no names of contacts cited during the interview. The network data are complete for almost every respondent—a commendable achievement given the nature and complexity of the questions, and the business leaders being interviewed.

Scaling the Network Data

It is not uncommon to see categorical network data scaled in an ad hoc way to compute network metrics. Relations can be dichotomized into present versus absent—with a strong response category coded as 1, and all others as 0—or assigned a level of strength from the number of response categories (e.g., 1 for "especially close" in the Chinese network module, .75 for "close," .50 for "less close," and .25 for "distant").

An alternative is to infer relation strength from the way respondents use response categories. The general idea, based on balance theory (Heider 1958; Doreian et al. 1996), is that the respondent's relationship with a contact should be proportional in strength to the strength of relations that respondent and contact have with other contacts. If I feel close to Jie, I expect the other people close to me to feel close to Jie. The people from whom I feel distant I expect to feel distant from Jie. For probability samples of disconnected networks, such as the General Social Survey, Burt and Guilarte (1986) proposed that an "anchor" contact be identified as the contact most strongly connected to the respondent. By balance theory, the strength of the respondent's relationship with the anchor contact should be proportional to the strength of his perceived relationship between anchor and each other contact named. Associations between categories of relationship can then be used to scale the categories relative to one another.

Figure A10 shows the results for the 2012 network data (cf. Burt, 2010:290–292, for similar results within a management population). The anchor contact for each respondent is a person with whom the respondent has the strongest direct and indirect connection. Rows in the Figure A10 table distinguish categories of relation strength between respondents and their anchor contact. The 700 respondents cited a total of 4,464 contacts, one of whom per respondent is an anchor contact. The other cited contacts are distributed across the columns in the Figure A10 table according to their connection with the respondent's anchor contact. The graphic in Figure A10 shows the results of fitting a one-dimensional loglinear association model to the frequencies in the table (Goodman 1981). There are three broad levels of connection: At the top of the scale, "especially close" relations are strong, whether they are respondent to contact, or contact to contact. In the middle are "close," "less close," and something "neither distant nor especially close." "Distant" relations are together at the bottom of the scale. When scaled to vary from zero to one, the scores in Figure A10 define the following category scores: Especially close (1.0 with contacts, .99 between contacts), close (.57), neither close nor distant between contacts (.44), less close (.29), and distant (.06 with contacts, .00 between

Table A1 Descriptive Statistics on Network Metrics Computed from the Scaled 2012 Network Data

	Managers in Two American Firms		Chinese Entrepreneurs			
	Firm A	Firm B	Mean	Standard Deviation	Min	Max
Network Size (number of cited contacts)	9.09	7.07	6.38	1.48	3	12
Structural Embedding (mean number of contacts connected to respondent's contacts)	3.55	3.31	2.97	1.16	0.00	8.33
Network Density (mean connection strength between contacts)	.43	.49	.47	.18	.00	1.00
Effective Size (network size adjusted down for redundant contacts)	6.52	4.35	3.66	1.44	1.00	8.17
Network Constraint (zero to one, lack of structural holes among contacts)	.42	.49	.57	.14	.20	1.00
Network Betweenness (zero to one, monopoly access to structural holes between contacts)	.46	.37	.37	.19	.05	1.00

contacts). From left to right in Figure A10, the loglinear scores are −.677, −.599, −.270, −.058, .127, .734, and .743. Scaled category scores are computed as a loglinear score plus .677, quantity divided by (.743 + .677).

The final result is a symmetric, square matrix of variables measuring the strength of connections between respondent and each cited contact, and between every pair of cited contacts. Table A1 contains descriptive statistics on network indices computed from the matrix for each respondent. The listed indices are often used to measure the advantage provided by a network: size, structural embedding, density, constraint, effective size, and betweenness. These measures are widely available in network analysis software packages (Burt 2010: 293–300). The .47 mean density and .57 mean network constraint for the Chinese entrepreneurs are close to the respective means of .42 and .51 reported by Batjargal et al. (2013:1036) for sample entrepreneurs in China, France, Russia, and the United States, and similar to results in the first two columns of Table A1 for managers in two U.S. firms.

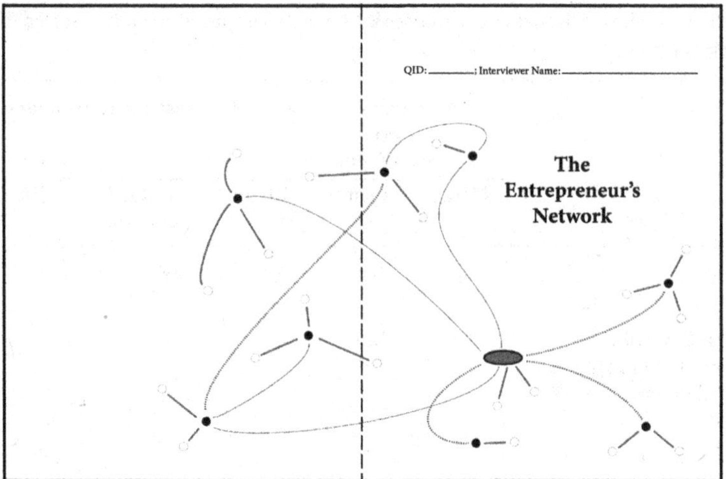

Figure A1 Network Booklet (English Translation)

1.Business Time Line

This first question asks you to look back through time to identify significant events in the history of your business.

A. Begin by defining the time-line. The line on the bottom of your worksheet represents time. Today, 2017, is at the extreme right. **At the extreme left, under "business founded," please write the year in which you founded your firm.** No need for months, just round to whole years. If you operate multiple firms, please complete the time line for the largest of your firms. As a guide, an illustrative time-line is provided at the top of the worksheet for a hypothetical business. The business was founded in 1997.

B. **In the middle of the line, write the year half-way between the founding date and today.** For the example firm in the box at the top of the worksheet, half-way is 2007 (2017 minus 1997 is 20, half of which is 10, so half-way is 1997 plus 10, or 2007). Again, just round to whole years.

C. **Write in the year at the two quarters.** For the example firm, a quarter is half of 10, which is 5, so the two quarters are marked 2002 and 2012. Again, just round to whole years.

D. **Using the four dates as a frame of reference, think about the most important event you experienced in building this business.** We rely on your judgment to determine what events are significant, but examples could include events like the ones that happened to the example firm at the top of your worksheet. After the firm was founded in 1997, the owner secured a relationship with a key technology partner in 1998. The business prospered. To expand faster, a bank loan was obtained in 2004. In 2005, the firm had to deal with the problem that a critical supplier was purchased so it was no longer available. A new supplier was arranged and the business grew into its first export contract in 2009. Four years later, in 2013, a contract was secured with the current primary export customer. **In your judgment, what was the one most important event in building this business? Indicate the year and nature of the event on the time line for your business.**

E. **Over the history of your business, what other significant events—besides founding the business, and the event you just mentioned—occurred in building the business?** Please limit yourself to four or fewer significant events, and please be sure to include the year in which each event took place.

You have a lot of space, so don't worry about scratching things out.

Business Time Line Worksheet

Time line for an Example Firm

Time Line for Your Firm

INTERVIEWER - Within this box, write under each event the order in which the event was mentioned. After founding, the most important event is event #1. Next mentioned event is #2, and so on.

Figure A2 Business Time Line (pp. 2–3)

Business Network
(hand over NETWORK WORKSHEET)

The next five questions generate a summary picture of the business network. To draw the picture, you will be asked about people, but we do not want to know any one's name. I will go through this network worksheet with you, asking about people who were useful to your business in one way or another. Without mentioning anyone's name to me, please write on your worksheet the names of people who come to mind in response to the questions. We will create a list of names then refer to people by their order on the list. No names. We need the worksheet to complete the list of contacts for the next section of the interview. You will keep the worksheet to yourself.

2. Let me begin with an example so you can see how the interview protects your confidentiality at the same time that a picture of the business network emerges. Your business time line shows that your firm was founded in (say founding year) **Please think back to your activities in founding the firm. Who was the one person who was most valuable to you in founding the firm?**

Please write in the box below the person's name so you can refer back to him or her later in the interview. Use any symbol that identifies the person for you-–an ideograph, first name, initials, any name that will let you identify the person.z

3. Now please do the same thing for each of the significant events you listed on your business time line. The first significant event you listed was (say first event) in (say year). Who was the person most valuable to you during that event? Please write on the first line below the person's name. The person most valuable in this event could be the same person who was most valuable to you in founding the firm. You would just enter the name again.

If you listed a second significant event, who was the person most valuable to you during the second event? Again, this could be the same person who was most valuable to you in the first event.

Third event?

Fourth?

Fifth?

INTERVIEWER: Check box if you had to probe to get a name for this event.

4. People can be helpful in many ways. **The first person you mentioned was particularly valuable when the business was founded in (insert year). Very briefly, what did the person do that was so helpful?** REPEAT FOR EACH CONTACT LISTED ON PAGE 4, WRITING RESPONSES ON "EVENTS SHEET." LEAVE EVENTS SHEET INSERTED BETWEEN PAGES 4 AND 5 WHEN FINISHED.

5. **Shifting now to business this year, and thinking about people inside or outside your firm, who are the three or four people who have been most valuable to your business activities this year?** Again, no need to say names. Just write their names in the boxes to the right so you can remember them later in the interview. Of course, these people valuable this year could be some of the same people you mentioned as valuable during significant events in the past.

6. In contrast to people who help and are valued in your business activities, there are usually some people who make life difficult. **Without mentioning the person's name, who was the most difficult person to deal with in your business activities this year?** Just jot a name or initials in the box below. Only you are going to know who this person is.

Interviewer follows up, and has respondent write response on interviewer's questionnaire: **Without mentioning the name, what did this person do that made things difficult for your business activities this year?**

7. **Shifting to happier thoughts, who do you think was your most valuable senior employee this year?** If the people you already listed as most valuable include your most valuable employee, just enter the person's again in the box to the right.

Figure A3 Name Generators (pp. 4–7)

(hand over ROSTER WORKSHEET)

The remaining network questions are about the people you named. This final worksheet is a list of names that gets inserted in the next few pages of the interview so that you can see the names as you answer some quick questions about the people. When the roster worksheet is pulled away, there is no indication of who the people are.

For example, to indicate the gender of each person named on the next page, you insert the list of names (insert blank list under next page), circle the gender of each person, and when the list is removed, there is no indication of the people named. You keep the roster worksheet, so the names remain confidential with you.

You could have named up to 12 people on the network worksheet. Most business leaders we survey name fewer than 12 because some people are named on more than one question. **Please write each person you named from first to last on the roster worksheet, making sure that no name appears more than once and no lines are skipped between names.**

For example, write in the first space on the roster worksheet the name of the person you named in Question 2 as valuable to you when you founded the firm.

In the second space, write the name of the person you named in Question 3 as most valuable during the first significant event for the firm. If the person named in the first event is the same person named in founding the firm, skip to the next name you mentioned. The list should contain each different person you named.

Continue entering names until you finish with the person named in Question 7 as the most valuable employee.

8. Now that you have a list of contacts on the roster worksheet, please look it over quickly. **Is there anyone particularly significant for your business who has not been mentioned?** If yes, please enter their names at the bottom of the list. There are many people you could mention. These would just be people particularly significant for your business. The roster can hold a maximum of 14 names.

Now that we have a network roster, I can record your responses to the network questions while protecting your confidentiality. I assume that contact 1, the first person on your roster worksheet, was the person named as most valuable during the founding of your firm. Correct?

What number on your roster worksheet is the person you named as most valuable during the first significant event in your firm's history? Interviewer: continue through Question 7 on the previous two pages.

Interviewer hand over questionnaire and ask respondent to insert roster worksheet to answer Question 9. When finished go to next page.

Figure A3 *continued*

9. Man or woman?
(circle answer)

		cut away grey section of page
1. man woman	1._______________	
2. man woman	2._______________	
3. man woman	3._______________	
4. man woman	4._______________	
5. man woman	5._______________	
6. man woman	6._______________	
7. man woman	7._______________	
8. man woman	8._______________	
9. man woman	9._______________	
10. man woman	10._______________	
11. man woman	11._______________	
12. man woman	12._______________	
13. man woman	13._______________	
14. man woman	14._______________	

BUSINESS NETWORK WOKSHEET
(This sheet remains with the respondent.)

The next five questions generate a summary picture of the business network. To draw the picture, you will be asked about people, but we do not want to know any one's name. I will go through this network worksheet with you, asking about people who were useful to your business in one way or another. without mentioning anyone's name to me, please write on your worksheet the names of people who come to mind in response to the questions. We will create a list of names then refer to people by their order on the list. No names. We need the worksheet to complete the list of contacts for the next section of the interview. You will keep the worksheet to yourself.

2. Let me begin with an example so you can see how the interview protects your confidentiality at the same time that a picture of the business network emerges. Your business time line shows that your firm was founded in (say founding year) . **Please think back to your activities in founding the firm. Who was the one person who was most valuable to you in founding the firm?**

Please write in the box below the person's name so you can refer back to him or her later in the interview. Use any symbol that identifies the person for you— an ideograph, first name, initials, any name that will let you identify the person.

3. Now please do the same thing for each of the significant events you listed on your business time line. The first significant event you listed was   (say first event)   in (say year) . Who was the person most valuable to you during that event? Please write on the first line below the person's name. The person most valuable in this event could be the same person who was most valuable to you in founding the firm. You would just enter the name again.

If you listed a second significant event, who was the person most valuable to you during the second event? Again, this could be the same person who was most valuable to you in the first event.

Third event?

Fourth?

Fifth?

4. Question about how event contacts were helpful.

5. **Shifting now to business this year, and thinking about people inside or outside your firm, who are the three or four people who have been most valuable to your business activities this year?** Again, no need to say names. Just write their names in the boxes to the right so you can remember them later in the interview. Of course, these people valuable this year could be some of the same people you mentioned as valuable during signfiicant events in the past.

6. In contrast to people who help and are valued in your business activities, there are usually some people who make life difficult. **Without mentioning the person's name, who was the most difficult person to deal with in your business activities this year?** Just jot a name or initials in the box below. Only you are going to know who this person is.

Interviewer follows up, and has respondent write response on interviewer's questionnaire: **Without mentioning the name, what did this person do that made things difficult for your business activities this year?**

Write response on interviewer's questionnaire.

7.**Shifting to happier thoughts, who do you think was your most valuable senior employee this year?** If the people you already listed as most valuable include your most valuable employee, just enter the person's name again in the box to the right.

Figure A4 Name Generator Worksheet

NETWORK ROSTER WORKSHEET
(This sheet remains with the respondent.)

first person named — 1. _______________________

second person named — 2. _______________________

third person named — 3. _______________________

4. _______________________

fifth person named — 5. _______________________

6. _______________________

7. _______________________

eighth person named — 8. _______________________

9. _______________________

10. _______________________

11. _______________________

and so on.

12. _______________________

Please make sure
that no one is listed twice, and
there are no blank lines between names

13. _______________________

14. _______________________

Figure A5 Network Roster

EVENTS WORKSHEET   QID: _________

LINE UP THIS SHEET WITH THE NAMES ON PAGE 4. (1) FOR THE FIRST CONTACT, ASK: "The first person you mentioned was particularly valuable when the business was founded in (insert year). Very briefly, what did the person do that was so helpful? WRITE WHAT THE RESPONDENT SAYS ON THE LINE TO THE RIGHT BELOW, THEN CHECK WHICH OF THE FOUR OPTIONS IN THE BOX BEST DESCRIBES WHAT MADE THE CONTACT VALUABLE. (2) MOVE TO NEXT CONTACT, ASKING: **Thinking about the especially important event in (insert year), what did the person do that was so helpful in that event? Again, very briefly** (3–6) REPEAT FOR EACH CONTACT ON PAGE 4.

| P   E   R   O | founding ______________________________ |

P - contact provided resource (money, land, skills, permits, etc.)
E - contact provided emotional support
R - contact made referral to someone else who provided resource
O - contact did something else

| P   E   R   O | event 1 ______________________________ |

| P   E   R   O | event 2 ______________________________ |

P E R O	event 3 __________________________
P E R O	event 4 __________________________
P E R O	event 5 __________________________

Figure A6 Events Worksheet

COMMS CARD

FACE TO FACE

VIDEO CALL

VOICE (by phone or computer, for example, WeChat)

TEXT (email)

TEXT (other, for example instant messaging, or some other text exchange)

SOMETHING ELSE (please specify)

Figure A7 Name Interpreter Communications Card

ROLES CARD

family — the person is your parent, spouse, or child, or more distant family relative

neighbor — the person lives in same neighborhood

party — the person is a member of the party

childhood — you and the person knew each other when you were children

classmate — you and the person were in school together

military — you and the person met each other during your military service

colleague — the person works in your current company

past colleague — you and the person met each other in a company where you worked previously

other — the person is none of the above (What is the person to you?)

Figure A8 Name Interpreter Roles Card

Now about the strength
of your relationship
with each person ...

Circle the option that best describes your connection with each person.

Are you **especially close** in the sense that this is one of your closest contacts,

or are you merely **close** in the sense that you enjoy the person, but don't count him or her among your closest contacts,

or are you **less than close** in the sense that you don't mind working with the person, but you have no wish to develop a friendship,

or are you **distant** in the sense that you really don't enjoy spending time with the person unless it is necessary?

10. How Close Are You with Each Person?
(circle best approximation)

1.	especially close	close	less close	distant
2.	especially close	close	less close	distant
3.	especially close	close	less close	distant
4.	especially close	close	less close	distant
5.	especially close	close	less close	distant
6.	especially close	close	less close	distant
7.	especially close	close	less close	distant
8.	especially close	close	less close	distant
9.	especially close	close	less close	distant
10.	especially close	close	less close	distant
11.	especially close	close	less close	distant
12.	especially close	close	less close	distant
13.	especially close	close	less close	distant
14.	especially close	close	less close	distant

cut away grey
section of page

1. __________
2. __________
3. __________
4. __________
5. __________
6. __________
7. __________
8. __________
9. __________
10. __________
11. __________
12. __________
13. __________
14. __________

Figure A9 Name Interpreters (pp. 8–23)

Beyond emotional closeness,

there is duration,

and

frequency.

Duration is your best guess—in whole years—of how long you have known the person from today back to when you first met the person.

Frequency is your best guess of how often you had any discussion (face-to-face or electronic) with the person during the last six months: almost every business day, almost every week, almost every month....

11. How Long
Have You Known
Each Person?
(Best guess in whole years..
Enter "1" for less than a year)

1.	about________ years
2.	about________ years
3.	about________ years
4.	about________ years
5.	about________ years
6.	about________ years
7.	about________ years
8.	about________ years
9.	about________ years
10.	about________ years
11.	about________ years
12.	about________ years
13.	about________ years
14.	about________ years

12. On Average,
How Often Do You Talk To Each?
(circle best approximation; any discussion)

1.	daily	weekly	monthly	less often
2.	daily	weekly	monthly	less often
3.	daily	weekly	monthly	less often
4.	daily	weekly	monthly	less often
5.	daily	weekly	monthly	less often
6.	daily	weekly	monthly	less often
7.	daily	weekly	monthly	less often
8.	daily	weekly	monthly	less often
9.	daily	weekly	monthly	less often
10.	daily	weekly	monthly	less often
11.	daily	weekly	monthly	less often
12.	daily	weekly	monthly	less often
13.	daily	weekly	monthly	less often
14.	daily	weekly	monthly	less often

cut away grey
section of page

1.________________
2.________________
3.________________
4.________________
5.________________
6.________________
7.________________
8.________________
9.________________
10.________________
11.________________
12.________________
13.________________
14.________________

Figure A9 *continued*

With modern technology, people can communicate in many ways (hand over COMMS SHEET). During the last year, how have you communicated with the listed people?

13. Communication Channels
(Circle as many as apply. If you have not communicated with a person during the last year, just leave the line blank.)

cut away grey section of page

1. face-to-face	video call	voice	text (email)	text (other)	something else (How?________)	1. ________________
2. face-to-face	video call	voice	text (email)	text (other)	something else (How?________)	2. ________________
3. face-to-face	video call	voice	text (email)	text (other)	something else (How?________)	3. ________________
4. face-to-face	video call	voice	text (email)	text (other)	something else (How?________)	4. ________________
5. face-to-face	video call	voice	text (email)	text (other)	something else (How?________)	5. ________________
6. face-to-face	video call	voice	text (email)	text (other)	something else (How?________)	6. ________________
7. face-to-face	video call	voice	text (email)	text (other)	something else (How?________)	7. ________________
8. face-to-face	video call	voice	text (email)	text (other)	something else (How?________)	8. ________________
9. face-to-face	video call	voice	text (email)	text (other)	something else (How?________)	9. ________________
10. face-to-face	video call	voice	text (email)	text (other)	something else (How?________)	10. ________________
11. face-to-face	video call	voice	text (email)	text (other)	something else (How?________)	11. ________________
12. face-to-face	video call	voice	text (email)	text (other)	something else (How?________)	12. ________________
13. face-to-face	video call	voice	text (email)	text (other)	something else (How?________)	13. ________________
14. face-to-face	video call	voice	text (email)	text (other)	something else (How?________)	14. ________________

Figure A9 *continued*

What about trust? Consider the
extent to which you trust each of the listed
people. [Respondent reads the below text.]

For example, suppose one of the people asked
for your help. The help is not extreme, but it is
substantial. It is a level of help you cannot offer
to many people. To what extent would you trust
each person to give you all the information you
need to decide on the help? For example, if the
person was asking for a loan, would they fully
inform you about the risks of them being able to
repay the loan? If the person was asking to you
give a job to one of their relatives, would they
fully inform you about their relative's poor work
attitude or weak abilities, or other qualities that
would make you prefer not to hire the relative?

**For each person, circle the option that best
describes your view.**

Circle a 5 if you have no question that the person
would give to you all the information they have.

At the other extreme, circle a 1 if you believe that the
person might wish to inform you, but in the past has
often misled people from whom he asked favors.

Or, circle 4, 3, or 2 if your opinion is somewhere
between the extremes.

14. Trust
(circle best approximation)

	high trust				low trust
1.	5	4	3	2	1
2.	5	4	3	2	1
3.	5	4	3	2	1
4.	5	4	3	2	1
5.	5	4	3	2	1
6.	5	4	3	2	1
7.	5	4	3	2	1
8.	5	4	3	2	1
9.	5	4	3	2	1
10.	5	4	3	2	1
11.	5	4	3	2	1
12.	5	4	3	2	1
13.	5	4	3	2	1
14.	5	4	3	2	1

cut away grey
section of page

1. _______________
2. _______________
3. _______________
4. _______________
5. _______________
6. _______________
7. _______________
8. _______________
9. _______________
10. _______________
11. _______________
12. _______________
13. _______________
14. _______________

Figure A9 *continued*

Collaboration requires more than trust in the information a person will give you. It requires trust that the other person will be able to do his or her share of work, and be honest about costs. [Respondent reads the below text.]

Consider the extent to which you would be willing to collaborate in a business venture with each of the listed people.

For example, suppose one of your contacts came to you with a business idea, asking you to enter a joint venture with him or her to develop and launch the idea. The idea looks good to you and you have the resources to participate in the venture —— but is the contact the right person to work with? Can you trust the person to do his or her share of work, or hire the right people to do their share of the work? Can you trust him or her to keep honest accounts of costs and income?

For each person, circle the option that best describes your view.

Circle a 5 if you would definitely enter a joint venture with the person to develop and launch a good idea.

At the other extreme, circle a 1 if you would definitely not enter the joint venture, even if the venture seems promising.

Or, circle 4, 3, or 2 if your opinion is somewhere between the extremes.

15. Collaborate?
(circle best approximation)

	Definitely Yes				Definitely No
1.	5	4	3	2	1
2.	5	4	3	2	1
3.	5	4	3	2	1
4.	5	4	3	2	1
5.	5	4	3	2	1
6.	5	4	3	2	1
7.	5	4	3	2	1
8.	5	4	3	2	1
9.	5	4	3	2	1
10.	5	4	3	2	1
11.	5	4	3	2	1
12.	5	4	3	2	1
13.	5	4	3	2	1
14.	5	4	3	2	1

cut away grey section of page

1.____________
2.____________
3.____________
4.____________
5.____________
6.____________
7.____________
8.____________
9.____________
10.____________
11.____________
12.____________
13.____________
14.____________

Figure A9 *continued*

16. Are you familiar with the word "guanxi?"

(Interviewer circle answer)   yes   no

16b. If no, skip to question 16c. If yes, ask:
When there is guanxi between two people, that tells you certain things about their relationship. In your own words, how would you describe to a foreigner the relationship between two people who have guanxi with each other? (Interviewer, write response here.)

____

____

____

16c. In general, people say that guanxi exists when two people feel morally obligated to help one another without the expectation of a direct compensation. **Look over the list of your business contacts. Thinking of guanxi as feeling a moral obligation to help each other, with whom do you feel you have the strongest guanxi? Just read the number next to the name of the person.** (Interviewer, write "1" in response line for named person.)

16d. **Are there any other people on the list with whom you have guanxi almost as strong as with the person you just named, contact "number named in question 16c"?** (Interviewer, write "2" in response lines for named people.)

16e. **In terms of the general understanding of guanxi as feeling a moral obligation to help each other, with which people on the list do you definitely NOT have guanxi?** (Interviewer, write "3" in response lines for each named person.)

Responses

1. __________
2. __________
3. __________
4. __________
5. __________
6. __________
7. __________
8. __________
9. __________
10. __________
11. __________
12. __________
13. __________
14. __________

cut away grey section of page

1. __________________
2. __________________
3. __________________
4. __________________
5. __________________
6. __________________
7. __________________
8. __________________
9. __________________
10. __________________
11. __________________
12. __________________
13. __________________
14. __________________

Figure A9 *continued*

People can be connected in many ways. Here are some (hand over ROLE SHEET). In what ways are you connected with each of the listed people?

cut away grey section of page

17. Connections

(Circle as many as apply. It is possible for a connection to be none of these things, where upon fill in the blank after "other.")

1. family   neighbor party   childhood   classmate military colleague past colleague other_________   1._________________
2. family   neighbor party   childhood   classmate military colleague past colleague other_________   2._________________
3. family   neighbor party   childhood   classmate military colleague past colleague other_________   3._________________
4. family   neighbor party   childhood   classmate military colleague past colleague other_________   4._________________
5. family   neighbor party   childhood   classmate military colleague past colleague other_________   5._________________
6. family   neighbor party   childhood   classmate military colleague past colleague other_________   6._________________
7. family   neighbor party   childhood   classmate military colleague past colleague other_________   7._________________
8. family   neighbor party   childhood   classmate military colleague past colleague other_________   8._________________
9. family   neighbor party   childhood   classmate military colleague past colleague other_________   9._________________
10. family   neighbor party   childhood   classmate military colleague past colleague other_________   10._________________
11. family   neighbor party   childhood   classmate military colleague past colleague other_________   11._________________
12. family   neighbor party   childhood   classmate military colleague past colleague other_________   12._________________
13. family   neighbor party   childhood   classmate military colleague past colleague other_________   13._________________
14. family   neighbor party   childhood   classmate military colleague past colleague other_________   14._________________

Figure A9 *continued*

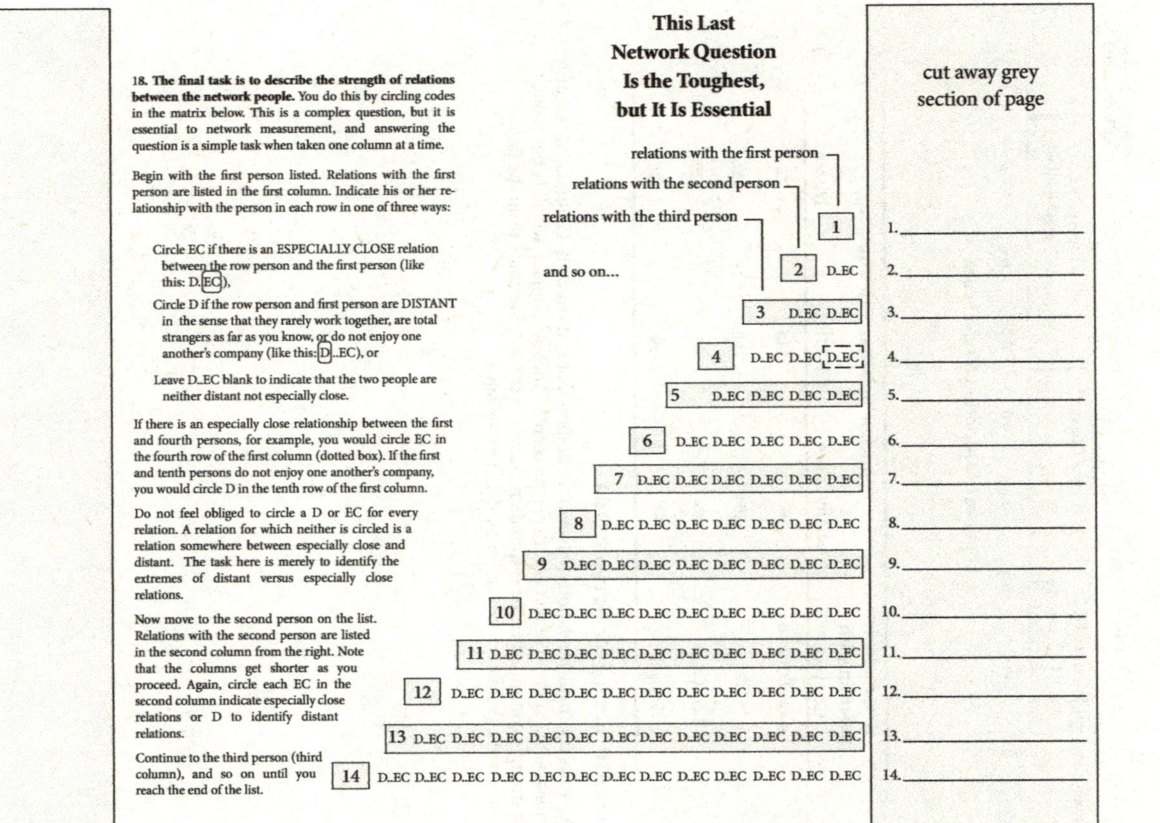

Figure A9 *continued*

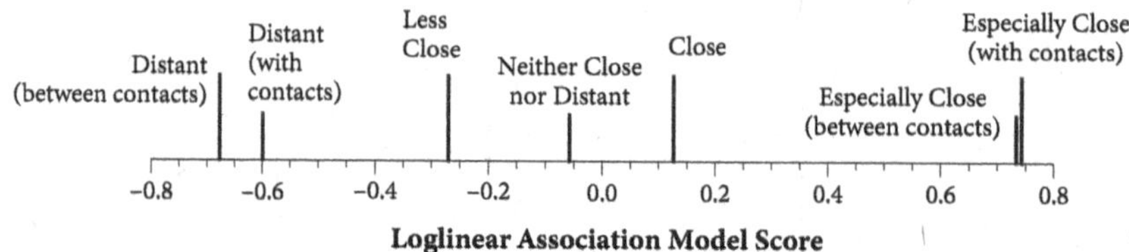

Respondent Relation with Contact	Anchor Relation with Contact		
	Especially Close	Middling	Distant
Especially Close	690	146	86
Close	1294	260	462
Less Close	209	95	219
Distant	37	39	226

Figure A10   Scaling the Network Data

Note: Rows distinguish relations between the respondent and contacts. Columns distinguish relations between each contact and the respondent's "anchor" contact, which is the contact most strongly connected to the respondent. Scores in the graphic come from the first dimension of a loglinear association model fit to the table

Descriptive Statistics

Tables of means, standard deviations, and correlations are presented here with titles indicating the tables in the text where they are used.

Table B.1 Descriptive Statistics for Table 2.1

	Mean	S.D.	Correlations		
Trust	4.97	1.05	1.00		
Number Third Parties	2.99	1.77	.35	1.00	
Event Contact	.66	.48	.53	.15	1.00
Interaction Term	.86	.74	.49	.52	.84	1.00

Note: Statistics are computed across 7166 relationships cited by 700 respondents in the 2012 survey and 384 respondents in the 2018 survey (no re-interviewed respondents). Number of third parties is used as raw scores for mean and standard deviation, then as log scores, ln (TP+1), for correlations (as in the Table 2.1 predictions).

Table B.2 Descriptive Statistics for Tables 4.2 and 4.3

		Mean	S.D.	1	2	3	4	5	6	7
1	Trust	4.03	1.01	—	.24	.29	.45	.29	.22	.09
2	Structural embedding (count)	2.88	2.05	.24	—	.93	.10	.05	.06	.68
3	Structural embedding (weighted)	2.07	1.61	.29	.93	—	.14	.06	.09	.72
4	All guanxi	0.29	0.45	.45	.03	.05	—	.29	.74	−.01
5	Strongest guanxi	0.15	0.35	.34	.03	.04	.65	—	−.43	.01
6	Other guanxi	0.14	0.35	.24	.01	.02	.64	−.17	—	−.02
7	Network density	38.7	22.0	.09	.68	.72	−.01	.00	−.02	—

Note: Statistics are computed across 2702 relationships cited by 384 respondents in the 2018 survey. Row variables and correlations below the diagonal are based on respondent definitions of which contacts are guanxi. Above the diagonal, correlations are based on guanxi inferred from respondents naming contacts valued for helping the respondent manage significant events in the history of the respondent's business. Structural embedding is used as raw scores for means and standard deviations, then used as log scores for correlations (as in the Model M1 to M6 predictions): ln (1 + count or weighted sum of indirect connections through third parties). Network density is the average connection strength between an entrepreneur's contacts multiplied by 100 to vary from zero to 100 (displayed on the vertical axis in Figure 4.5).

Table B.3 Descriptive Statistics of Table 4.4 and 4.5

		Mean	S.D.	1	2	3	4	5	6	7	8	9	10	11	12	13	14
1	Return on assets	22.22	14.20	1.00													
2	S. guanxi embedding (count third parties)	3.11	2.08	−.21	1.00												
3	S. guanxi embedding (weighted sum TP)	2.30	1.67	−.20	.94	1.00											
4	Embedded guanxi Eq. 1	2.24	1.50	−.21	.83	.90	1.00										
5	Guanxi bridges, Eq. 2	.75	.63	.23	−.65	−.69	−.74	1.00									
6	Net Constraint (exclude top guanxi)	45.49	17.76	−.20	.30	.35	48	−.42	1.00								
7	Female	16	.36	−.03	.03	.03	.01	.00	.02	1.00							
8	Age (years)	43.56	7.04	.03	.05	.11	.11	−.05	.01	−.22	1.00						
9	Founder	.84	.37	.07	−.05	.02	.07	.03	.00	−.01	.35	1.00					
10	Education (years)	15.19	2.33	−.04	.20	.20	.18	−.17	.18	.02	−.32	−.17	1.00				
11	Party member	.12	.33	−.09	.17	.17	.15	−.05	.09	−.05	.10	.03	.06	1.00			
12	Assets at founding (millions of CNY)	12.80	32.82	.01	.24	.30	.30	−.19	.15	−.10	.13	.10	.13	.02	1.00		
13	Years to profitability	2.04	2.95	−.10	−.01	−.03	−.08	−.03	−.11	−.06	−.04	−.42	.02	−.02	−.06	1.00	
14	IT	.50	.50	.17	.02	.00	.02	−.01	−.00	−.01	−.25	−.03	.32	.02	−.03	−.09	1.00
15	Hangzhou	.33	47	−.25	.14	.12	.18	−.07	.13	.09	−.15	.01	.14	.19	−.19	−.16	−.01

Note: There are 384 observations on respondents in the 2018 survey (except 381 on strongest guanxi embedding, see footnote 15 in Chapter 4). Correlations are computed with pairwise deletion. Variables 2 and 3 measure embedding around entrepreneur's strongest guanxi for Table 4.4. For Table 4.5, variable 4 is average embedding around entrepreneur's guanxi (equation 1), and variable 5 is the summed lack of embedding around entrepreneur's guanxi (equation 2). Means and standard deviations are based on raw network scores. Correlations are based on log network scores as in the Model M7 to M14 predictions.

Table B.4 Descriptive Statistics for Table 5.7

	Mean	S.D.	Correlations				
Days between meetings	22.04	28.19	1.00				
Days (alternative)	14.45	12.66	.78	1.00			
Bridge, not guanxi	.23	.42	.42	.35	1.00		
Guanxi, embedded	.21	.41	−.18	−.17	−.28	1.00	
Guanxi, bridge	.08	.27	.04	.15	−.16	−.15	1.00
Embedded guanxi (Eq. 1)	2.07	1.61	−.47	−.48	−.69	.31	−.38

Note: Statistics are computed across 2.702 relationships cited by 384 respondents in the 2018 survey. Days between meetings are 1, 7, 30, 90 for survey response categories daily, weekly, monthly, and less often. "Days alternative" is the same but with the 90-day category re-coded as 30. "Bridge not guanxi," "embedded guanxi," and "bridge guanxi" are dummy variables defined as discussed in the text. Reference category is embedded relations that are not guanxi. Structural embedding is the sum of weighted indirect connections between respondent and contact (third row in Table B.2). Structural-embedding raw scores are used to compute means and standard deviations and log, ln (raw+1), scores are used to compute correlations as in the Model M15 to M17 predictions.

Table B.5 Descriptive Statistics for Table 5.8

		Mean	S.D.	1	2	3	4	5	6	7
1	Trust	4.03	1.01	1.00						
2	Structural embedding (weighted)	2.07	1.61	.29	1.00					
3	Guanxi	0.29	0.45	.45	.05	1.00				
4	Guanxi x structural embedding	.01	.32	.06	.54	.06	1.00			
5	Family	.08	.27	.21	−.02	.35	−.07	1.00		
6	Just Friend	.08	.28	.15	−.22	.20	−.29	−.09	1.00	
7	Classmate	.12	.32	.18	.16	.18	.14	−.05	−.11	1.00
8	Texting	.46	.50	.16	.00	.14	−.08	.00	.23	−.01

Note: Statistics are computed across 2702 relationships cited by 384 respondents in the 2018 survey. Structural embedding is used as raw scores for means and standard deviations, then used as log scores for correlations (as in the Table 5.8 predictions): ln (1 + weighted sum of indirect connections through third parties). Guanxi is a dummy variable distinguishing contacts cited as strongest or other guanxi. The interaction variable, number 4, is the product of guanxi and the log of structural embedding. The remaining variables are dummy variables distinguishing family, just friend, classmates, or contacts with whom the respondent communicates by text.

Table B.6 Descriptive Statistics for Table 5.9

		Mean	S.D.	1	2	3	4	5	6	7	8
1	Return on Assets	22.22	14.20	1.00							
2	Guanxi bridges (Eq. 2)	.75	.53	.23	1.00						
3	Network Constraint	45.49	17.75	−.20	−.42	1.00					
4	Multiplexity general	.62	.43	.06	.33	−.15	1.00				
5	Multiplexity family	.24	.37	.06	.17	−.05	.47	1.00			
6	Multiplexity just friends	.19	.33	.19	.41	−.31	.40	−.18	1.00		
7	Multiplexity classmate	.21	.36	−.14	−.16	.18	.39	−.19	−.27	1.00	
8	Multiplexity texting	.52	.47	.08	.29	−.17	.23	.05	.36	−.06	1.00

Note: Statistics are computed across 384 respondents in the 2018 survey. Return on assets is variable 1 in Table B.3. Guanxi bridges and network constraint are variables 5 and 6 in Table B.3. Means and standard deviations are computed from raw scores for variables 2 and 3, then log scores for the correlations, as in the Table 5.9 predictions. Variables 4 through 8 measure the proportion of guanxi bridges that are multiplex with the indicated foundation relationship. "Multiplexity general" counts a relationship as multiplex if it is with family, or a classmate, or a contact who is just a friend.

Table B.7 Descriptive Statistics for Table 5.9

	1	2	3	4	5	6	7	8
Female	−.03	.005	.02	.10	.02	.01	.11	.12
Age (years)	.03	−.05	.01	−.10	.04	−.07	−.09	−.17
Founder	.07	.03	.001	.04	.20	−.11	−.03	−.03
Education (years)	−.04	−.17	.18	−.07	−.12	−.12	.18	.01
Party Member	−.09	−.05	.09	−.04	.02	−.10	.04	.08
Founding Assets (millions of CNY)	.01	−.19	.15	−.13	−.06	−.22	.14	−.29
Years to Profitability	−.10	−.03	−.11	−.05	−.12	.02	.03	−.11
IT	.17	−.01	−.005	.03	.02	.01	.03	.005
Hangzhou	−.25	−.07	.13	.12	.09	−.04	.12	.39

Note: Statistics are computed across 384 respondents in the 2018 survey. These are correlations between the eight variables in Table B.6 (columns) and the nine control variables in Table B.3 (rows). Correlations among the control variables are given in Table B.3.

Table B.8 Descriptive Statistics for Table 6.3

Predictors	Mean	S.D.	1	2	3
1. Language complexity	53.73	30.60	1.00		
2. Number of characters in description	20.42	15.15	.86	1.00	
3. Hangzhou (versus Shanghai & Ningbo)	.35	.48	.07	−.07	1.00
Network Characteristics					
4. Relatively closed network, no bridges	.13	.33	−.23	−.22	.14
5. Relatively closed network, bridges	.15	.36	−.19	−.20	−.05
6. Relatively closed network, guanxi bridge	.23	.42	−.11	−.11	.12
7. Relatively open network, no bridges	.05	.22	−.13	−.17	.19
8. Relatively open network, bridges	.08	.28	−.03	−.02	−.10
9. Relatively open network, guanxi bridge	.35	.48	.48	.49	−.20

continued

Table B.8 *continued*

Predictors	Mean	S.D.	1	2	3
Business Characteristics					
10. Information technology (versus manufacturing)	.51	.50	−.08	−.09	−.03
11. Current asset value (100,000 CNY)	.23	2.11	−.07	−.06	−.05
12. Small firm (versus not small)	.44	.50	.23	.25	−.17
13. Return on assets (last three years)	22.28	14.39	.21	.24	−.26
14. Years since founding (in decades)	10.74	5.64	.02	.04	−.05
15. Research and development dept.	.55	.50	.07	.07	.20
16. Founder still runs the business	.84	.37	−.05	−.06	.02
Personal Characteristics					
17. Female	.16	.37	.03	.00	.09
18. Age (in decades)	43.41	6.82	−.10	−.04	−.15
19. College degree	.61	.49	−.25	−.26	.04
20. Years of education	15.21	2.33	−.28	−.30	.14
21. Household annual income (10,000 CNY)	17.55	23.40	−.15	−.18	.26
22. Happiness	3.78	.51	−.18	−.17	.06

Note: Statistics are computed across 365 respondents in the 2018 survey who provided a guanxi text description. Complexity is the dependent variable in Model M18. Number of characters is the dependent variable in Model M19.

Table B.9 Descriptive Statistics for Table 6.3 (continued from Table B.8)

Variables	4	5	6	7	8	9	10	11	12	13	14	15	16	17	18	19	20	21
Network Characteristics																		
4	1.00																	
5	−.16	1.00																
6	−.20	−.23	1.00															
7	−.09	−.11	−.14	1.00														
8	−.12	−.13	−.17	−.08	1.00													
9	−.27	−.32	−.39	−.18	−.23	1.00												
Business Characteristics																		
10	−.06	.03	.01	−.01	−.06	.04	1.00											
11	−.01	.13	−.03	.00	−.02	−.06	−.06	1.00										
12	−.03	−.16	−.02	−.17	−.01	.25	−.09	−.09	1.00									
13	−.11	−.12	−.09	−.10	.02	.28	.17	−.08	.23	1.00								
14	.07	.03	−.14	.08	−.01	.01	−.24	.22	−.16	−.14	1.00							
15	−.01	−.02	.02	.01	.07	−.05	.05	.06	−.41	−.09	.13	1.00						
16	.03	−.05	.03	.05	−.06	−.01	−.03	.04	.02	.07	−.15	−.07	1.00					
Personal Characteristics																		
17	.08	−.05	.01	.07	−.06	−.03	−.01	−.04	.11	−.03	−.10	−.08	−.01	1.00				
18	.04	.03	−.04	.01	.02	−.03	−.25	.20	−.05	.03	.40	.04	.35	−.22	1.00			
19	.05	.10	.01	−.03	−.06	−.08	.36	.07	−.26	−.03	−.09	.10	−.19	−.02	−.27	1.00		
20	.09	.12	.03	−.01	−.04	−.16	.32	.04	−.27	−.04	−.17	.10	−.17	.02	−.32	.73	1.00	
21	.20	−.06	.01	.19	−.09	−.14	−.02	.13	−.30	−.05	.01	.24	.15	−.04	.20	.15	.20	1.00
22	.11	.05	−.01	.09	.08	−.20	.02	.04	−.12	−.05	−.01	−.04	.03	−.03	.03	.13	.13	.00

Table B.10 Descriptive Statistics for Table 7.1

	Mean	S.D.	1	2	3	4	5	6	7	8	9	10	11	12	13
1. COVID contact	.08	.27	—												
2. Hangzhou respondent	.51	.50	−.02	—											
3. Months of lockdown	2.93	3.89	.01	−.76	—										
4. Bridge (no mutuals)	.09	.29	.24	−.02	−.05	—									
5. Log weighted indirect	.93	.50	−.20	.02	.17	−.60	—								
6. Contact frequency	2.37	.92	.19	.02	−.02	.17	−.36	—							
7. Emotional closeness	3.07	.66	.02	−.03	.06	.02	.19	−.30	—						
8. Cited on an event	.52	.50	−.26	.03	−.02	−.13	.12	−.06	−.01	—					
9. Cited as most valued	.49	.50	−.25	.01	.03	−.19	.20	−.20	−.16	−.06	—				
10. Years known	9.51	4.27	.12	−.16	.07	.16	−.10	.03	.48	.01	−.34	—			
11. Family	.10	.30	.01	−.02	.05	.10	.05	−.29	.42	−.12	−.21	.31	—		
12. Colleague, current	.45	.50	−.22	.09	.00	−.29	.47	−.46	−.14	.09	.43	−.39	−.22	—	
13. Colleague, previous	.10	.30	−.02	.04	.00	.06	−.06	.22	.01	.10	−.14	.15	−.09	−.17	—

Note: Statistics are computed across 3726 relationships cited by 371 respondents in the 2021 survey. Variables are defined in Table 7.1.

Table B.11 Descriptive Statistics for Table 7.3

		Mean	S.D.	1	2	3	4
1	Trust	3.99	0.79	—			
2	Structural embedding (count)	3.28	2.11	.10	—		
3	Structural embedding (weighted)	1.87	1.36	.23	.87	—	
4	Contact is cited as guanxi (strongest or almost as strong)	0.21	0.41	.56	−.00	.06	—

Note: Statistics are computed across 3,726 relationships cited by 371 respondents in the 2021 survey. Variables are defined as in Table B.2.

Table B.12 Descriptive Statistics for Tables 7.4 and 7.6

	Mean	S.D.	1	2	3	4	5	6	7	8	9	10	11
1. Guanxi 2021	.25	.43	—										
2. Guanxi 2018	.32	.47	.47	—									
3. Structural embedding	.95	.61	.03	.13	—								
4. Contact is family	.07	.25	.30	.36	.04	—							
5. Just friend	.09	.28	.06	.11	−.22	−.08	—						
6. Classmate	.11	.32	.10	.17	.20	−.04	−.11	—					
7. Comms. channels	3.05	1.05	.15	.19	.18	.04	−.04	.09	—				
8. IT	.58	.49	.04	−.02	−.01	.02	.11	.02	.08	—			
9. Hangzhou	.49	.50	.07	.00	.16	.06	−.08	.15	.31	−.05	—		
10. Months closed	1.84	2.02	−.09	.01	−.09	−.06	.06	−.11	−.28	−.01	−.85	—	
11. Guanxi bridge 2021	.11	.31	.60	.31	−.08	.33	.08	.04	.07	.02	.09	−.10	—
12. Figure 7.4	1.97	1.01	.42	.89	−.28	.31	.18	.09	.10	−.02	−.08	.06	.31

Note: Statistics are computed across 622 relationships matched across both surveys. Variables are defined in Tables 7.4 and 7.6. Variable "Figure 7.4" is the four categories across the horizontal in Figure 7.4.

Topics Implicit in the Descriptions

In Chapter 6, we stay close to the spoken word. Descriptions are compared in terms of the frequency with which key words and kinds of words are used. A virtue of such analysis, especially for non-native speakers, is that it requires few subjective decisions from the analyst. A disadvantage is that it can miss cases where different words are used to describe the same topic. If we loosen our grasp on specific word choices, we can compare entrepreneurs based on the topics implicit in their descriptions of guanxi. What topics emerge? How are those topics connected with text complexity (the dimension of language differentiation primarily associated with networks in Chapter 6)? Topic models are a popular method for answering such questions.

Topic modelling is readily available in Stata's implementation of Latent Dirichlet Allocation (LDA) topic modelling, developed by Blei et al. (2003; see LDA in Wikipedia). DiMaggio et al. (2013) offer an applied introduction, and Schwarz (2018) describes his implementation in Stata (ldagibbs command). The idea for our data is that the 365 entrepreneur descriptions of guanxi are each a mixture of underlying topics—some topics more prominent in one description than in another, but all topics potentially present in each description. For example, Mr. Sun today emphasizes confidence in the support of guanxi contacts. In a conversation next week, he talks about reliability. In both cases, trust is an implicit topic. The statistical task is to map specific words into a known number of unobserved topics and, in doing so, define the topics implicit in each description. Words can reflect multiple topics, and words that frequently co-occur in the same descriptions are likely to indicate the same topic—a loose analog to the multidimensional word map in Figure 6.4.

Relative to our analysis of spoken words in Chapter 6, topic modelling involves more subjective judgement. The number of topics and certain clustering parameters have to be defined in advance. More importantly, the extent to which two topics are meaningfully different is also a matter of analyst discretion. One of this book's co-authors speaks Chinese, but the other does not. For this initial exploration of topic modelling, we translated the Chinese texts into English using Deepl's subscription service, so we could both make independent, subjective judgements about the resulting topics. The results of our exploratory analysis with the English translations did not encourage further topic modelling with software keyed to Chinese, yet the results are worth reporting, if only to corroborate our analyses in Chapter 6.

Results

We have to define the number of topics before running the analysis. From past research, we expect guanxi descriptions to reflect themes of warmth, obligation, and trust (Bian 2019). If the three themes are always discussed together, they would define one broad topic reflected across all guanxi texts. At the other extreme, if the three themes are also discussed by respondents individually—one person emphasizing warmth, another focusing on obligation, another on trust—while others discuss the themes in all possible combinations, the result could be as many as seven distinct topics. We did not expect that level of fragmentation, since the analysis in Chapter 6 shows one primary dimension of variable complexity (Figure 6.2). Still, to allow for variation around the core themes, we extracted six topics—and later show that extracting just three yields a similar conclusion, in keeping with the three principal component factors in Table C.3 that underlie the six topics.

The analysis produces two files: A 365 × 6 data matrix of "topic probabilities," where cell i, j is the probability that entrepreneur i's text reflects topic j. Second, a K × 6 data matrix of "word probabilities" in which cell k, j is the probability that word k reflects topic j, with k being one of K unique words in the pool of all unique words in the 365 texts. After pre-processing, we have a total of 5187 words, of which 608 are unique (K = 608).[1]

Word Probabilities

Table C.1 lists the six topics, T1 through T6, extracted from the guanxi texts. Cell k, j of the table contains the probability that word k reflects topic j. The table contains all words that have more than a .02 probability of reflecting one or more topics. For each topic, these probabilities sum to 1.0 across the 608 unique words, so the probabilities for individual words are often small. The .02 cutoff is arbitrary. It includes multiple keywords for each topic, and is well below the largest probabilities for each topic. To facilitate identification of keywords, probabilities below .02 are excluded from the table. Words are listed down the rows in descending order of their cumulative probability across all six topics, shown in the right-most column. For example, "relationship," in the third row of the table, has a .065 probability of reflecting Topic T5 and a .094 probability of reflecting Topic T6. The .183 sum in the final column is the sum of these two values plus the sum of probabilities (each less than .02) for "relationship" reflecting the remaining four topics.

Topics can be interpreted in terms of the words with the highest probability of reflecting each topic. For example, Topic T3 seems most similar to a general guanxi topic. Its key indicators are "contact," "mutual," "trust," "intimate," and "frequent." These are not far removed from qualitative studies emphasizing themes of warmth, obligation, and trust. The key words for the other topics are more generic in their reference to relationships: "other," "people," "relationship," "help," "friend," "contact," and "together." Words lower in the table have consistently lower probabilities across topics. In short, the topics look like fine-grained variations on a broader theme of close relationships.

The fact that the third topic T3 reflects the general guanxi theme is irrelevant to its descriptive importance. Topics in a model have no order in terms of descriptive power. This is unlike factor analysis in which the first factor describes the most variance within

---

[1] The pre-processing involves use of the TXTTOOL command in Stata to convert to lower case and remove punctuation, special characters, and extra white spaces (Williams and Williams 2014). We also remove words shorter than four letters and often-used stopwords that emerged as obscuring topic content. The removed stopwords are: each, even, have, just, make, many, more, same, such, that, there, there's, they, this, those, very, what, when, will, and your. The probability-distribution parameters alpha and beta are set to .5 and .1 respectively. In search of broad topics, .5 for alpha is twice the default magnitude, allowing for multiple broad topics reflected in each text. To check on topic breadth, we also ran analyses with alpha set to .10, which generated more narrow, text-specific topics. We re-ran the analysis several times to remove function words emerging as spurious key words, and assess the results of changes in the number of topics and breadth of topics. For reliable comparisons between runs, each run begins with the same arbitrary seed (3449) initializing the random number generator.

Table C.1 Strongest Word Probabilities for the Six Topics

word	T1	T2	T3	T4	T5	T6	sum
other		0.142			0.207		0.367
people	0.038	0.054		0.089			0.203
relationship				0.065		0.094	0.183
help					0.146		0.178
friend						0.072	0.101
contact			0.059	0.027			0.097
together	0.035	0.052					0.089
common	0.085						0.088
work		0.067					0.079
close	0.052						0.066
interest	0.040						0.062
trust			0.057				0.059
mutual			0.058				0.059
intimate			0.046				0.049
connection				0.027			0.047
frequent			0.044				0.046
life		0.034					0.045
support					0.024		0.041
something	0.026						0.040
deeper				0.03			0.037
certain		0.024					0.035
communication			0.029				0.033
between				0.023			0.033
well					0.031		0.033
business						0.028	0.031
closer			0.022				0.029
goal	0.025						0.027
phone			0.021				0.023
intimacy			0.022				0.023
give					0.021		0.022

and across indicators, the second less, and so on. In topic modelling, for a fixed number of topics, the same underlying topic may appear in different positions across runs—first in one pass, fourth in another, or anywhere among the six.

Topic Probabilities

A second strategy for interpreting topics is to look at context: Who are the people, or what are the situations, in which a topic is most likely to be mentioned? We look at context in Table C.2 and Table C.3. The analysis produces six topic probabilities for each entrepreneur, each indicating the presence of each topic in the entrepreneur's guanxi description. These probabilities sum to 1.0 across the six topics. In other words, every text has a nonzero probability of reflecting one or more topics, and the probability for a topic can be high for an entrepreneur who focuses on that topic.

Table C.2 shows descriptive statistics for the six topics. Probabilities for every topic vary across the sample entrepreneurs, from near zero to high values. Correlations between topic probabilities are primarily negative, indicating that a text reflecting one topic strongly tends not to reflect the others. For example, consider Topic T3, which seems in Table C.1 to be a general guanxi topic. Here are two texts with high probabilities of reflecting topic three:

> Frequent contact; face-to-face, voice, text, more mutual trust.

> Relationships definitely have more contact, more dinners, more events, more frequent gatherings, it's a place of trust.

The shorter text has the highest probability for reflecting Topic T3 (.66 probability). The speaker is one of the dots to the left in Figure 6.2. He is an entrepreneur in a relatively closed network (50.7 network constraint) who used a list of terms to describe guanxi (47.8 complexity on the horizontal axis in Figure 6.2). The second text is from an entrepreneur at the high end of the complexity continuum to the right in Figure 6.2. He operates in a relatively open network in which his strongest guanxi is a bridge (33.8 network constraint; he is one of the solid dots in Figure 6.2B) and he offers a relatively complex description of guanxi (89.7 complexity on horizontal axis in Figure 6.2).

Putting these data in context, Table C.3 shows factor loadings for a principal factor analysis of the six topics combined with key variables from our prior text analysis: The two multidimensional scaling dimensions in Figure 6.2 (complexity across the horizontal and a secondary dimension up the vertical), the length of an entrepreneur's text (in Chinese characters), the level of closure around the entrepreneur (network constraint, closely associated with complexity in Figure 6.3), and a dummy variable distinguishing the entrepreneurs with relatively open networks whose strongest guanxi is a bridge (Figure 6.2B).

Table C.2 Descriptive Statistics for Topic Probabilities

	T1	T2	T3	T4	T5	T6
T1	1.00					
T2	−.02	1.00				
T3	−.20	−.26	1.00			
T4	−.20	−.17	−.18	1.00		
T5	−.30	−.08	−.25	−.36	1.00	
T6	−.17	−.36	−.17	.03	−.25	1.00
Mean	.16	.17	.16	.16	.19	.15
S.D.	.12	.11	.14	.12	.16	.12
Minimum	.03	.03	.03	.04	.02	.02
Maximum	.80	.68	.66	.69	.72	.81

Note: These correlations, means, and standard deviations are computed across the 365 probabilities that measure the extent to which each text reflects each of the six topics.

Table C.3 Correlations Between Topic Probabilities and Key Variables in Chapter 6 Text Analysis

	Factor 1	Factor 2	Factor 3
Probability of Topic T1	−.11	−.26	−.73
Probability of Topic T2	.17	.39	−.63
Probability of Topic T3	−.49	−.32	.21
Probability of Topic T4	.51	−.41	.15
Probability of Topic T5	−.20	.87	.35
Probability of Topic T6	.23	−.44	.50
Text Complexity (horizontal in Figure 6.2)	.83	.14	.00
Secondary Dimension (vertical in Figure 6.2)	−.22	.59	.18
Text Character Count	.83	.07	.05
Network Constraint	−.70	−.11	−.02
Guanxi Network Categories across Figure 4.7	.78	.05	.01
Number Guanxi Bridges in Figure 6.2	.67	.10	−.02

Note: These are correlations (factor loadings with uncorrelated factors) between the row variables and the first three principal factors extracted from the row variables. First three factors describe 68 percent of the indicator variance (35 percent, 19 percent, and 14 percent, respectively, then 11 percent, 10 percent, and 8 percent for factors four, five, and six). Number of guanxi bridges is zero, one (hollow dots in Figure 6.2B), or more than one (solid dots in Figure 6.2B).

By including six variables from Chapter 6 in the Table C.3 factor analysis, we bias the factors toward our earlier results. But the presenting issue is not to discover the factor structure of topic probabilities. We already have the topics defined in Table C.1. The presenting issue is to learn what topic probabilities contribute beyond what we already know from studying word counts and text complexity.

Complexity remains the primary dimension in the data. The strongest correlations with the strongest principal component, Factor 1, are complexity and the length of a text (correlations of .83). The factor is positively associated with entrepreneurs in open networks containing guanxi bridges (correlations of .78 and .67, bottom rows of the table), and negatively associated with network constraint (−.70 correlation). Topics T3 and T4 are strongly linked to the complexity dimension. Topic T3—the general guanxi topic in Table C.1—is negatively associated with Factor 1 (−.49), while Topic T4 has a positive correlation with the factor (.51). In other words, text complexity obscures the key words that describe guanxi, which are, on average, more obvious in less complex texts. The longer of the two guanxi texts quoted above is an example: it has a high probability of reflecting Topic T3, and also has relatively high probabilities for reflecting Topics T4 and T6.

Conclusion

The search for abstract topics reflected in the guanxi texts adds shadings to the conclusions already in hand from Chapter 6. Topic probabilities are closely associated with the two dimensions of differentiation in Figure 6.2. Topics T3 and T4 covary with the dominant complexity dimension along the horizontal axis. Topic T5 covaries with the minor vertical axis. Topics T1, T2, and T5 show little correlation with the key variables from Chapter 6, and covary primarily with the third and least-descriptive principal component factor in Table C.3.

In sum, topic modeling confirms what we learned from word counts and text complexity, while it is useful in identifying particularly good indicator texts. However, the fine-grain distinctions between topics add little beyond what we already know. Of course, we know that only because we looked.

Note on Variations

We ran variations on the topic model, but reached similar conclusions, so we do not report the results. We mention two variations here.

One variation was to run the model with the same parameters but limit the extracted topics to three, given that the principal component analysis of topic probabilities in Table C.3 suggests a three-topic structure. Topics T4 and T3 appear as positive and negative variations on Factor 1. Topic T5 corresponds to Factor 2. T6, T1 and T2 map onto Factor 3—one positively and two negatively. The results of the three-topic model are shadings on a broad theme of positive relationships. Indicator words for the first topic (corresponding to Table C.1) include together, common, close, work, mutual, and trust. For the second topic: other, help, people, and support. For the third: relationship, people, friend, and connection. The longer guanxi text quoted earlier in this Appendix has high probabilities of reflecting all three topics (.63, .15, and .23, respectively). When topic probabilities are factor analyzed with key variables from the earlier analysis, text complexity is strongly correlated with the probability of the third topic (.82 correlation) and the secondary dimension in Figure 6.2 is strongly correlated with the probability of the second topic (.99 correlation). The first of the three topics corresponds to the general guanxi topic, with indicator words similar to Topic T3 (Table C.1), and it is most apparent in low-complexity guanxi texts (Table C.3).

A second variation to note is our exploration of less broadly defined topics. To check whether the broad topics were obscuring subsample differences between kinds of entrepreneurs, we re-ran the analysis extracting narrower topics. Topic breadth decreases as the probability-distribution parameter, alpha, is lowered. Smaller values of alpha skew the distribution of topic probabilities, making topics more text-specific, which in our data means more entrepreneur-specific. In Stata's LDA procedure, the default value of alpha is .25. To extract more narrow topics, we set it to .10. All other parameters remained the same.

The resulting topics are more narrowly defined. The mean minimum topic probability of .028 in Table C.2 decreases to .005, and the mean maximum of .728 increases to .944. Topics are more likely to be absent from a text, and if present, more likely to be highly present.

But the conclusions are similar. Replicating Table C.3, the principal factor (30 percent of indicator variance) measures text complexity (.85 correlation with the horizontal axis in Figure 6.2), and the next factor (18 percent of indicator variance) measures variation on the vertical axis in Figure 6.2 (.65 correlation). A pair of narrowly defined topics vary positively/negatively with the complexity factor in Figure 6.2 (akin to Topics T3 and T4 in Table C.2). Another pair of more narrowly defined topics vary positively/negatively with the secondary factor in Figure 6.2 (akin to Topics T5 and T6 in Table C.2). More specifically, probabilities for topics in the tables in this appendix are correlated with probabilities for corresponding topics more narrowly defined: T6 with the fifth narrow topic (.76 correlation). T5 with the sixth narrow topic (.93 correlation). T4 with the first narrow topic (.67 correlation). T3 with the second narrow topic (.91 correlation). T2 with the third narrow topic (.73 correlation). The weakest, though still strong, correlation is between probabilities for Topic T1 and the fourth narrow topic (.58 correlation). Topic T1 is a particularly generic one, defined by its absence in the factor analysis (negative or negligible loadings in Table C.2), with key indicator words in Table C.1 of "common," "close," "interest," and "people."

References

Abascal, Maria, and Delia Baldassarri. 2015. "Love thy neighbor? Ethnoracial diversity and trust reexamined." *American Journal of Sociology* 121(3): 722–782.

Alós-Ferrer, Carlos, and Federica Farolfi. 2019. "Trust games and beyond." *Frontiers in Neuroscience* 13(3): Article 887.

Aral, Sinan, and Marshall Van Alstyne. 2011. "Networks, information and brokerage: The diversity-bandwidth tradeoff." *American Journal of Sociology* 117(1): 90–171.

Asch, Solomon E. 1951. "Effects of group pressure upon the modification and distortion of judgments." pp. 177–190 in *Groups, Leadership and Men*, edited by Harold Guetzkow. Pittsburg, PA: Carnegie Press.

Bailey, Stefanie and Peter V. Marsden. 1999. "Interpretation and interview context: Examining the general social survey name generator using cognitive methods." *Social Networks* 21(3): 287–309.

Barbalet, Jack. 2021a. *The Theory of Guanxi and Chinese Society.* Oxford, UK: Oxford University Press.

Barbalet, Jack. 2021b. "Where does guanxi come from? Bao, shu and renqing in Chinese connections." *Asian Journal of Social Science* 49(1): 31–37.

Barley, William C., Jeffrey W. Treem, and Paul M. Leonardi. 2020. "Experts at coordination: Examining the performance, production, and value of process expertise." *Journal of Communication* 70(1): 60–89.

Baruch, Yahuda. 1999. "Response rate in academic studies — a comparative analysis." *Human Relations* 52(4): 421–438.

Batjargal, Bat. 2007a. "Comparative social capital: networks of entrepreneurs and venture capitalists in China and Russia." *Management and Organization Review* 3(3): 397–419.

Batjargal, Bat. 2007b. "Internet entrepreneurship: Social capital, human capital, and performance of internet ventures in China." *Research Policy* 36(5): 605–618.

Batjargal, Bat. 2010. "The effects of network's structural holes: Polycentric institutions, product portfolio, and new venture growth in China and Russia." *Strategic Entrepreneurship Journal* 4(2): 146–163.

Batjargal, Bat, Michael A. Hitt, Anne S. Tsui, Jean-Luc Arregle, Justin W. Webb, and Toyah L. Miller. 2013. "Institutional polycentrism, entrepreneur's social networks, and new venture growth." *Academy of Management Journal* 56(4): 1024–1049.

Baum, Joel A. C., Bill McEvily, and Tim J. Rowley. 2012. "Better with age? Tie longevity and the performance implications for bridging and closure." *Organization Science* 23(2): 529–546.

Berg, Joyce, John Dickhaut, and Kevin McCabe. 1995. "Trust, reciprocity, and social history." *Games and Economic Behavior* 10(1): 122–142.

Bernstein, Lisa. 1992. "Opting out of the legal system: Extralegal contractual relations in the diamond industry." *Journal of Legal Studies* 21(1): 115–157.

Bernstein, Lisa. 2015. "Beyond relational contracts: Social capital and network governance in procurement contracts." *Journal of Legal Analysis* 7(2): 561–621.

Bian, Yanjie. 1997. "Bringing strong ties back in: Indirect ties, network bridges, and job searches in China." *American Sociological Review* 62(3): 366–385.

Bian, Yanjie. 2018. "The prevalence and the increasing significance of *guanxi.*" *China Quarterly* 235: 597–621.

Bian, Yanjie. 2019. *Guanxi: How China Works.* London: Polity Press.

Bian, Yanjie, and Lulu Li. 2012. "The Chinese General Social Survey (2003–8)." *Chinese Sociological Review* 45(1): 70–97.

Bian, Yanjie, and Man Shuai. 2019. "Elective affinity between *guanxi* favouritism and market rationality: *Guanxi* circles as governance structure in China's private firms." *Asia Pacific Business Review* 26(2): 149–168.

Bian, Yanjie, and Wenbin Wang. 2016. "The social capital for self-employment in transitional China," pp. 21–35 in *Rethinking Social Capital and Entrepreneurship in Greater China*, edited by Jenn-Hwan Wang and Ray-May Hsung. New York: Routledge.

Bidart, Claire, and Johanne Charbonneau. 2011. "How to generate personal networks: Issues and tools for a sociological perspective." *Field Methods* 23(3): 266–286.

Blau, Peter M. 1955. *The Dynamics of Bureaucracy: A Study of Interpersonal Relations in Two Government Agencies.* Chicago, IL: University of Chicago Press.

Blau, Peter M. 1964. *Exchange and Power in Social Life.* New York: John Wiley.

Blau, Peter M. 1974. "Presidential address: Parameters of social structure" *American Sociological Review* 39(5): 615–635.

Blau, Peter M., and Joseph Schwartz. 1984. *Crosscutting Social Circles: Testing a Macrosociological Theory of Intergroup Relations.* New York: Academic Press.

Blei, David M., Andrew Y. Ng, and Michael I. Jordon. 2003. "Latent Dirichlet allocation." *Journal of Machine Learning Research* 3: 993–1022.

Boissevain, Jeremy. 1974. *Friends of Friends: Networks, Manipulators and Coalitions.* Oxford, UK: Basil Blackwell.

Borgatti, Stephen P. 2002. *NetDraw.* Boston, MA: Analytic Technologies.

Borgatti, Stephen P., and Daniel Halgin. 2011. "On network theory." *Organization Science* 22(5): 1165–1181.

Bott, Elizabeth. 1957. *Family and Social Network: Roles, Norms, and External Relationships in Ordinary Urban Families.* London: Tavistock.

Bowlby, John. 1969. *Attachment and Loss, Vol 1: Attachment.* New York: Basic Books.

Brashears, Matthew E. 2011. Small networks and high isolation? A reexamination of American discussion networks. *Social Networks* 33(4): 331–341.

Brashears, Matthew E., and Eric Quintane. 2015. "The microstructures of network recall: How social networks are encoded and represented in human memory." *Social Networks* 41 (May): 113–128.

Brashears, Matthew E., and Eric Quintane. 2018. "The weakness of tie strength." *Social Networks* 55 (October): 104–115.

Breiger, Ronald. 1974. "The duality of persons and groups." *Social Forces* 53(2): 181–190.

Burger, Martijn J., and Vincent Buskens. 2009. "Social context and network formation: An experimental study." *Social Networks* 31: 63–75.

Burt, Ronald S. 1983. "Distinguishing relational contents." pp. 35–74 in *Applied Network Analysis*, edited by Ronald S. Burt and Michael J. Minor. Beverly Hills, CA: Sage.

Burt, Ronald S. 1984. "Network items and the General Social Survey." *Social Networks* 6(3): 293–339.

Burt, Ronald S. 1990. "Kinds of relations in American discussion networks." pp. 411–451 in *Structures of Power and Constraint*, edited by Craig Calhoun, Marshall W. Meyer, and W. Richard Scott. New York: Cambridge University Press.

Burt, Ronald S. 1992. *Structural Holes*. Cambridge, MA: Harvard University Press.

Burt, Ronald S. 1998. "The gender of social capital." *Rationality and Society* 10(1):5–46.

Burt, Ronald S. 1999. "The social capital of opinion leaders." *Annals of the American Academy of Political and Social Science* 566(Nov): 37–54.

Burt, Ronald S. 2000. "The network structure of social capital." *Research in Organizational Behavior* 22: 345–423.

Burt, Ronald S. 2001. "Attachment, decay, and social network." *Journal of Organizational Behavior* 22(6): 619–643.

Burt, Ronald S. 2004. "Structural holes and good ideas." *American Journal of Sociology* 110(2):349–399.

Burt, Ronald S. 2005. *Brokerage and Closure*. New York: Oxford University Press.

Burt, Ronald S. 2010. *Neighbor Networks*. New York: Oxford University Press.

Burt, Ronald S. 2012. "Network-related personality and the agency question: Multirole evidence from a virtual world." *American Journal of Sociology* 118(3): 543–591.

Burt, Ronald S. 2017. "Social network and temporal discounting." *Network Science* 5(4): 411–440.

Burt, Ronald S. 2019a. "Network disadvantaged entrepreneurs: density, hierarchy, and success in China and the West." *Entrepreneurship Theory and Practice* 43(1): 19–50.

Burt, Ronald S. 2019b. "The networks and success of female entrepreneurs in China." *Social Networks* 58: 37–49.

Burt, Ronald S. 2021. "Structural holes, capstone, cautions, and enthusiasms." pp. 384–416 in *Personal Networks*, edited by Mario L. Small, Brea L. Perry, Bernice A. Pescosolido, and Edward B. Smith. Cambridge, UK: Cambridge University Press.

Burt, Ronald S. 2026. "Fragile brokerage." in *Social Networks*, edited by Tommy Andersson and Christofer Edling. New York: Oxford University Press.

Burt, Ronald S., and Bat Batjargal. 2019. "Comparative network research in China." *Management and Organization Review* 15(1): 3–29.

Burt, Ronald S., Yanjie Bian, and Sonja Opper. 2018. "More or less guanxi: Trust is 60% network context, 10% individual differences." *Social Networks* 54(July): 12–25.

Burt, Ronald S., and Katarzyna Burzynska. 2017. "Chinese entrepreneurs, social networks, and *guanxi*." *Management and Organization Review* 13(2): 221–260.

Burt, Ronald S., and Miguel G. Guilarte. 1986. "A note on scaling the General Social Survey network item response categories." *Social Networks* 8(4): 387–396.

Burt, Ronald S., Martin Kilduff, and Stefano Tasselli. 2013. "Social network analysis: Foundations and frontiers on advantage." *Annual Review of Psychology* 64: 527–547.

Burt, Ronald S., and Jennifer Merluzzi. 2014. "Embedded brokerage: hubs versus locals." pp. 161–177 in *Contemporary Perspectives on Organizational Social Networks*, edited by Daniel J. Brass, Giuseppe Labianca, Ajay Mehra, Daniel S. Halgin, and Stephen P. Borgatti. Bingley, UK: Emerald.

Burt, Ronald S., and Ray Reagans. 2022. "Team talk: Learning, jargon, and structure versus the pulse of the network." *Social Networks* 70(July): 375–392.

Burt, Ronald S., and Sonja Opper. 2017. "Early network events in the later success of Chinese entrepreneurs." *Management and Organization Review* 13(3): 497–537.

Burt, Ronald S., and Sonja Opper. 2024. "*Guanxi* and structural holes: Strong bridges from relational embedding." *American Journal of Sociology* 131(1): 1–43.

Burt, Ronald S., and Sonja Opper. 2026. "Evaluation in network context." in *Oxford Handbook of Organisational Social Evaluations*, edited by Rupert Younger and Anastasiya Zavyalova. Oxford, UK: Oxford University Press.

Burt, Ronald S., Sonja Opper, and Hakan J. Holm. 2022. "Cooperation beyond the network." *Organization Science* 33(2): 495–517.

Burt, Ronald S., Sonja Opper, and Na Zou. 2021. "Social network and family business: Uncovering hybrid family firms." *Social Networks* 65(May): 141–156.

Burt, Ronald S., and Thomas Schott. 1985. "Relation contents in multiple networks." *Social Science Research* 14(4): 287–308.

Burt, Ronald S., and Giuseppe Soda. 2017. "Social origins of great strategies." *Strategy Science* 2(4): 226–233.

Burt, Ronald S., and Song Wang. 2022. "Bridge supervision: Correlates of a boss on the far side of a structural hole." *Academy of Management Journal* 65(6): 1835–1853.

Buskens, Vincent, and Arnout van de Rijt. 2008. "Dynamics of networks if everyone strives for structural holes." *American Journal of Sociology* 114(2): 371–407.

Carnabuci, Gianluca, and Eric Quintane. 2023. "When people build networks that hurt their performance: Structural holes, cognitive style, and the unintended consequences of person-network fit." *Academy of Management Journal* 66(5): 1360–1383.

Carter, Dorothy R., Leslie A. DeChurch, Michael T. Braun, and Noshir S. Contractor. 2015. "Social network approaches to leadership: An integrative conceptual review." *Journal of Applied Psychology* 100(3): 597–622.

Cartwright, Dorwin, and Frank Harary. 1956. "Structural balance: A generalization of Heider's theory." *Psychological Review* 63(5): 277–293.

Casciaro, Tiziana, Francesca Gino, and Maryam Kouchaki. 2014. "The contaminating effects of building instrumental ties: How networking can make us feel dirty." *Administrative Science Quarterly* 59(4): 705–735.

Centola, Damon, and Michael Macy. 2007. "Complex contagions and the weakness of long ties." *American Journal of Sociology* 113(3): 702–734.

Centola, Damon. 2018. *How Behavior Spreads*. Princeton, NJ: Princeton University Press.

Chang, Kuang-Chi. 2011. "A path to understanding *guanxi* in China's transitional economy: Variations on network behavior." *Sociological Theory* 29(4): 315–339.

Chen, Chao C., Xiao-Ping Chen, and Shengsheng Huang. 2013. "Chinese *guanxi*: An integrative review and new directions for future research." *Management and Organization Review* 9(1): 167–207.

Chen, Chen. 2019. "A comparative study on English and Chinese kinship terms and their translation strategies." *Theory and Practice in Language Studies* 9(9): 1237–1242.

Chen, Xiao-Ping, and Chao C. Chen. 2004. "On the intricacies of the Chinese *guanxi*: A process model of *guanxi* development." *Asia Pacific Journal of Management* 21: 305–324.

Chua, Roy Y. J., Michael W. Morris, and Paul Ingram. 2009. "*Guanxi* vs. networking. Distinctive configurations of affect- and cognition-based trust in the networks of Chinese vs. American managers." *Journal of International Business Studies* 40(3): 490–509.

Coase, Ronald 1937. "The nature of the firm." *Economica* 4(16) 386–405.

Coleman, James S. 1988. "Social capital in the creation of human capital." *American Journal of Sociology* 94(S), S95–S120.

Coleman, James S. 1990. *Foundations of Social Theory*. Cambridge, MA: Harvard University Press.

Cross, Rob, Stephen P. Borgatti, and Andrew Parker. 2001. "Beyond answers: Dimensions of the advice network." *Social Networks* 23(3): 215–235.

Dane, Erik. 2020. "Suddenly everything became clear. How people make sense of epiphanies surrounding their work and careers." *Academy of Management Discoveries* 6(1): 39–60.

Dane, Erik, Markus Baer, Hannes Leroy, Richard Swartz, & Aleksandra Wrobel. In Press. "Gaining career purpose through lightning bolts: Examining the strength and psychological foundations for work-related epiphanies." *Journal of Management* In Press.

Danescu-Niculescu-Mizil, Cristian, Lillian Lee, Bo Pang, Jon Kleinberg. 2012. "Echoes of power: Language effects and power differences in social interaction." Proc. 21st International World Wide Web Conference.

de Vaan, Mathijs, Balazs Vedres, and David Stark. 2015. "Game changer: The topology of creativity." *American Journal of Sociology* 120(4):1144–1194.

DiMaggio, Paul, Manish Nag, and David Blei. 2013. "Exploiting affinities between topic modeling and the sociological perspective on culture: Application to newspaper coverage of U.S. government arts funding." *Poetics* 41: 570–606.

DiMaggio, Paul. 1997. "Culture and cognition." *Annual Review of Sociology* 23: 263–287.

Doreian, Patrick, Roman Kapuscinski, David Krackhardt, and Janusz Szczypula. 1996. "The history of balance through time." *Journal of Mathematical Sociology* 21(1–2): 113–131.

Dunning, John H., and Changsu Kim. 2007. "The cultural roots of *guanxi*." *World Economy* 30(2): 329–341.

Easley, David, and Jon Kleinberg. 2010. *Networks, Crowds, and Markets*. New York: Cambridge University Press.

Ekeh, Peter P. 1974. *Social Exchange Theory*. Cambridge, MA: Harvard University Press.

Ellickson, Robert C. 1991. *Order without Law*. Cambridge, MA: Harvard University Press.

Ermisch, John, and Diego Gambetta. 2010. "Do strong family ties inhibit trust?" *Journal of Economic Behavior and Organization* 75(3): 365–376.

Ertug, Gokhan, Julia Brennecke, and Stefano Tasselli. 2023. "Theorizing about the implications of multiplexity: An integrative typology." *Academy of Management Annals* 17(2): 626–654.

Falk, Armin, Anke Becker, Thomas Dohmen, David Huffman, and Uwe Sunde. 2023. "The preference survey module: A validated instrument for measuring risk, time, and social preferences." *Management Science* 69(4): 1935–1950.

Fan, Ying. 2002. "*Guanxi*'s consequences: Personal gains at social cost." *Journal of Business Ethics* 38(4): 371–380.

Farh, Jiing-Lih., Anne S. Tsui, Katherine Xin, and Bor-Shiuan Cheng. 1998. "The influence of relational demography and *guanxi*: the Chinese case." *Organization Science* 9(4): 471–488.

Fehr, Ernst, Urs Fischbacher, Bernhard von Rosenbladt, Jurgen Schupp, and Gert Wagner. 2002. "A nation-wide laboratory: Examining trust and trustworthiness by integrating behavioral experiments into representative surveys." *Schmollers Jahrbuch* 122: 519–542.

Fei, Xiatong. 1992 [1947]. *From the Soil: Foundations of Chinese Society*. Translated by Gary G. Hamilton and Wang Zheng. Berkeley: University of California Press.

Feld, Scott L. 1981. "The focused organization of social ties." *American Journal of Sociology* 86(5): 1015–1035.

Feltham, Eric, Laura Forastiere, and Nicholas A. Christakis. 2025. "Cognitive representations of social networks in isolated villages." *Nature Human Behavior* 9: 1737–1753.

Festinger, Leon, Stanley Schachter, and Kurt Back. 1950. *Social Pressures in Informal Groups*. New York: Harper.

Fischer, Claude S. 1982. *To Dwell among Friends: Personal Networks in Town and City*. Chicago, IL: University of Chicago Press.

Fischer, Claude S. 2009. "The 2004 GSS finding of shrunken social networks: An artifact?" *American Sociological Review* 74(August): 657–669.

Fischer, Claude S., and Shria Offer. 2020. "Who is dropped and why? Methodological and substantive accounts for network loss." *Social Networks* 61(May): 78–86.

Fleming, Lee, and Matt Marx. 2006. "Managing creativity in small worlds." *California Management Review* 48(4): 6–27.

Fleming, Lee, Santiago Mingo, and David Chen. 2007. "Collaborative brokerage, generative creativity, and creative success." *Administrative Science Quarterly* 52(4): 443–475.

Frank, Robert H., Thomas Gilovich, and Dennis T. Regan. 1993. "The evolution of one-shot cooperation: An experiment." *Ethology and Sociobiology* 14(4): 247–256.

Freeman, Linton C. 1977. "A set of measures based on betweenness." *Sociometry* 40(1): 35–41.

Gargiulo, Martin, and Mario Benassi. 2000. "Trapped in your own net? Network cohesion, structural holes, and the adaptation of social capital." *Organization Science* 11(2): 183–196.

Gluckman, Max. 2012 [1965]. *Politics, Law and Ritual in Tribal Society*. New York: Routledge.

Gold, Thomas, Doug Guthrie, and David Wank. 2002. "An introduction to the study of guanxi." pp. 3–20 in *Social Connections in China*, edited by Thomas Gold, Doug Guthrie, and David Wank. New York: Cambridge University Press.

Goldberg, Amir, Sameer B. Srivastava, V. Govind Manian, William Monroe, and Christopher Potts. 2016. "Fitting in or standing out? The tradeoffs of structural and cultural embeddedness." *American Sociological Review* 81(6): 1190–1222.

Gondal, Neha. 2022. "Multiplexity as a lens to investigate the cultural meaning of interpersonal ties." *Social Networks* 68(January): 209–217.

Gong, Ting. 2004. "Dependent judiciary and unaccountable judges: Judicial corruption in contemporary China." *The China Review* 4(2): 33–54.

Goodman, Leo A. 1981. "Association models and the bivariate normal for contingency tables with ordered categories." *Biometrika* 68(2): 347–355.

Gouldner, Alvin W. 1957. "Cosmopolitans and locals: Toward an analysis of latent social roles." *Administrative Science Quarterly* 2(3): 281–306.

Goyal, Sanjeev, Marco J. van der Leij, and Jose Luis Moraga-Gonzalez. 2006. "Economics: An emerging small world." *Journal of Political Economy* 114(2): 403–412.

Goyal, Sanjeev, and Fernando Vega-Redondo. 2007. "Structural holes in social networks." *Journal of Economic Theory* 137(1): 460–492.

Granovetter, Mark. 1973. "The strength of weak ties." *American Journal of Sociology* 78(6): 1360–1380.

Granovetter, Mark. 1974. *Getting a Job*. Cambridge, MA: Harvard University Press.

Granovetter, Mark. 1982. "The strength of weak ties: A network theory revisited." pp. 105–130 in *Social Structure and Network Analysis*, edited by Peter V. Marsden and Nan Lin. Beverly Hills, CA: Sage.

Granovetter, Mark. 1985. "Economic action, social structure, and embeddedness." *American Journal of Sociology* 91(3): 481–510.

Granovetter, Mark. 1992. "Problems of explanation in economic sociology." pp. 29–56 in *Networks and Organizations*: edited by Nitin Nohria, and Robert G. Eccles. Boston, MA: Harvard Business School Press.

Greif, Avner. 1989. "Reputation and coalitions in medieval trade: Evidence on the Maghribi traders." *Journal of Economic History* 49(4): 857–882.

Guilbeault, Douglas, and Damon Centola. 2021. "Topological measures for identifying and predicting the spread of complex contagions." *Nature Communications* 12(1): 4430.

Gulati, Ranjay, Maxim Sytch, and Adam Tatarynowicz. 2012. "The rise and fall of small worlds: Exploring the dynamic of social structure." *Organization Science* 23(2): 449–471.

Guo, Chun and Jane K. Miller. 2010. "*Guanxi* dynamics and entrepreneurial firm creation and development in China." *Management and Organization Review* 6(2): 267–291.

Guo, Man, Wen Long, Yanqiang Zhang, and Wei Zhang. 2026. "Who knows more? The role of structural hole spanners in accurate information identification on social media." *Asia-Pacific Basic Financial Journal* 93: In Press.

Guthrie, Doug. 1998. "The declining significance of *guanxi* in China's economic transition." *China Quarterly* 154: 254–282.

Halevy, Nir, Eileen Y. Chou, Emma E. Levine, and Maurice Schweitzer. 2025. "Brokered distances: Trust in brokers within and between organizations." *Organizational Psychology Review* 15(2): 156–180.

Halevy, Nir, Eliran Halali, and Julian J. Zlatev. 2019. "Brokerage and brokering: An integrative review and organizing framework for third party influence." *Academy of Management Annals* 13(1): 215–239.

Hardin, Russell. 1991. "Trusting persons, trusting institutions." pp. 185–209 in *Strategy and Choice*, edited by Richard J. Zeckhauser. Cambridge, MA: MIT Press.

Hayek, Friedrich A. 1937. "Economics and knowledge." *Economica* 4(13): 33–54.

Hayek, Friedrich A. 1945. "The use of knowledge in society." *American Economic Review* 35(4): 519–530.

Heider, Fritz. 1958. *The Psychology of Interpersonal Relations*. New York: John Wiley.

Hinde, Robert A. 1966. *Animal Behavior: A Synthesis of Ethology and Comparative Psychology*. New York: McGraw-Hill.

Hong, Jingzhu, Barney Tan, Evelyn Ng, Robert M. Davison, and Louie Wong. 2025. "The impact of social media on digital guanxi development in the Chinese workplace: A technology affordance perspective." *International Journal of Information Management* 84: 102933.

Horn, Gabriel. 2004. "Pathways of the past: The imprint of memory." *Nature Reviews Neuroscience* 5(2): 108–120.

Huang, Chin-Lan, Cindy K. Huang, Chin-Lan, Cindy K. Chung, Natalie H. Hui, Yi-Cheng Lin, Yi-Tai Seih, Ben C. P. Lam, Wei-Chuan Chen, Michael H. Bond, and James W. Pennebaker. 2012. "The development of the Chinese linguistic inquiry and word count dictionary." *Chinese Journal of Psychology* 54(2): 185–201.

Huang, Phillip. 1990. *The Peasant Family and Rural Development in the Yangzi Delta, 1350–1988*. Stanford, CA: Stanford University Press.

Hwang, Kwang-kuo. 1987. "Face and favor: The Chinese power game." *American Journal of Sociology* 92(4): 944–974.

Hwang, Kylie Jiwon, and Damon J. Phillips. 2024. "Entrepreneurship as a response to labor market discrimination for formerly incarcerated people." *American Journal of Sociology* 130(1): 88–146.

Inglehart, Ronald et al. (eds). 2014. World Values Survey: Round Six - Country-Pooled Datafile Version: www.worldvaluessurvey.org/WVSDocumentationWV6.jsp. Madrid: JD Systems Institute.

Ingram, Paul, and Michael W. Morris. 2010. "Do people mix at mixers? Structure, homophily, and the 'life of the party.'" *Administrative Science Quarterly* 52(4): 558–585.

Ireland, Molly E., Richard B. Slatcher, Paul W. Eastwick, Lauren E. Scissors, Eli J. Finkel, and James W. Pennebaker. 2011. "Language style matching predicts relationship initiation and stability." *Psychological Science* 22(1): 39–44.

Islam, Rabiul, and Greg Walkerden. 2014. "How bonding and bridging networks contribute to disaster resilience and recovery on the Bangladeshi coast." *International Journal of Disaster Risk Reduction* 10, Part A (December): 281–291.

Jacobs, J. Bruce. 1979. "A preliminary model of particularistic ties in Chinese political alliances: Kan-ch'ing and Kuan-hsi in a rural Taiwanese township." *China Quarterly* 78(2): 237–273.

Jacobs, J. Bruce. 1980. *Local Politics in a Rural Chinese Cultural Setting*. Canberra, Australia: Australia National University.

Jang, Sujin. 2017. "Cultural brokerage and creative performance in multicultural teams." *Organization Science* 29(6): 993–1009.

Jannace, Diego, and Ronald S. Burt. 2024. "Contingent bridge supervision: New evidence and cautions for network theory." *Social Networks* 78: 253–264.

Ji, Yingchun, and Xiaogang Wu. 2018. "New gender dynamics in post-reform China: Family, education, and labor market." *Chinese Sociological Review* 50(3): 231–239.

Jo, Jae Kwon, David A. Harrison, and Steven M. Gray. 2021. "The ties that cope? Reshaping social connections in response to pandemic distress." *Journal of Applied Psychology* 106(9): 1267–1282.

Johnson, Noel D., and Alexandra A. Mislin. 2011. "Trust games: A meta-analysis." *Journal of Economic Psychology* 32(5): 865–889.

Katz, Elihu, and Paul F. Lazarsfeld. 1955. *Personal Influence*. New York: Free Press.

Kilduff, Martin, and David Krackhardt. 2009. *Interpersonal Networks in Organizations: Cognition, Personality, Dynamics, and Culture*. New York: Cambridge University Press.

Kim, Minjae, and Roberto M. Fernandez. 2023. "What makes weak ties strong?" *Annual Review of Sociology* 49: 177–193.

Kipnis, Andrew B. 1997. *Producing Guanxi: Sentiment, Self, and Subculture in a North China Village*. Durham, NC: Duke University Press.

Kleinberg, Jon. 2000. "Navigation in a small world." *Nature* 406(6798): 845.

Kleinberg, Jon. 2026. "Algorithmic perspectives on social networks." in *Social Networks*, edited by Tommy Andersson and Christofer Edling. New York: Oxford University Press.

Kleinberg Jon, Siddharth Suri, Éva Tardos, and Tom Wexler. 2008. "Strategic network formation with structural holes." *Proceedings of 9th ACM Conference on Electronic Commerce*.

Kollock, Peter. 1994. "The emergence of exchange structures: An experimental study of uncertainty, commitment, and trust." *American Journal of Sociology* 100(2): 313–345.

Krackhardt, David. 1987. "Cognitive social structures." *Social Networks* 9(2): 109–134.

Krackhardt, David. 1992. "The strength of strong ties: The importance of Philos in organizations." pp. 216–239 in *Networks and Organizations*, edited by Nitin Nohria, and Robert G. Eccles. Boston, MA: Harvard Business School Press.

Krackhardt, David. 1999. "The ties that torture: Simmelian tie analysis in organizations." *Research in the Sociology of Organizations* 16(1): 183–210.

Kuwabara, Ko, Robb Willer, Michael W. Macy, Rie Masima, Shigeru Terai, and Toshio Yamagishi. 2007. "Culture, identity, and structure in social exchange: A web-based trust experiment in the United States and Japan." *Social Psychology Quarterly* 70(1): 461–479.

Kwon, Seok-Woo, Emanuela Rondi, Daniel Z. Levin, Alfredo De Massis, and Daniel J. Brass. 2020. "Network brokerage: An integrative review and future research agenda." *Journal of Management* 46(6): 1092–1120.

Lardy, Nicholas. 2019. *The State Strikes Back: The End of Economic Reform in China?* Washington, DC: Peterson Institute for International Economics.

Latour, Bruno. 2008. "A cautious Prometheus? A few steps toward a philosophy of design (with special attention to Peter Sloterdijk)." Keynote lecture for the Networks of Design meeting of the Design History Society, Falmouth, UK. http://www.bruno-latour.fr/sites/default/files/112-DESIGN-CORNWALL-GB.pdf

Laumann, Edward O. 1973. *Bonds of Pluralism.* New York: Wiley?

Lazega, Emmanuel, Tom A. B. Snijders, and Rafael P. M. Wittek. 2022, Eds. *A Research Agenda for Social Networks and Social Resilience.* Cheltenham, UK: Edward Elgar.

Lee, Nancy Howell. 1969. *The Search for an Abortionist.* Chicago, IL: University of Chicago Press.

Lee, Seungyoon, and Cheolhan Lee. 2015. "Creative interaction and multiplexity in intraorganizational networks." *Management Communication Quarterly* 29(1): 56–83.

Lee, Yonghoon G., and Martin Gargiulo. 2022. "Escaping the survival trap: Network transition among early-career freelance songwriters." *Administrative Science Quarterly* 67(2): 339–377.

Leonardi, Paul M. 2015. "Ambient awareness and knowledge acquisition: Using social media to learn 'who knows what' and 'who knows whom.'" *MIS Quarterly* 39(4): 747–762.

Levinthal, Daniel A., and James G. March. 1993. "The Myopia of Learning." *Strategic Management Journal* 14(S2): 95–112.

Li, Hongbin, Lingsheng Meng, Qian Wang, and Li-An Zhou. 2008. "Political connections, financing and firm performance: Evidence from Chinese private firms." *Journal of Development Economics* 87(2): 283–299.

Li, Julie Juan, Laura Poppo, and Kevin Zheng Zhou. 2008. "Do managerial ties in China always produce value? Competition, uncertainty, and domestic vs. foreign firms." *Strategic Management Journal* 29(4): 383–400.

Li, Peter Ping, Steven Zhou, Abby Zhou, and Zhangbo Yang. 2019. "Reconceptualizing and redirecting research on *guanxi*: "*Guan-Xi*" interaction to form a multicolored Chinese knot." *Management and Organization Review* 15(3): 1–35.

Li, Xiaoguang, and Yanjie Bian. 2024. "*Guanxi* networks in China: A thematic review of *guanxi* scholarship in the past decade." *Chinese Journal of Sociology* 10(4): 531–562.

Lin, Nan. 2001a. *Social Capital: A Theory of Social Structure and Action.* New York: Cambridge University Press.

Lin, Nan. 2001b. "*Guanxi*: A conceptual analysis." pp. 153–166 in *The Chinese Triangle of Mainland, Taiwan, and Hong Kong: Comparative Institutional Analysis*: edited by Alvin Y. So, Nan Lin, and Dudley Poston. Westport, CT: Greenwood.

Lin, Nan. 2018. *Guanxi*: Social relationships based on sentiment (renqing). Unpublished Paper, April 5, Sociology Department, Duke University.

Lingo, Elizabeth Long, and Sioban O'Mahony. 2010. "Nexus work: Brokerage on creative projects." *Administrative Science Quarterly* 55(1): 47–81.

Lizardo, Omar. 2024. "Two-mode relational similarities." *Social Networks* 76(January): 34–41.

Luo, Jar-Der, Meng-Yu Cheng, and Tian Zhang. 2016. "*Guanxi* circle and organizational citizenship behavior: Context of a Chinese workplace." *Asia Pacific Journal of Management* 33: 649–671.

Luo, Yadong. 2003. "Industrial dynamics and managerial networking in an emerging market: The case of China." *Strategic Management Journal* 24(13): 1315–1327.

Luo, Yadong. 2008. "The changing culture and business behavior: The perspective of intertwinement between *guanxi* and corruption." *International Business Review* 17(2): 188–193.

Luo, Yadong, Ying Huang, and Stephanie Lu Wang. 2011. "*Guanxi* and organizational performance: A meta-analysis." *Management and Organization Review* 8(1): 139–172.

March, James G. 1991. "Exploration and exploitation in organizational learning." *Organization Science* 2(1): 71–87.

Marsden, Peter V. 1987. "Core discussion networks of Americans." *American Sociological Review* 52(1): 122–131.

Marsden, Peter V. 2011. "Survey methods for network data." pp. 370–388 in *The SAGE Handbook of Social Network Analysis*, edited by John P. Scott, and Peter J. Carrington. Thousand Oaks, CA: Sage Publications.

Marsden, Peter V., and Karen E. Campbell. 1984. "Measuring tie strength." *Social Forces* 63(2): 482–501.

Masuda, Yuta J., Yuqing Liu, Sheila M.W. Reddy, Kenneth A. Frank, Kyle Burford, Jonathan R.B. Fisher, and Jensen Montambault. 2018. "Innovation diffusion within large environmental NGOs through informal network agents." *Nature Sustainability* 1(4): 190–197.

Mauss, Marcel. (1925)1967. *The Gift*, translated by Ian Cunnison. New York: W. W. Norton.

McEvily, Bill, Jonathan Jaffee, and Marco Tortoriello. 2012. "Not all bridging ties are equal: Network imprinting and firm growth in the Nashville legal industry, 1933–1978." *Organization Science* 23(2): 547–563.

Mehra, Ajay, Martin Kilduff, and Daniel J. Brass. 2001. "The social networks of high and low self-monitors: Implications for workplace performance." *Administrative Science Quarterly* 46(1): 121–146.

Mellahi, Kamel, and Lloyd C. Harris. 2016. "Response rates in business and management research: An overview of current practice and suggestions for future direction." *British Journal of Management* 27(2): 426–437.

Menon, Tanya, and Jeffrey Pfeffer. 2003. "Valuing internal vs. external knowledge: Explaining the preference for outsiders." *Management Science* 49(4): 497–543.

Merluzzi, Jennifer, and Ronald S. Burt. 2021. "One path does not fit all: A career path approach to the study of professional women entrepreneurs." *Entrepreneurship Theory and Practice* 45(6): 1366–1383.

Merton, Robert K. 1949. "Patterns of influence: Local and cosmopolitan influentials." pp. 441–474 in *Social Theory and Social Structure*, 3rd ed. (1968), edited by Robert K. Merton. New York: Free Press.

Merton, Robert K. 1961. "Singletons and multiples in scientific discovery: A chapter in the sociology of science." *Proceedings of the American Philosophical Society* 105(5): 470–486.

Merton, Robert K. 1984. "Socially expected durations: A case study of concept formation in sociology." pp. 262–283 in *Conflict and Consensus*, edited by Walter W. Powell and Richard Robbins. New York: Free Press.

Merton, Robert K., and Elinor Barber. 2004. *The Travels and Adventures of Serendipity.* Princeton, NJ: Princeton University Press.

Meyerson, Debra, Karl E. Weick, and Roderick M. Kramer. 1996. "Swift trust and temporary groups." pp. 166–195 in *Trust in Organizations*, edited by Roderick M. Kramer and Tom R. Tyler. Thousand Oaks, CA: Sage.

Milgram, Stanley. 1967. "The small-world problem." *Psychology Today* 1(1): 61–67.

Mill, John Stuart. 1987 [1848]. *Principles of Political Economy.* Fairchild, NJ: Augustus M. Kelley.

Mitchell, J. Clyde. 1969, Ed. *Social Networks in Urban Situations.* Manchester, UK: Manchester University Press.

Morgan, Gareth. 1986. *Images of Organization.* Thousand Oaks, CA: Sage.

Neal, Zachary P. 2022. "Sometimes weak ties are just weak." *Science* (eLetters) 377: osf. io/preprints/osf/j5ue4_v1/

Neal, Zachary P. 2024. "The not-so-forbidden triad: Evaluating the assumptions of the strength of weak ties." *Network Science* 12(3): 289–304.

Nee, Victor, and Sonja Opper. 2010. "Political capital in a market economy." *Social Forces* 88(5): 2105–2133.

Nee, Victor, and Sonja Opper. 2012. *Capitalism from Below. Markets and Institutional Change in China.* Cambridge, MA: Harvard University Press.

Nolan, Jane, and Chris Rowley. 2020. "Whither guanxi and social networks in China? A review of theory and practice." *Asia Pacific Business Review* 26(2): 113–123.

Nunn, Nathan, and Leonard Wantchekon. 2011. "The slave trade and the origins of mistrust in Africa." *American Economic Review* 101(7): 3221–3252.

Offer, Shira, and Claude S. Fischer. 2018. "Difficult people: Who is perceived to be demanding in personal networks and why are they there?" *American Sociological Review* 63(1): 111–142.

Opper, Sonja, and Ronald S. Burt. 2021. "Social network and temporal myopia." *Academy of Management Journal* 64(3): 741–771.

Opper, Sonja, Victor Nee, and Hakan J. Holm. 2017. "Risk aversion and *guanxi* activities: A behavioral analysis of CEOs in China." *Academy of Management Journal* 60(4): 1504–1530.

Opper, Sonja, Sandeep Devanatha Pillai, and Enying Zheng. 2025. "Historical foundations of regional absorptive capacity." Paper presented at annual meetings of the Strategic Management Society.

Opper, Sonja, and Na Zou. 2024. "Trust in difficult people: A social network perspective." *Journal of Management Studies* 61(7): 2885–2918.

Ou, Carol Xiaojuan, Paul A. Pavlou, and Robert M. Davison. 2014. "Swift guanxi in online marketplaces: The role of computer-mediated communication technologies." *MIS Quarterly* 38(1): 209–230.

Padgett, John F. 2026a. *Organizational Invention in Renaissance Florence*. New York: Oxford University Press.

Padgett, John F. 2026b. "Historical introduction and overview." in *Social Networks*, edited by Tommy Andersson and Christofer Edling. New York: Oxford University Press

Park, Seung Ho, and Yadong Luo. 2001. "Guanxi and organizational dynamics: Organizational networking in Chinese firms." *Strategic Management Journal* 22(5): 455–477.

Peng, Mike W., and Yadong Luo. 2000. "Managerial ties and firm performance in a transition economy: The nature of a micro-macro link." *Academy of Management Journal* 43 (3): 486–501.

Pennebaker, James W., Ryan L. Boyd, Kayla Jordan, and Kate Blackburn. 2015. *The Development and Psychometric Properties of LIWC2015*. Austin: University of Texas at Austin.

Perry, Brea L., Bernice A. Pescosolido, and Stephen P. Borgatti. 2018. *Egocentric Network Analysis*. New York: Cambridge University Press.

Perry-Smith, Jill E. 2006. "Social yet creative: The role of social relationships in facilitating individual creativity." *Academy of Management Journal* 49(1): 85–101.

Perry-Smith, Jill E., and Pier Vittorio Mannucci. 2017. "From creativity to innovation: The social network drivers of the four phases of the idea journey." *Academy of Management Review* 42(1): 53–79.

Pontikes, Elizabeth G. 2012. "Two sides to the same coin: How ambiguous classification affects multiple audiences' evaluations." *Administrative Science Quarterly* 57(1): 81–118.

Powell, Walter W., Douglas R. White, Kenneth W. Koput, and Jason Owen-Smith. 2005. "Network dynamics and field evolution: The growth of interorganizational collaboration in the life sciences." *American Journal of Sociology* 110(4): 1132–1205.

Putnam, Robert. 1993. *Making Democracy Work*. Princeton (NJ): Princeton University Press.

Putnam, Robert. 2000. *Bowling Alone*. New York: Simon and Schuster.

Putnam, Robert. 2007. "E pluribus unum: Diversity and community in the twenty-first century." *Scandinavian Political Studies* 30(2): 137–174.

Qiu, Lin, Jiahui Lu, Jonathan Ramsay, Shanshan Yang, Weina Qu, and Tingshao Zhu. 2017. "Personality expression in Chinese language use." *International Journal of Psychology* 52(6): 463–472.

Quintane, Eric, and Gianluca Carnabuci. 2016. "How do brokers broker? Tertius gaudens, tertius iungens, and the temporality of structural holes." *Organization Science* 27(6): 1343–1360.

Rahman, Hatim A., and Stephen R. Barley. 2017. "Situated redesign in creative occupations – An ethnography of architects." *Academy of Management Discoveries* 3(4): 404–424.

Reagans, Ray, and Bill McEvily. 2003. "Network structure and knowledge transfer: The effects of cohesion and range." *Administrative Science Quarterly* 48(2): 240–267.

Rodan, Simon, and Charles Galunic. 2004. "More than network structure: How knowledge heterogeneity influences managerial performance and innovativeness." *Strategic Management Journal* 25(6): 541–562.

Rousseau, Denise, Sim B. Sitkin, Ronald S. Burt, and Colin F. Camerer. 1998. "Not so different after all: A cross-disciplinary review of trust." *Academy of Management Review* 23(3): 393–404.

Ruan, Danching. 1998. "The content of the General Social Survey discussion networks: An exploration of the General Social Survey discussion name generator in a Chinese context." *Social Networks* 20(3): 247–264.

Ryall, Michael D., and Olav Sorenson. 2007. "Brokers and competitive advantage." *Management Science* 53(4): 566–583.

Salganik, Matthew J., Peter Sheridan Dodds, and Duncan J. Watts. 2006. "Experimental study of inequality and unpredictability in an artificial culture market." *Science* 311(5762): 854–856.

Samila, Sampsa, Alexander Oettl, and Sharique Hasan. 2022. "Helpful behavior and the duration of collaborative ties." *Organization Science* 33(5): 1816–1836.

Schilke, Oliver, Martin Reimann, and Karen S. Cook. 2021. "Trust in social relations." *Annual Review of Sociology* 47:239–259.

Schumpeter, Joseph A. 1934 [1911]. *The Theory of Economic Development*, translated by Redvers Opie. Cambridge, MA: Harvard University Press.

Schwarz, Carlo. 2018. "Idagibbs: A command for topic modeling in Stata using latent Dirichlet allocation." *The Stata Journal* 18(1): 101–117.

Smith, Adam. 1937 [1776]. *An Inquiry into the Nature and Causes of the Wealth of Nations*. New York: Random House.

Smith, Edward Bishop, Tanya Menon, and Leigh Thompson. 2012. "Status differences in the cognitive activation of social networks." *Organization Science* 23(1): 67–82.

Soda, Giuseppe, Pier Vittorio Mannucci, and Ronald S. Burt. 2021. "Networks, creativity, and time: Staying creative through brokerage and network rejuvenation." *Academy of Management Journal* 64(4): 1164–1190.

Soda, Giuseppe, Alessandro Usai, and Akbar Zaheer. 2004. "Network memory: The influence of past and current networks on performance." *Academy of Management Journal* 47(6): 893–906.

Sorenson, Olav, and Toby E. Stuart. 2008. "Bringing the context back in: Settings and the search for syndicate partners in venture capital investment networks." *Administrative Science Quarterly* 53(2): 266–294.

Srivastava, Sameer B., Amir Goldberg, V. Govind Manian, and Christopher Potts. 2018. "Enculturation trajectories: Language, cultural adaptation, and individual outcomes in organizations." *Management Science* 64(3): 1348–1364.

Stigler, George J. 1961. "The economics of information." *Journal of Political Economy* 69(3): 213–225.

Stigler, Stephen M. 1980. "Stigler's law of eponymy." *Transactions of the New York Academy of Sciences* 39(1): 147–157.

Stinchombe, Arthur L. 1965. "Social structure and organizations," pp. 142–194 in *Handbook of Organizations*, edited by James G. March. Chicago, IL: Rand McNally.

Stovel, Katherine, Benjamin Golub, and Eva M. Meyersson Milgrom. 2011. "Stabilizing brokerage." *Proceedings of the National Academy of Sciences* 104: 21326–21332.

Stovel, Katherine, and Lynette Shaw. 2012. "Brokerage." *Annual Review of Sociology* 38: 139–158.

Stuart, Toby E., and Olav Sorenson. 2007. "Strategic networks and entrepreneurial ventures." *Strategic Entrepreneurship Journal* 1(3–4): 211–227.

Suchman, Mark. 1995. "Managing legitimacy: Strategic and institutional approaches." *Academy of Management Review* 20: 571–610.

Swedberg, Richard. 1990. *Economics and Sociology*. Princeton, NJ: Princeton University Press.

Szulanski, Gabriel. 2003. *Sticky Knowledge*. Thousand Oaks, CA: Sage.

Tasselli, Stefano, and Martin Kilduff. 2021. "Network agency." *Academy of Management Annals* 15(1): 68–110.

Ter Wal, Anne L. K., Oliver Alexy, Jörn Block, and Philipp G. Sandner. 2016. "The best of both worlds: The benefits of open-specialized and closed-diverse syndication networks for new ventures' success." *Administrative Science Quarterly* 61(3): 393–432.

Tortoriello, Marco. 2015. "The social underpinnings of absorptive capacity: The moderating effects of structural holes on innovation generation based on external knowledge." *Strategic Management Journal* 36(4): 586–597.

Tortoriello, Marco, and David Krackhardt. 2010. "Activating cross-boundary knowledge: The role of Simmelian ties in the generation of innovations." *Academy of Management Journal* 53(1): 167–181.

Tortoriello, Marco, Giuseppe Soda, and Manuel Gomez-Solorzano. In Press. "The ties that nurture: Expressive Simmelian ties, instrumental brokerage, and individual performance." *Academy of Management Journal*, In Press.

Tortoriello, Marco, Ray Regans, and Bill McEvily. 2012. "Bridging the knowledge gap: The influence of strong ties, network cohesion, and network range on the transfer between organization units." *Organization Science* 23(4): 1024–1039.

Tsui, Aanne S., and Jiing-Lih Farh. 1997. "Where *guanxi* matters: Relational demography and *guanxi* in the Chinese context." *Work and Occupations* 24(1): 56–79.

Uzzi, Brian. 1996. "The sources and consequences of embeddedness for the economic performance of organizations." *American Sociological Review* 61(4): 674–698.

Uzzi, Brian. 1997. "Social structure and competition in interfirm networks: The paradox of embeddedness." *Administrative Science Quarterly* 42(1): 35–67.

Verbrugge, Lois M. 1979. "Multiplexity in adult friendships." *Social Forces* 57(4): 1286–1309.

Völker, Beate. 2023. "Networks in lockdown: the consequences of COVID-19 for social relationships and feelings of loneliness." *Social Networks* 72(January): 1–12.

von Hippel, Eric. 1994. "Sticky information and the locus of problem solving: implications for innovation." *Management Science*, 40(4): 429–439.

Walder, Andrew G. 1986. *Communist Neo-traditionalism: Work and Authority in Chinese Industry*. Berkeley: University of California Press.

Wang, Jenn-Hwan, and Ray-May Hsung. 2016. *Rethinking Social Capital and Entrepreneurship in Greater China*. New York: Routledge.

Wang, Jenn-Hwan, Tsung-Yuan Chen, and Ray-May Hsung. 2016. "Introduction: Guanxi matters? Rethinking social capital and entrepreneurship in greater China," pp. 1–18 in *Rethinking Social Capital and Entrepreneurship in Greater China*, edited by Jenn-Hwan Wang and Ray-May Hsung. New York: Routledge.

Watts, Duncan J. 1999. "Networks, dynamics, and the small-world phenomenon." *American Journal of Sociology* 105(2): 493–527.

Watts, Duncan J., and Steven H. Strogatz. 1998. "Collective dynamics of 'small-world' networks." *Nature* 393: 440–442.

Wellman, Barry. 1979. "The community question: The intimate networks of East Yorkers." *American Journal of Sociology* 84(5): 1201–1231.

Williams, Unislawa, and Sean P. Williams. 2014. "Txttool: Utilities for text analysis in Stata." *The Stata Journal* 14(4): 817–829.

Xiao, Zhixing, and Anne S. Tsui. 2007. "When brokerage may not work: The cultural contingency of social capital in Chinese high-tech firms." *Administrative Science Quarterly* 52(1): 1–31.

Xin, Katherine R., and Jone L. Pearce. 1996. "*Guanxi*: Connections as substitutes for formal institutional support." *Academy of Management Journal* 39(6): 1641–1658.

Yamagishi, Toshio, and Midori Yamagishi. 1994. "Trust and commitment in the United States and Japan." *Motivation and Emotion* 18: 9–66.

Yan, Pu, and Taha Yasseri. 2017. "Two diverging roads: A semantic network analysis of Chinese social connection ('*Guanxi*') on Twitter." *Frontiers in Digital Humanities* 4: 11.

Yan, Yunxiang. 1998. *The Flow of Gifts: Reciprocity and Social Networks in a Chinese Village*. Stanford, CA: Stanford University Press.

Yang, Longqi, David Holtz, Sonia Jaffe, Siddharth Suri, Shilpi Sinha, Jeffrey Weston, Connor Joyce, Neha Shah, Kevin Sherman, Brent Hecht, and Jame Teevan. 2022. "The effects of remote work on collaboration among information workers." *Nature, Human Behavior* 6: 43–54.

Yang, Mei-Hui. 1994. *Gifts, Favors, and Banquets*. Ithaca, NY: Cornell University Press.

Yeung, Irene Y. M., and Rosalie L. Tung. 1996. "Achieving business success in Confucian societies: The importance of *Guanxi* (connections)." *Organizational Dynamics* 25(2): 54–65.

Zaheer, Akbar, and Giuseppe Soda. 2009. "Network evolution: The origins of structural holes." *Administrative Science Quarterly* 54(1): 1–31.

Zerubavel, Eviatar. 1991. *The Fine Line*. New York: Free Press.

Zhang, Jing, and Poh-Kam Wong. 2008. "Networks vs. market methods in high-tech venture fundraising: The impact of institutional environment." *Entrepreneurship and Regional Development* 20(5): 409–430.

Zhang, Grace O. 2015. *Elastic Language*: How and Why We Stretch Our Worlds. New York: Cambridge University Press.

Zhao, Chenlin, and Ronald S. Burt. 2018. "A note on business survival and social network." *Management and Organization Review* 14(2): 377–394.

Zuzul, Tiona, Emily Cox Pahnke, Jonathan Larson, Patrick Bourke, Nicholas Caurvina, Neha Parikh Shah, Fereshteh Amini, Jeffrey Weston, Youngser Park, Joshua Vogelstein, Christopher White, Carey E. Priebe. 2025. "Dynamic silos: Increased modularity and decreased stability in intraorganizational communication networks during the COVID-19 pandemic." *Management Science* 71(4): 3428–3448.

Index

For the benefit of digital users, indexed terms that span two pages (e.g., 52–53) may, on occasion, appear on only one of those pages.

Tables and figures are indicated by *t* and *f* following the page number.